I can cook with whatever's on hand!

Four Knights of the Apocalypse

31901068000001

Nakaba Suzuki Presents

1

✦ Contents ✦

Four Knights
Of The Apocalypse

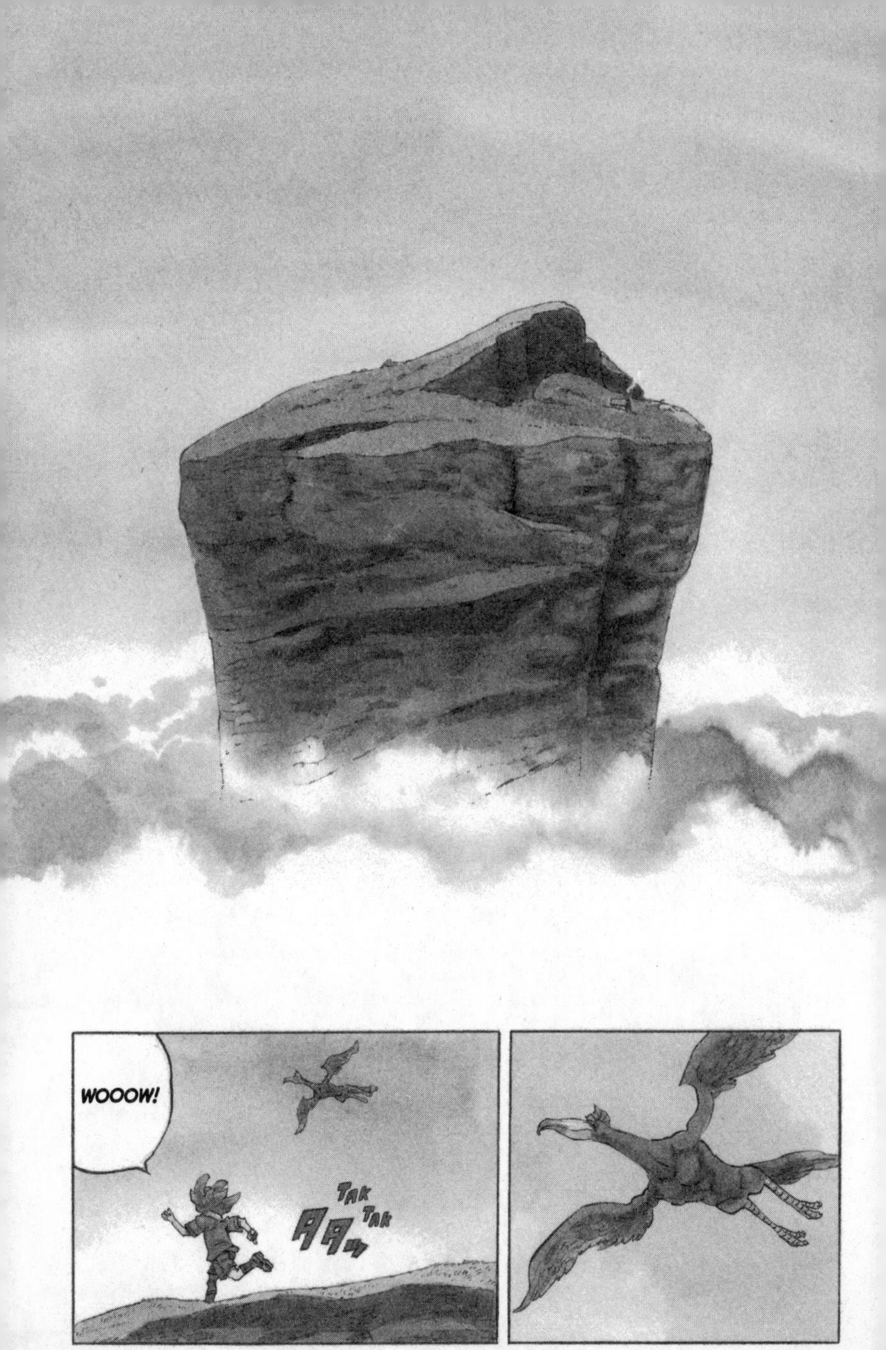
WOOOW!
TAK TAK

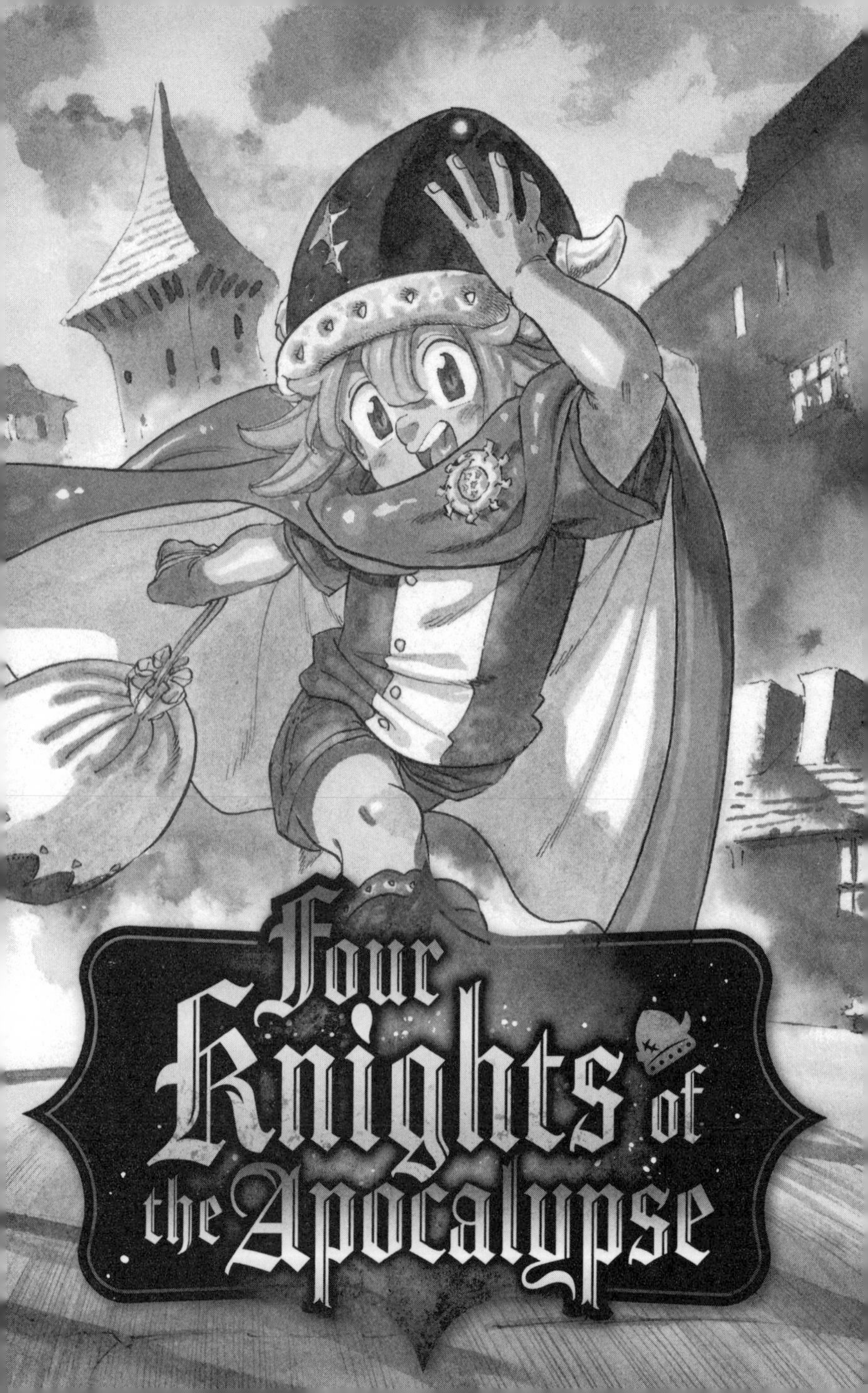
Four Knights of the Apocalypse

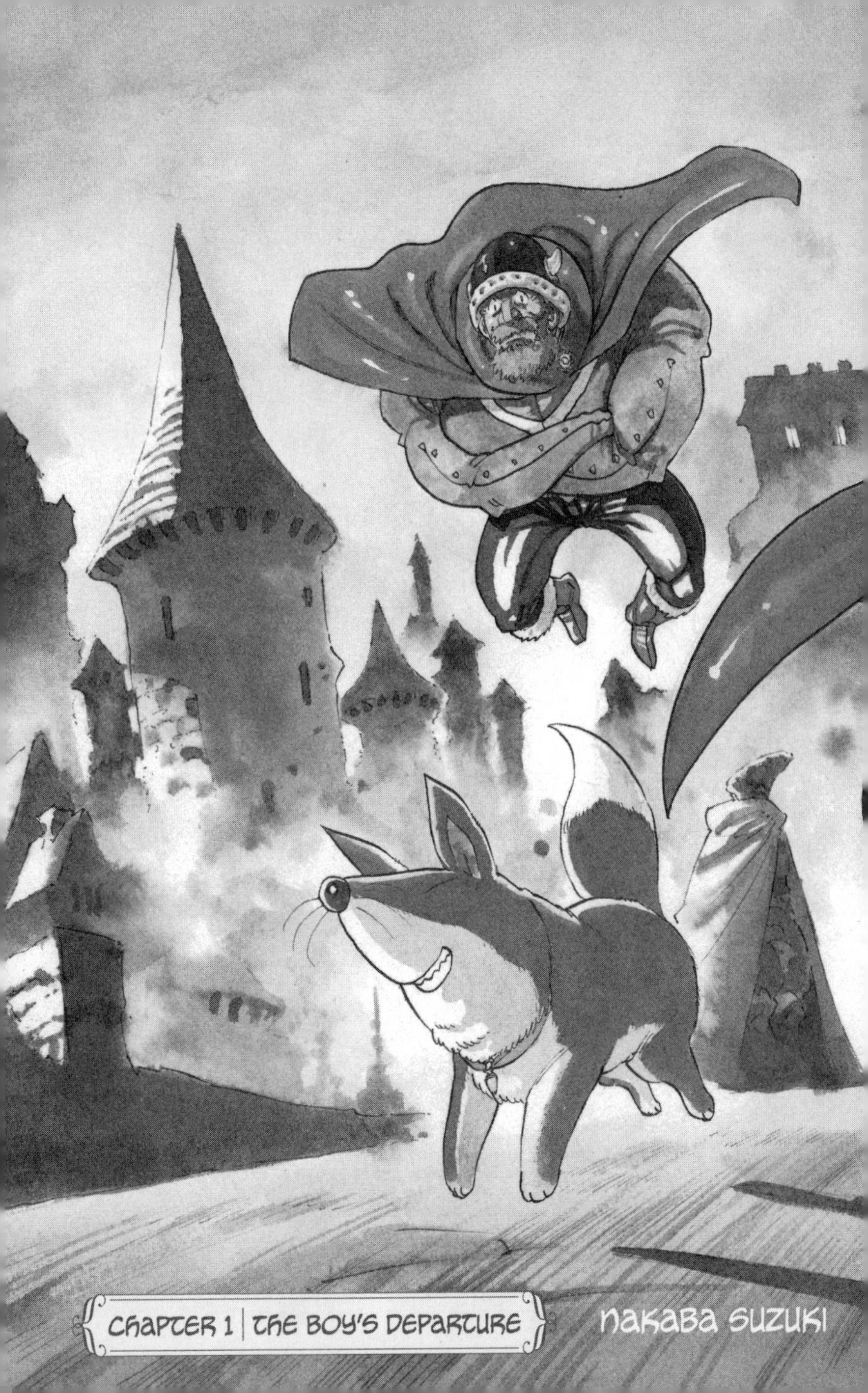
CHAPTER 1 | THE BOY'S DEPARTURE
NAKABA SUZUKI

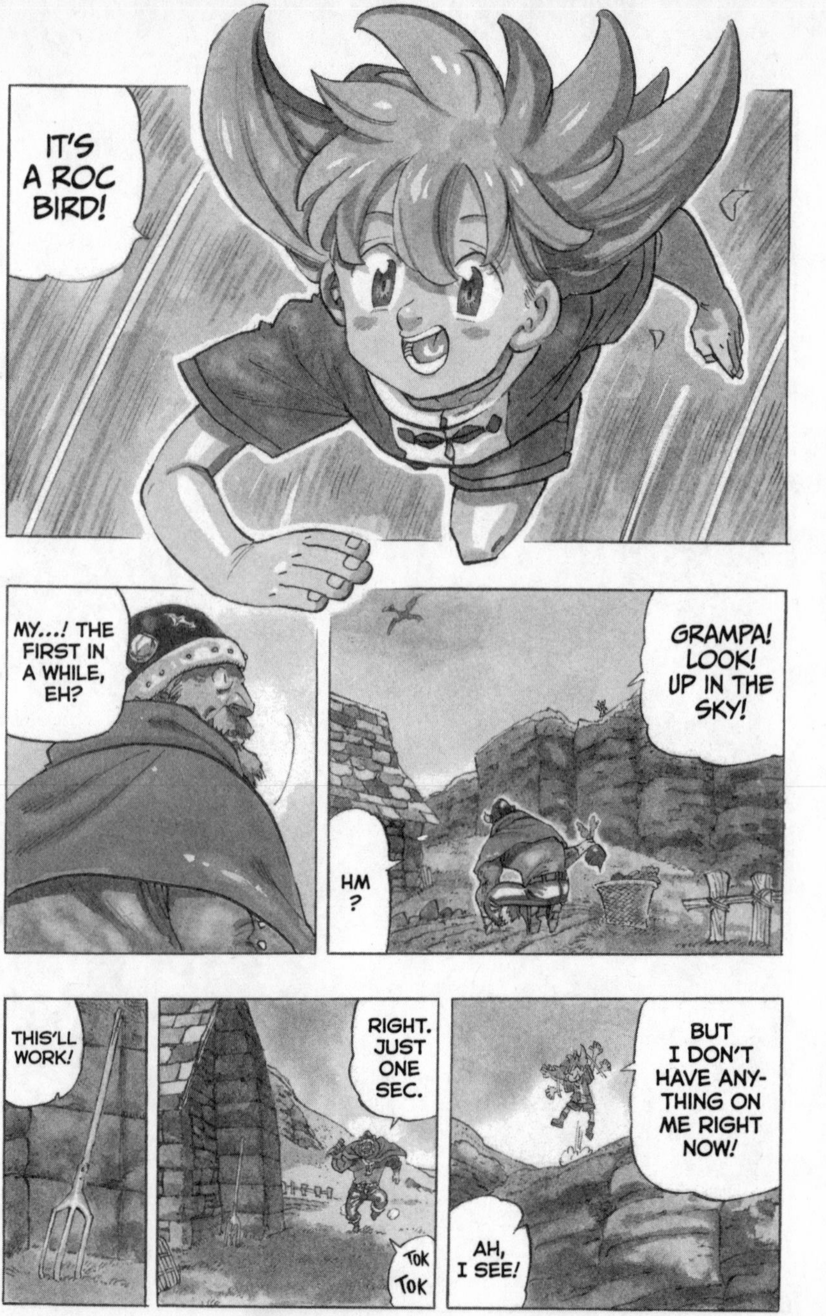
IT'S A ROC BIRD!
GRAMPA! LOOK! UP IN THE SKY!
HM?
MY...! THE FIRST IN A WHILE, EH?
BUT I DON'T HAVE ANYTHING ON ME RIGHT NOW!
AH, I SEE!
RIGHT. JUST ONE SEC.
TOK TOK
THIS'LL WORK!

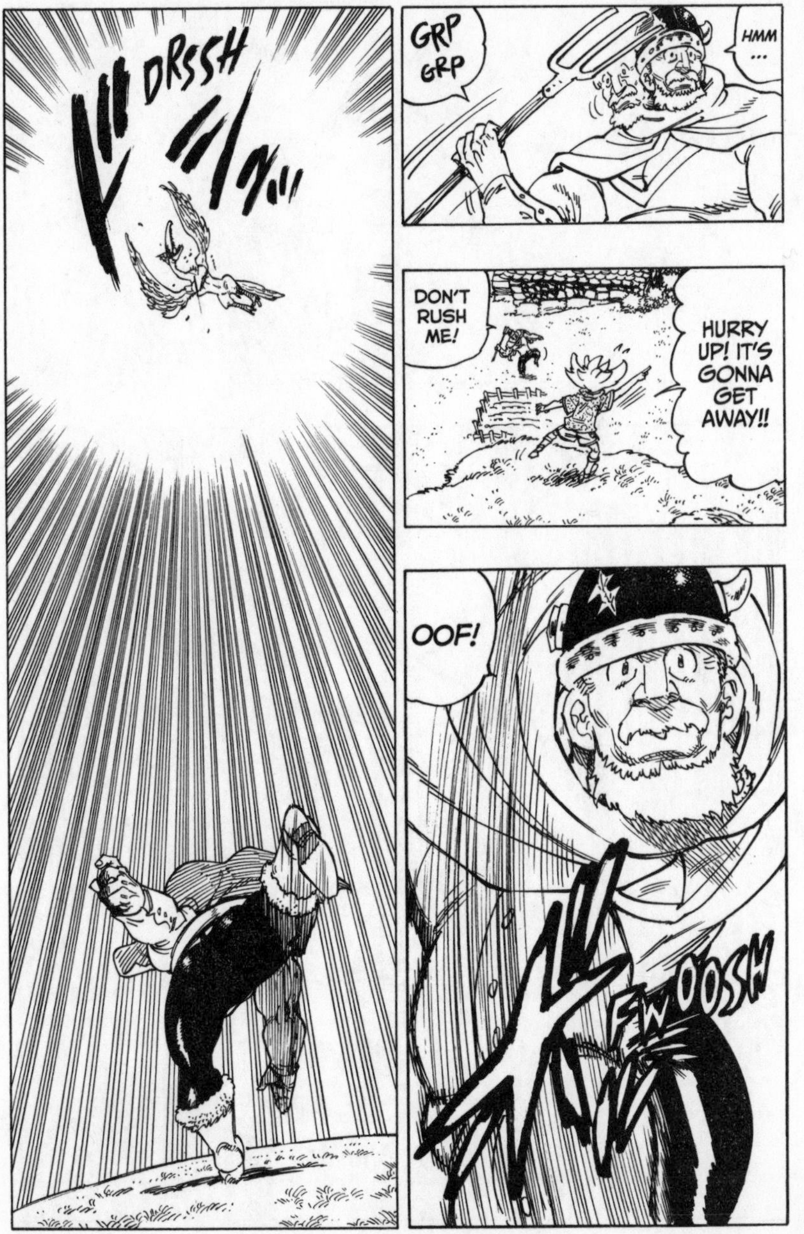
HMM ...
GRP GRP
HURRY UP! IT'S GONNA GET AWAY!!
DON'T RUSH ME!
OOF!
FWOOSH
DRSSH

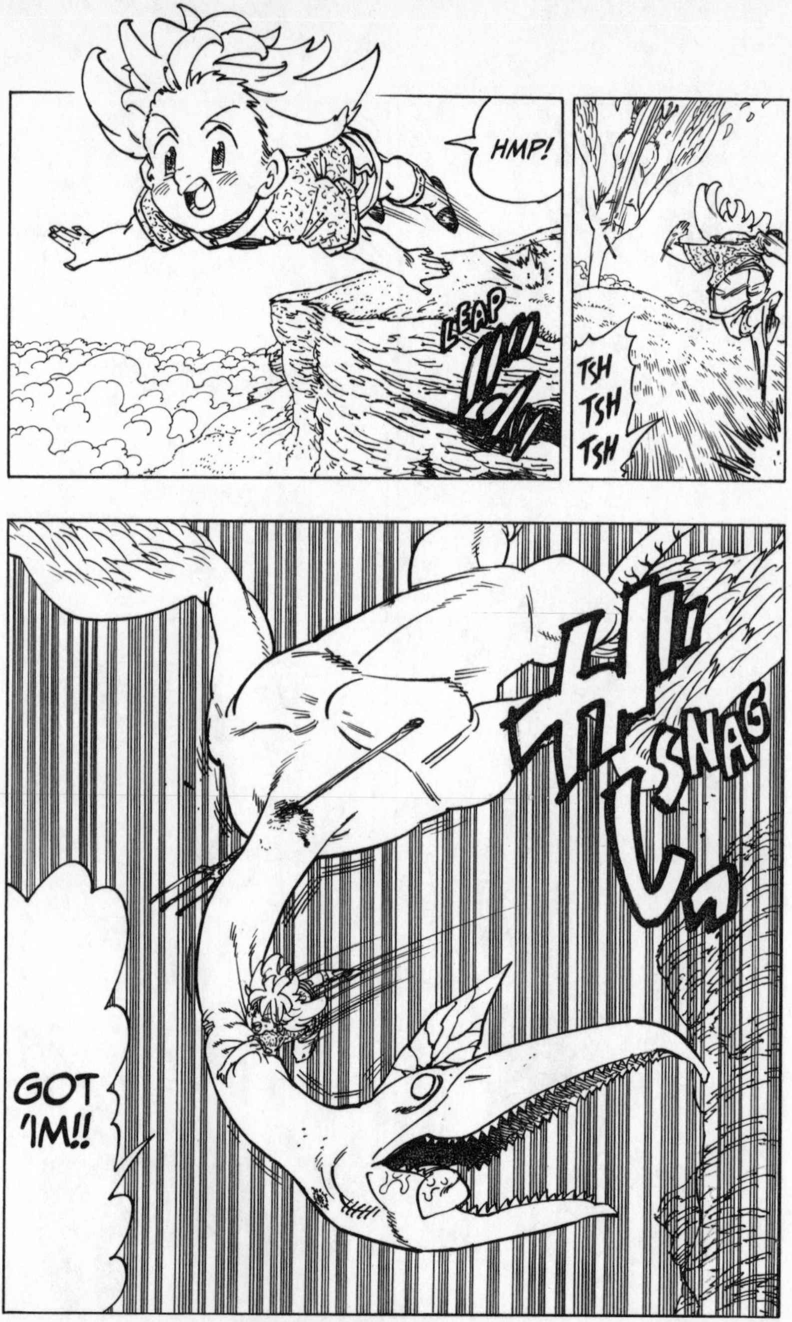
TSH
TSH
TSH
HMP!
LEAP
SNAG
GOT 'IM!!

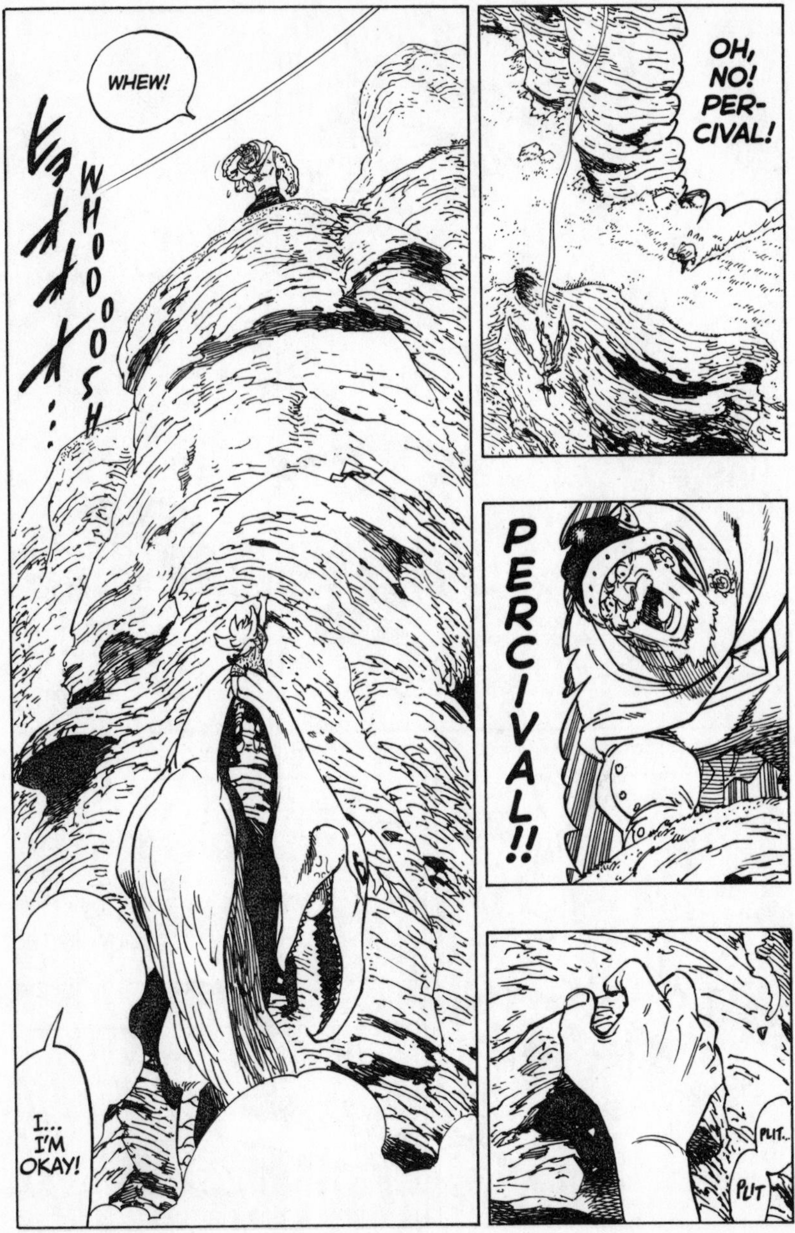
OH, NO! PERCIVAL!
PERCIVAL!!
PLIT...
PLIT
WHEW!
WHOOOOSH
I... I'M OKAY!

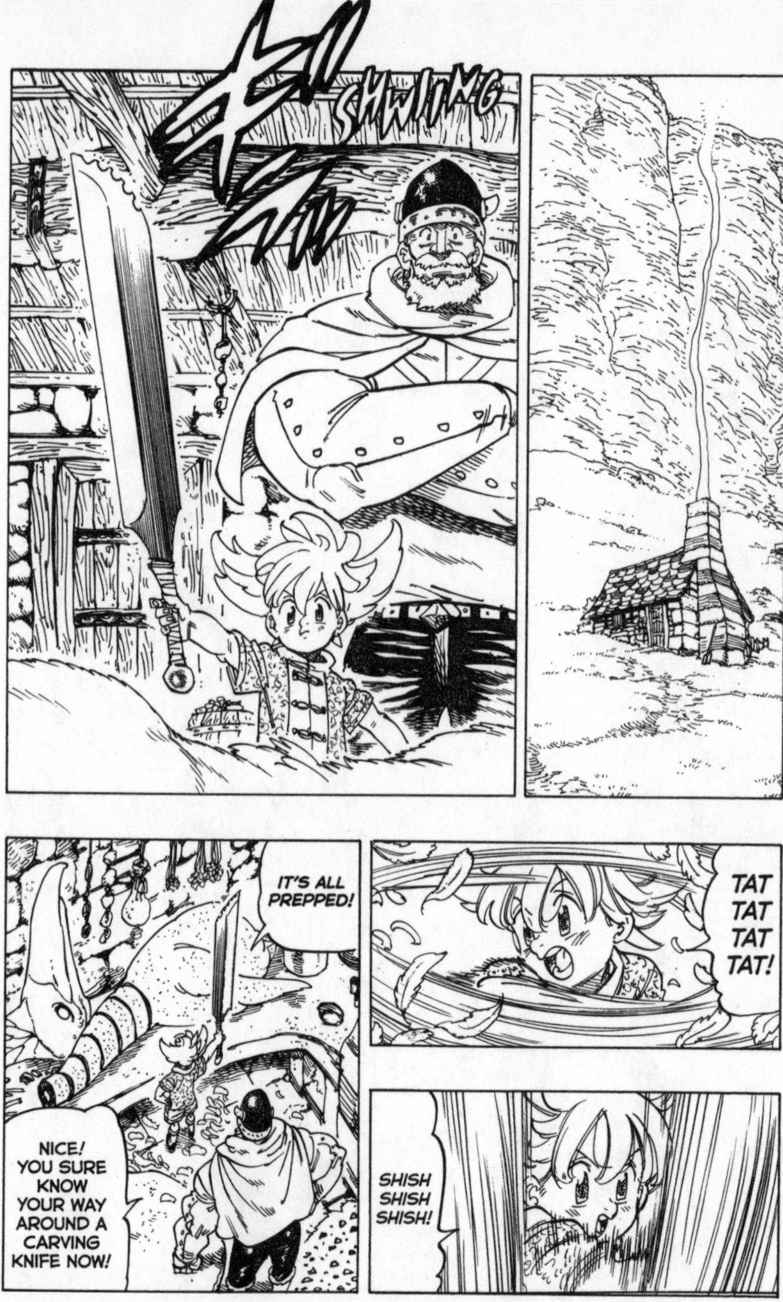
SHWING
TAT TAT TAT TAT!
SHISH SHISH SHISH!
IT'S ALL PREPPED!
NICE! YOU SURE KNOW YOUR WAY AROUND A CARVING KNIFE NOW!

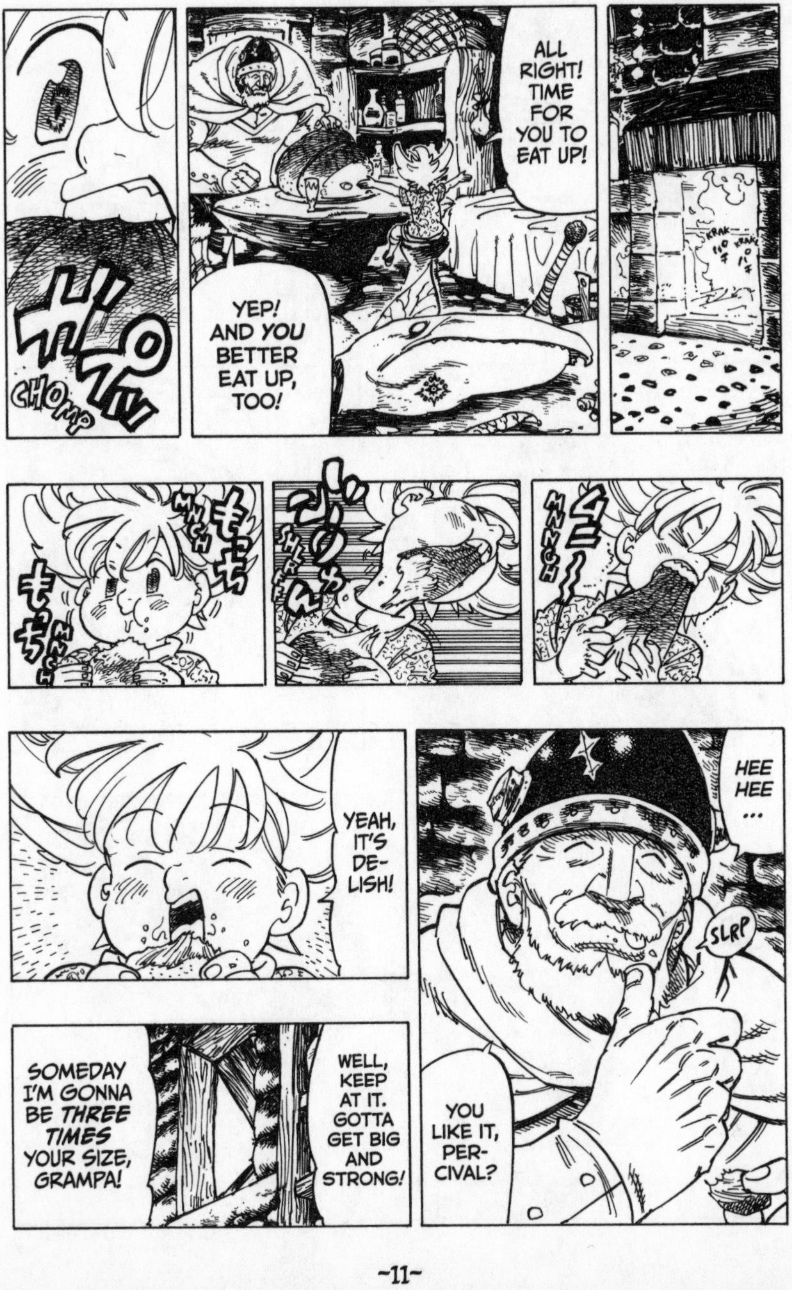
KRAK
KRAK
ALL RIGHT! TIME FOR YOU TO EAT UP!
YEP! AND *YOU* BETTER EAT UP, TOO!
CHOMP
MNNGH
SHLRP
MNCH
MNCH
HEE HEE ...
SLRP
YOU LIKE IT, PER-CIVAL?
YEAH, IT'S DE-LISH!
WELL, KEEP AT IT. GOTTA GET BIG AND STRONG!
SOMEDAY I'M GONNA BE *THREE TIMES* YOUR SIZE, GRAMPA!

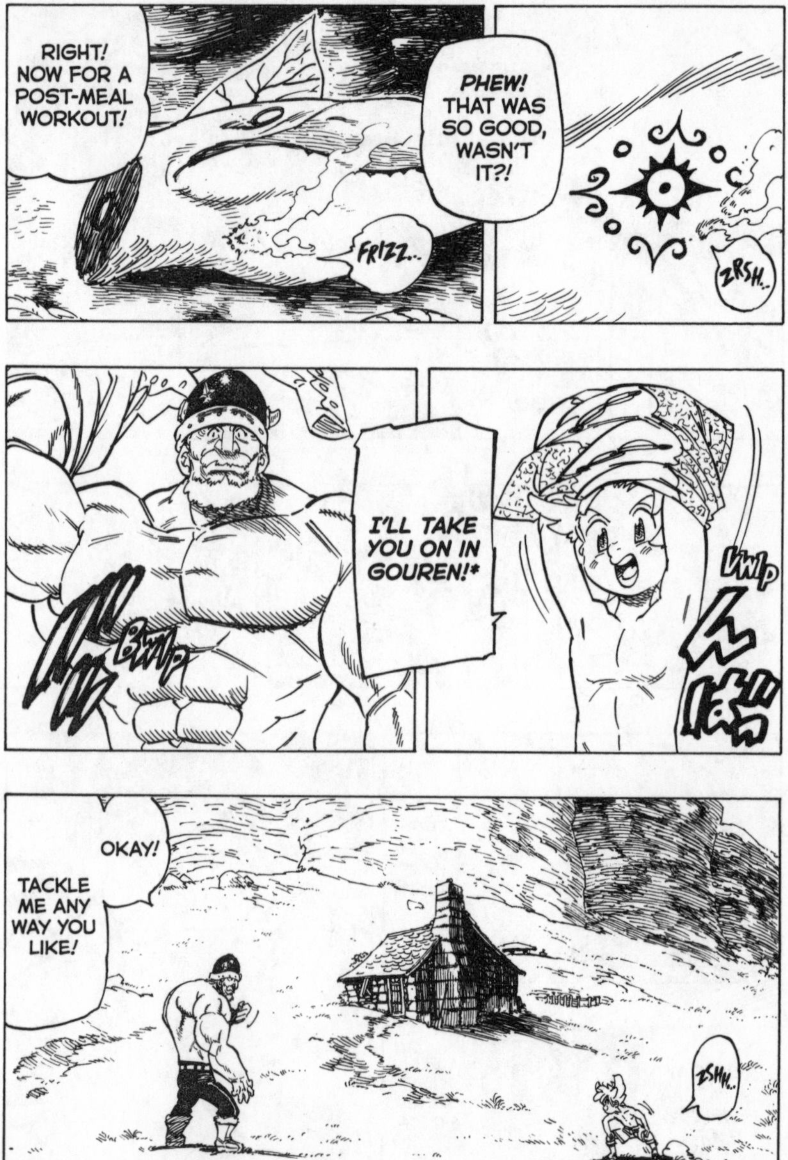
ZRSH...
PHEW! THAT WAS SO GOOD, WASN'T IT?!
RIGHT! NOW FOR A POST-MEAL WORKOUT!
FRIZZ...
VWIP
I'LL TAKE YOU ON IN GOUREN!*
ZSHH...
OKAY!
TACKLE ME ANY WAY YOU LIKE!

* A FORM OF TOPLESS WRESTLING ORIGINATING IN CELTIC LANDS.

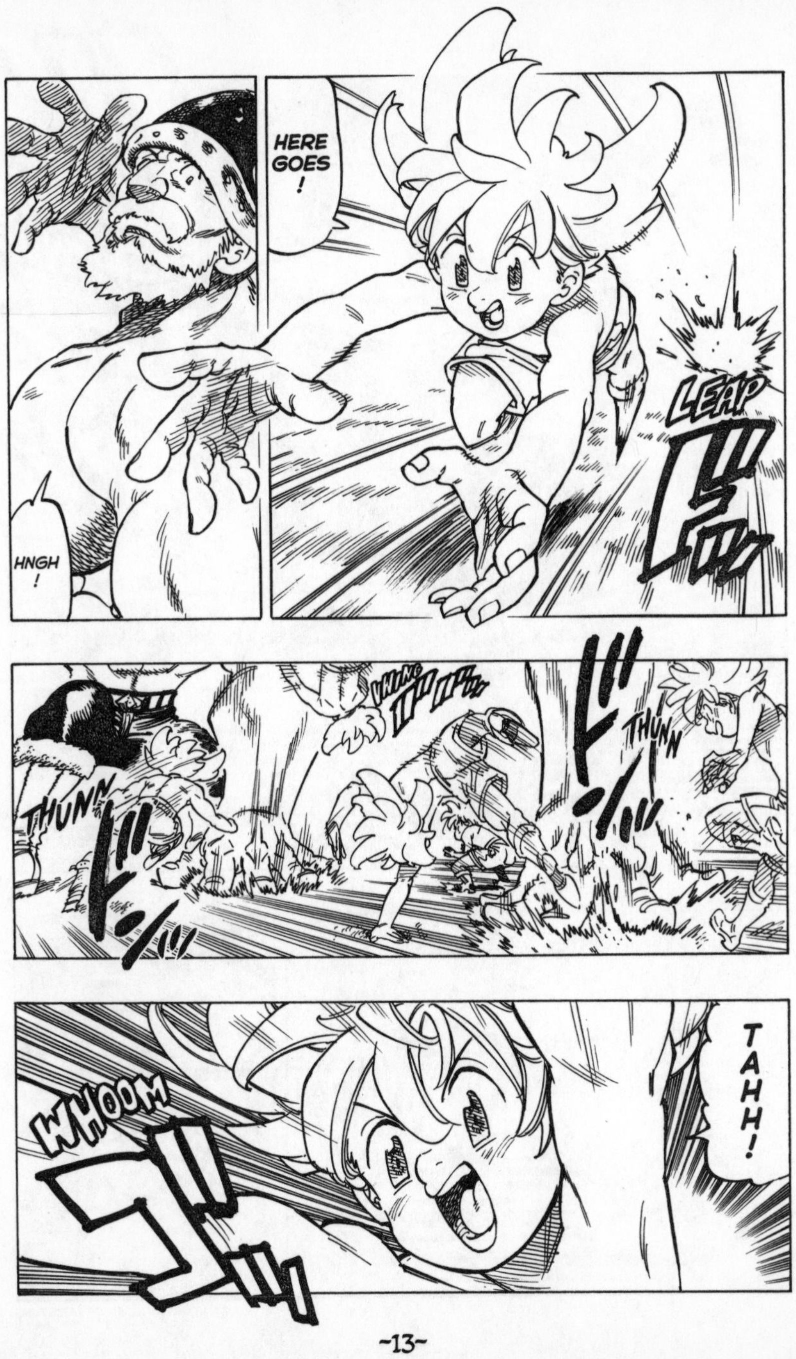
HERE GOES!
LEAP
HNGH!
THUNN
VHING
THUNN
TAHH!
WHOOM

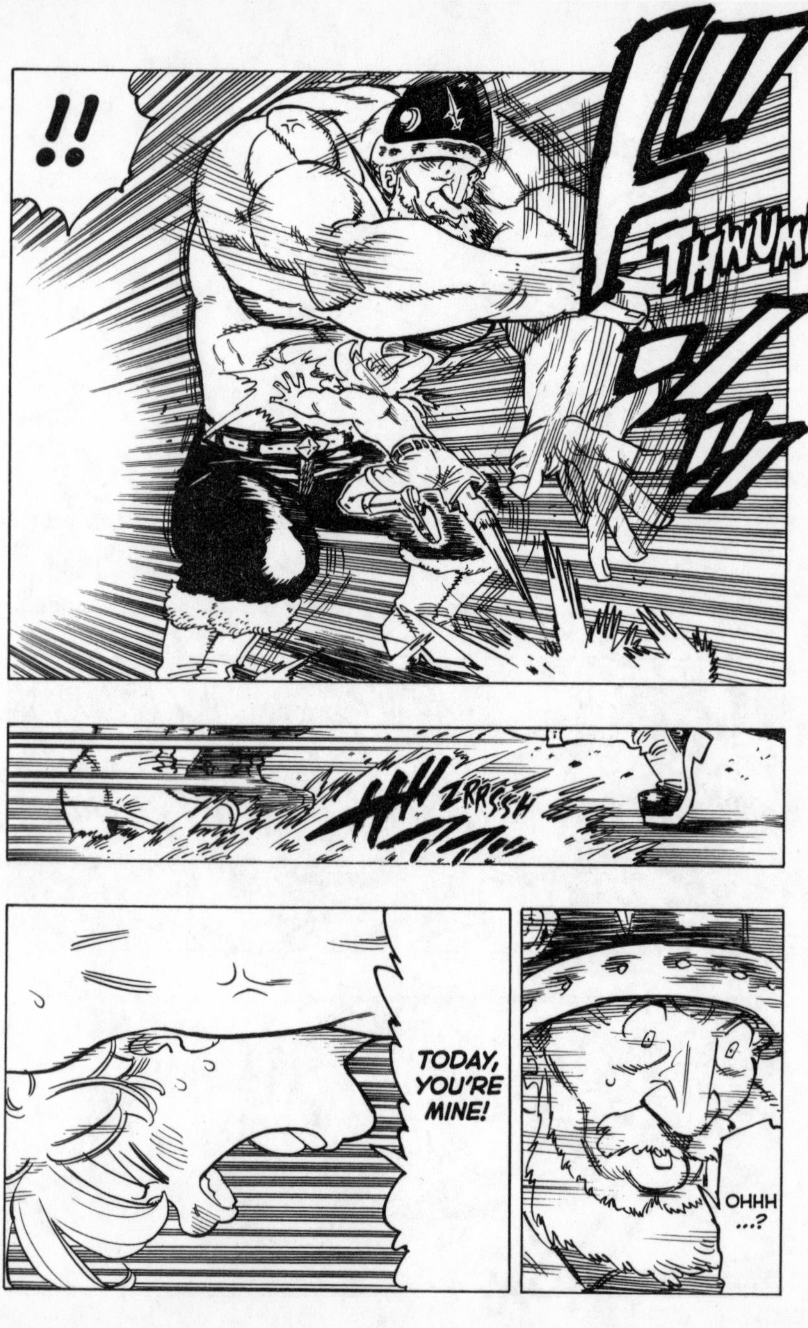
THWUMP
!!
ZRRSSH
OHHH
...?
TODAY, YOU'RE MINE!

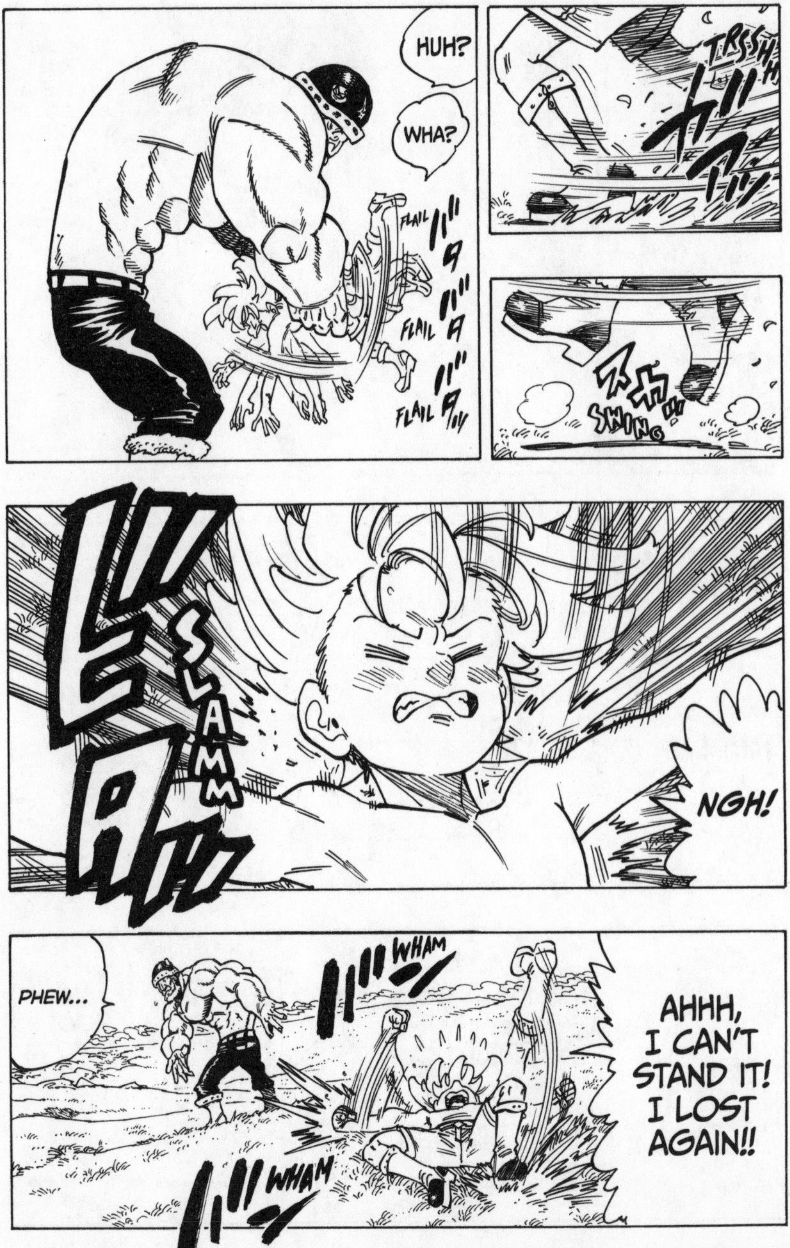
TRSSHH
SWING
HUH?
WHA?
FLAIL
FLAIL
FLAIL
SLAMM
NGH!
AHHH, I CAN'T STAND IT! I LOST AGAIN!!
WHAM
PHEW...
WHAM

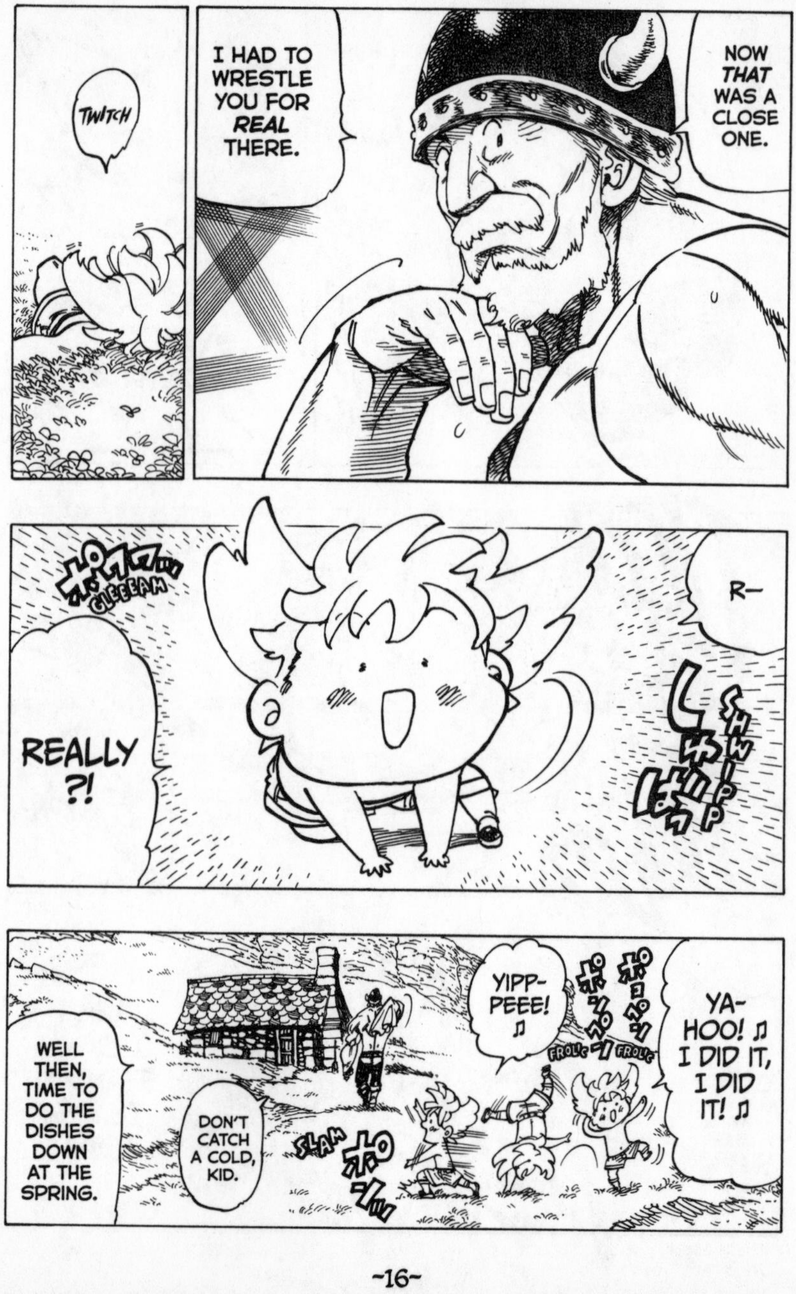
NOW THAT WAS A CLOSE ONE.
I HAD TO WRESTLE YOU FOR REAL THERE.
TWITCH
R—
SHWIPP
REALLY ?!
GLEEEAM
YA-HOO! ♫ I DID IT, I DID IT! ♫
FROLIC FROLIC
YIPP-PEEE! ♫
SLAM
DON'T CATCH A COLD, KID.
WELL THEN, TIME TO DO THE DISHES DOWN AT THE SPRING.

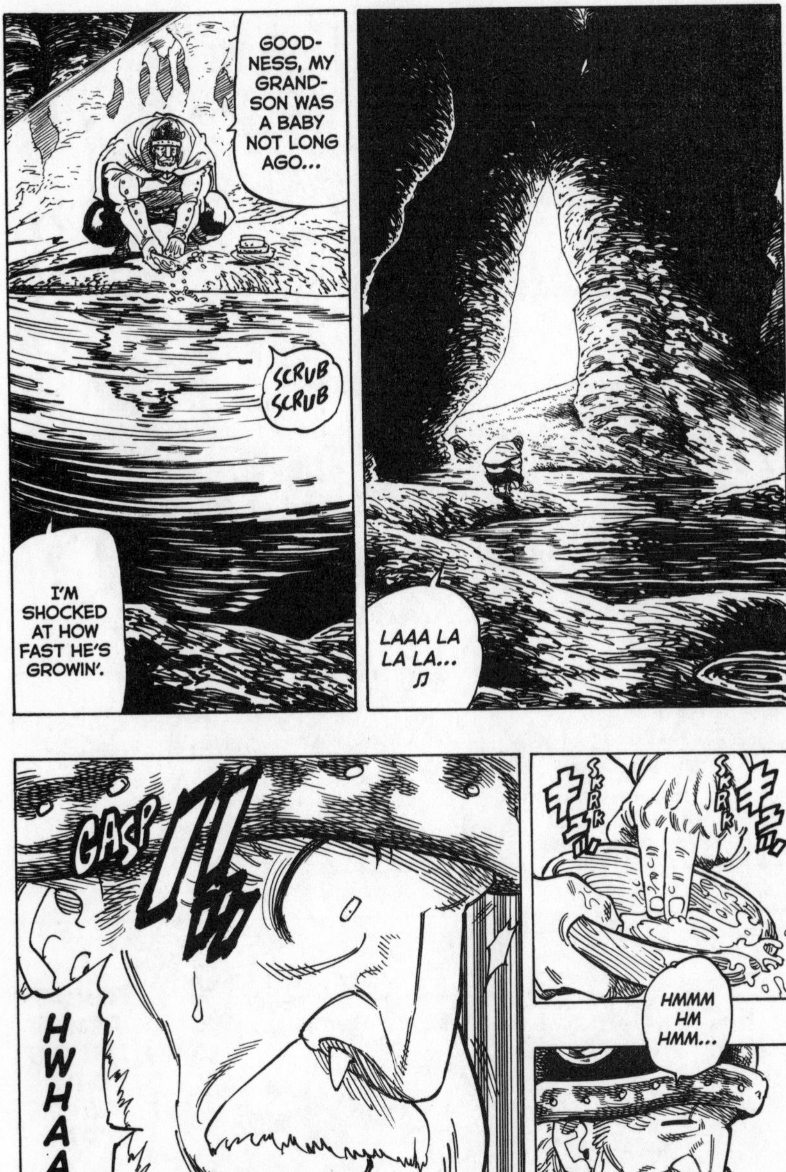
LAAA LA LA LA... ♫
GOODNESS, MY GRANDSON WAS A BABY NOT LONG AGO...
SCRUB SCRUB
I'M SHOCKED AT HOW FAST HE'S GROWIN'.
SKRK SKRK
HMMM HM HMM...
GASP
HWHAA?!

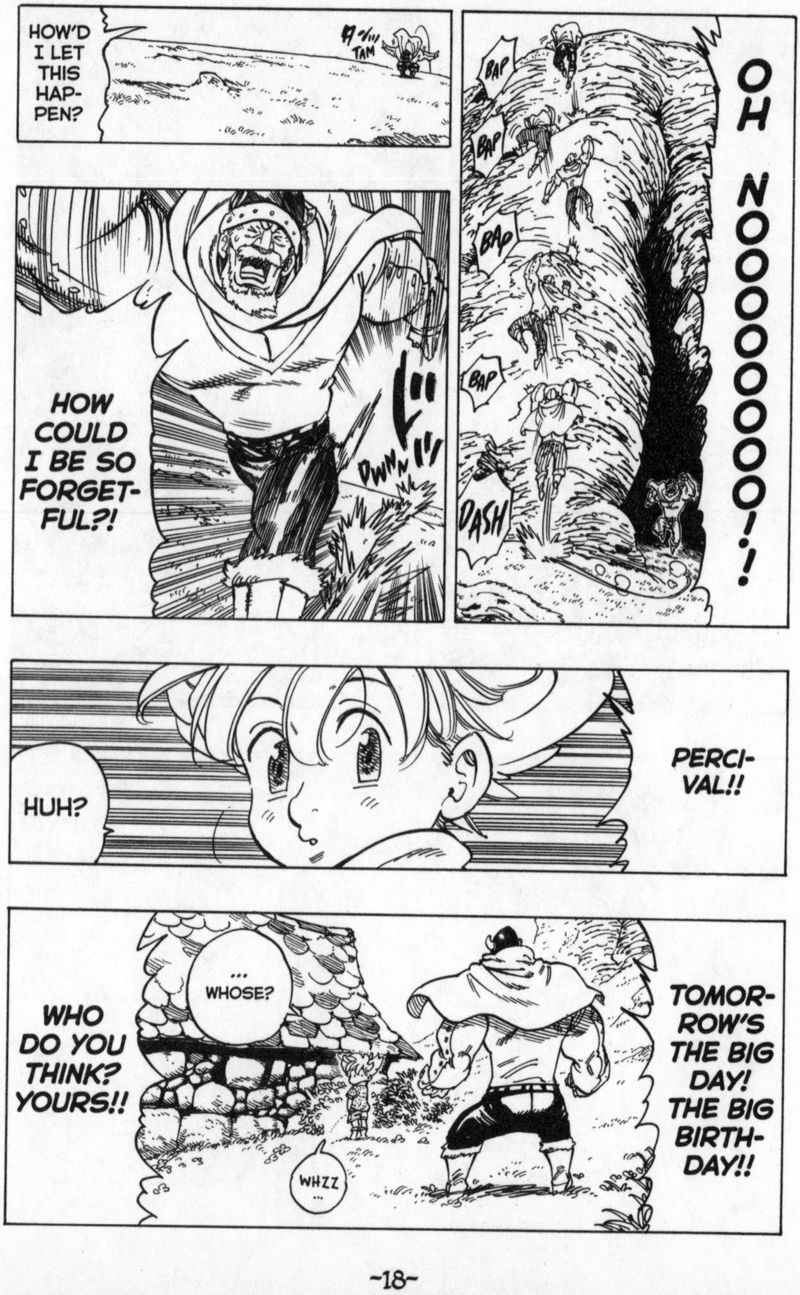

OH NOOOOOOOO!!
BAP
BAP
BAP
BAP
DASH
HOW'D I LET THIS HAPPEN?
TAM
HOW COULD I BE SO FORGETFUL?!
DWNN
PERCIVAL!!
HUH?
TOMORROW'S THE BIG DAY! THE BIG BIRTHDAY!!
... WHOSE?
WHO DO YOU THINK? YOURS!!
WHZZ ...

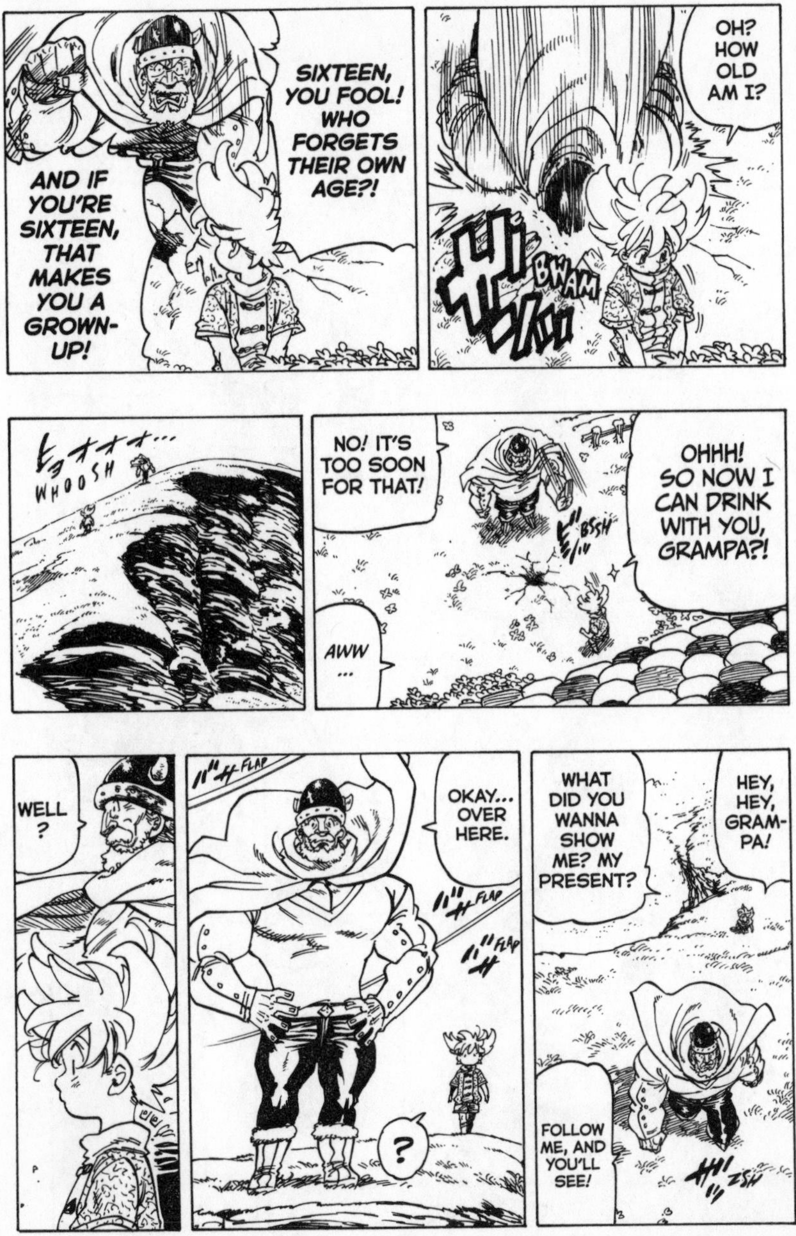

OH? HOW OLD AM I?
BWAM
SIXTEEN, YOU FOOL! WHO FORGETS THEIR OWN AGE?!
AND IF YOU'RE SIXTEEN, THAT MAKES YOU A GROWN-UP!
OHHH! SO NOW I CAN DRINK WITH YOU, GRAMPA?!
BSSH
NO! IT'S TOO SOON FOR THAT!
AWW...
ヒョオオオ…
WHOOSH
HEY, HEY, GRAMPA!
WHAT DID YOU WANNA SHOW ME? MY PRESENT?
FOLLOW ME, AND YOU'LL SEE!
ZSH
FLAP
OKAY... OVER HERE.
FLAP
FLAP
?
WELL?

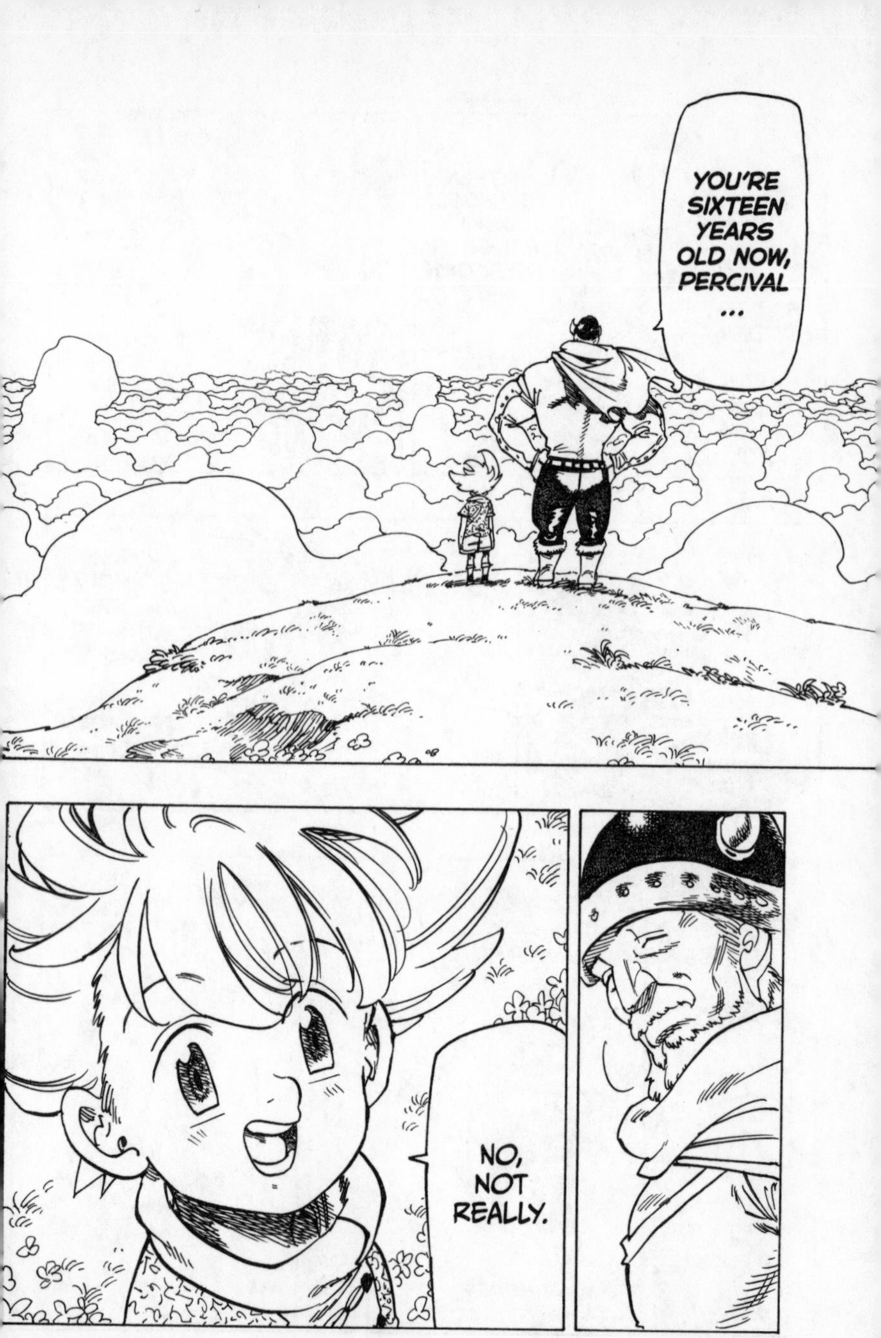
YOU'RE SIXTEEN YEARS OLD NOW, PERCIVAL...
NO, NOT REALLY.

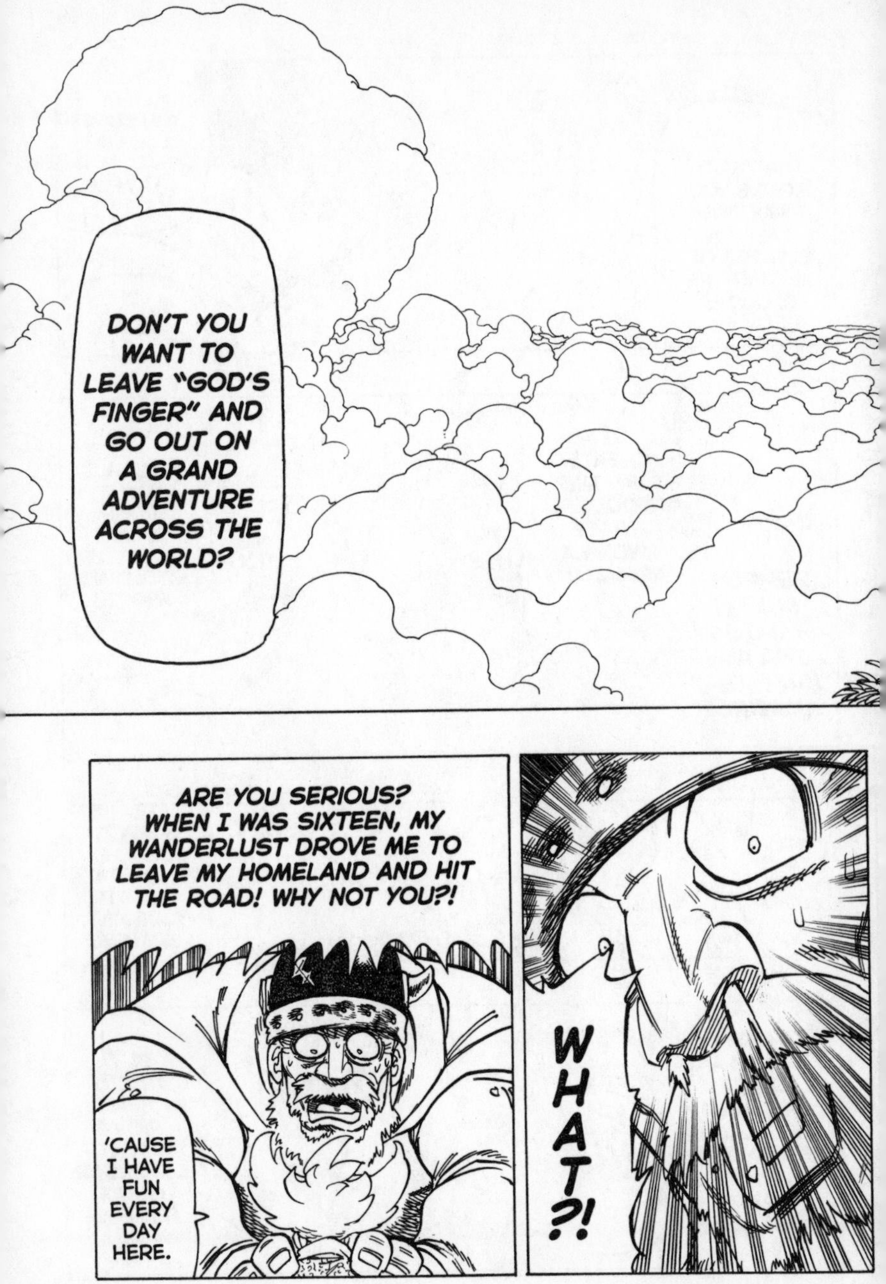
DON'T YOU WANT TO LEAVE "GOD'S FINGER" AND GO OUT ON A GRAND ADVENTURE ACROSS THE WORLD?
WHAT?!
ARE YOU SERIOUS? WHEN I WAS SIXTEEN, MY WANDERLUST DROVE ME TO LEAVE MY HOMELAND AND HIT THE ROAD! WHY NOT YOU?!
'CAUSE I HAVE FUN EVERY DAY HERE.

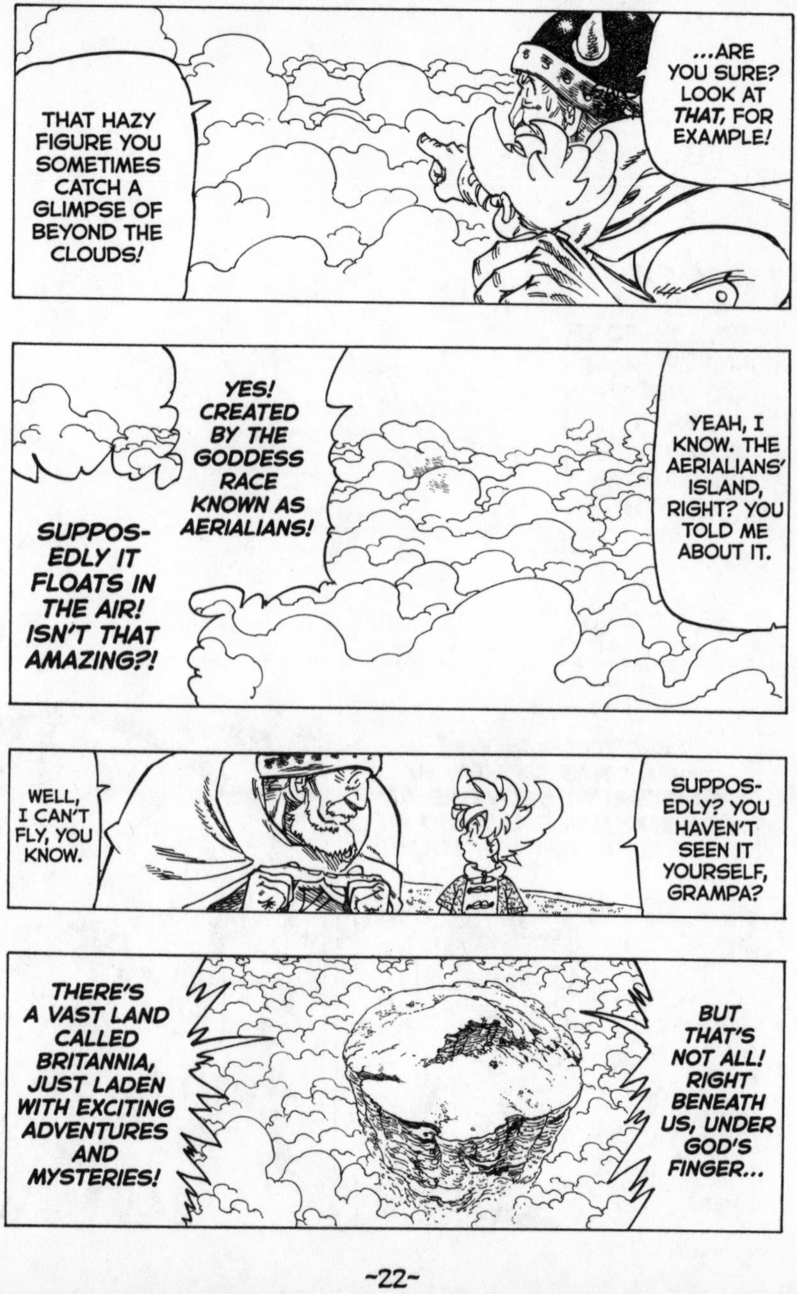
...ARE YOU SURE? LOOK AT *THAT,* FOR EXAMPLE!
THAT HAZY FIGURE YOU SOMETIMES CATCH A GLIMPSE OF BEYOND THE CLOUDS!
YEAH, I KNOW. THE AERIALIANS' ISLAND, RIGHT? YOU TOLD ME ABOUT IT.
YES! CREATED BY THE GODDESS RACE KNOWN AS AERIALIANS!
SUPPOS-EDLY IT FLOATS IN THE AIR! ISN'T THAT AMAZING?!
SUPPOS-EDLY? YOU HAVEN'T SEEN IT YOURSELF, GRAMPA?
WELL, I CAN'T FLY, YOU KNOW.
BUT THAT'S NOT ALL! RIGHT BENEATH US, UNDER GOD'S FINGER...
THERE'S A VAST LAND CALLED BRITANNIA, JUST LADEN WITH EXCITING ADVENTURES AND MYSTERIES!

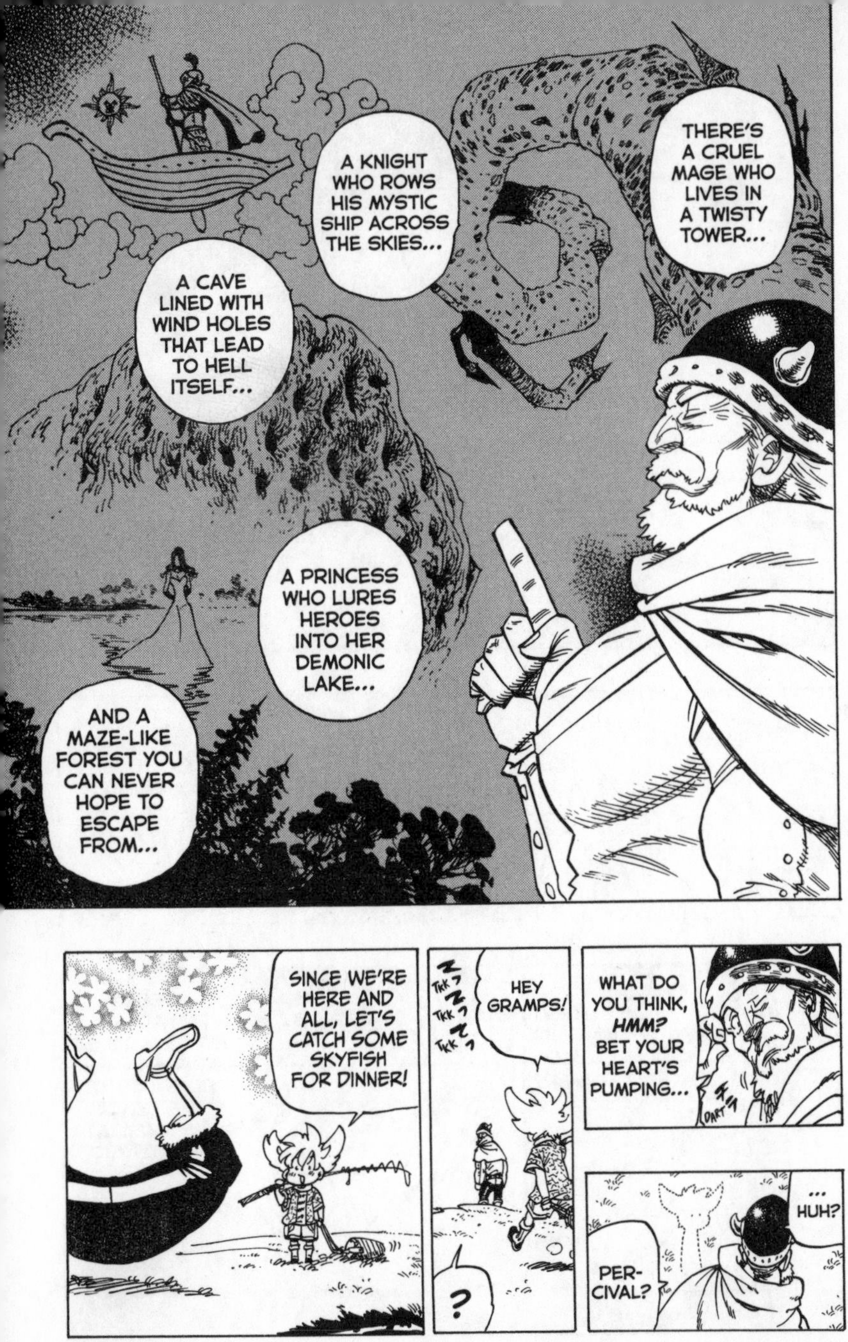
THERE'S A CRUEL MAGE WHO LIVES IN A TWISTY TOWER...
A KNIGHT WHO ROWS HIS MYSTIC SHIP ACROSS THE SKIES...
A CAVE LINED WITH WIND HOLES THAT LEAD TO HELL ITSELF...
A PRINCESS WHO LURES HEROES INTO HER DEMONIC LAKE...
AND A MAZE-LIKE FOREST YOU CAN NEVER HOPE TO ESCAPE FROM...
WHAT DO YOU THINK, *HMM?* BET YOUR HEART'S PUMPING...
DART
... HUH?
PER-CIVAL?
HEY GRAMPS!
TKK
TKK
TKK
?
SINCE WE'RE HERE AND ALL, LET'S CATCH SOME SKYFISH FOR DINNER!

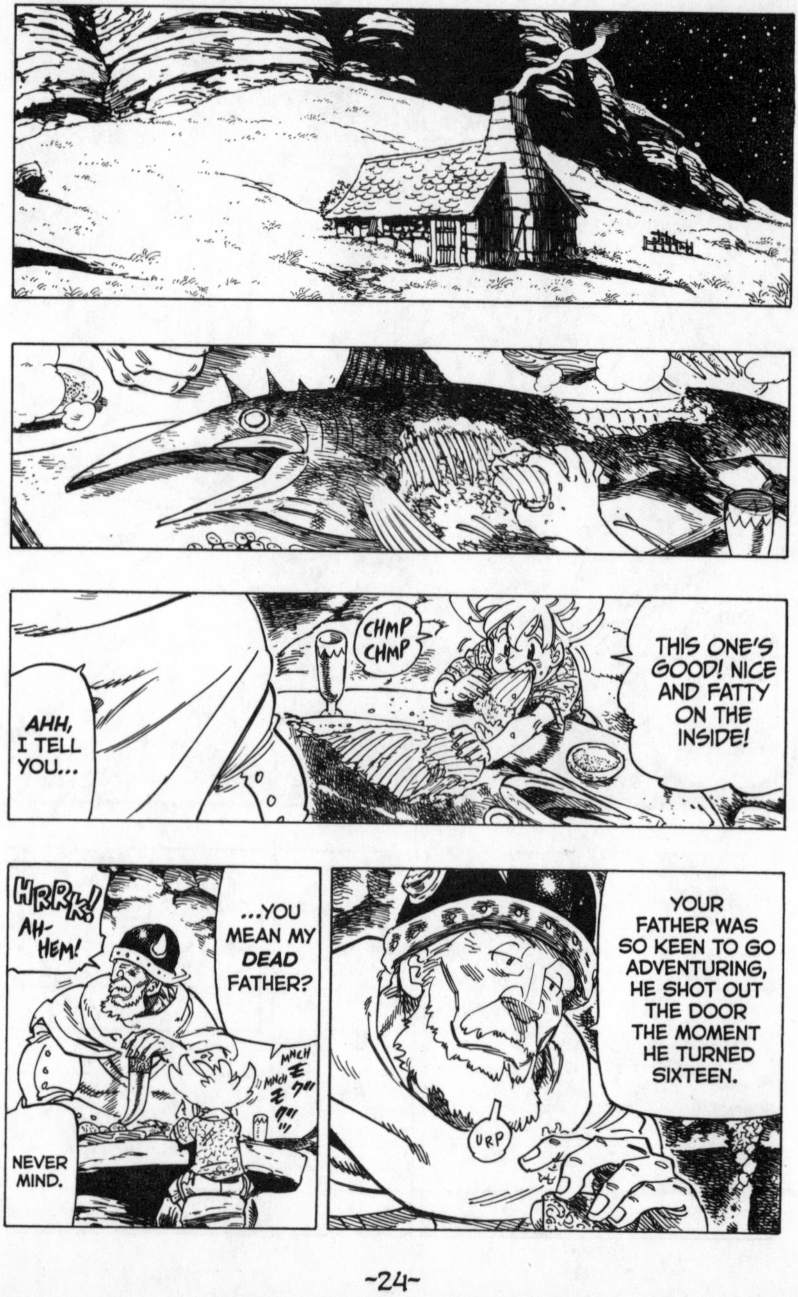
THIS ONE'S GOOD! NICE AND FATTY ON THE INSIDE!
CHMP CHMP
AHH, I TELL YOU...
YOUR FATHER WAS SO KEEN TO GO ADVENTURING, HE SHOT OUT THE DOOR THE MOMENT HE TURNED SIXTEEN.
URP
...YOU MEAN MY *DEAD* FATHER?
MNCH MNCH
HRRK! AH-HEM!
NEVER MIND.

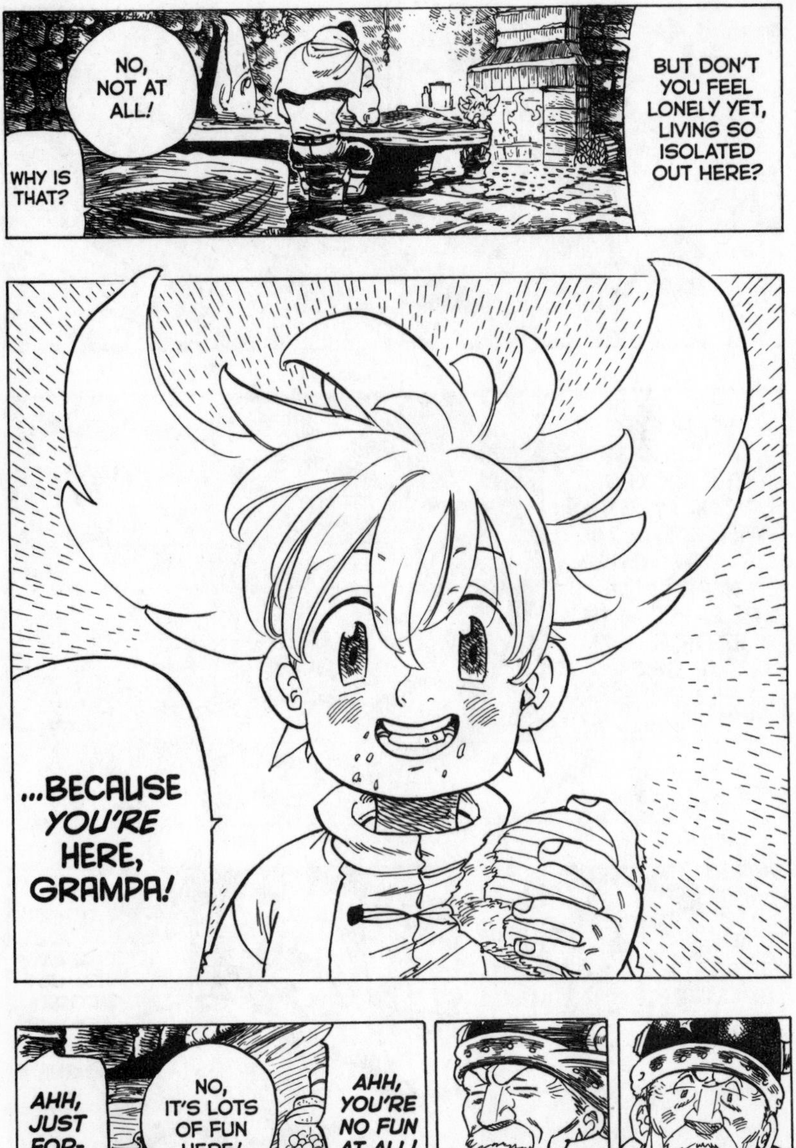

BUT DON'T YOU FEEL LONELY YET, LIVING SO ISOLATED OUT HERE?
NO, NOT AT ALL!
WHY IS THAT?
...BECAUSE YOU'RE HERE, GRAMPA!
TCH!
AHH, YOU'RE NO FUN AT ALL!
NO, IT'S LOTS OF FUN HERE!
AHH, JUST FOR-GET IT!!

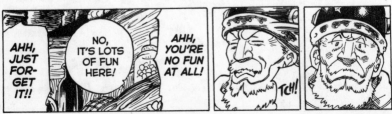

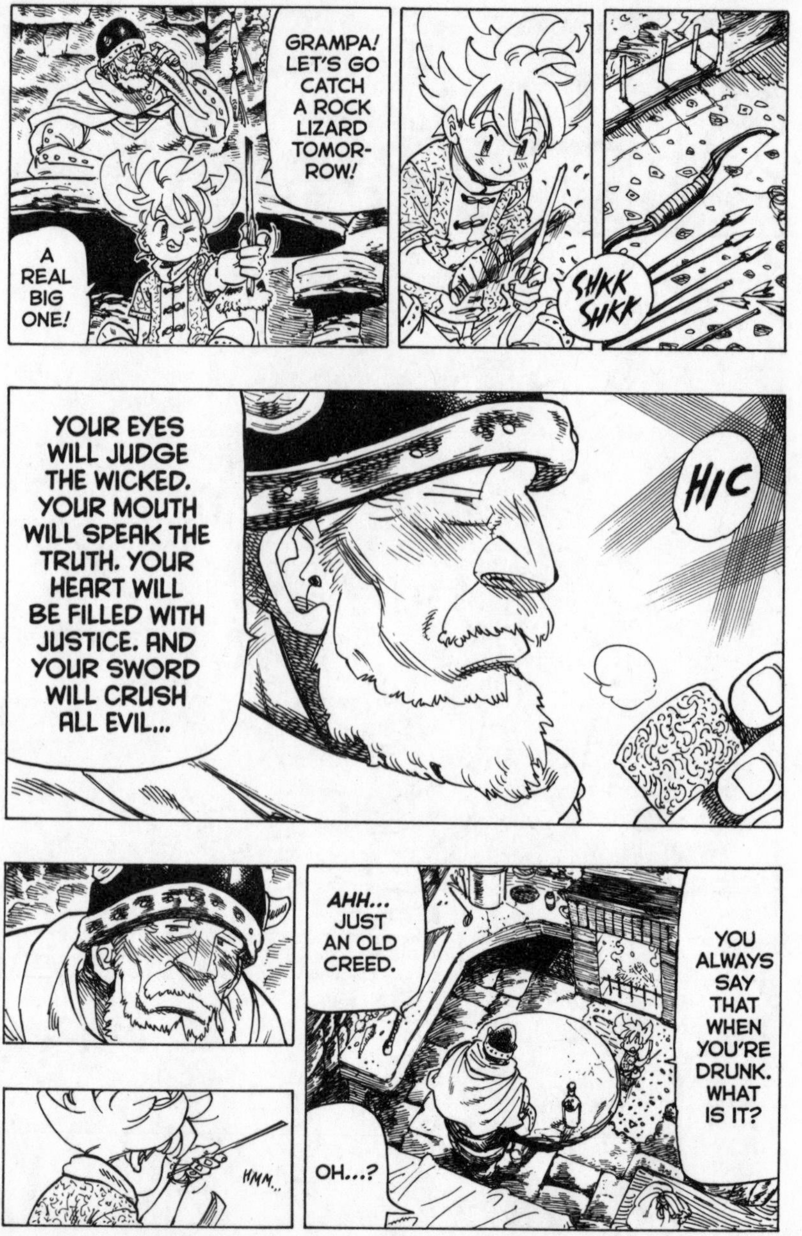
SHKK SHKK
GRAMPA! LET'S GO CATCH A ROCK LIZARD TOMORROW!
A REAL BIG ONE!
HIC
YOUR EYES WILL JUDGE THE WICKED. YOUR MOUTH WILL SPEAK THE TRUTH. YOUR HEART WILL BE FILLED WITH JUSTICE. AND YOUR SWORD WILL CRUSH ALL EVIL...
YOU ALWAYS SAY THAT WHEN YOU'RE DRUNK. WHAT IS IT?
AHH... JUST AN OLD CREED.
OH...?
HMM...

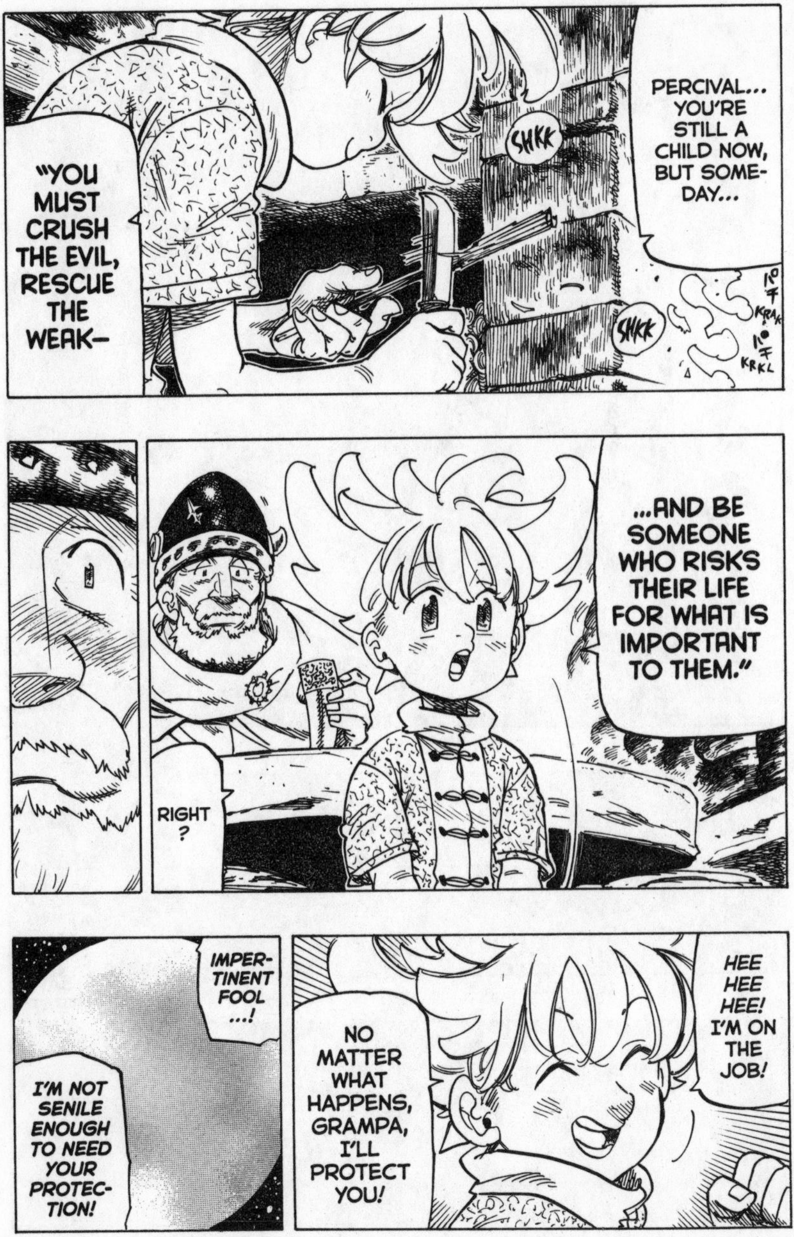
PERCIVAL... YOU'RE STILL A CHILD NOW, BUT SOMEDAY...
SHKK
SHKK
KRAK
KRKL
"YOU MUST CRUSH THE EVIL, RESCUE THE WEAK—
...AND BE SOMEONE WHO RISKS THEIR LIFE FOR WHAT IS IMPORTANT TO THEM."
RIGHT ?
HEE HEE HEE! I'M ON THE JOB!
NO MATTER WHAT HAPPENS, GRAMPA, I'LL PROTECT YOU!
IMPERTINENT FOOL ...!
I'M NOT SENILE ENOUGH TO NEED YOUR PROTECTION!

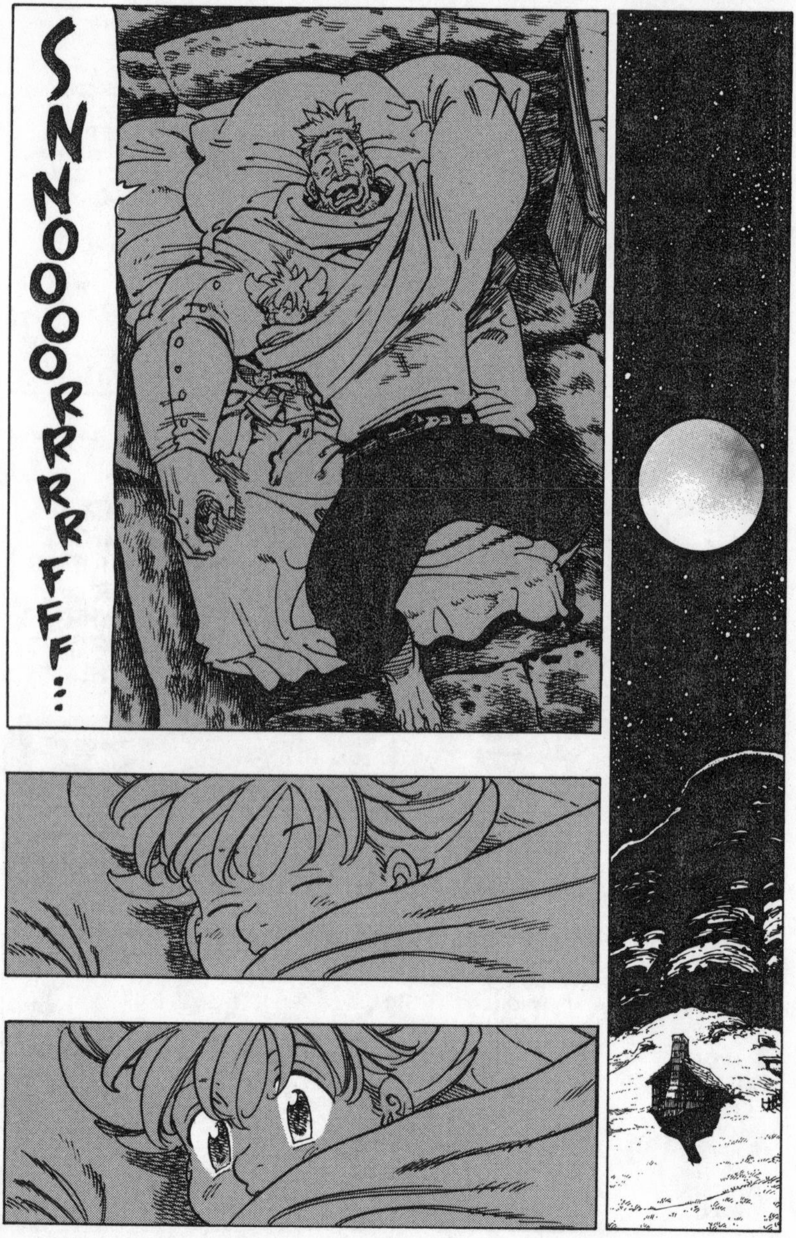
SNNOOOORRRRFFF...

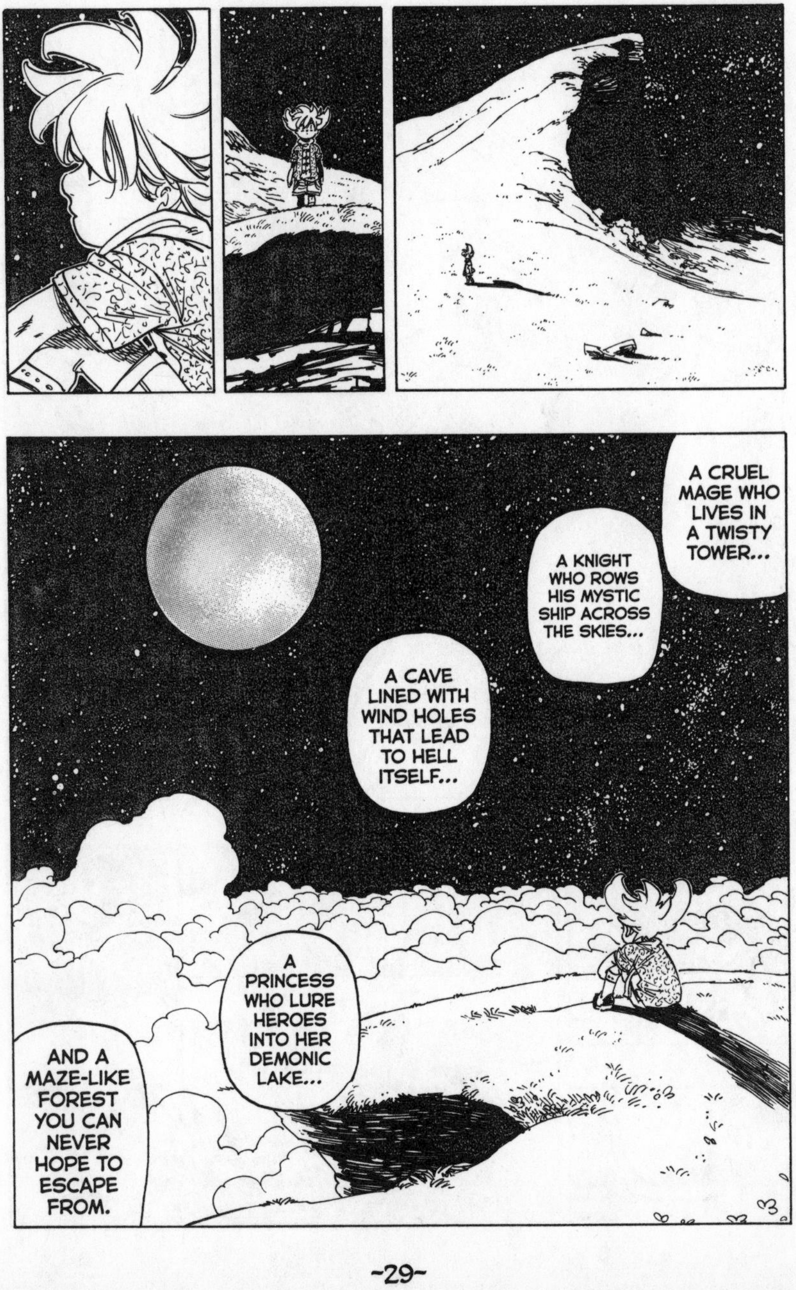
A CRUEL MAGE WHO LIVES IN A TWISTY TOWER...
A KNIGHT WHO ROWS HIS MYSTIC SHIP ACROSS THE SKIES...
A CAVE LINED WITH WIND HOLES THAT LEAD TO HELL ITSELF...
A PRINCESS WHO LURE HEROES INTO HER DEMONIC LAKE...
AND A MAZE-LIKE FOREST YOU CAN NEVER HOPE TO ESCAPE FROM.

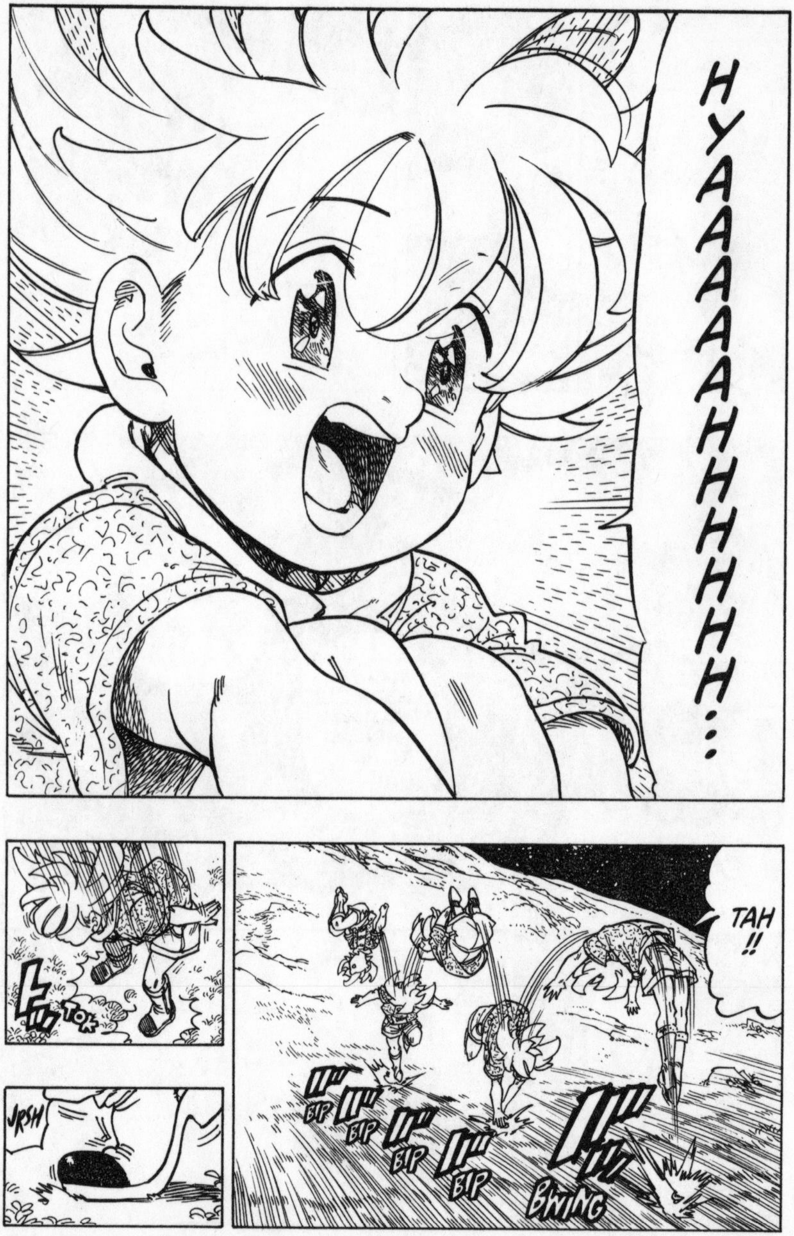

HYAAAAAHHHHHH...
TAH!!
BIP
BIP
BIP
BIP
BWING
TOK
JRSH

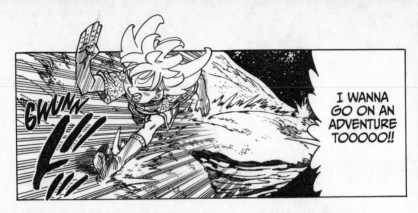

I WANNA GO ON AN ADVENTURE TOOOOO!!
GWUNN!!
I'M SO EXCIT-ED...
I CAN'T EVEN CONTAIN MYSELF!!
D-W-W-OOOOOOOOOOOOOOMMMM
TRIP
THWN
THWN
THWN
MNGH!
ZZZRRRRSSHN
HAAH
HAAH
HAAH
...
...BUT THAT'S OKAY.
I GOT GRAMPA WITH ME, SO...

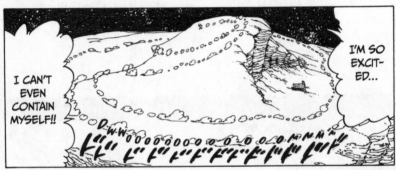

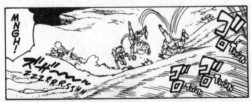

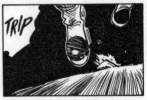

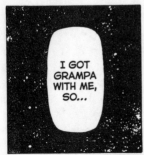

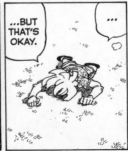

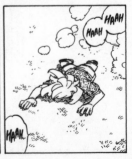

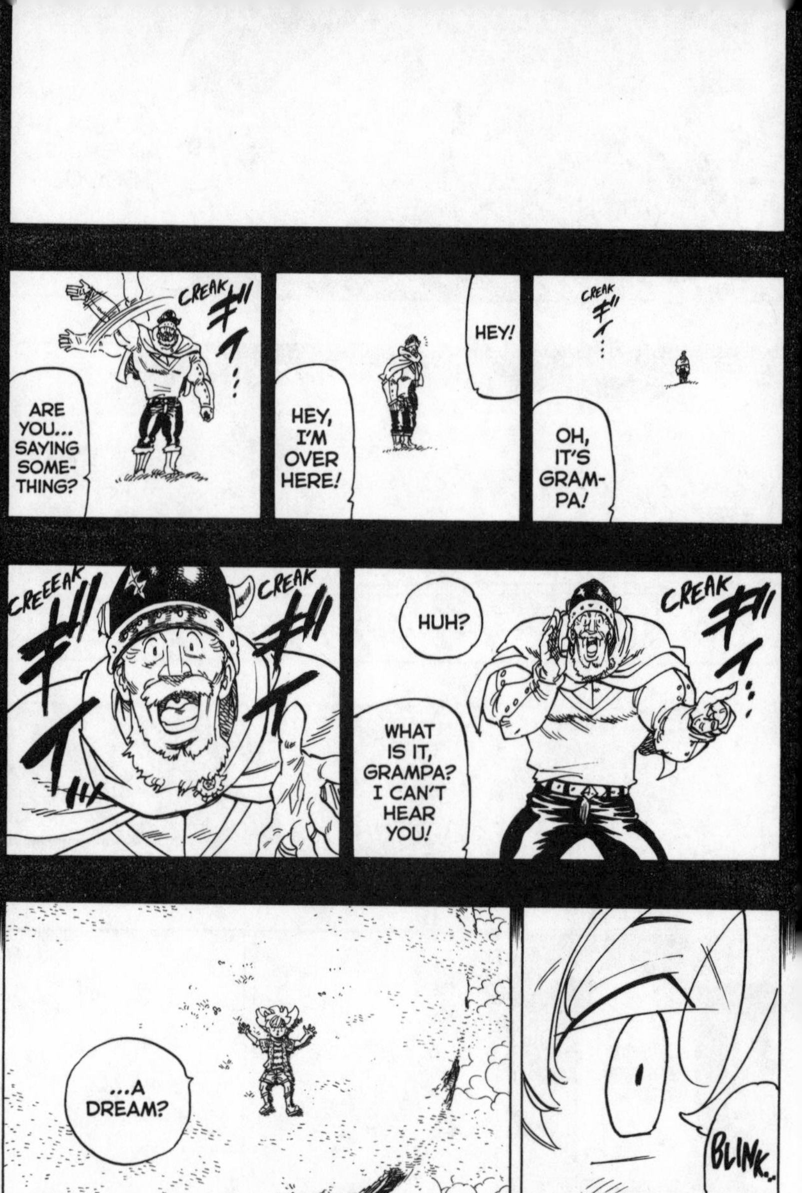
CREAK
OH, IT'S GRAMPA!
HEY!
HEY, I'M OVER HERE!
CREAK
ARE YOU... SAYING SOMETHING?
CREAK
HUH?
WHAT IS IT, GRAMPA? I CAN'T HEAR YOU!
CREAK
CREEEAK
BLINK..
...A DREAM?

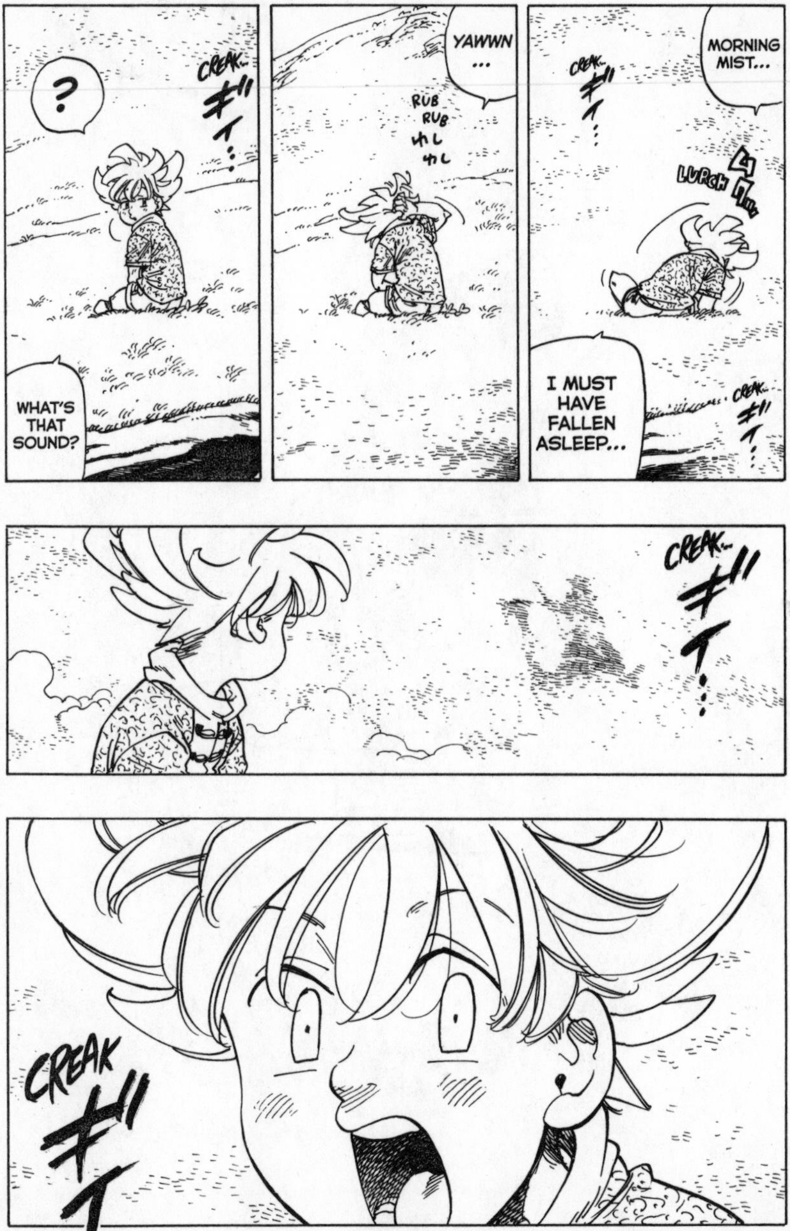
MORNING MIST...
CREAK... ギイ...
LURCH
I MUST HAVE FALLEN ASLEEP...
CREAK... ギイ...
YAWWN...
RUB RUB
?
CREAK... ギイ...
WHAT'S THAT SOUND?
CREAK... ギイ...
CREAK ギイ

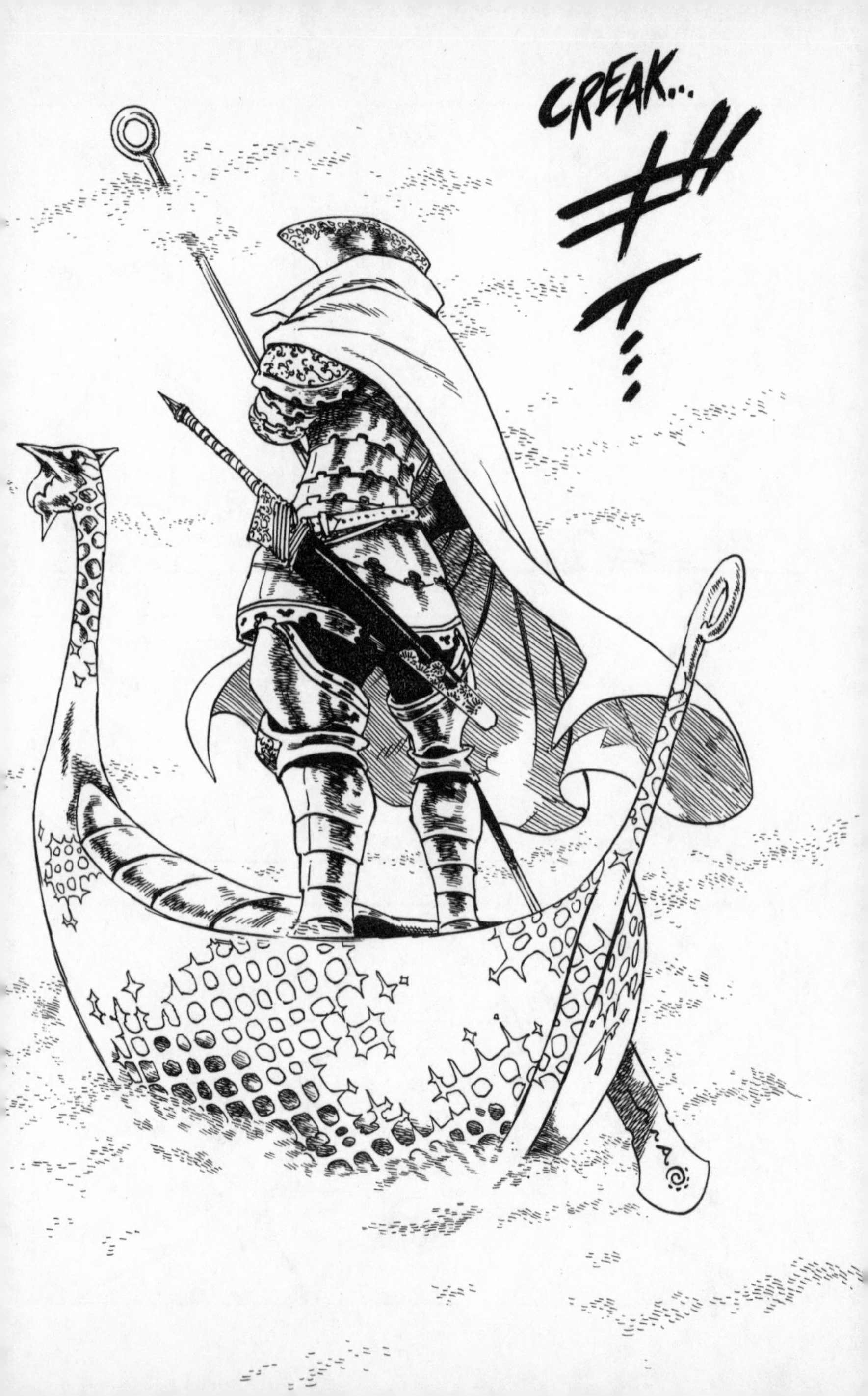
CREAK...
ギイ...

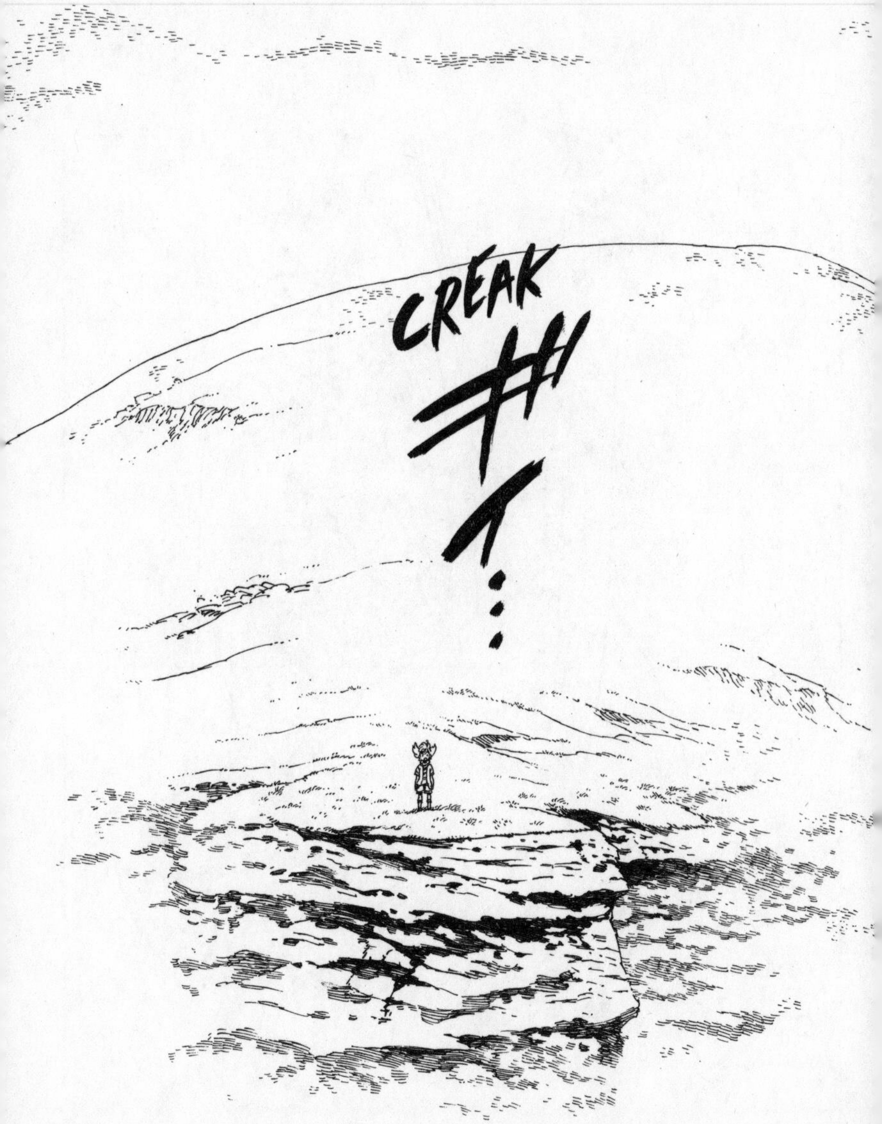
CREAK

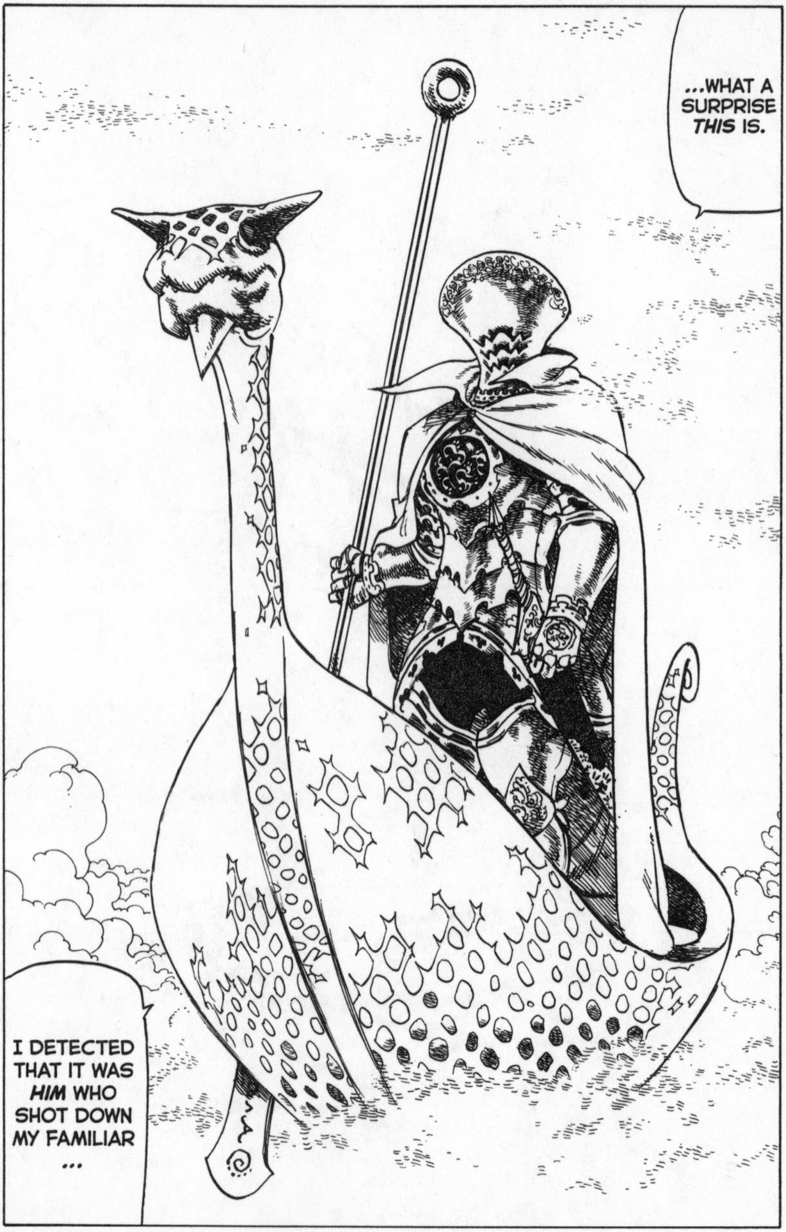
...WHAT A SURPRISE *THIS* IS.
I DETECTED THAT IT WAS *HIM* WHO SHOT DOWN MY FAMILIAR ...

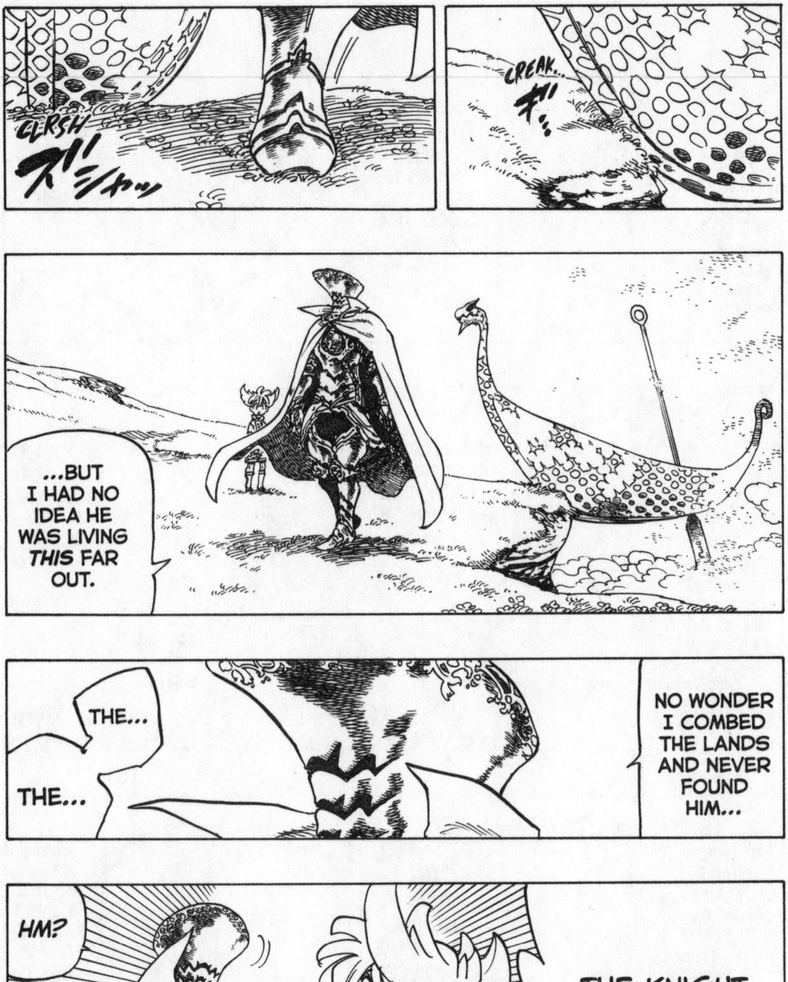
CREAK...
CLRSH
...BUT I HAD NO IDEA HE WAS LIVING *THIS* FAR OUT.
NO WONDER I COMBED THE LANDS AND NEVER FOUND HIM...
THE...
THE...
THE KNIGHT WHO ROWS HIS MYSTIC SHIP ACROSS THE SKIES!!
HM?
THAT STORY WAS REALLY TRUE!

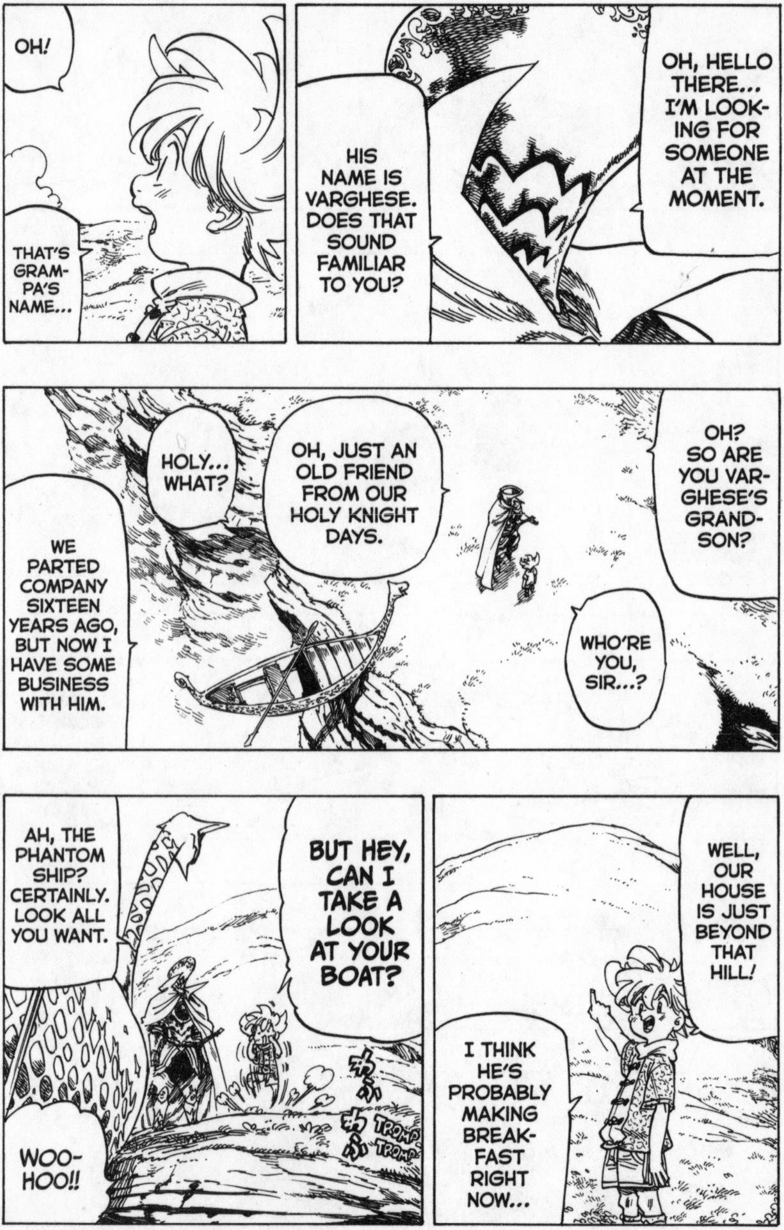
OH, HELLO THERE... I'M LOOKING FOR SOMEONE AT THE MOMENT.
HIS NAME IS VARGHESE. DOES THAT SOUND FAMILIAR TO YOU?
OH!
THAT'S GRAMPA'S NAME...
OH? SO ARE YOU VARGHESE'S GRANDSON?
WHO'RE YOU, SIR...?
OH, JUST AN OLD FRIEND FROM OUR HOLY KNIGHT DAYS.
HOLY... WHAT?
WE PARTED COMPANY SIXTEEN YEARS AGO, BUT NOW I HAVE SOME BUSINESS WITH HIM.
WELL, OUR HOUSE IS JUST BEYOND THAT HILL!
I THINK HE'S PROBABLY MAKING BREAKFAST RIGHT NOW...
BUT HEY, CAN I TAKE A LOOK AT YOUR BOAT?
AH, THE PHANTOM SHIP? CERTAINLY. LOOK ALL YOU WANT.
TROMP TROMP
WOO-HOO!!

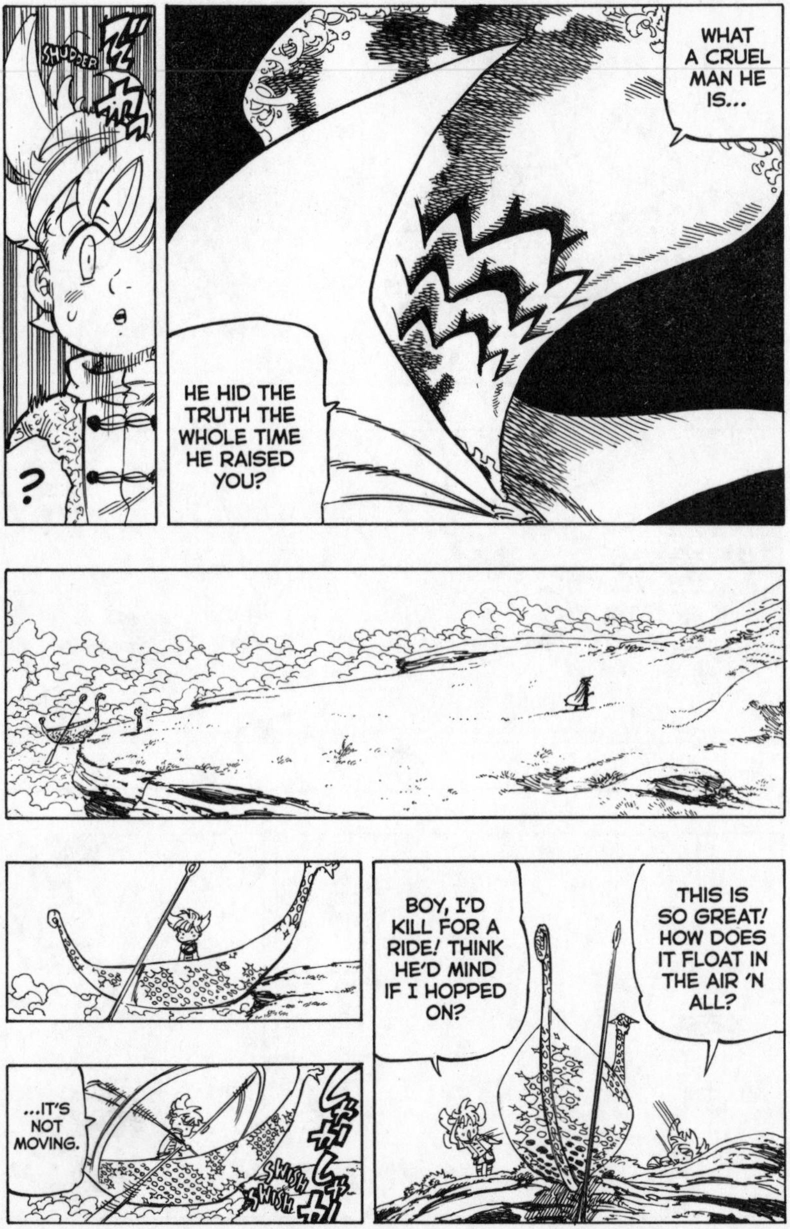
WHAT A CRUEL MAN HE IS...
HE HID THE TRUTH THE WHOLE TIME HE RAISED YOU?
SHUDDER
?
THIS IS SO GREAT! HOW DOES IT FLOAT IN THE AIR 'N ALL?
BOY, I'D KILL FOR A RIDE! THINK HE'D MIND IF I HOPPED ON?
...IT'S NOT MOVING.
SWISH
SWISH

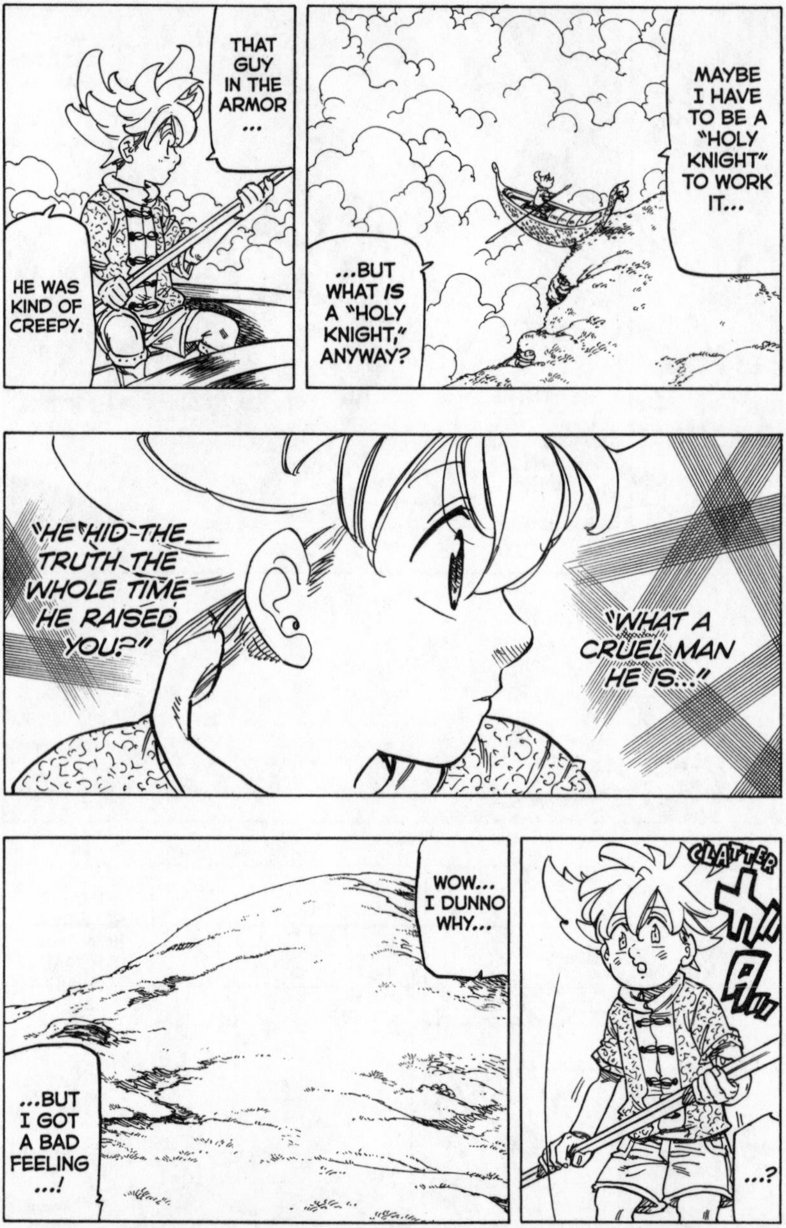
MAYBE I HAVE TO BE A "HOLY KNIGHT" TO WORK IT...
...BUT WHAT *IS* A "HOLY KNIGHT," ANYWAY?
THAT GUY IN THE ARMOR ...
HE WAS KIND OF CREEPY.
"HE HID THE TRUTH THE WHOLE TIME HE RAISED YOU?"
"WHAT A CRUEL MAN HE IS..."
CLATTER
...?
WOW... I DUNNO WHY...
...BUT I GOT A BAD FEELING ...!

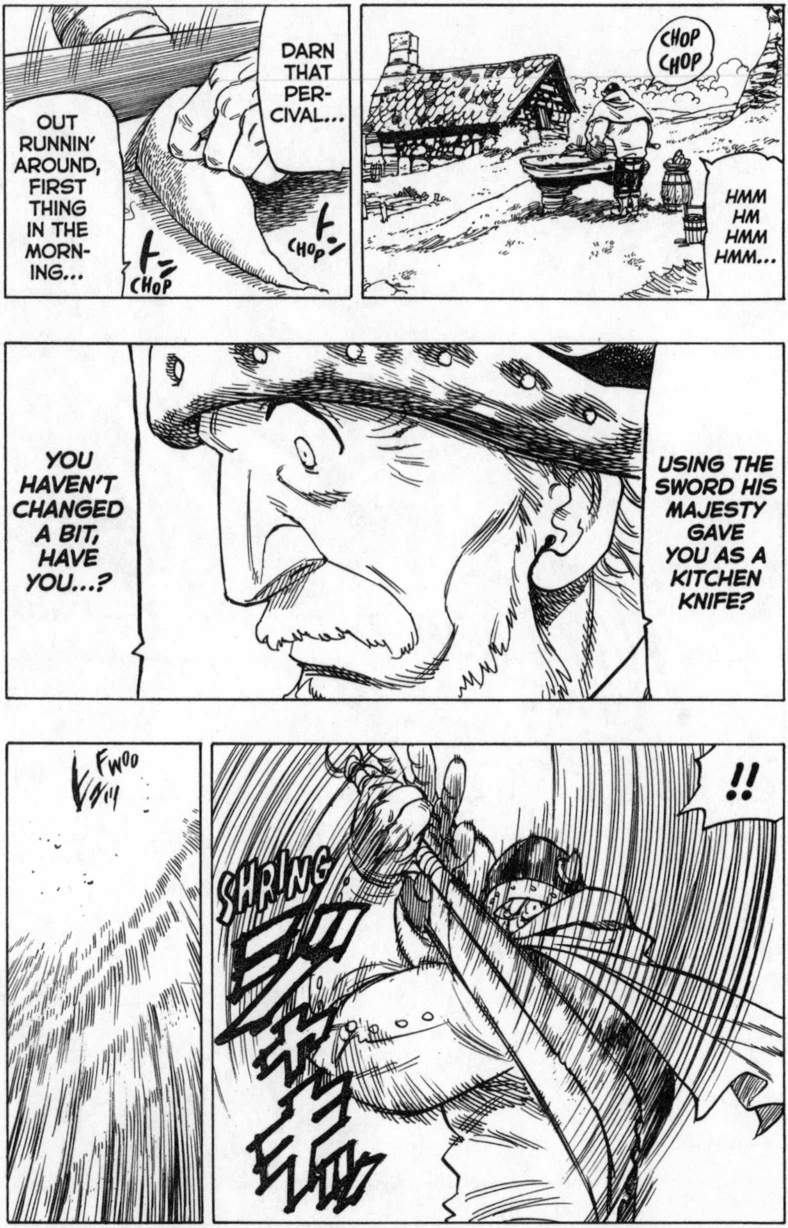
CHOP CHOP
HMM HM HMM HMM...
DARN THAT PERCIVAL...
OUT RUNNIN' AROUND, FIRST THING IN THE MORNING...
CHOP
CHOP
USING THE SWORD HIS MAJESTY GAVE YOU AS A KITCHEN KNIFE?
YOU HAVEN'T CHANGED A BIT, HAVE YOU...?
!!
SHRING
FWOO

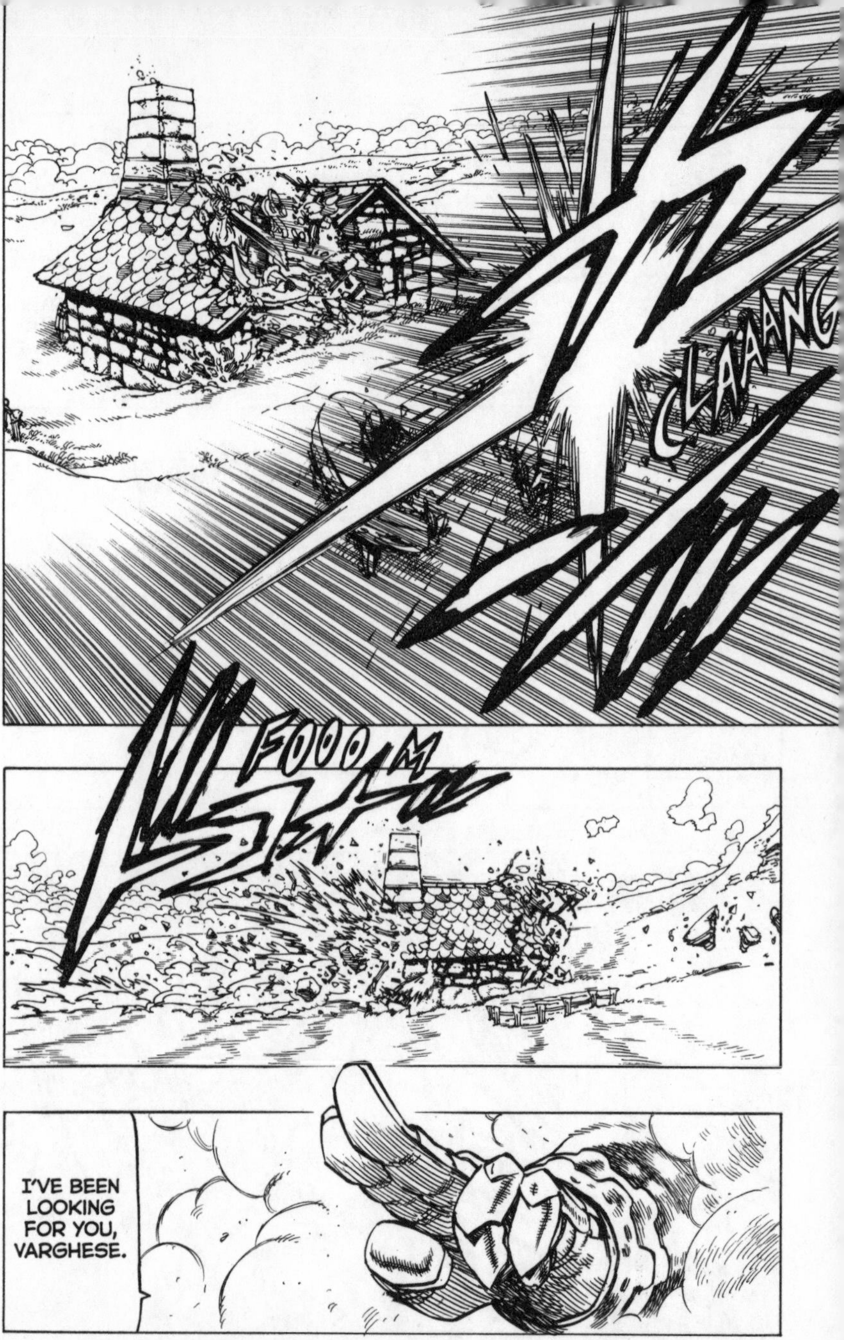
CLAAANG
FOOOM
I'VE BEEN LOOKING FOR YOU, VARGHESE.

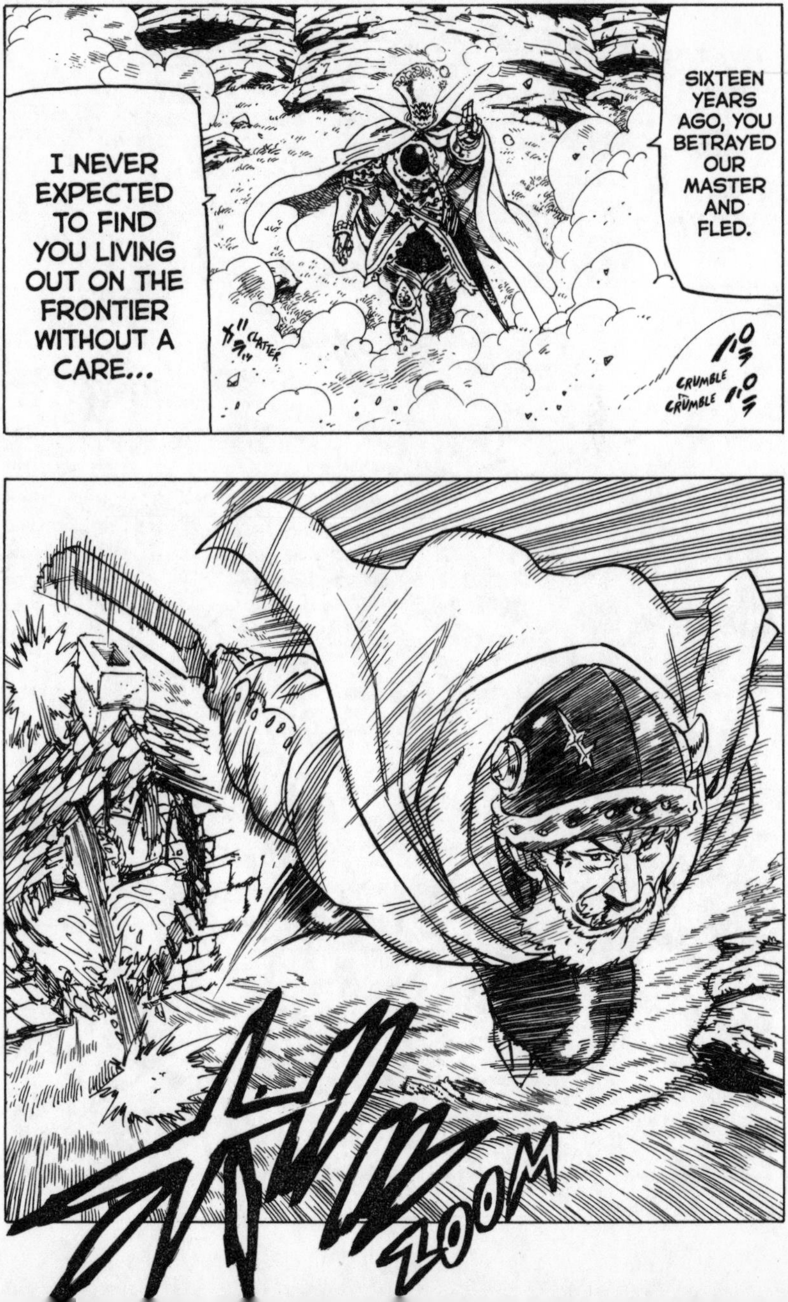
SIXTEEN YEARS AGO, YOU BETRAYED OUR MASTER AND FLED.
I NEVER EXPECTED TO FIND YOU LIVING OUT ON THE FRONTIER WITHOUT A CARE...
CRUMBLE
CRUMBLE
CLATTER
ZOOM

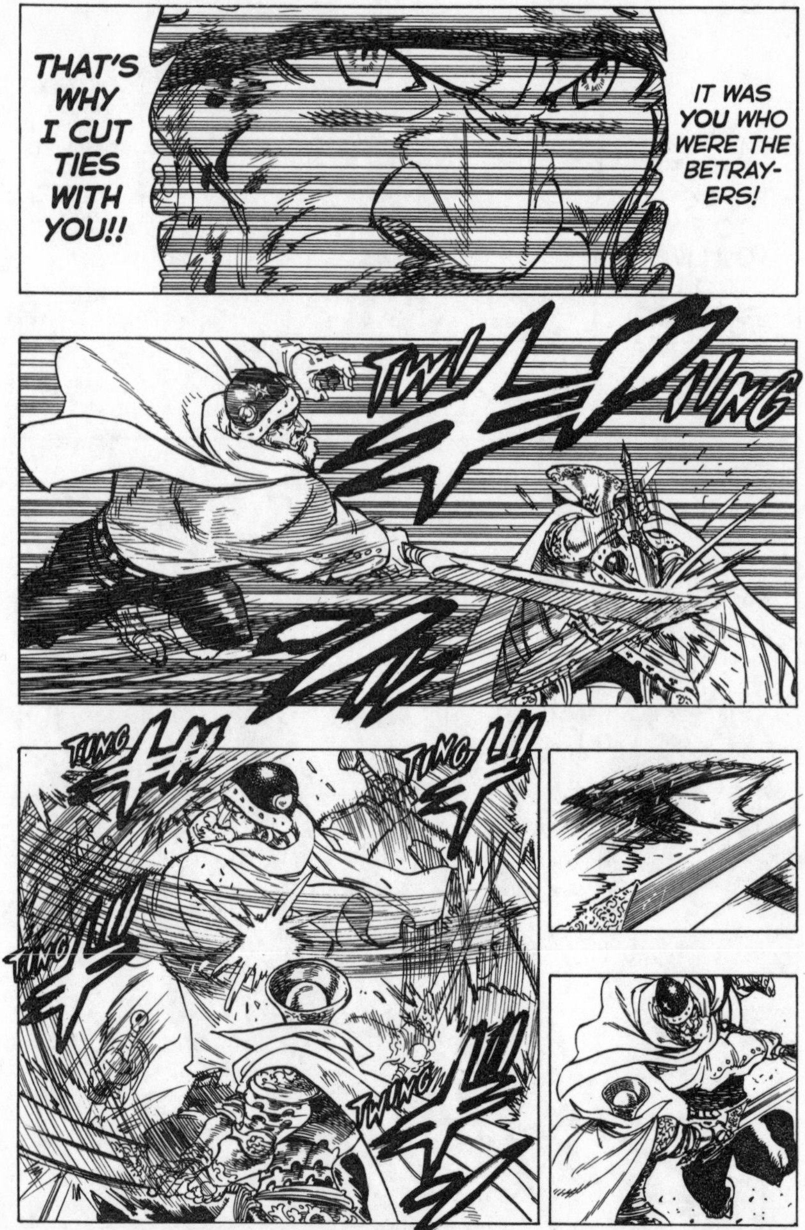
IT WAS YOU WHO WERE THE BETRAY-ERS!
THAT'S WHY I CUT TIES WITH YOU!!
TWIING
TWING!!
TWING!!
TWING!!
TWING!!

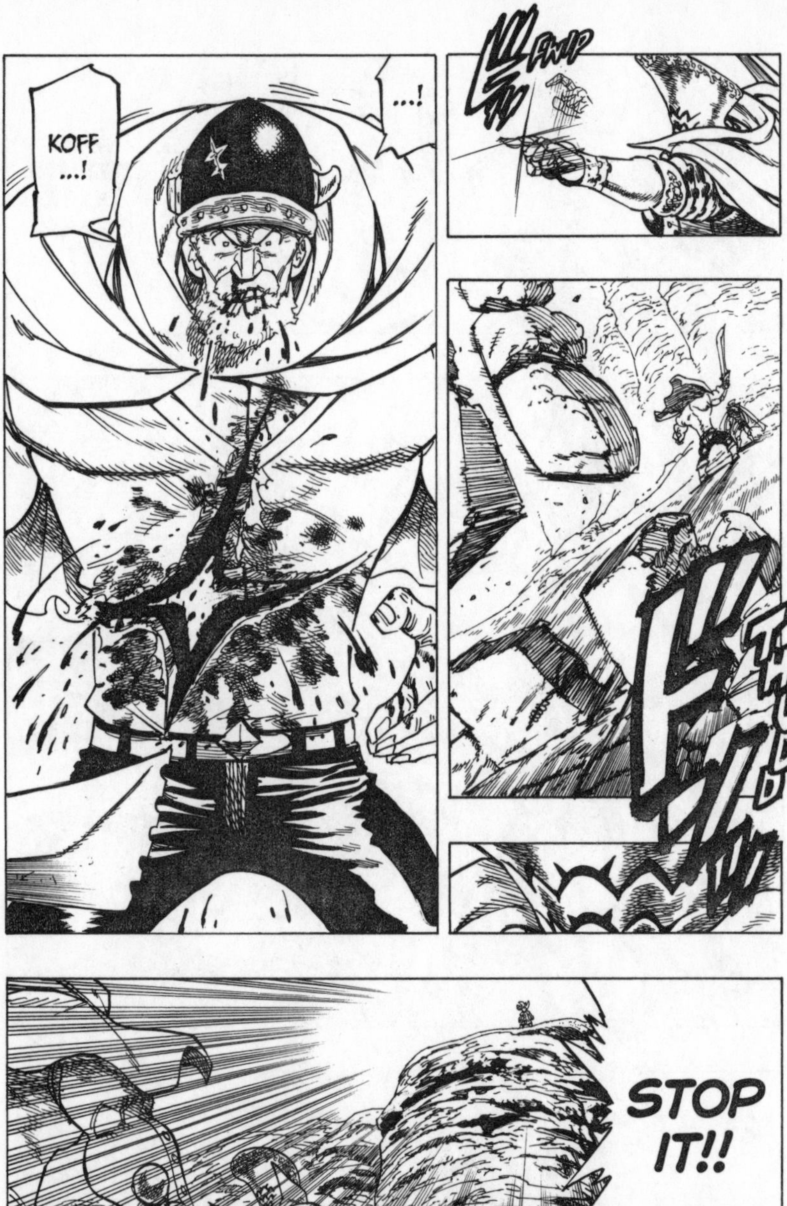
FWIP
THUDD
...!
KOFF ...!
STOP IT!!

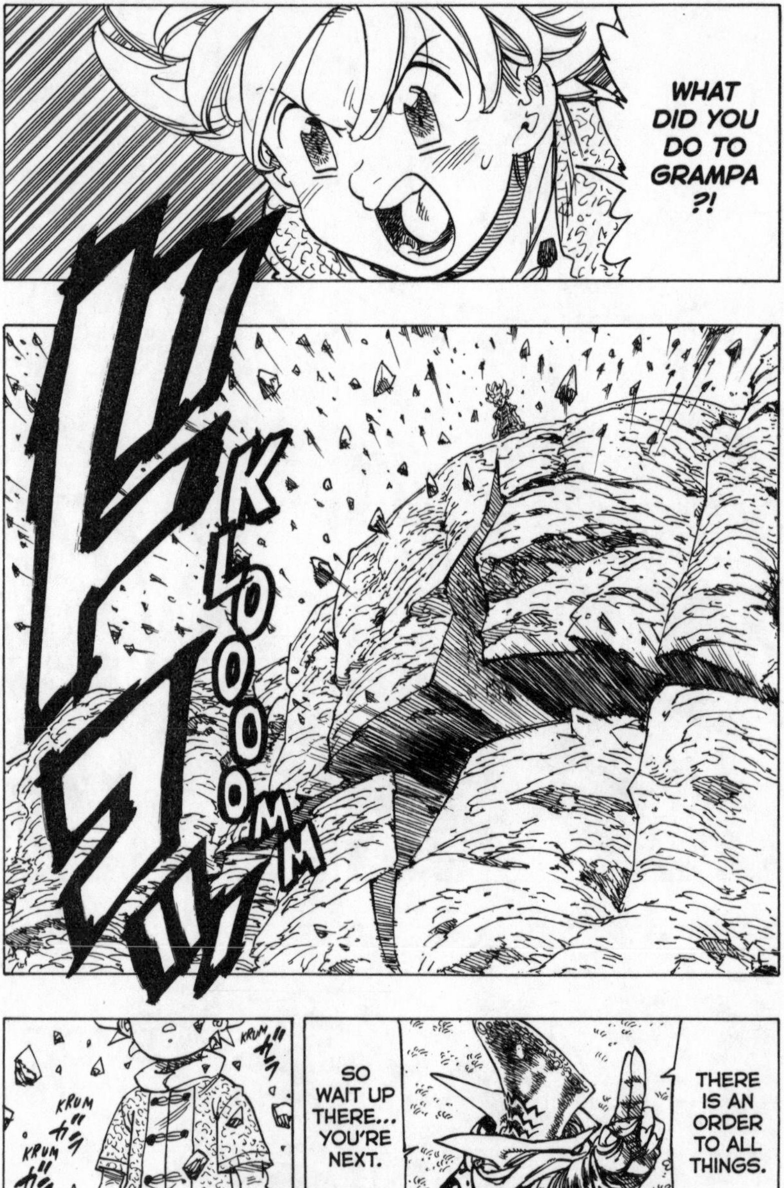

WHAT DID YOU DO TO GRAMPA?!
KLOOOOOMM
THERE IS AN ORDER TO ALL THINGS.
SO WAIT UP THERE... YOU'RE NEXT.
KRUM
KRUM
KRUM

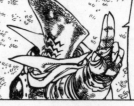

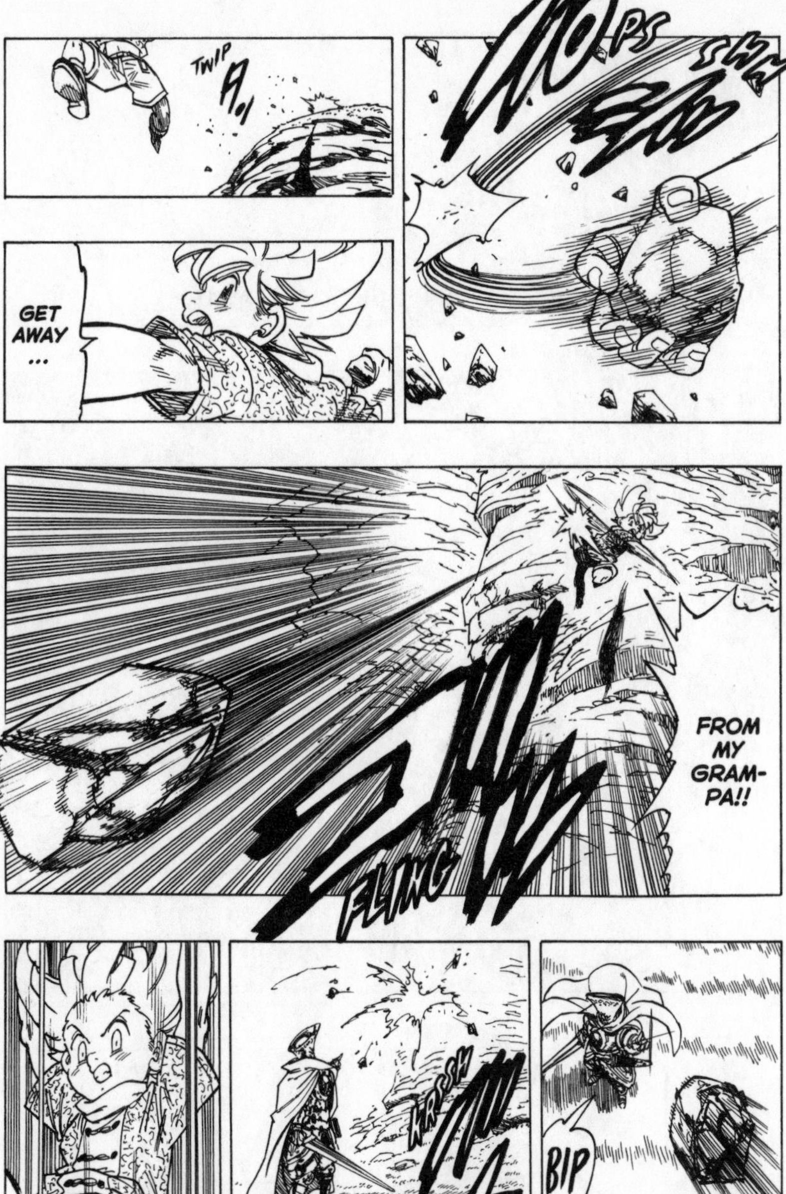
SWM
TWIP
GET AWAY ...
FROM MY GRAM-PA!!
FLING
BIP
KRSSH

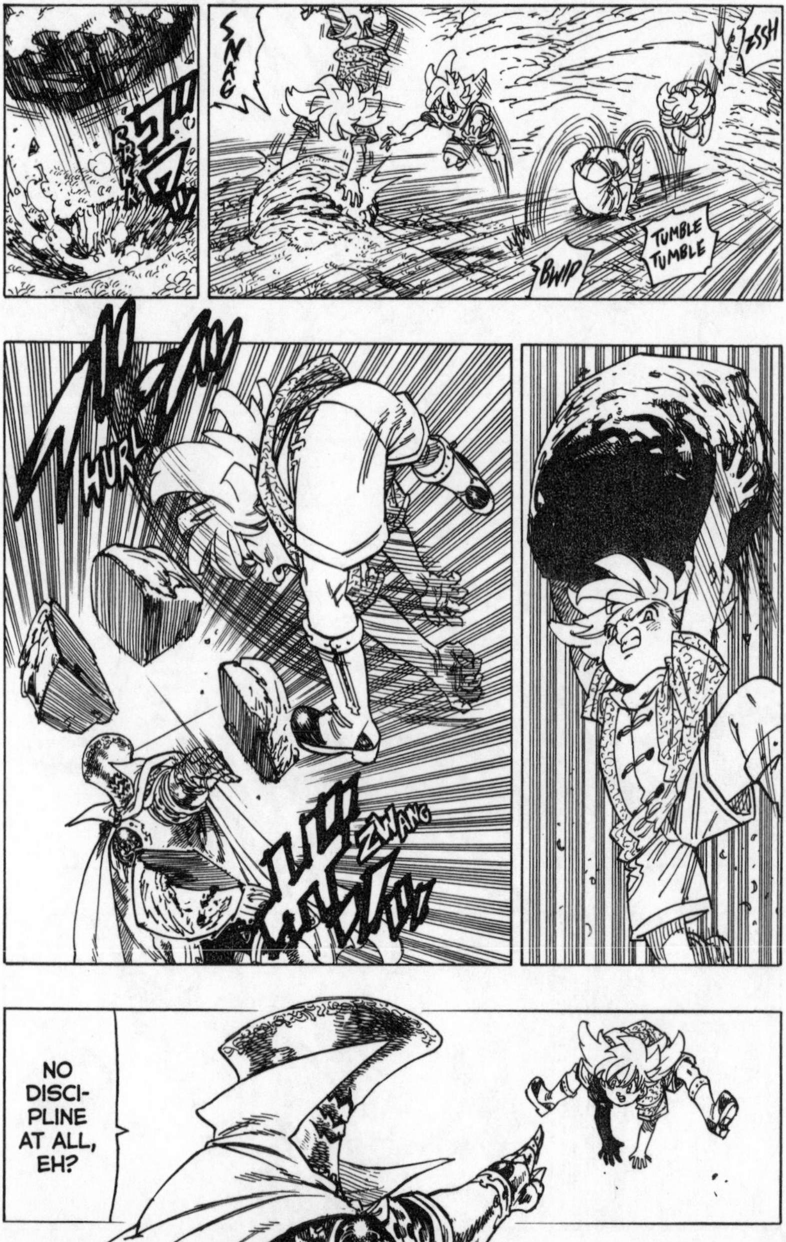
ESSH
SNAG
TUMBLE TUMBLE
BWIP
RRRK
HURL
ZWANG
NO DISCI-PLINE AT ALL, EH?

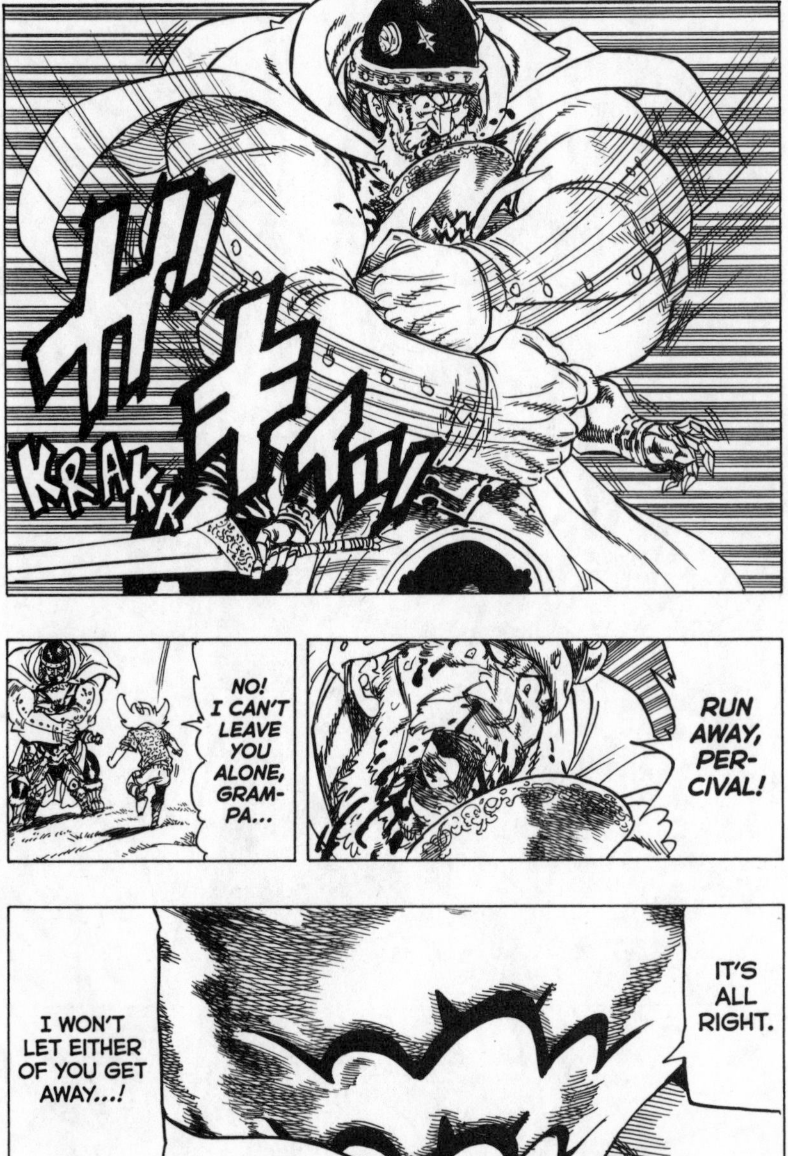
KRAKK
RUN AWAY, PER-CIVAL!
NO! I CAN'T LEAVE YOU ALONE, GRAM-PA...
IT'S ALL RIGHT.
I WON'T LET EITHER OF YOU GET AWAY...!

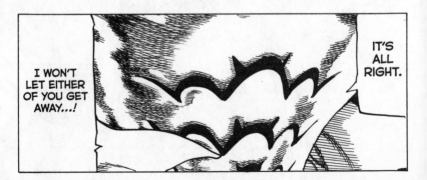

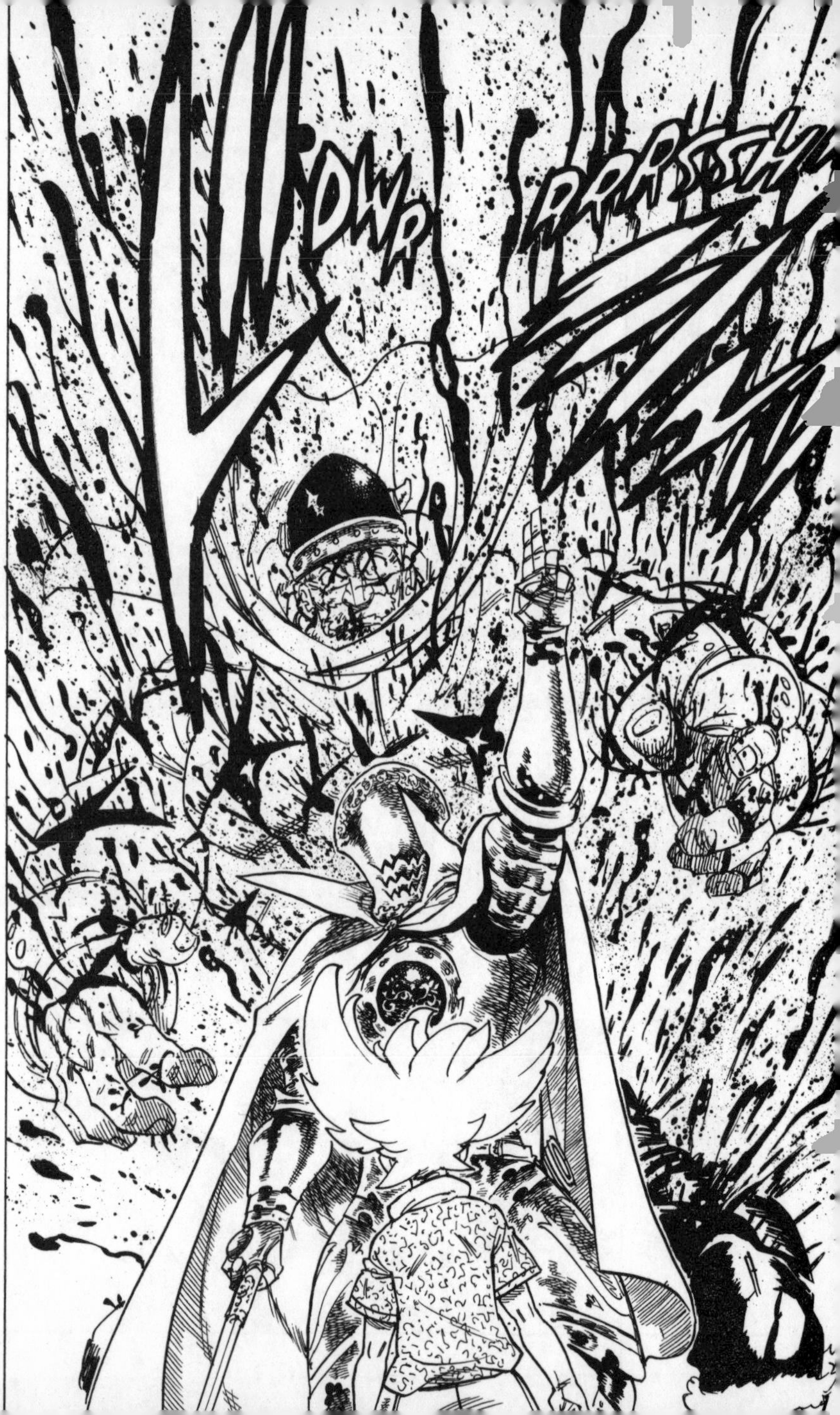
DWR

SLIPP

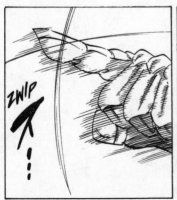

KWUMK

PER...

CI...

ZWIP

!!

HATE YOUR GRAMPA FOR THIS, NOT ME.

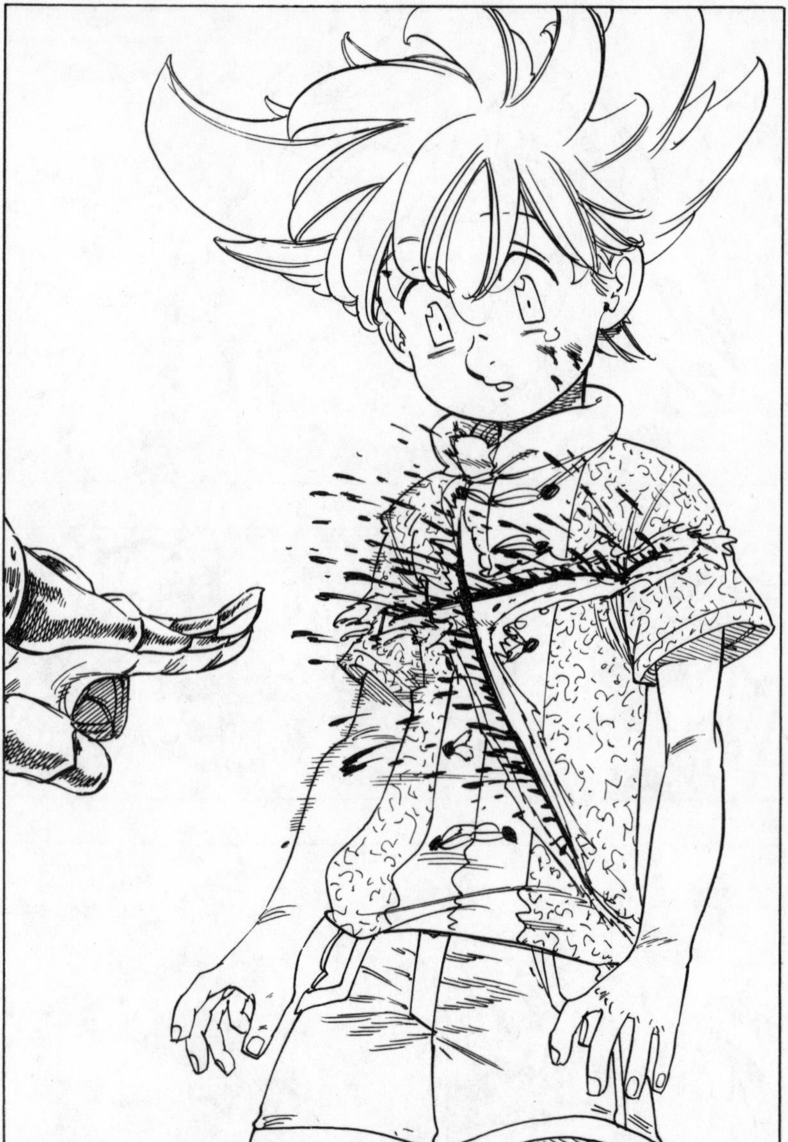

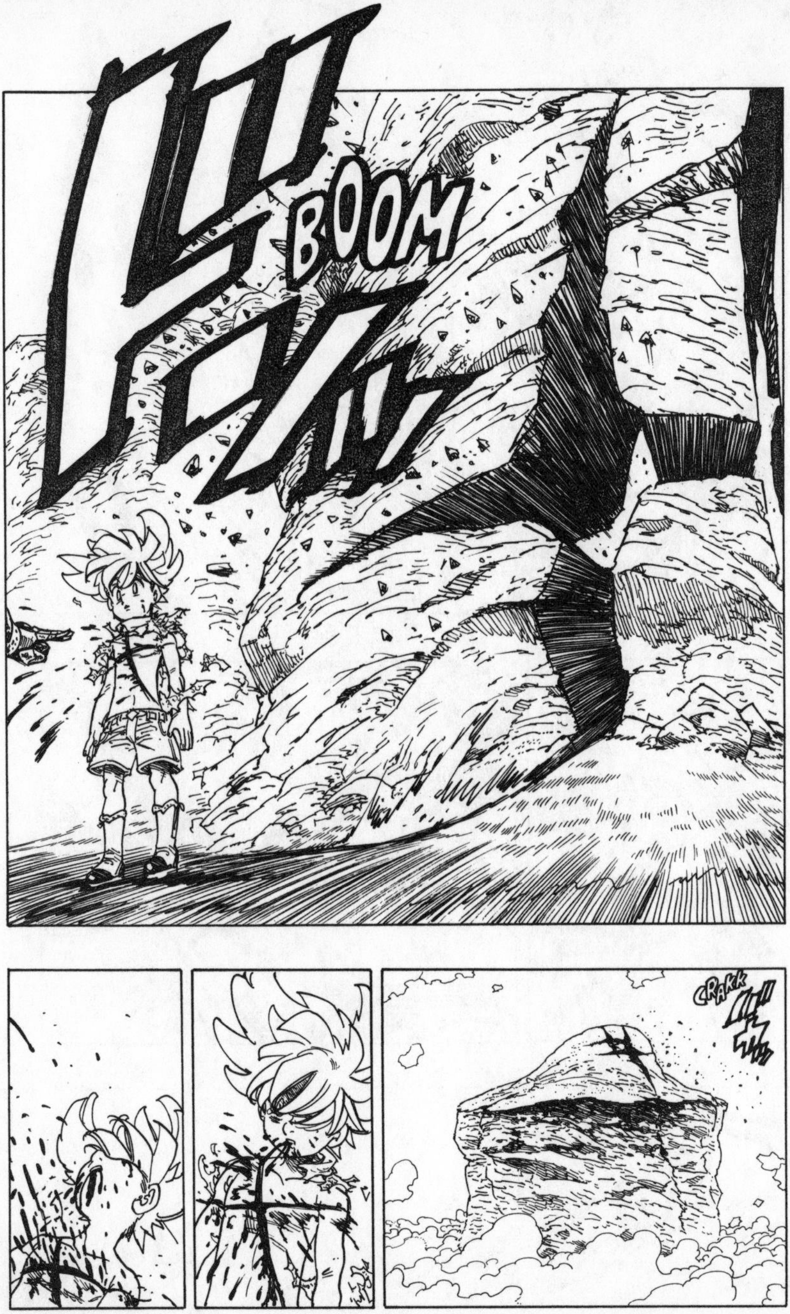
BOOM
CRAKK!!

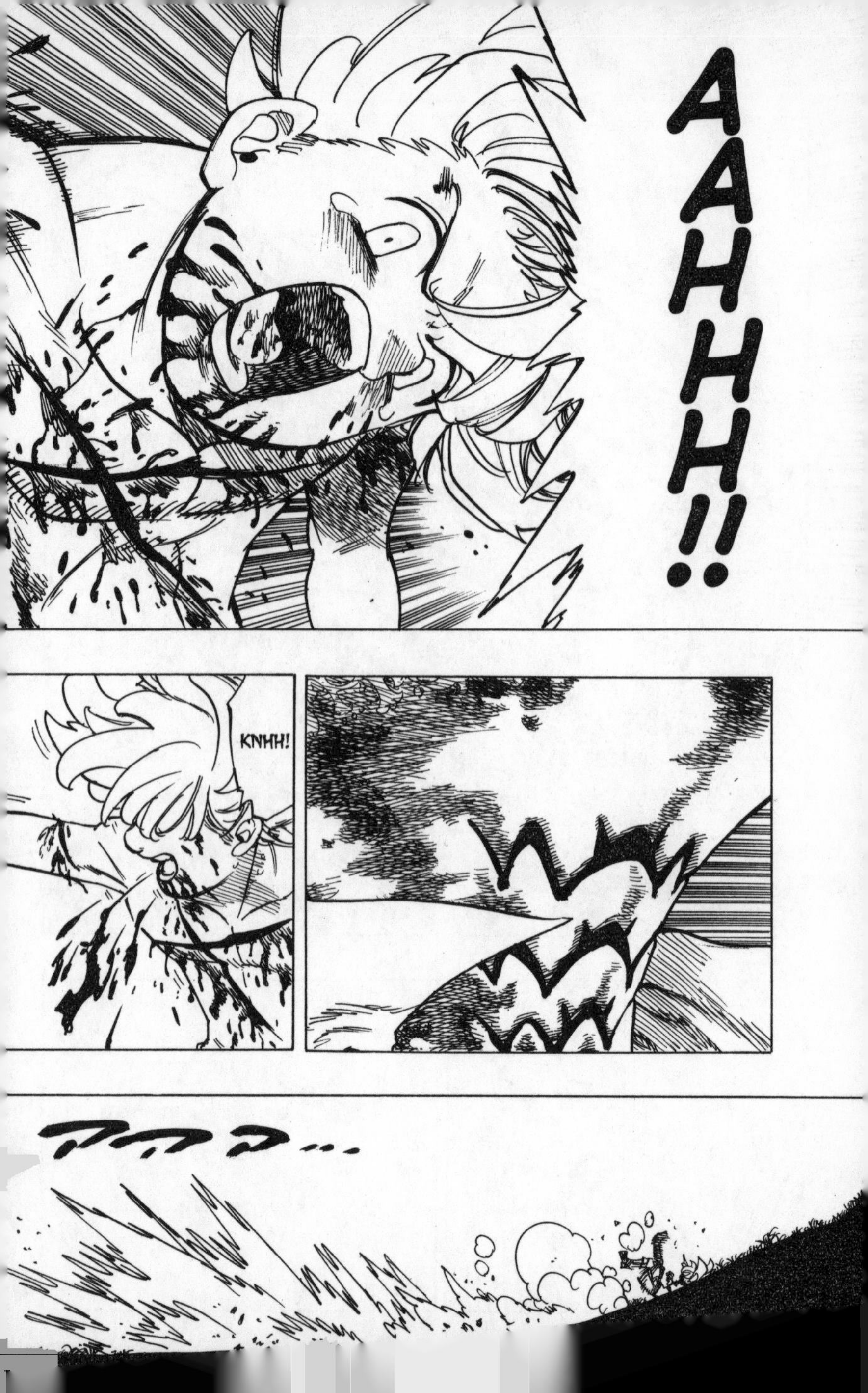
AAHHH!!
KNHH!

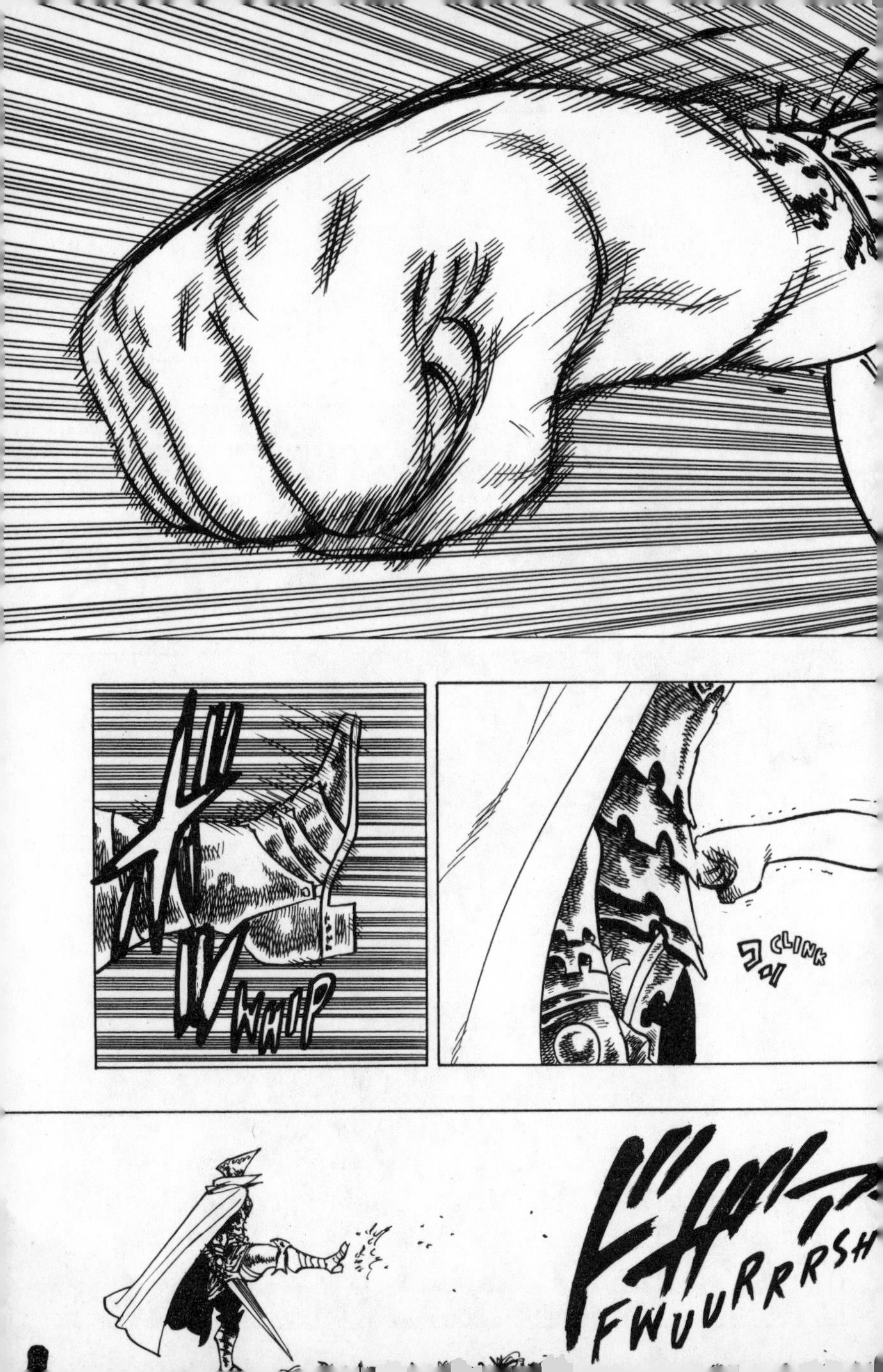
CLINK
WHIP
FWUURRRSH

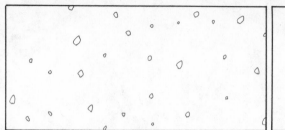

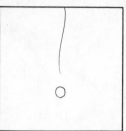

WHY'D... YOU COME TO KILL ME...AFTER ALL THIS TIME?

...IRON... SIDE...

A FEW DAYS AGO, WE WERE GIVEN A FOREBODING PROPHECY...

...ABOUT A GROUP WHO WILL DRIVE OUR LEADER, KING ARTHUR, TO HIS RUIN.

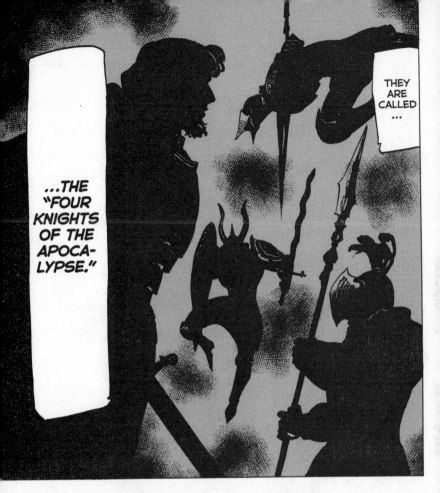

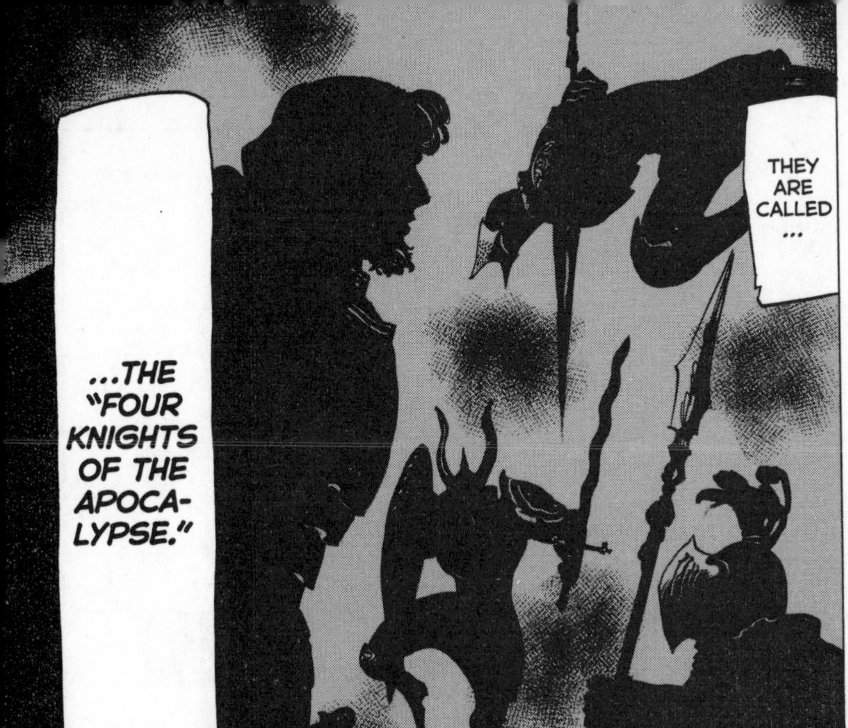
THEY ARE CALLED ...
...THE "FOUR KNIGHTS OF THE APOCA-LYPSE."

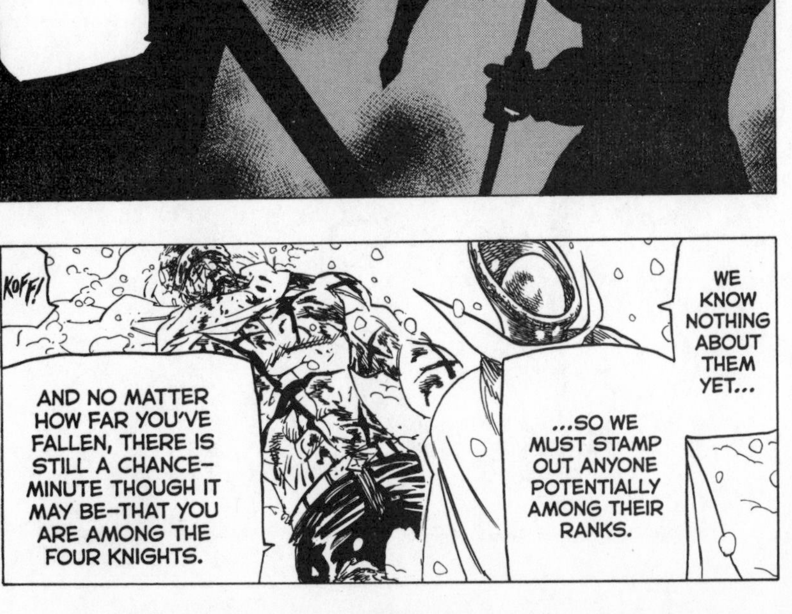
WE KNOW NOTHING ABOUT THEM YET...
...SO WE MUST STAMP OUT ANYONE POTENTIALLY AMONG THEIR RANKS.
KOFF!
AND NO MATTER HOW FAR YOU'VE FALLEN, THERE IS STILL A CHANCE-MINUTE THOUGH IT MAY BE-THAT YOU ARE AMONG THE FOUR KNIGHTS.

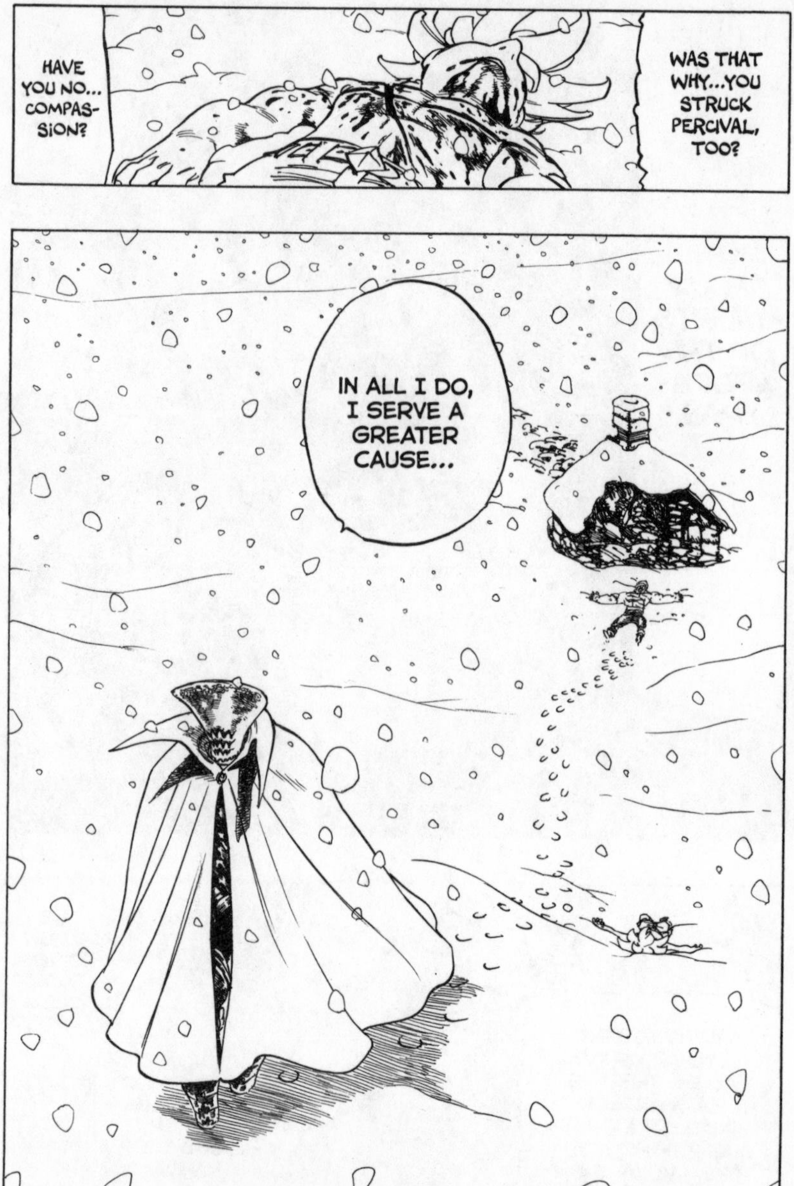
WAS THAT WHY...YOU STRUCK PERCIVAL, TOO?
HAVE YOU NO... COMPASSION?
IN ALL I DO, I SERVE A GREATER CAUSE...

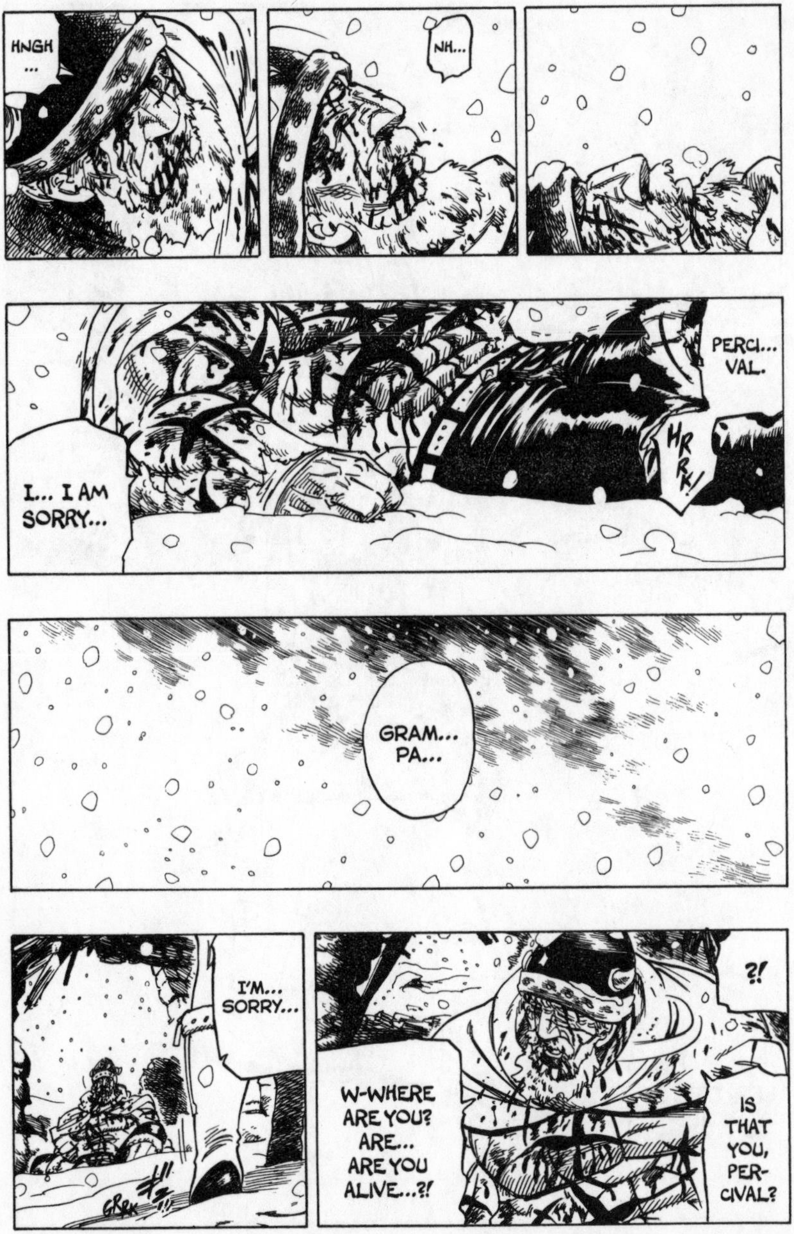
NH...
HNGH ...
PERCI... VAL.
HRRK!
I... I AM SORRY...
GRAM... PA...
?!
IS THAT YOU, PER-CIVAL?
W-WHERE ARE YOU? ARE... ARE YOU ALIVE...?!
I'M... SORRY...
GRRK

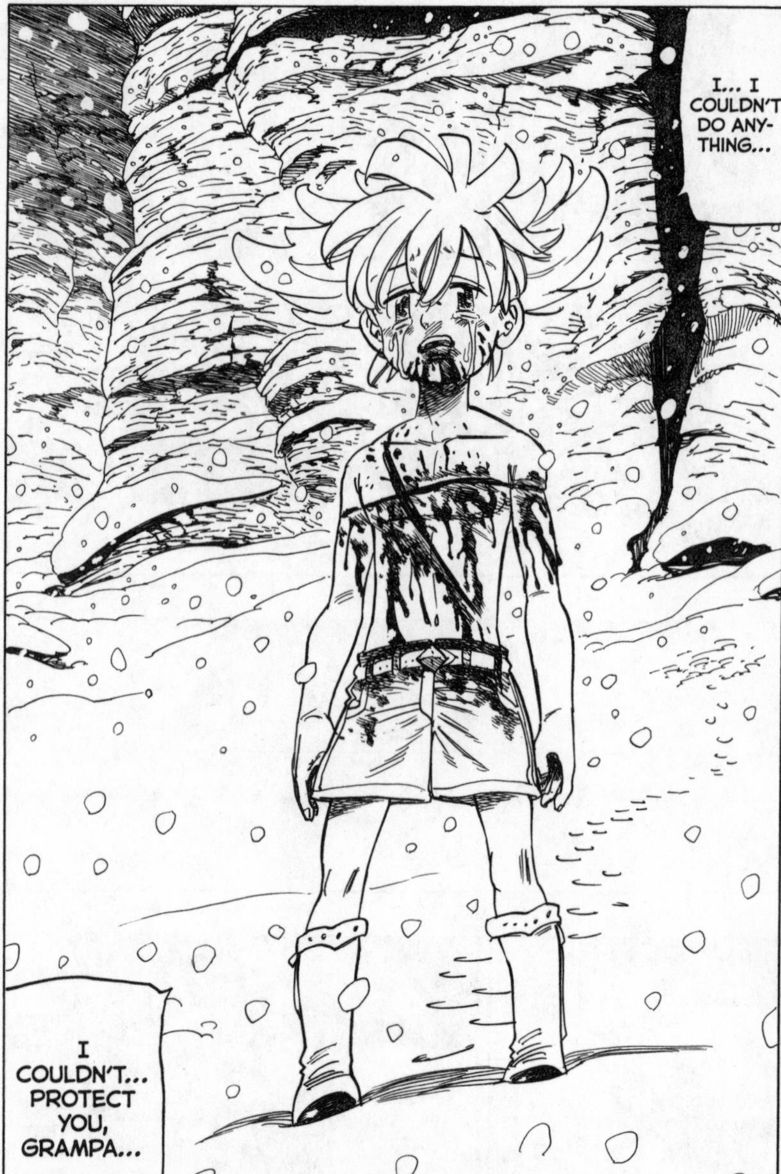
I... I COULDN'T DO ANYTHING...
I COULDN'T... PROTECT YOU, GRAMPA...

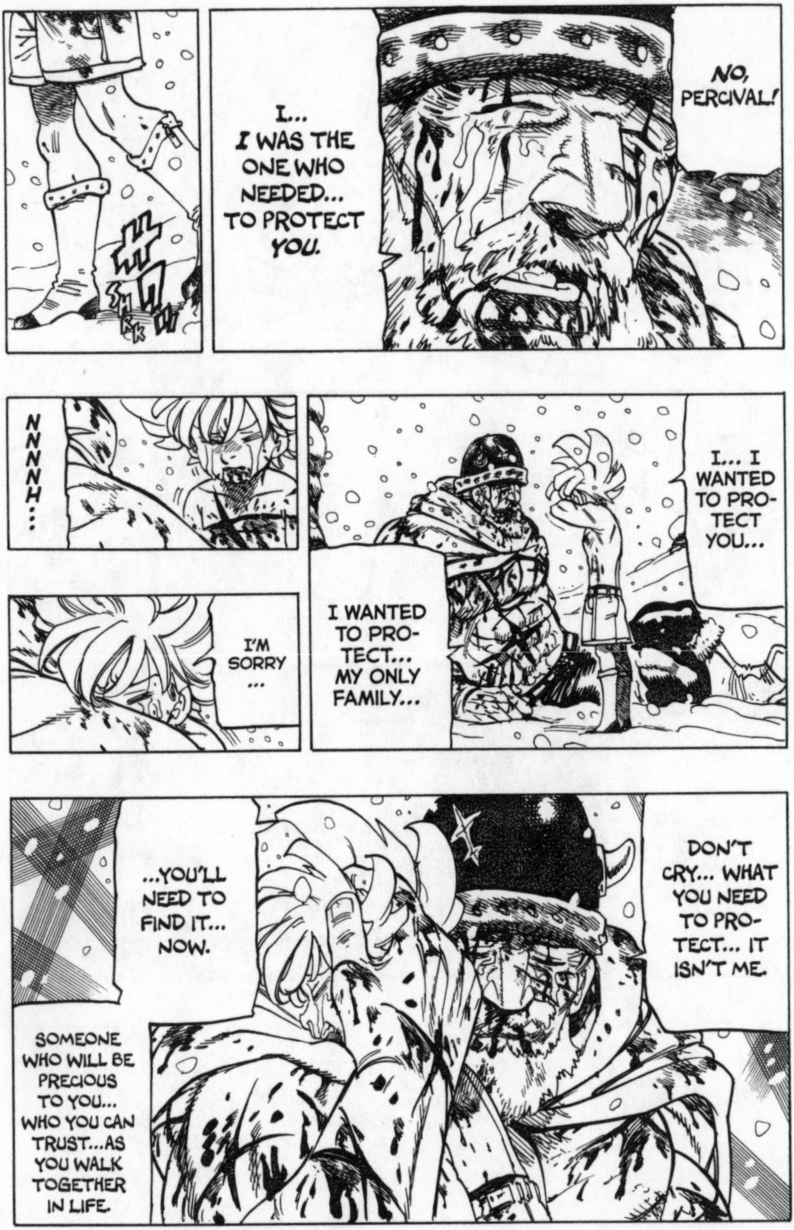
NO, PERCIVAL!
I... I WAS THE ONE WHO NEEDED... TO PROTECT YOU.
SHRK
I... I WANTED TO PRO-TECT YOU...
I WANTED TO PRO-TECT... MY ONLY FAMILY...
NNNNH...
I'M SORRY ...
DON'T CRY... WHAT YOU NEED TO PRO-TECT... IT ISN'T ME.
...YOU'LL NEED TO FIND IT... NOW.
SOMEONE WHO WILL BE PRECIOUS TO YOU... WHO YOU CAN TRUST...AS YOU WALK TOGETHER IN LIFE.

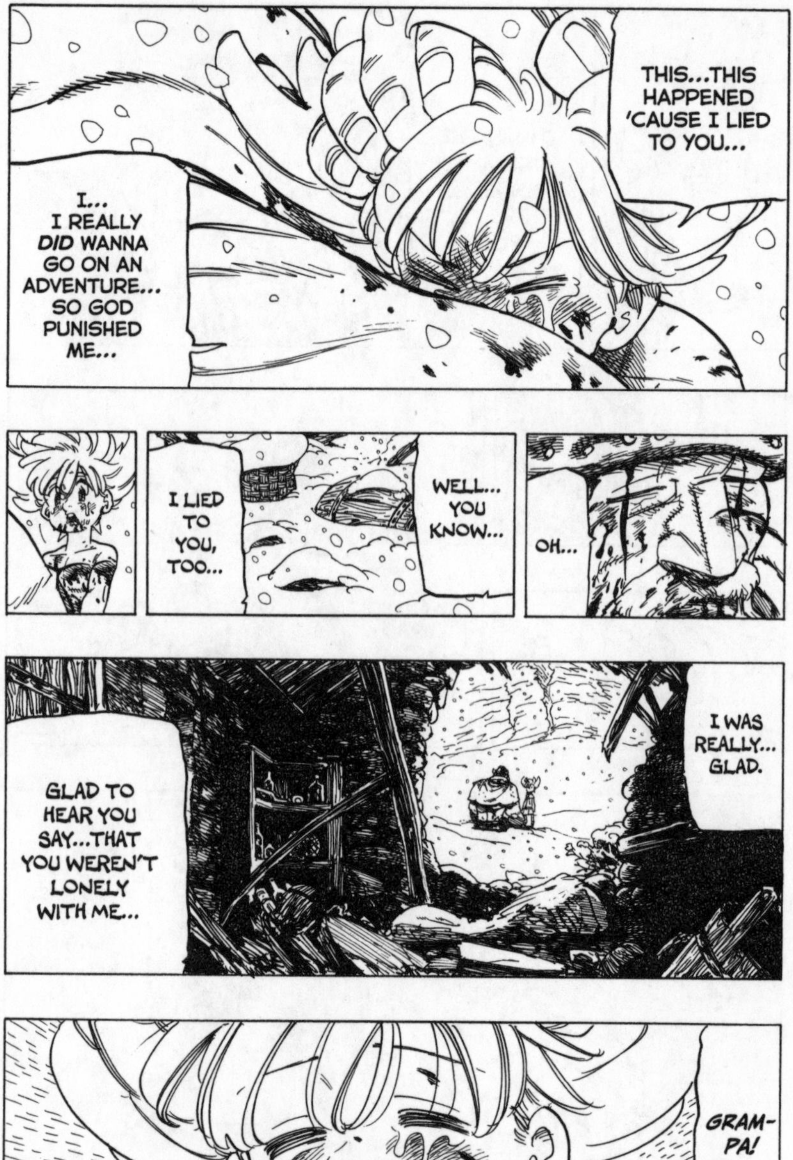
THIS...THIS HAPPENED 'CAUSE I LIED TO YOU...
I... I REALLY *DID* WANNA GO ON AN ADVENTURE... SO GOD PUNISHED ME...
OH...
WELL... YOU KNOW...
I LIED TO YOU, TOO...
I WAS REALLY... GLAD.
GLAD TO HEAR YOU SAY...THAT YOU WEREN'T LONELY WITH ME...
GRAM-PA!

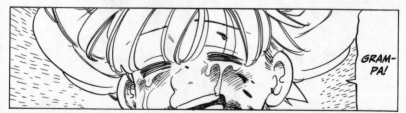

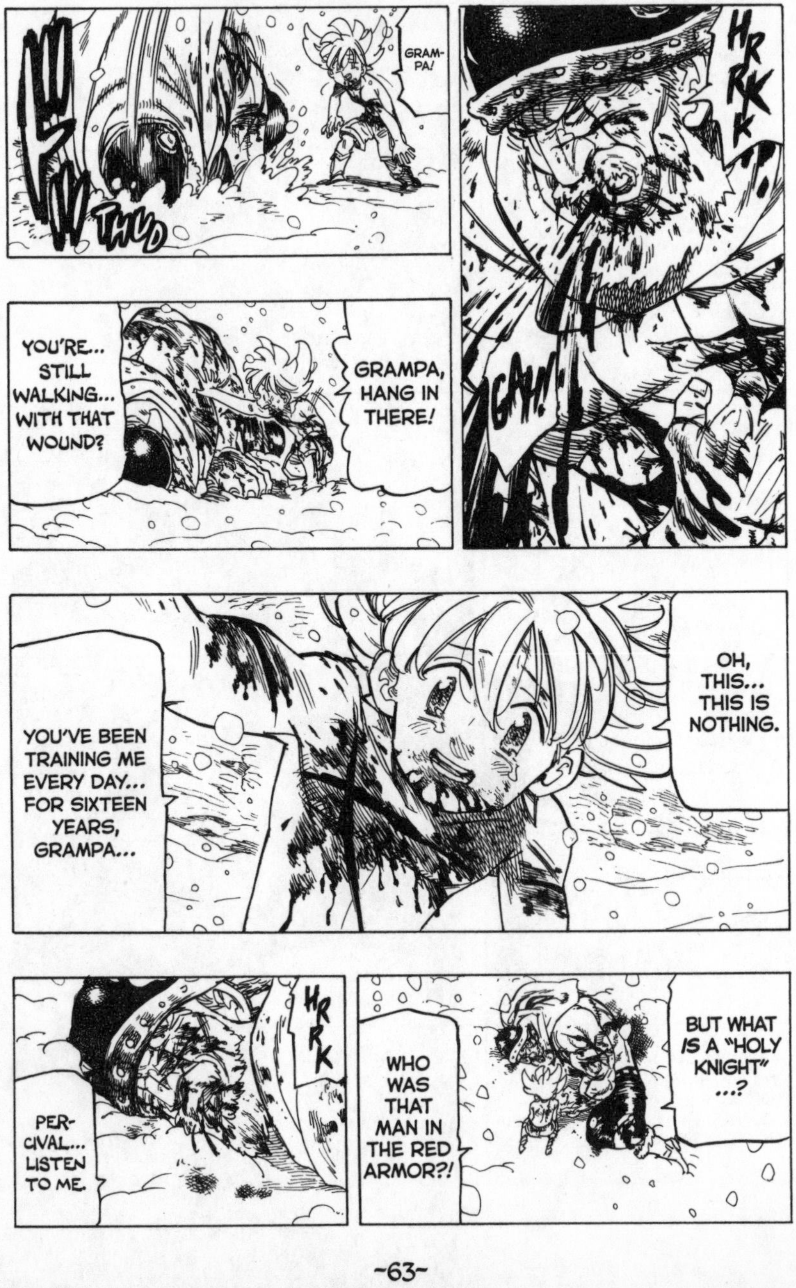
HRKK
GAH!
GRAMPA!
THUD
GRAMPA, HANG IN THERE!
YOU'RE... STILL WALKING... WITH THAT WOUND?
OH, THIS... THIS IS NOTHING.
YOU'VE BEEN TRAINING ME EVERY DAY... FOR SIXTEEN YEARS, GRAMPA...
BUT WHAT IS A "HOLY KNIGHT" ...?
WHO WAS THAT MAN IN THE RED ARMOR?!
HRK
PERCIVAL... LISTEN TO ME.

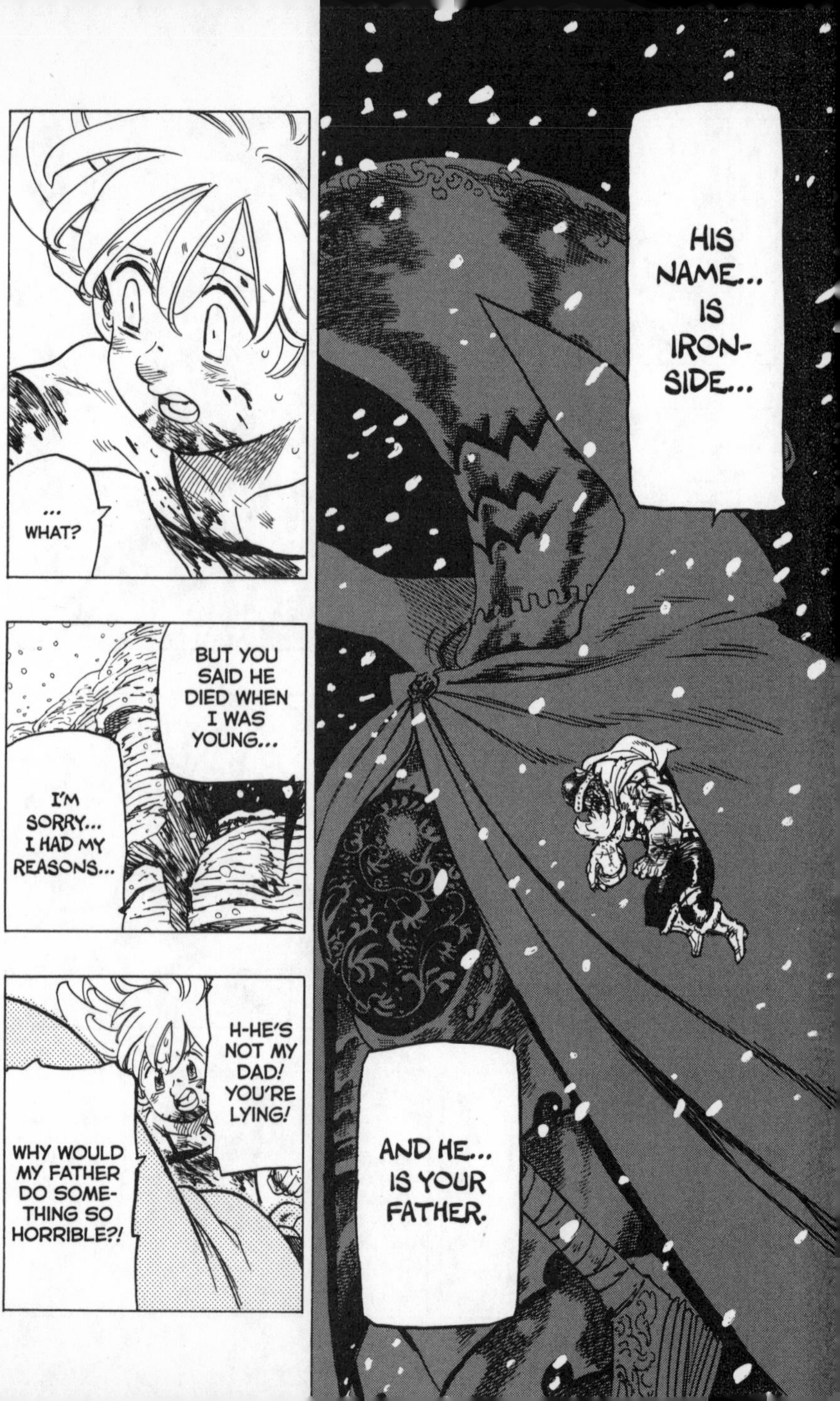

HIS NAME... IS IRON-SIDE...
AND HE... IS YOUR FATHER.
... WHAT?
BUT YOU SAID HE DIED WHEN I WAS YOUNG...
I'M SORRY... I HAD MY REASONS...
H-HE'S NOT MY DAD! YOU'RE LYING!
WHY WOULD MY FATHER DO SOME-THING SO HORRIBLE?!

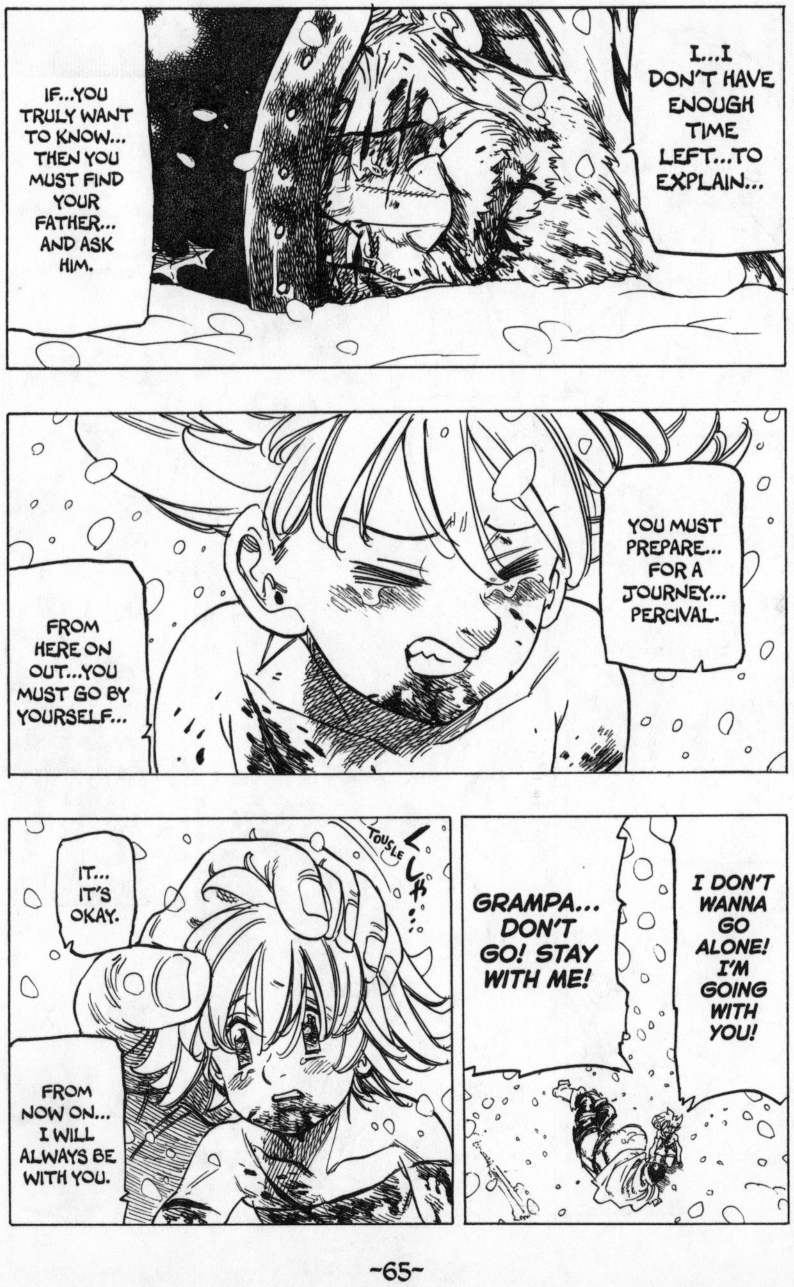
I...I DON'T HAVE ENOUGH TIME LEFT...TO EXPLAIN...
IF...YOU TRULY WANT TO KNOW... THEN YOU MUST FIND YOUR FATHER... AND ASK HIM.
YOU MUST PREPARE... FOR A JOURNEY... PERCIVAL.
FROM HERE ON OUT...YOU MUST GO BY YOURSELF...
I DON'T WANNA GO ALONE! I'M GOING WITH YOU!
GRAMPA... DON'T GO! STAY WITH ME!
TOUSLE
IT... IT'S OKAY.
FROM NOW ON... I WILL ALWAYS BE WITH YOU.

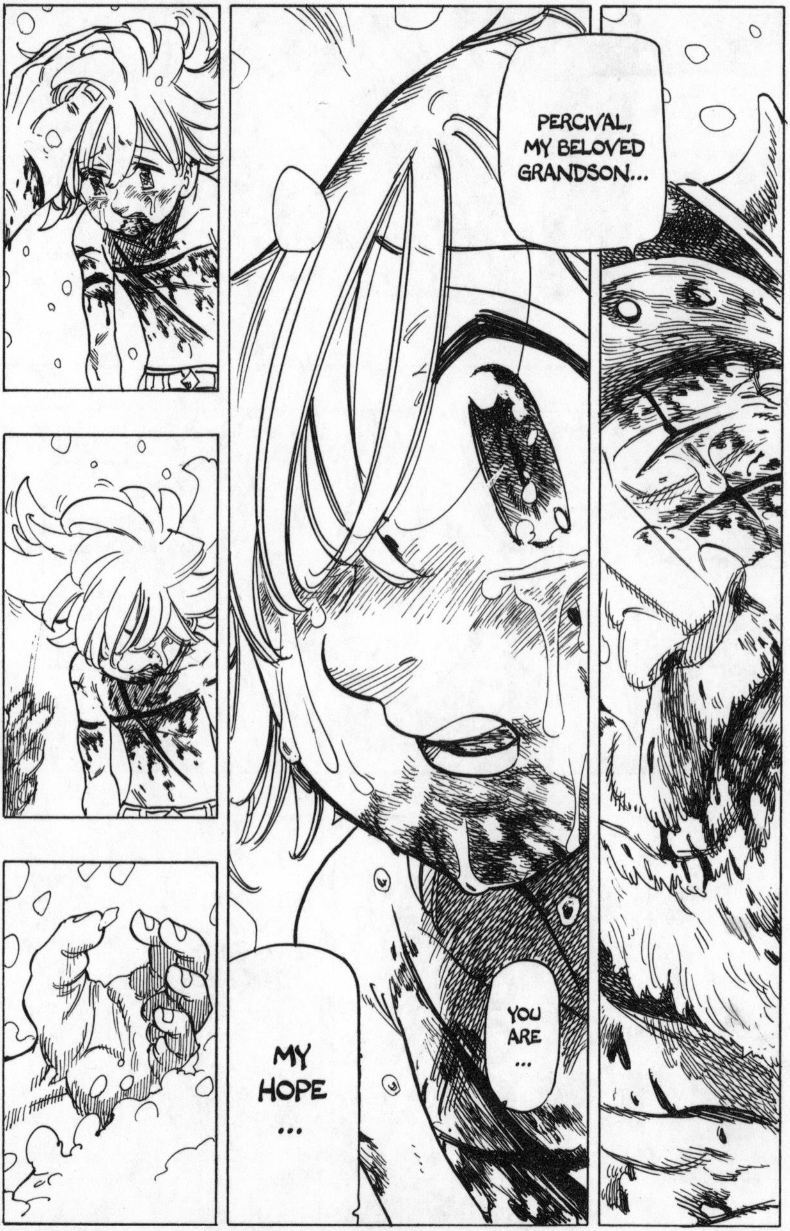
PERCIVAL, MY BELOVED GRANDSON...
YOU ARE ...
MY HOPE ...

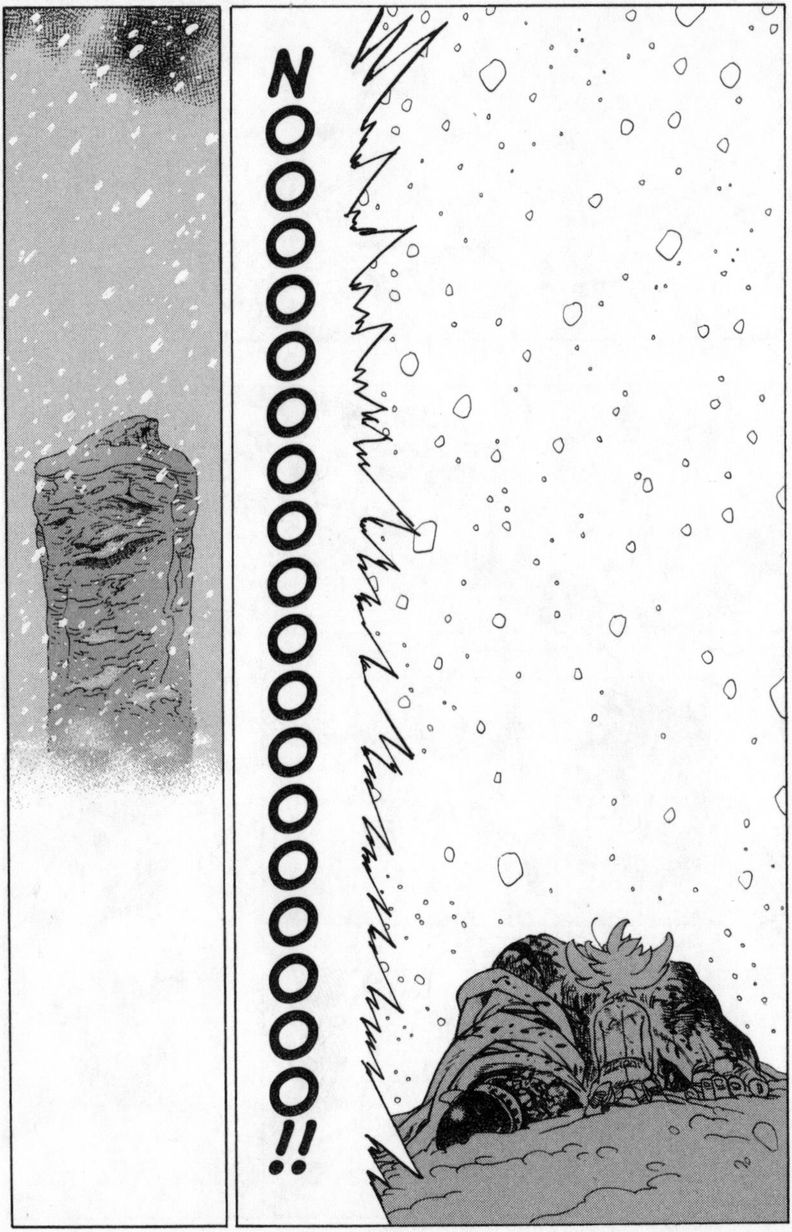
NOOOOOOOOOOOOOOOOOOOOO!!

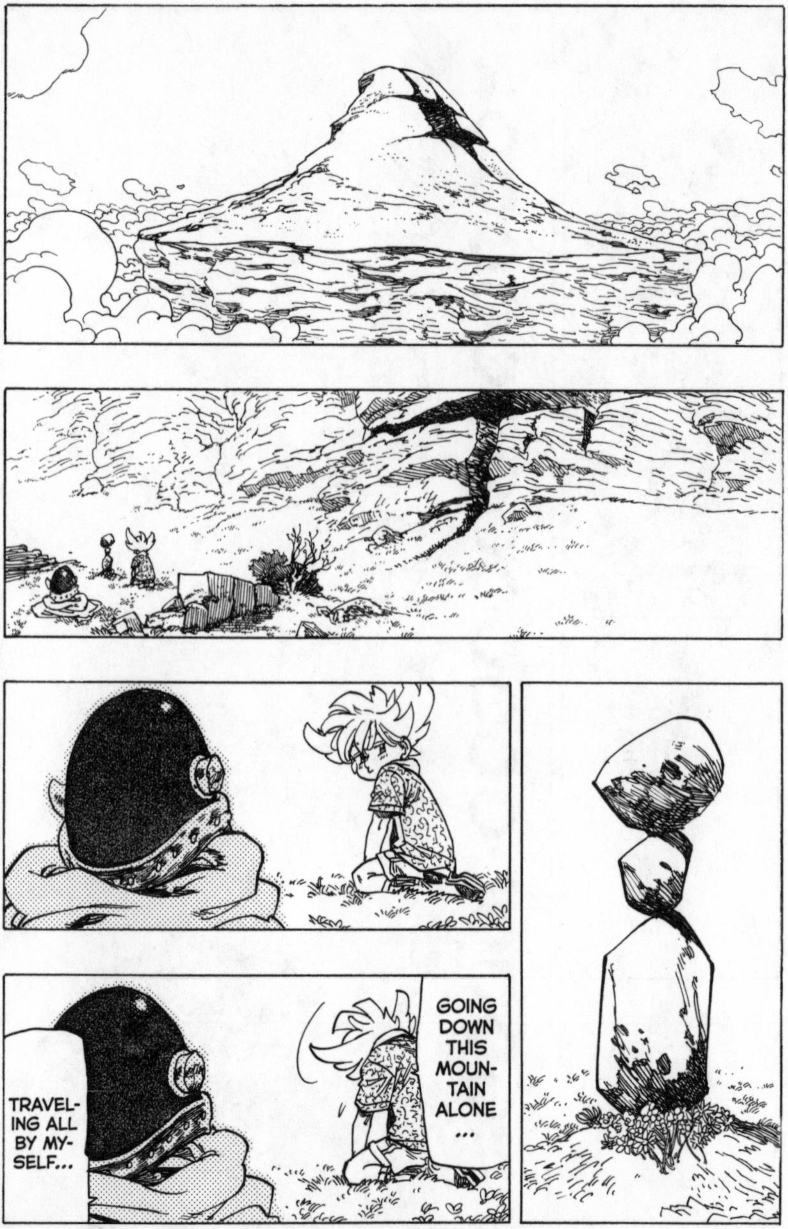
GOING DOWN THIS MOUNTAIN ALONE ...
TRAVELING ALL BY MYSELF...

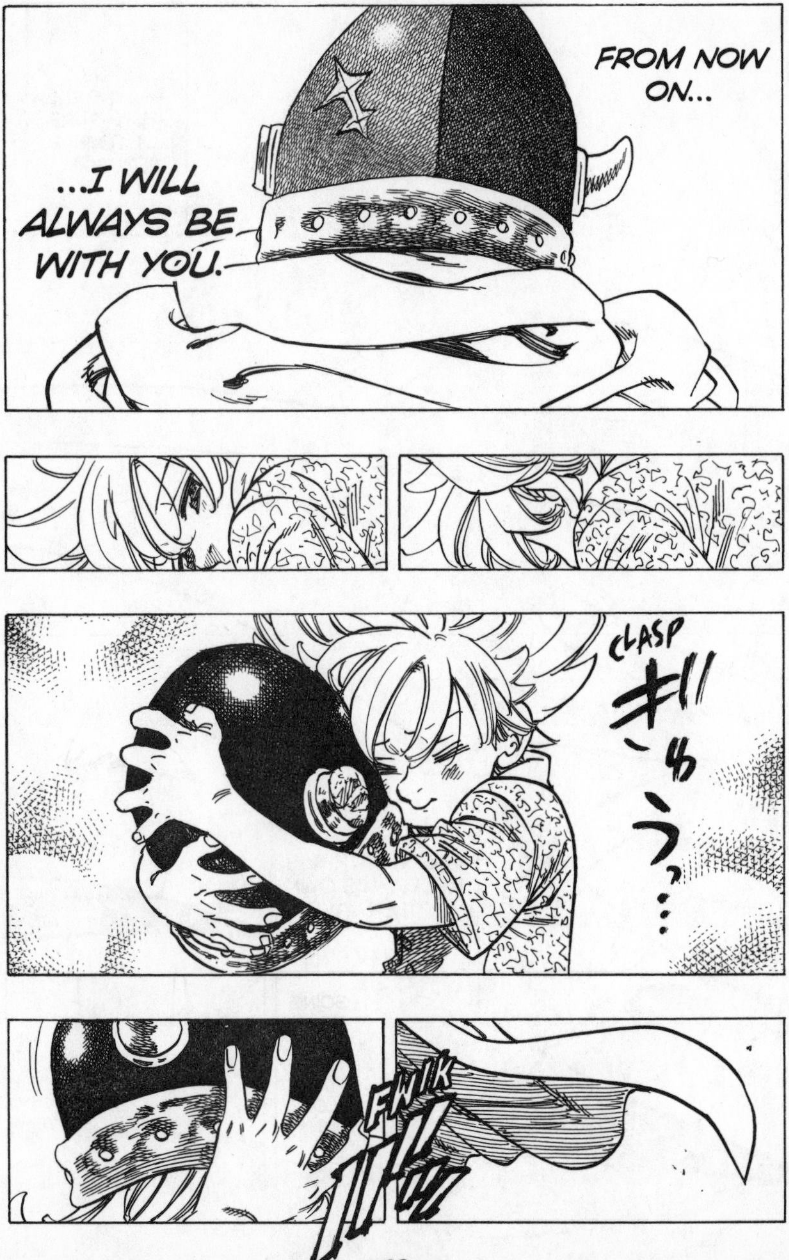
FROM NOW ON...
...I WILL ALWAYS BE WITH YOU.
CLASP
ぎゅう…
FWIK

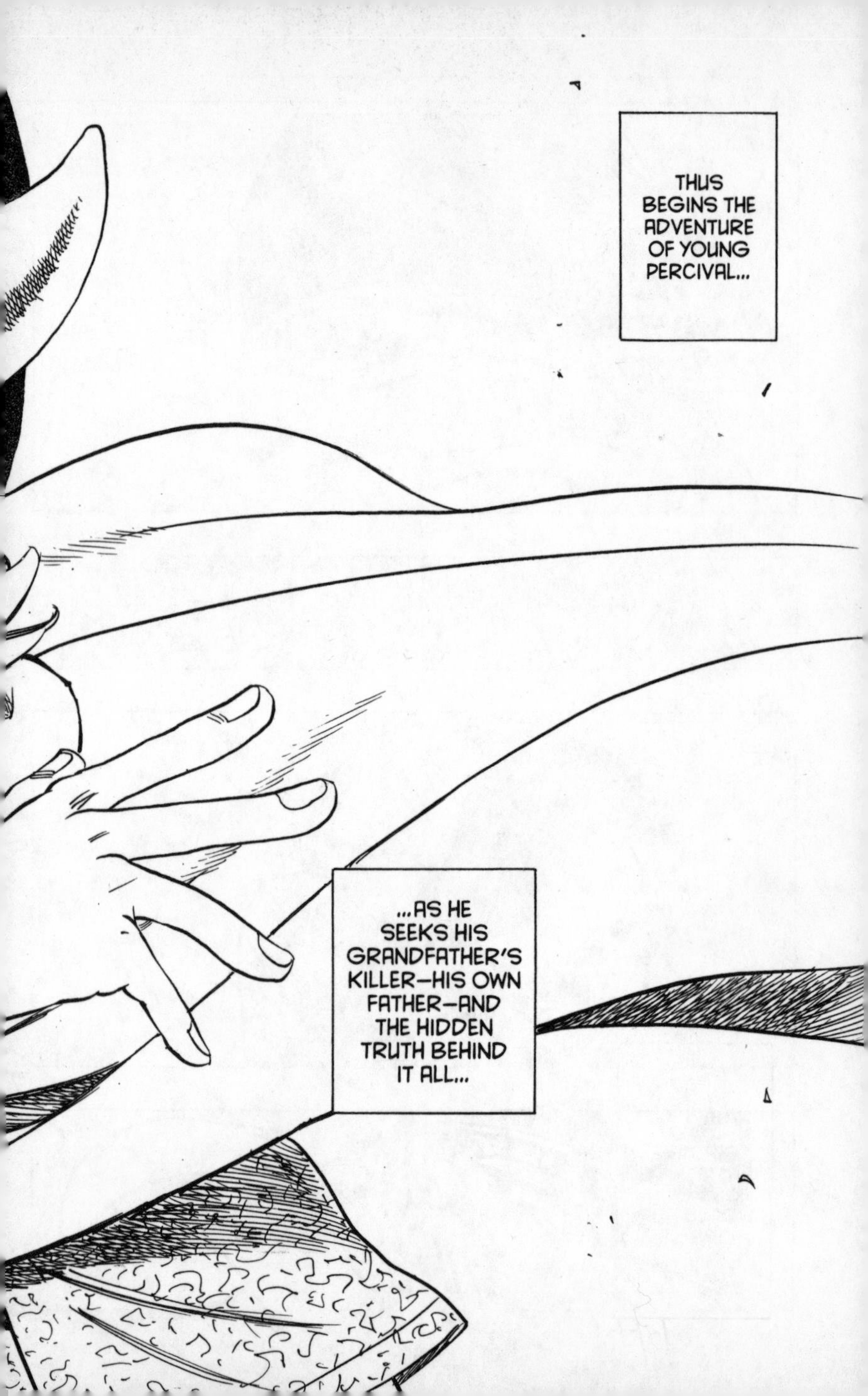
THUS BEGINS THE ADVENTURE OF YOUNG PERCIVAL...
...AS HE SEEKS HIS GRANDFATHER'S KILLER—HIS OWN FATHER—AND THE HIDDEN TRUTH BEHIND IT ALL...

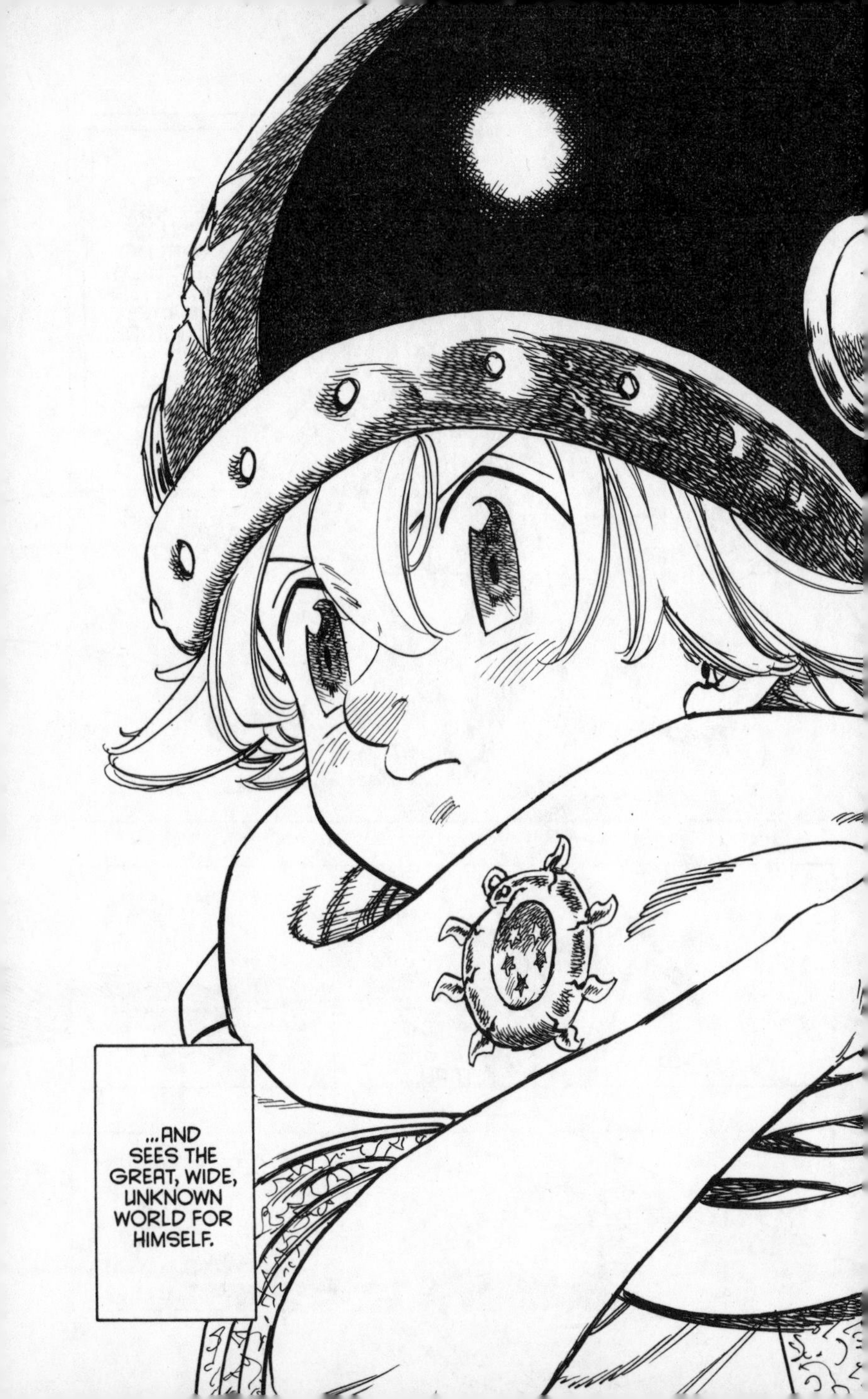
...AND SEES THE GREAT, WIDE, UNKNOWN WORLD FOR HIMSELF.

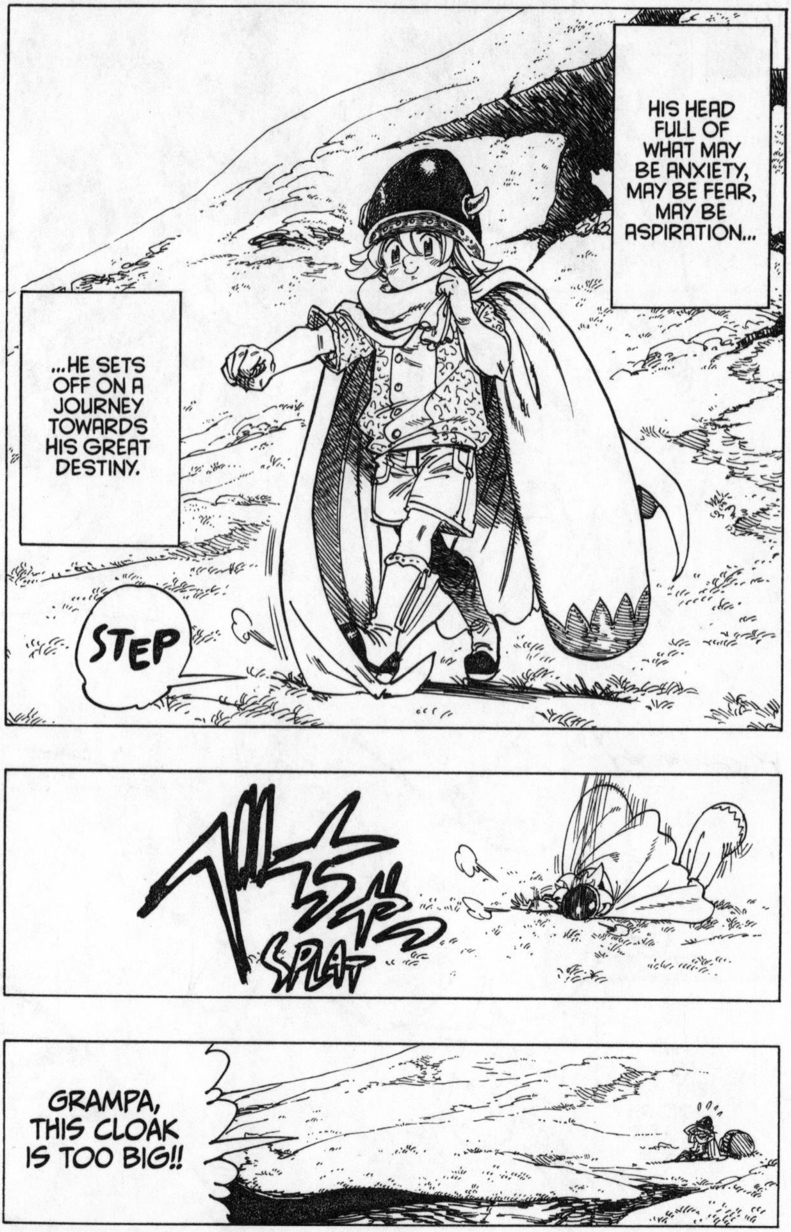
HIS HEAD FULL OF WHAT MAY BE ANXIETY, MAY BE FEAR, MAY BE ASPIRATION...
...HE SETS OFF ON A JOURNEY TOWARDS HIS GREAT DESTINY.
STEP
SPLAT
GRAMPA, THIS CLOAK IS TOO BIG!!

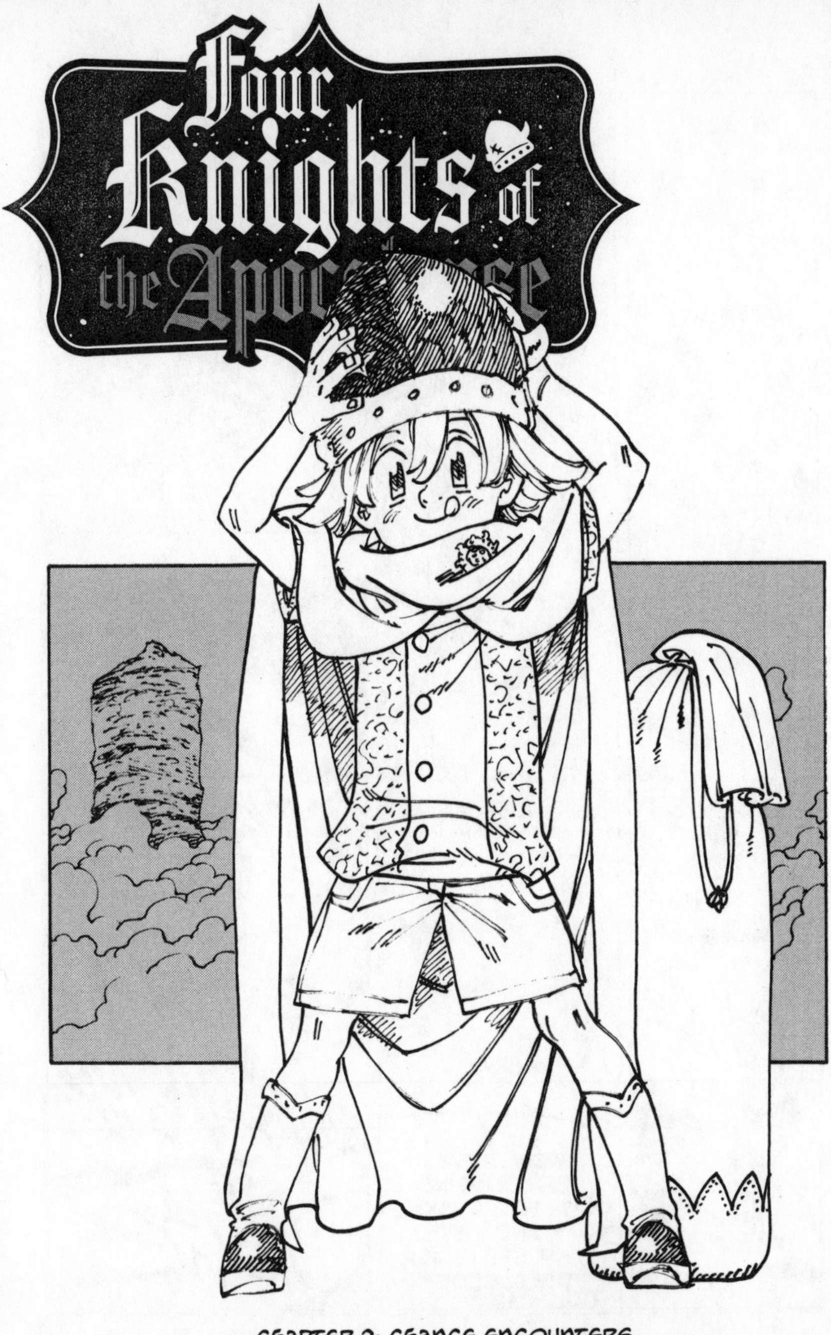
Four Knights of
the Apoc

CHAPTER 2: CHANCE ENCOUNTERS

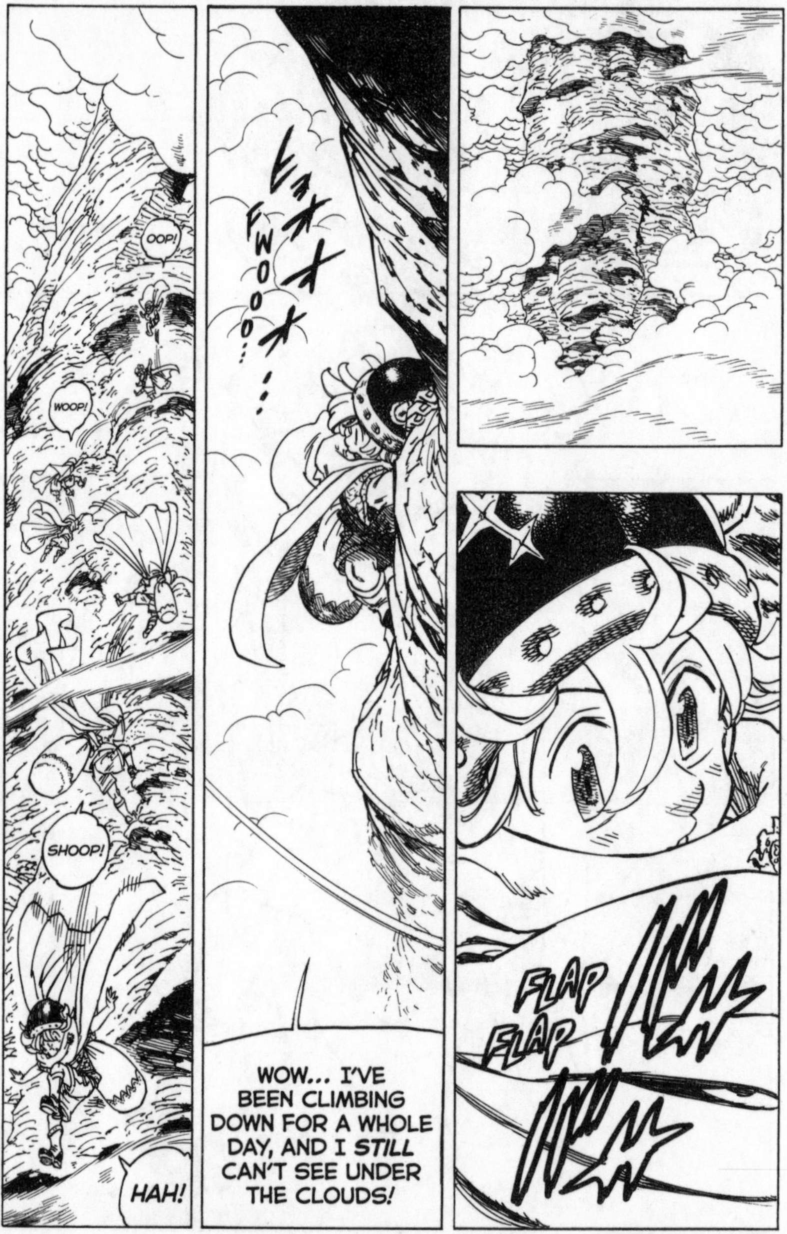
FLAP
FLAP
FWOOOO...
WOW... I'VE BEEN CLIMBING DOWN FOR A WHOLE DAY, AND I *STILL* CAN'T SEE UNDER THE CLOUDS!
OOP!
WOOP!
SHOOP!
HAH!

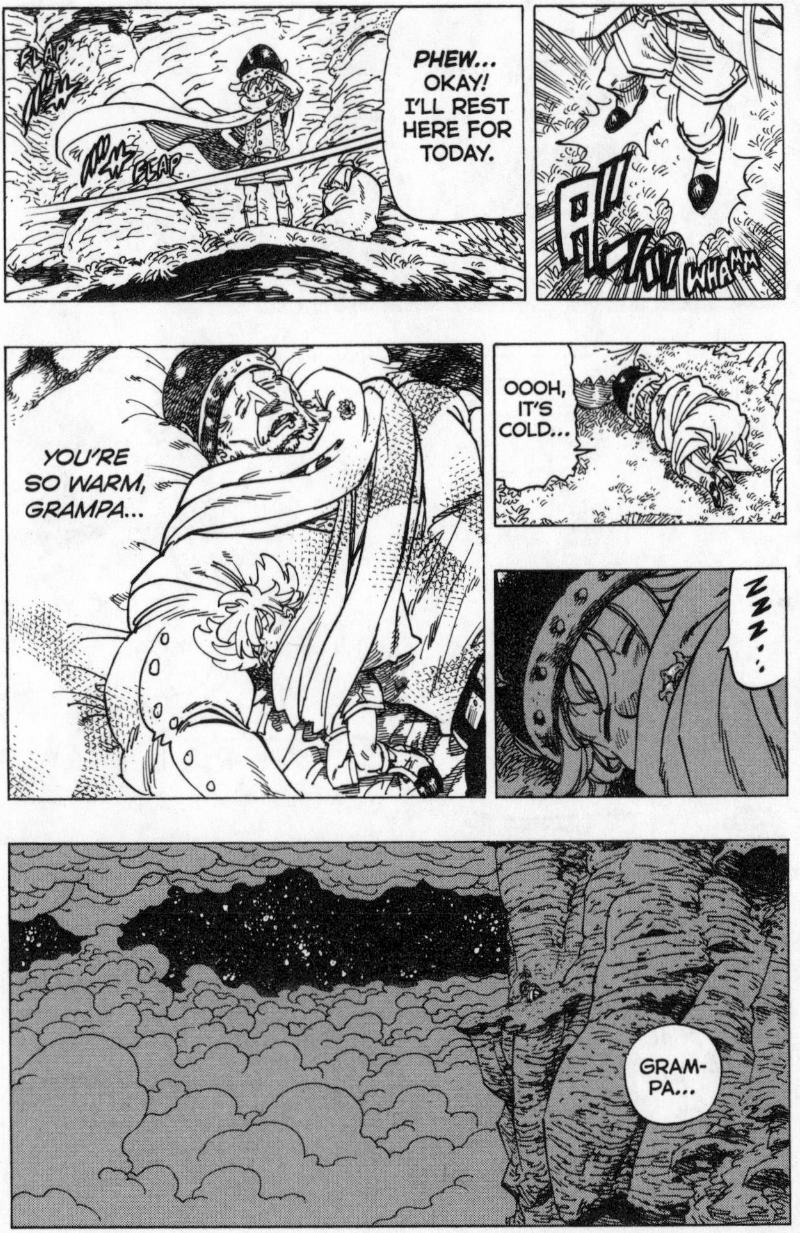
WHAMM
PHEW... OKAY! I'LL REST HERE FOR TODAY.
FLAP
FLAP
OOOH, IT'S COLD...
ZZZ...
YOU'RE SO WARM, GRAMPA...
GRAM-PA...

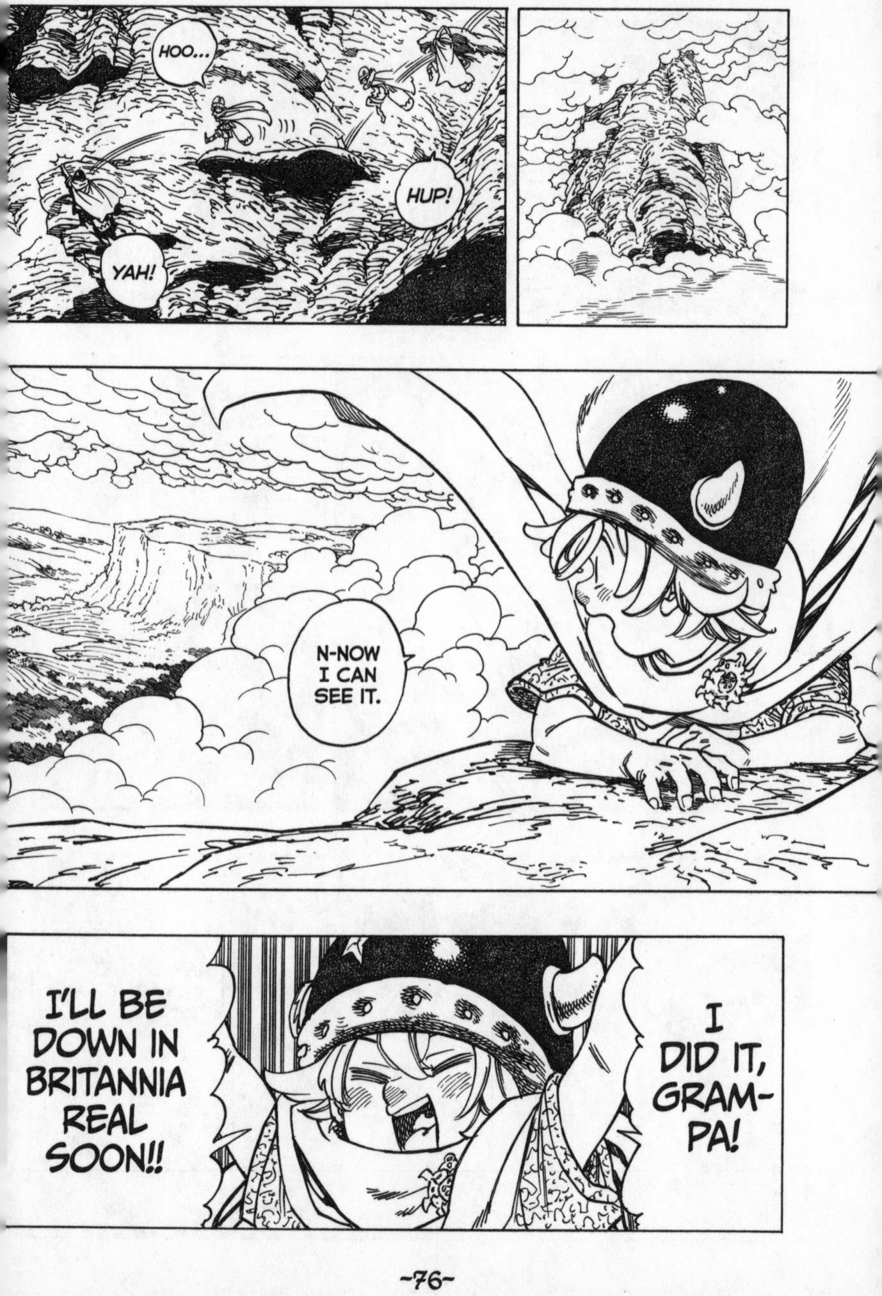
HOO...
HUP!
YAH!
N-NOW I CAN SEE IT.
I DID IT, GRAM-PA!
I'LL BE DOWN IN BRITANNIA REAL SOON!!

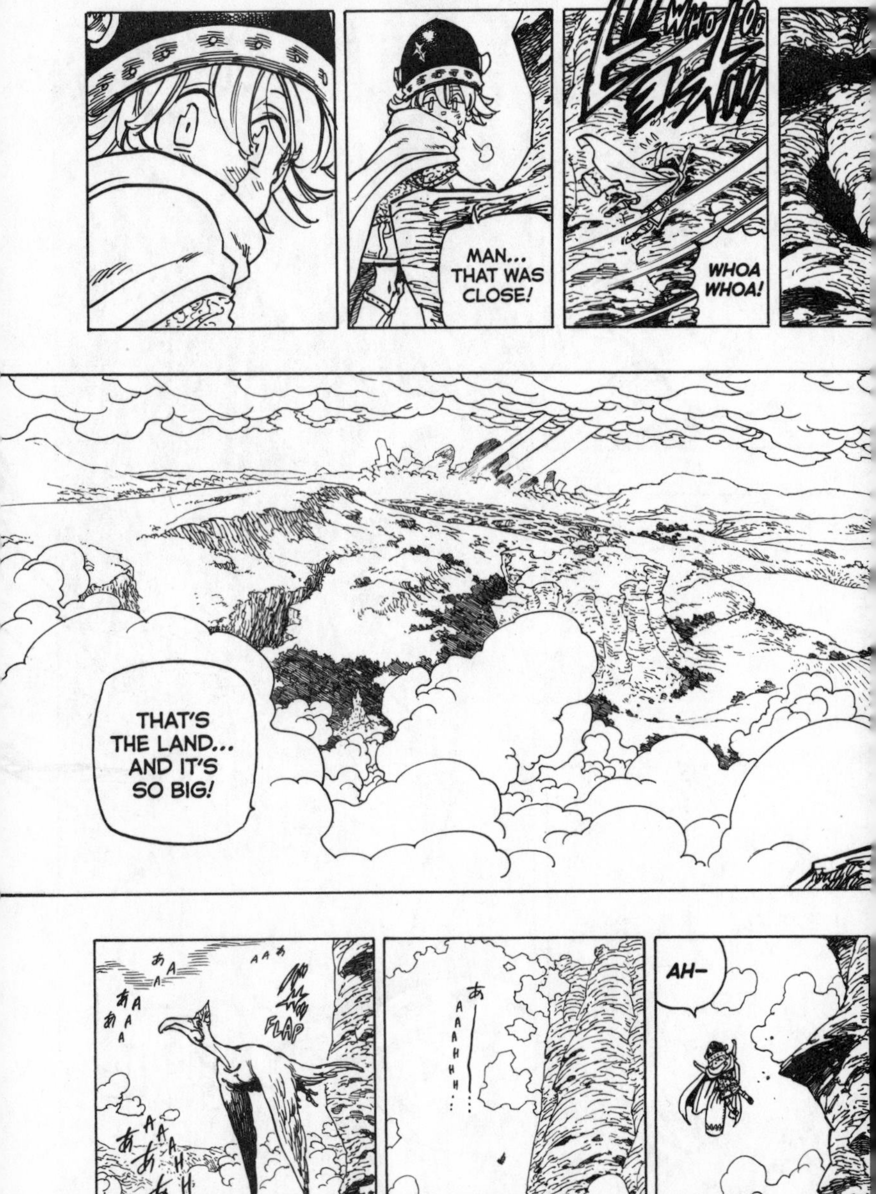
WHOA WHOA!
MAN... THAT WAS CLOSE!
THAT'S THE LAND... AND IT'S SO BIG!
AH-
FLAP

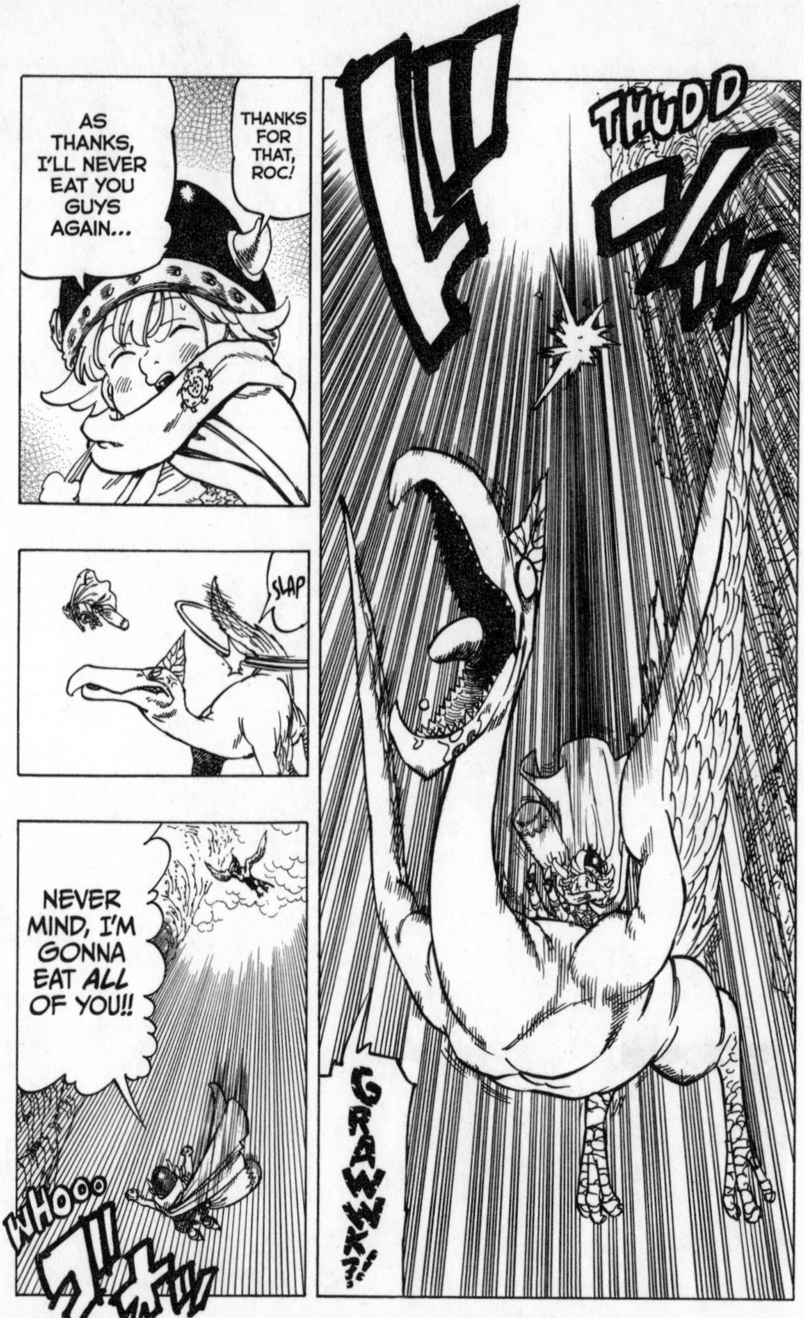
THUDD
GRAWWK?!
THANKS FOR THAT, ROC!
AS THANKS, I'LL NEVER EAT YOU GUYS AGAIN...
SLAP
NEVER MIND, I'M GONNA EAT *ALL* OF YOU!!
WHOOO

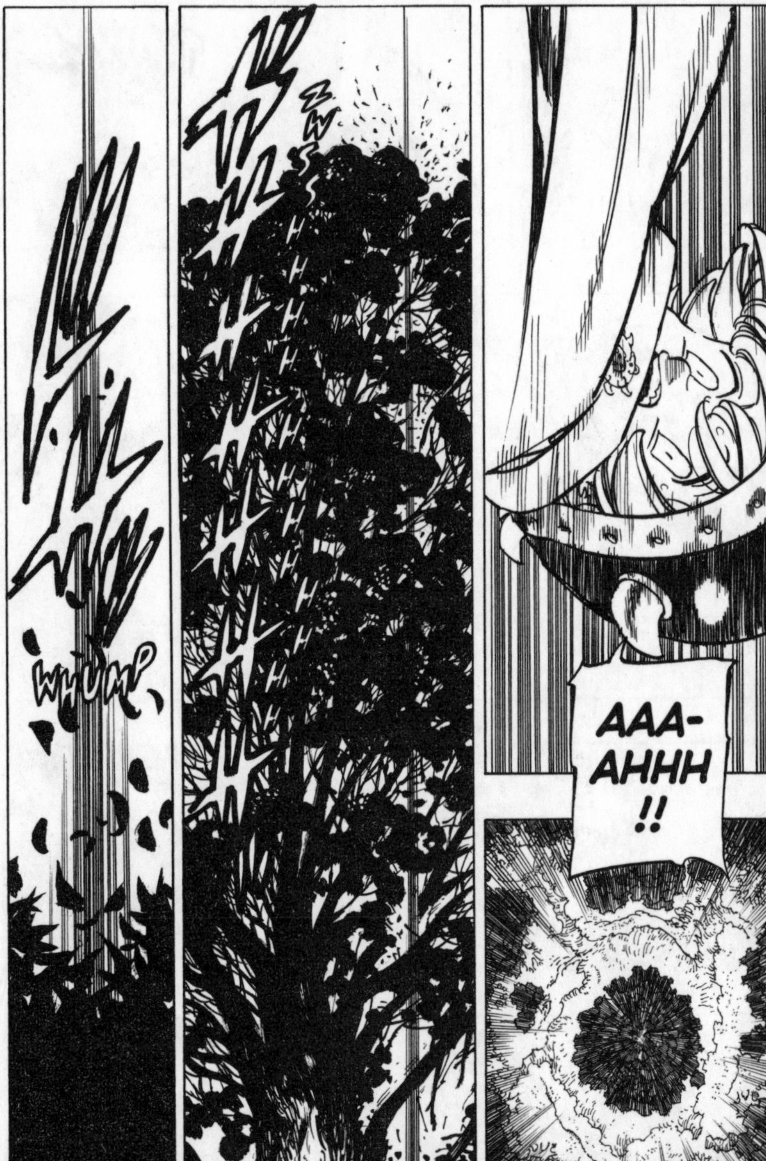
AAA-AHHH !!
WHUMP

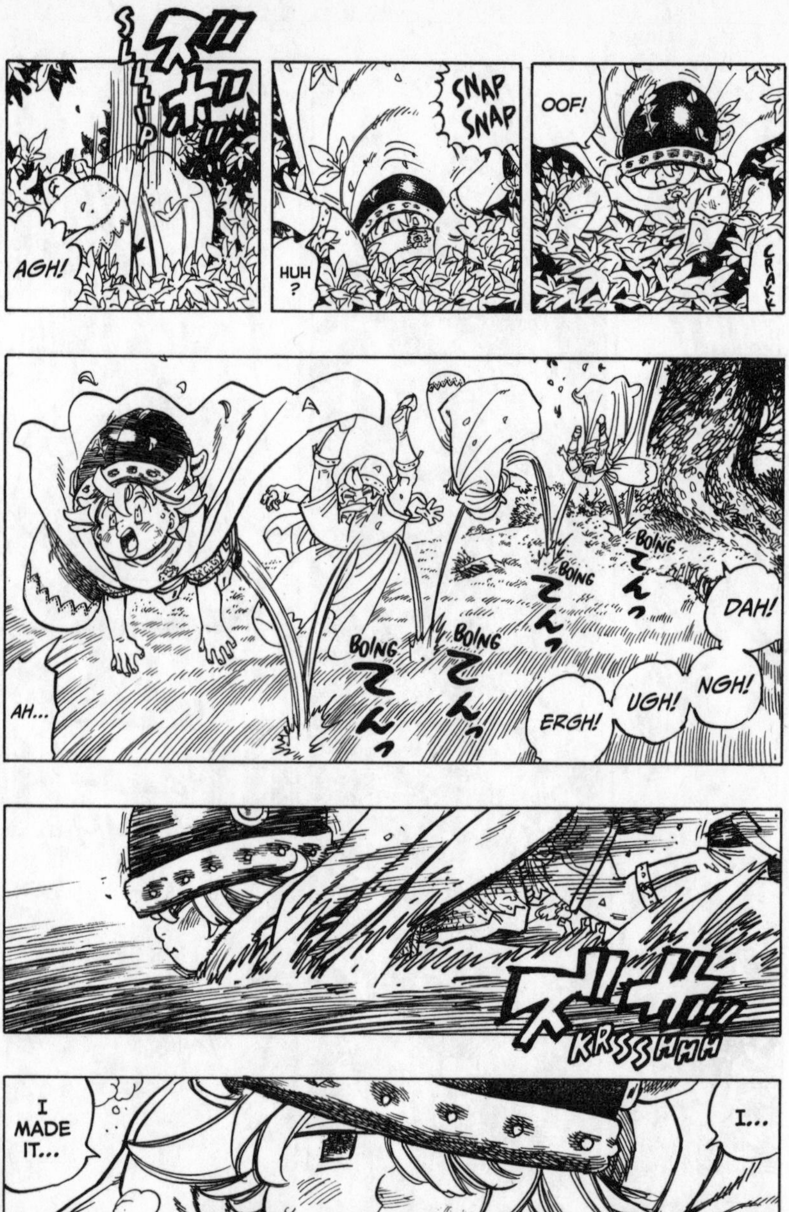

OOF!
CRAKK
SNAP SNAP
HUH?
SLLLP
AGH!
DAH!
NGH!
UGH!
ERGH!
BOING
BOING
BOING
BOING
AH...
KRSSHHH
I...
I MADE IT...

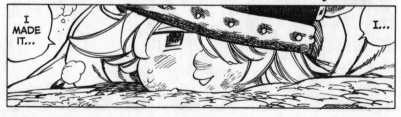

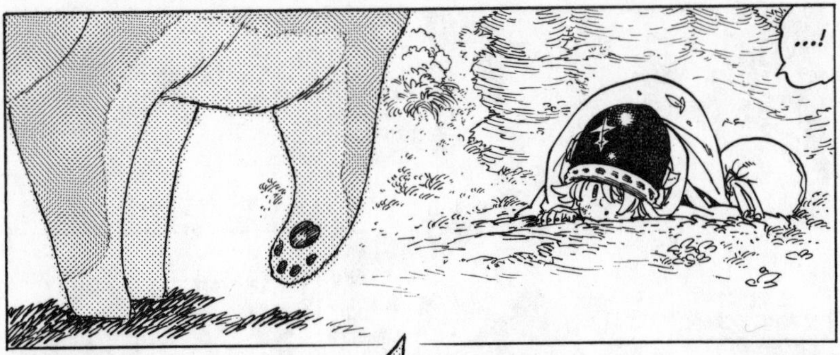
...!

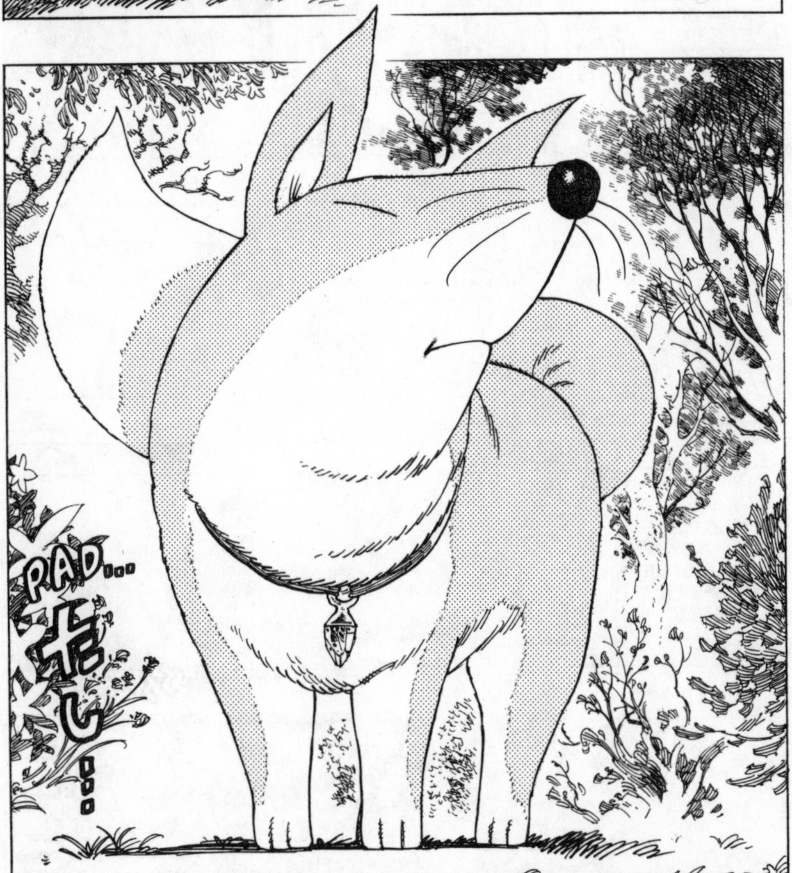
PAD...

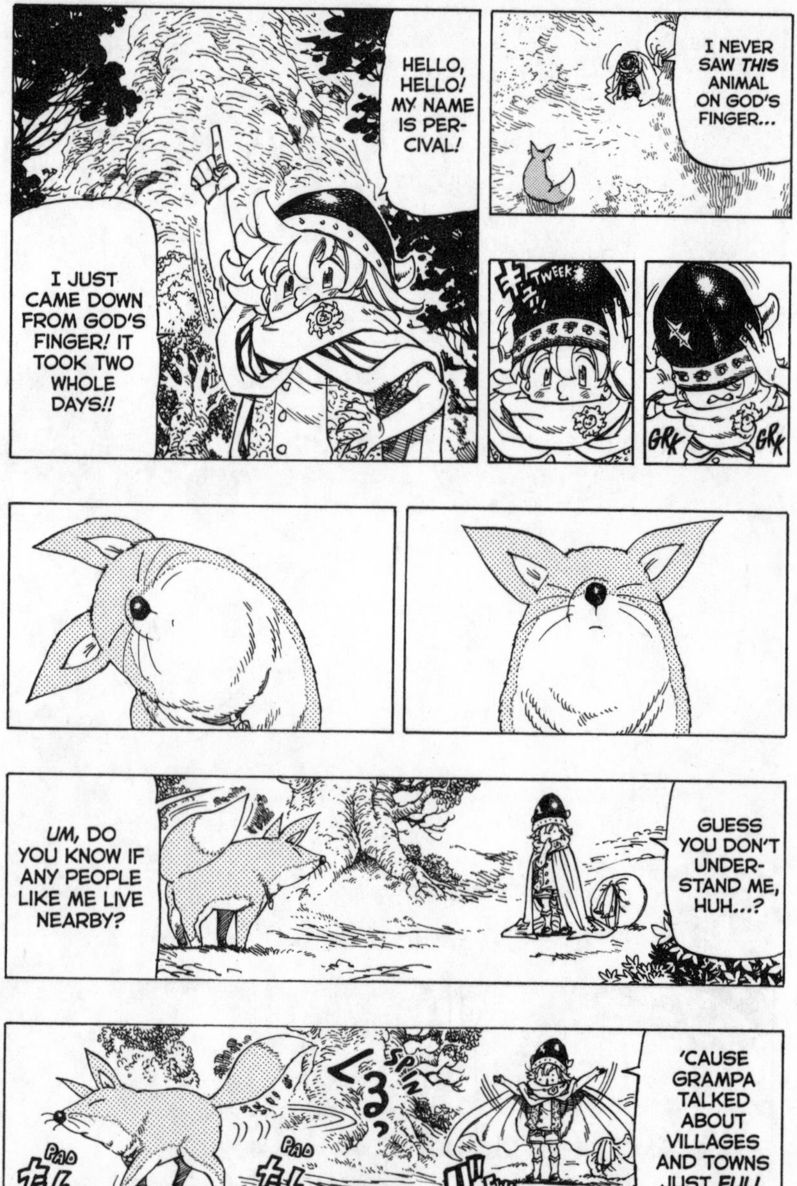
I NEVER SAW *THIS* ANIMAL ON GOD'S FINGER...
GRK
GRK
TWEEK
HELLO, HELLO! MY NAME IS PER-CIVAL!
I JUST CAME DOWN FROM GOD'S FINGER! IT TOOK TWO WHOLE DAYS!!
GUESS YOU DON'T UNDER-STAND ME, HUH...?
UM, DO YOU KNOW IF ANY PEOPLE LIKE ME LIVE NEARBY?
'CAUSE GRAMPA TALKED ABOUT VILLAGES AND TOWNS JUST *FULL* OF PEOPLE!
FWING
SPIN
PAO
PAO

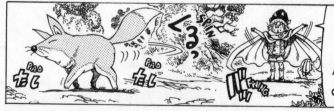

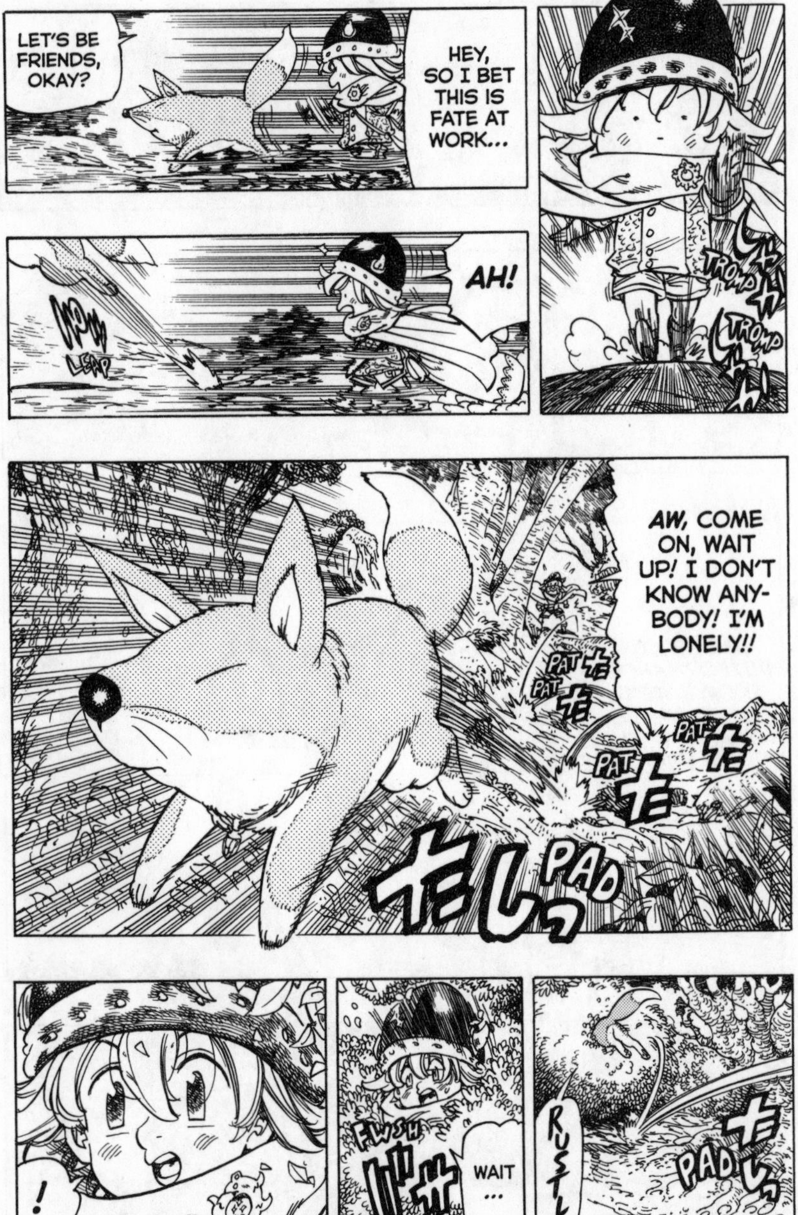
TROMP
TROMP
HEY, SO I BET THIS IS FATE AT WORK...
LET'S BE FRIENDS, OKAY?
AH!
LEAP
AW, COME ON, WAIT UP! I DON'T KNOW ANYBODY! I'M LONELY!!
PAT PAT
PAT PAT
PAD
RUSTL
PAD
FWSH
WAIT ...
!

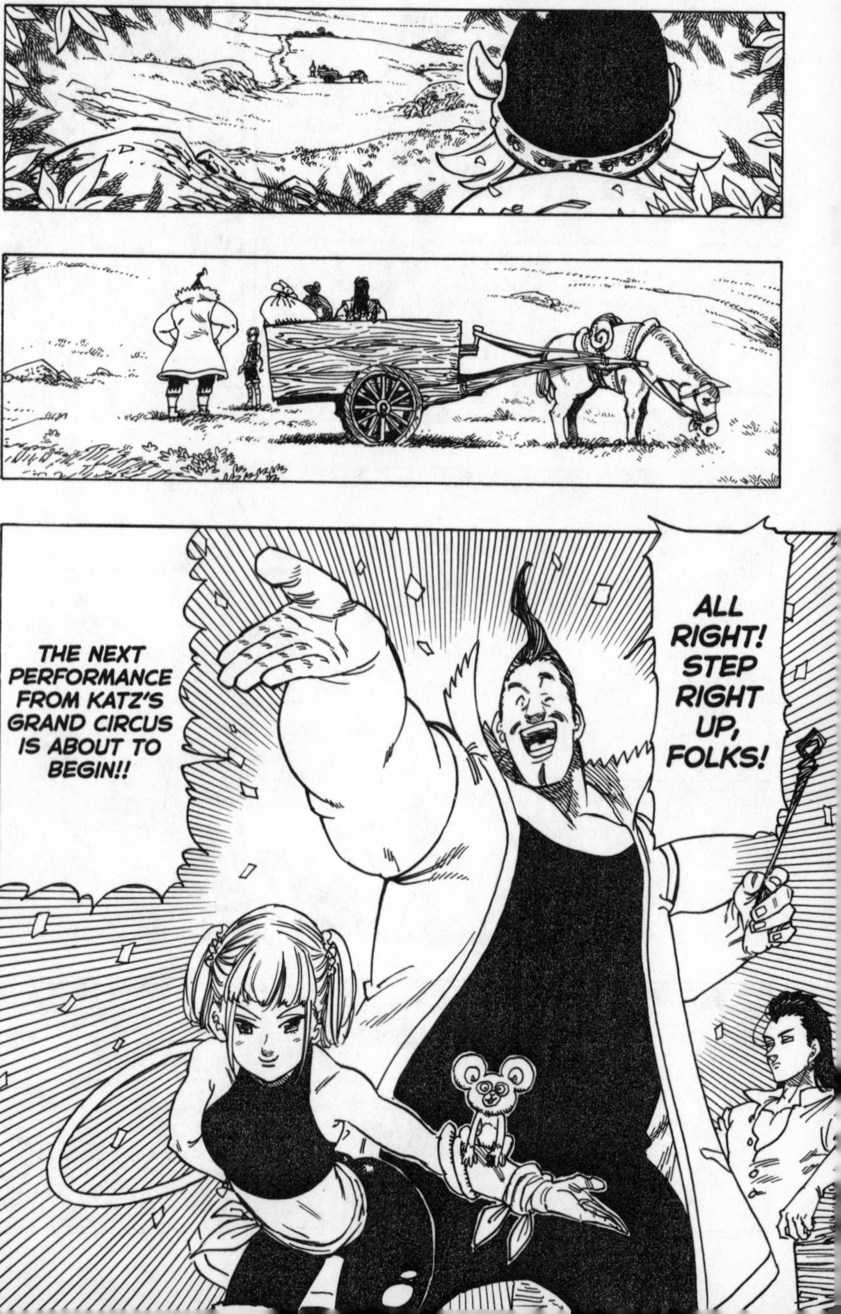
ALL RIGHT! STEP RIGHT UP, FOLKS!
THE NEXT PERFORMANCE FROM KATZ'S GRAND CIRCUS IS ABOUT TO BEGIN!!

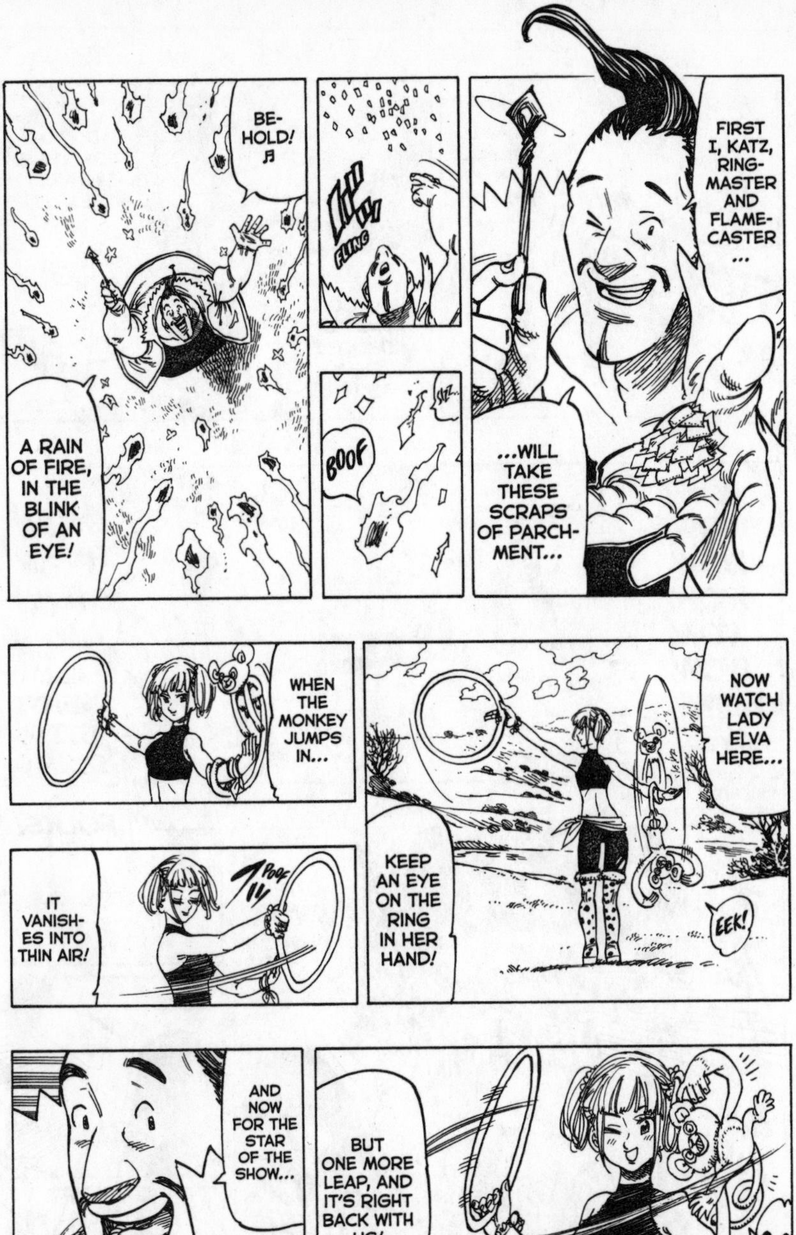
FIRST I, KATZ, RING-MASTER AND FLAME-CASTER ...
...WILL TAKE THESE SCRAPS OF PARCHMENT...
FLING
BOOF
BE-HOLD! ♬
A RAIN OF FIRE, IN THE BLINK OF AN EYE!
NOW WATCH LADY ELVA HERE...
KEEP AN EYE ON THE RING IN HER HAND!
EEK!
WHEN THE MONKEY JUMPS IN...
POOF
IT VANISH-ES INTO THIN AIR!
BUT ONE MORE LEAP, AND IT'S RIGHT BACK WITH US!
POP
AND NOW FOR THE STAR OF THE SHOW...

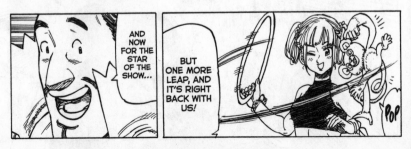

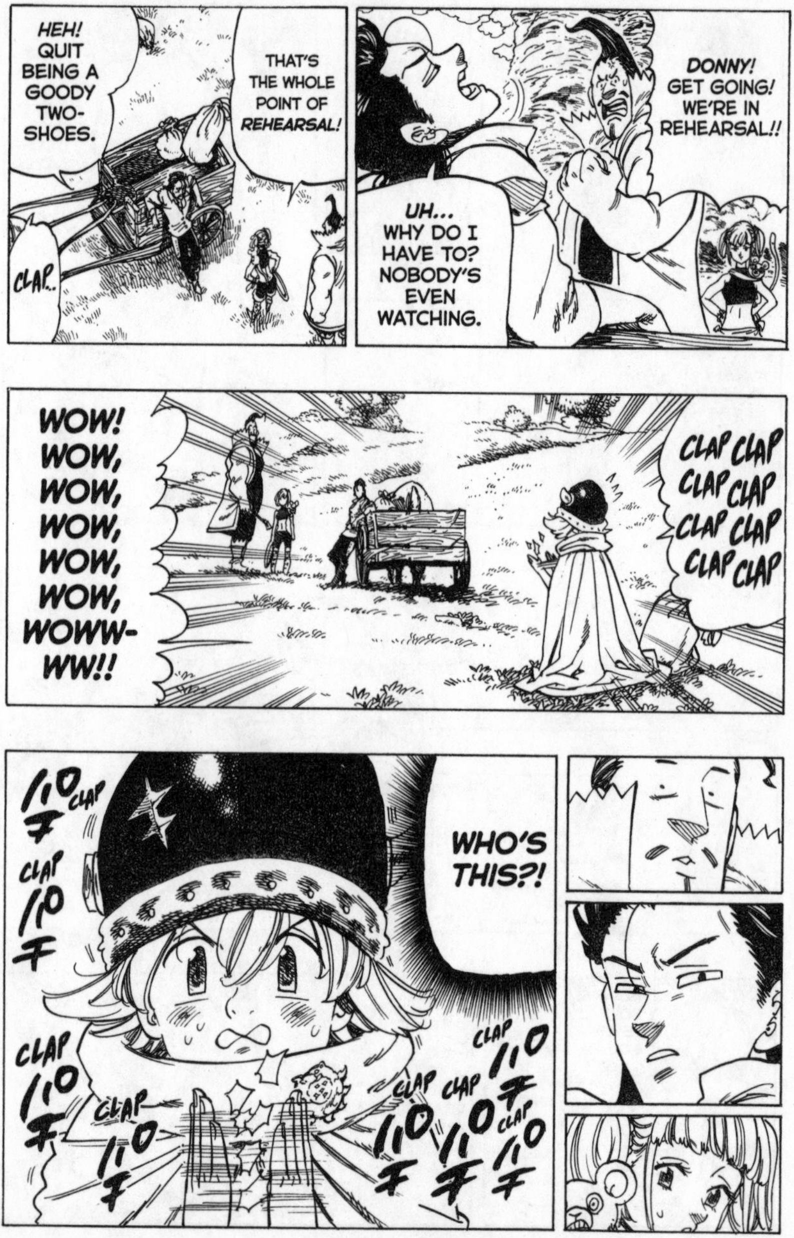
DONNY! GET GOING! WE'RE IN REHEARSAL!!
UH... WHY DO I HAVE TO? NOBODY'S EVEN WATCHING.
THAT'S THE WHOLE POINT OF REHEARSAL!
HEH! QUIT BEING A GOODY TWO-SHOES.
CLAP...
CLAP CLAP CLAP CLAP CLAP CLAP CLAP CLAP
WOW! WOW, WOW, WOW, WOW, WOW, WOWW-WW!!
WHO'S THIS?!
CLAP
CLAP
CLAP
CLAP
CLAP
CLAP
CLAP
CLAP

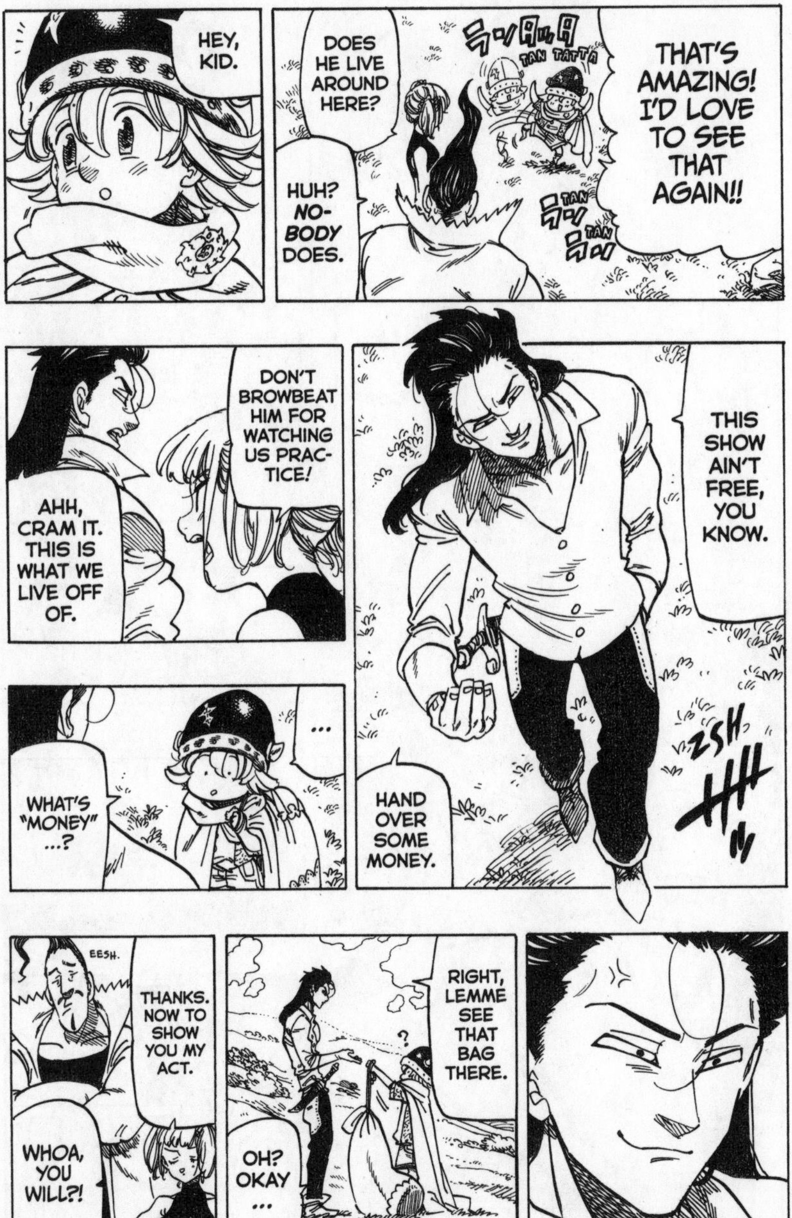
THAT'S AMAZING! I'D LOVE TO SEE THAT AGAIN!!
TAN TATTA
DOES HE LIVE AROUND HERE?
HUH? *NOBODY* DOES.
TAN TAN
HEY, KID.
THIS SHOW AIN'T FREE, YOU KNOW.
ZSH
HAND OVER SOME MONEY.
DON'T BROWBEAT HIM FOR WATCHING US PRACTICE!
AHH, CRAM IT. THIS IS WHAT WE LIVE OFF OF.
...
WHAT'S "MONEY" ...?
RIGHT, LEMME SEE THAT BAG THERE.
?
OH? OKAY ...
THANKS. NOW TO SHOW YOU MY ACT.
EESH.
WHOA, YOU WILL?!

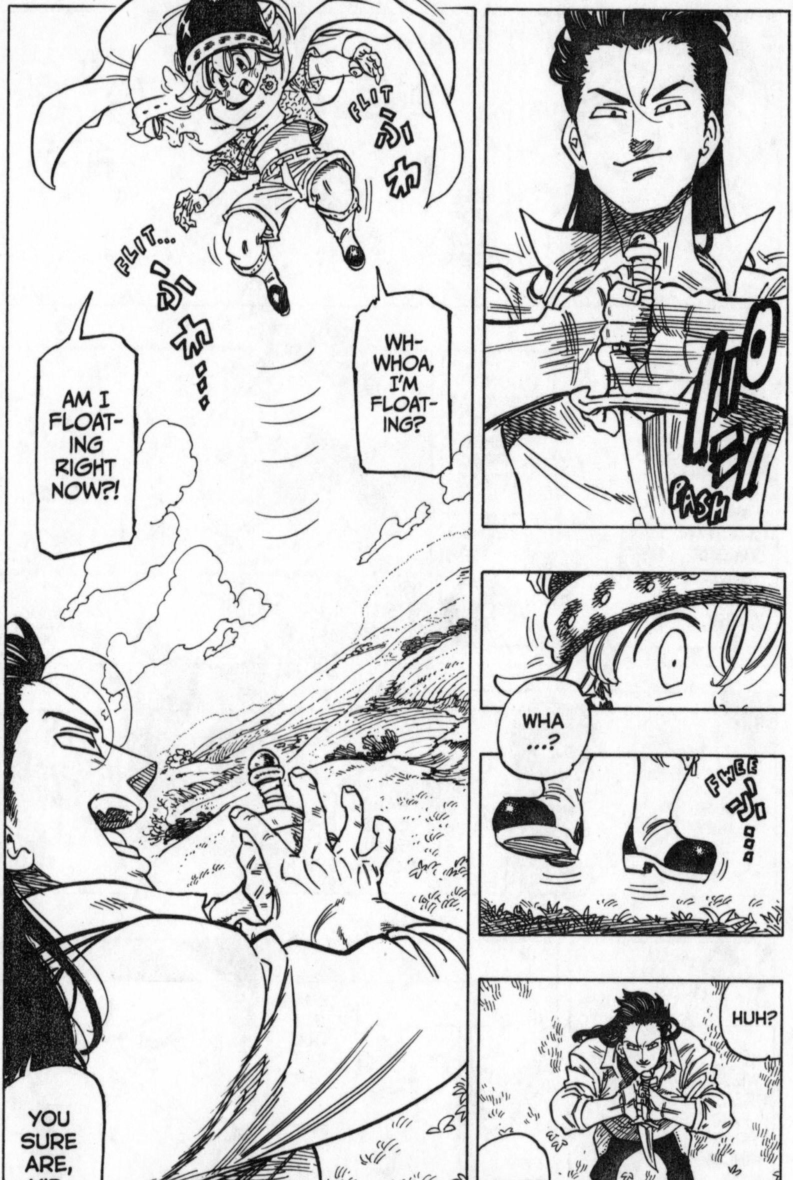
PASH
WHA ...?
FWEE
HUH?
HUH??
FLIT
FLIT...
WH- WHOA, I'M FLOAT- ING?
AM I FLOAT- ING RIGHT NOW?!
YOU SURE ARE, KID.

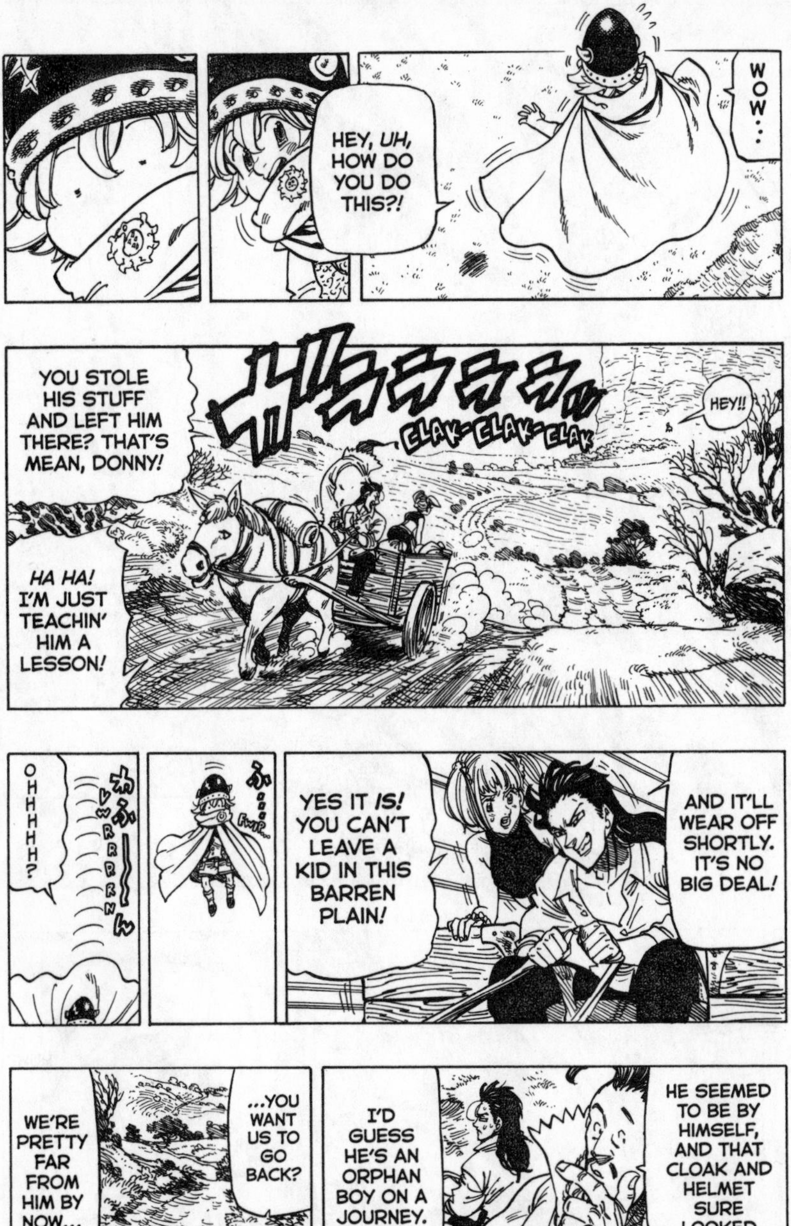
WOW...
HEY, UH, HOW DO YOU DO THIS?!
HEY!!
CLAK-CLAK-CLAK
YOU STOLE HIS STUFF AND LEFT HIM THERE? THAT'S MEAN, DONNY!
HA HA! I'M JUST TEACHIN' HIM A LESSON!
AND IT'LL WEAR OFF SHORTLY. IT'S NO BIG DEAL!
YES IT IS! YOU CAN'T LEAVE A KID IN THIS BARREN PLAIN!
FWIP...
WRRRRRN
OHHHHH?
HE SEEMED TO BE BY HIMSELF, AND THAT CLOAK AND HELMET SURE LOOKED OLD...
I'D GUESS HE'S AN ORPHAN BOY ON A JOURNEY.
...YOU WANT US TO GO BACK?
WE'RE PRETTY FAR FROM HIM BY NOW...

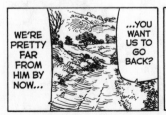

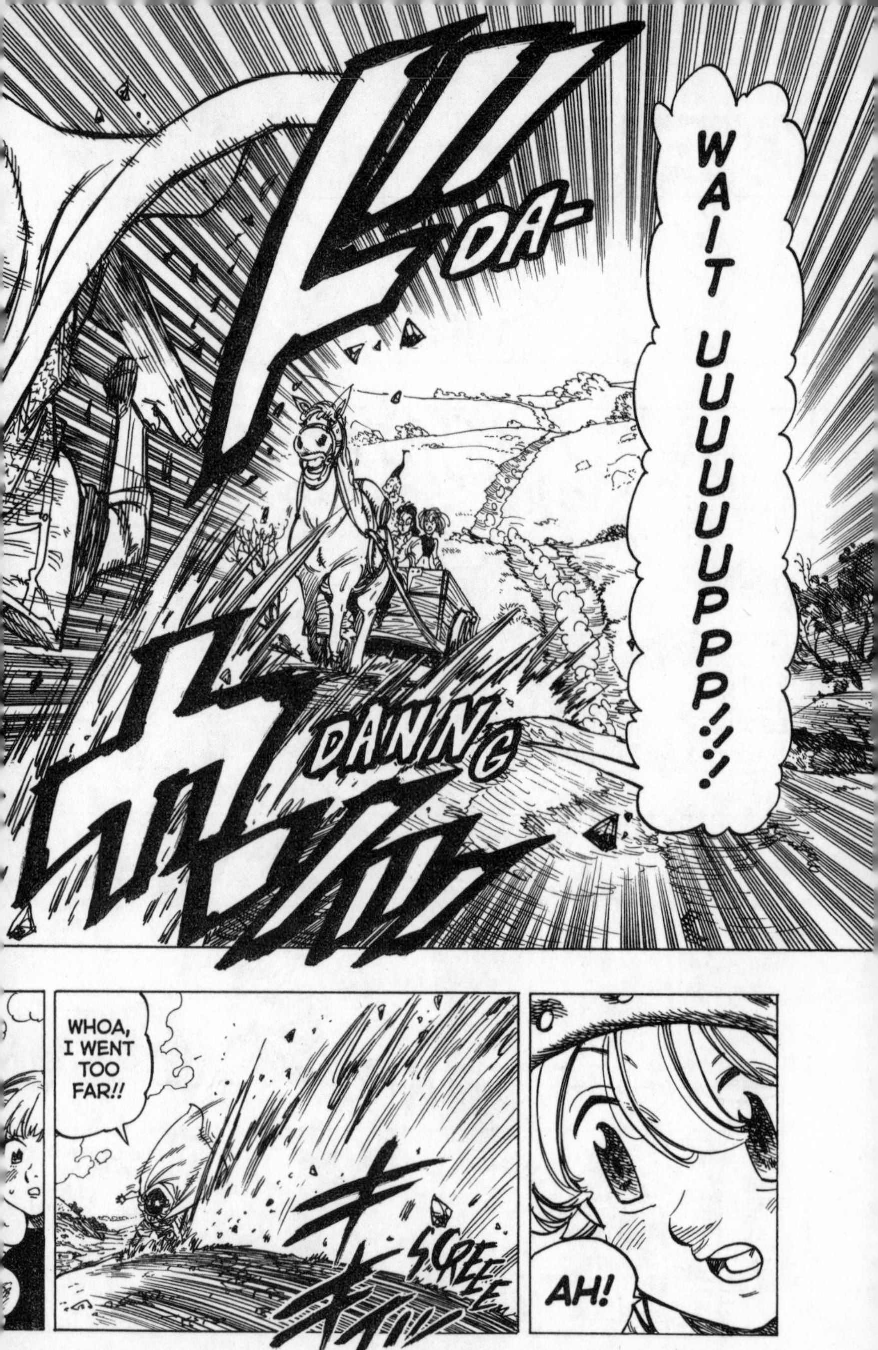
WAIT UUUUUUUPPP!!!
DA-
DANNG
AH!
SCREEE
WHOA, I WENT TOO FAR!!

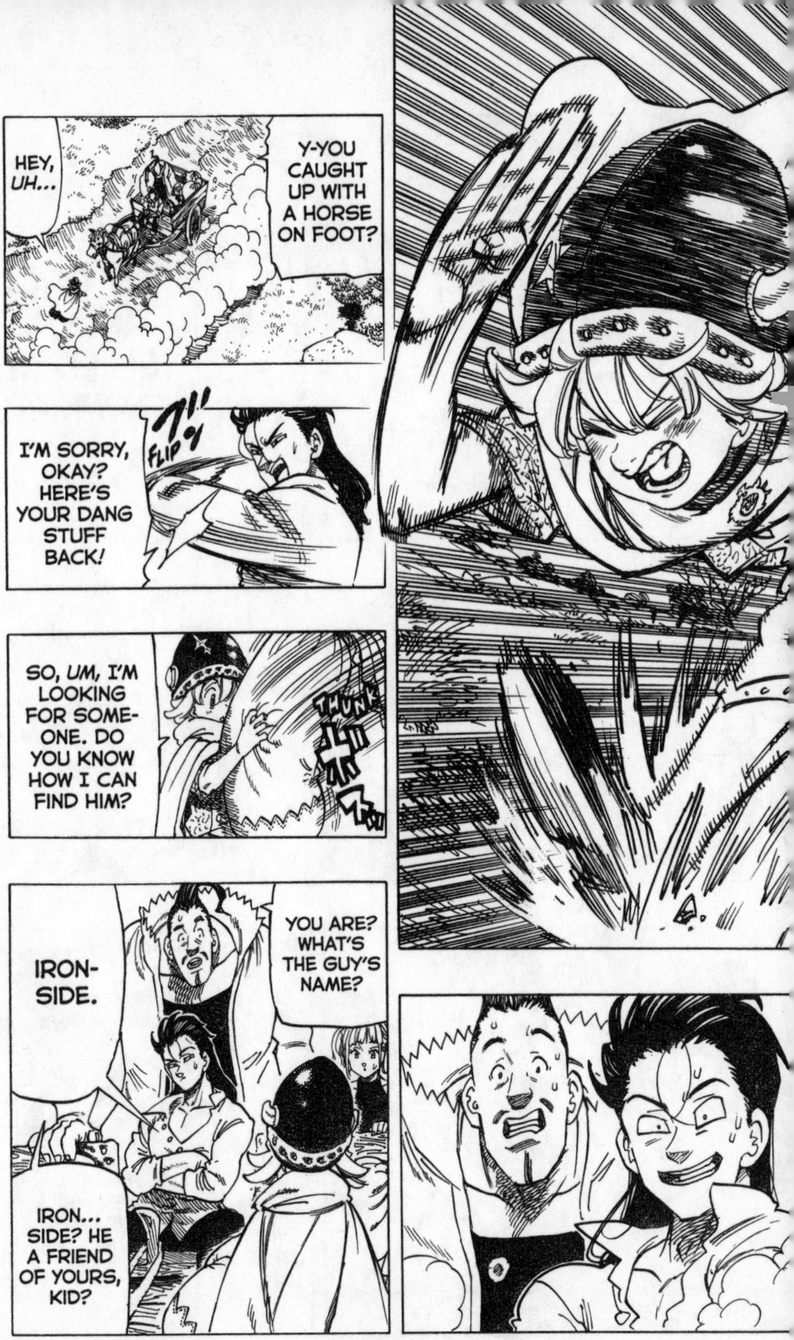
Y-YOU CAUGHT UP WITH A HORSE ON FOOT?
HEY, UH...
FLIP
I'M SORRY, OKAY? HERE'S YOUR DANG STUFF BACK!
THUNK
SO, UM, I'M LOOKING FOR SOME-ONE. DO YOU KNOW HOW I CAN FIND HIM?
YOU ARE? WHAT'S THE GUY'S NAME?
IRON-SIDE.
IRON... SIDE? HE A FRIEND OF YOURS, KID?

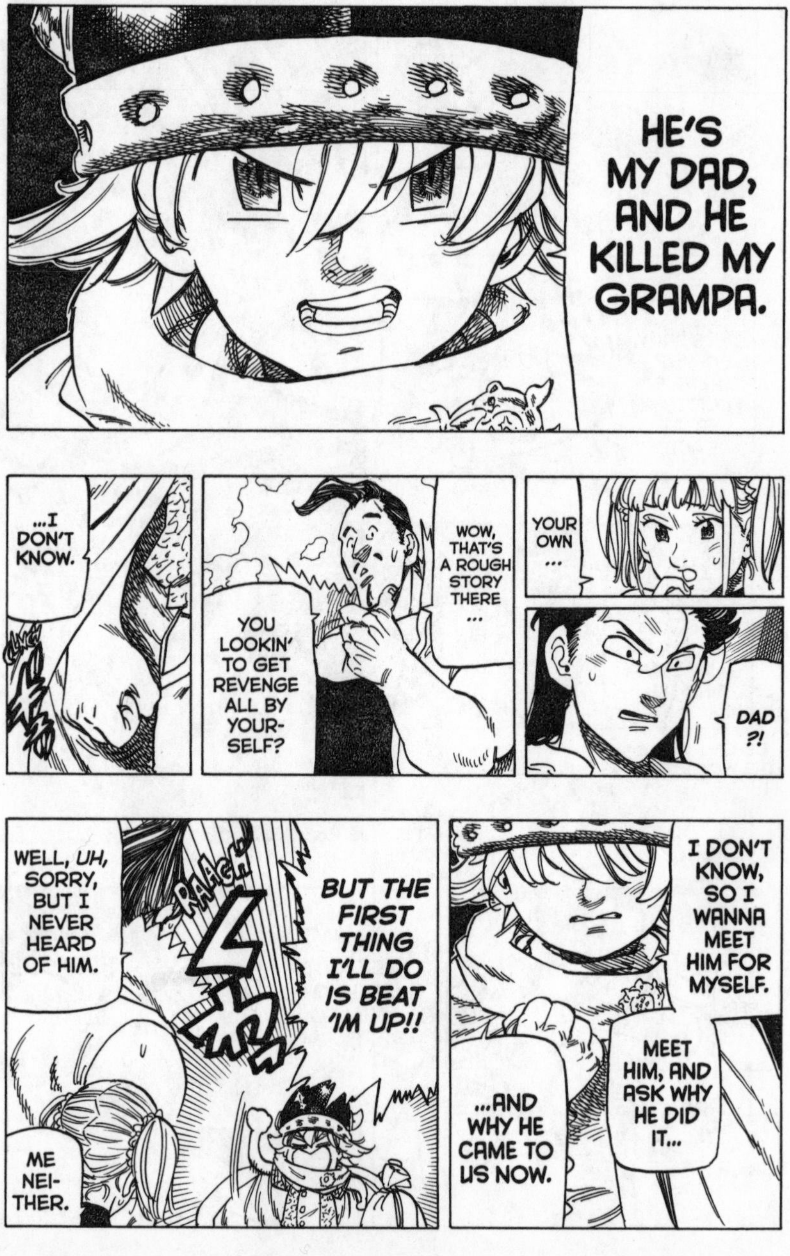
HE'S MY DAD, AND HE KILLED MY GRAMPA.
YOUR OWN ...
DAD ?!
WOW, THAT'S A ROUGH STORY THERE ...
YOU LOOKIN' TO GET REVENGE ALL BY YOURSELF?
...I DON'T KNOW.
I DON'T KNOW, SO I WANNA MEET HIM FOR MYSELF.
MEET HIM, AND ASK WHY HE DID IT...
...AND WHY HE CAME TO US NOW.
BUT THE FIRST THING I'LL DO IS BEAT 'IM UP!!
RAAGE
WELL, UH, SORRY, BUT I NEVER HEARD OF HIM.
ME NEITHER.

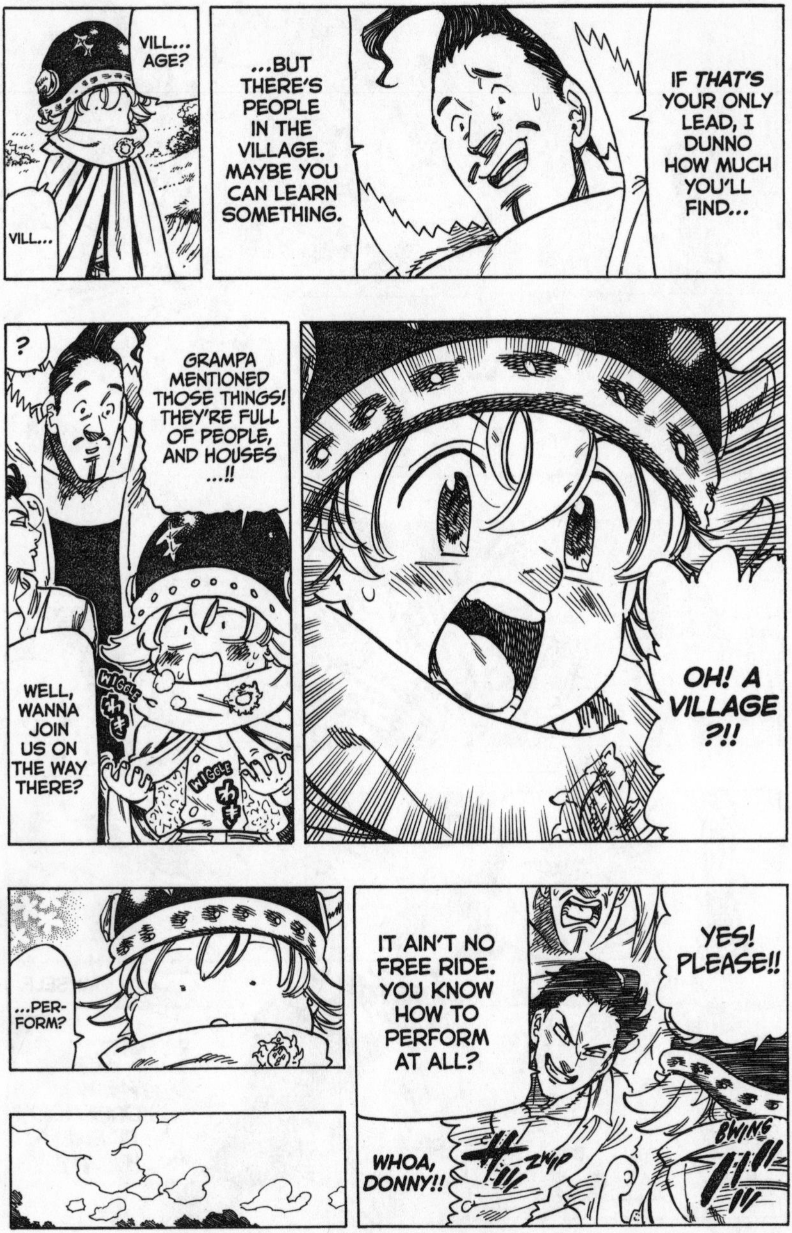
IF *THAT'S* YOUR ONLY LEAD, I DUNNO HOW MUCH YOU'LL FIND...
...BUT THERE'S PEOPLE IN THE VILLAGE. MAYBE YOU CAN LEARN SOMETHING.
VILL... AGE?
VILL...
OH! A VILLAGE ?!!
GRAMPA MENTIONED THOSE THINGS! THEY'RE FULL OF PEOPLE, AND HOUSES ...!!
?
WIGGLE
わき
WIGGLE
わき
WELL, WANNA JOIN US ON THE WAY THERE?
YES! PLEASE!!
IT AIN'T NO FREE RIDE. YOU KNOW HOW TO PERFORM AT ALL?
BWING
ZWIP
WHOA, DONNY!!
...PER-FORM?

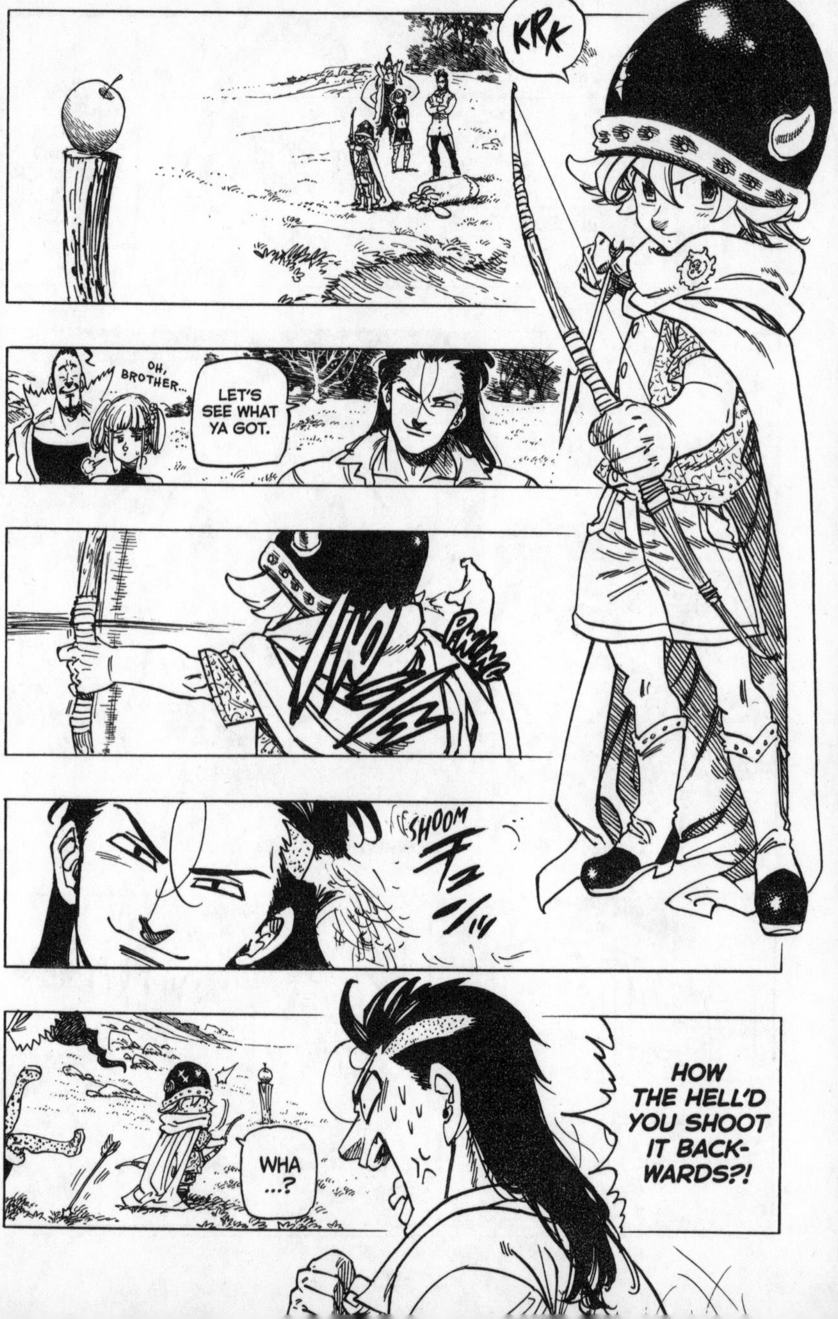
KRK
LET'S SEE WHAT YA GOT.
OH, BROTHER...
PWANG
SHOOM
HOW THE HELL'D YOU SHOOT IT BACK-WARDS?!
WHA ...?

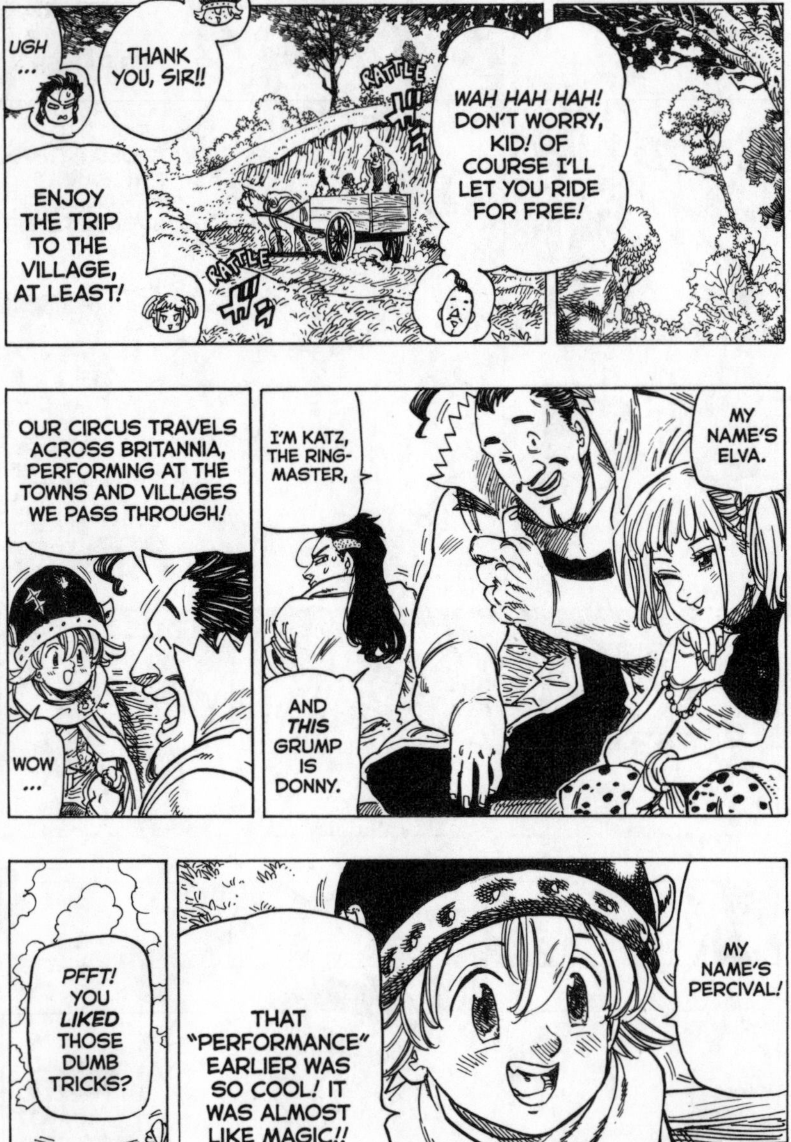
WAH HAH HAH! DON'T WORRY, KID! OF COURSE I'LL LET YOU RIDE FOR FREE!
RATTLE
THANK YOU, SIR!!
UGH ...
RATTLE
ENJOY THE TRIP TO THE VILLAGE, AT LEAST!
MY NAME'S ELVA.
I'M KATZ, THE RING-MASTER,
AND *THIS* GRUMP IS DONNY.
OUR CIRCUS TRAVELS ACROSS BRITANNIA, PERFORMING AT THE TOWNS AND VILLAGES WE PASS THROUGH!
WOW ...
MY NAME'S PERCIVAL!
THAT "PERFORMANCE" EARLIER WAS SO COOL! IT WAS ALMOST LIKE MAGIC!!
PFFT! YOU *LIKED* THOSE DUMB TRICKS?

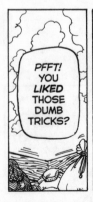

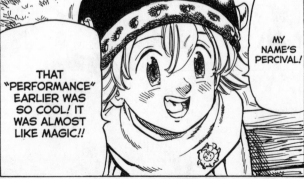

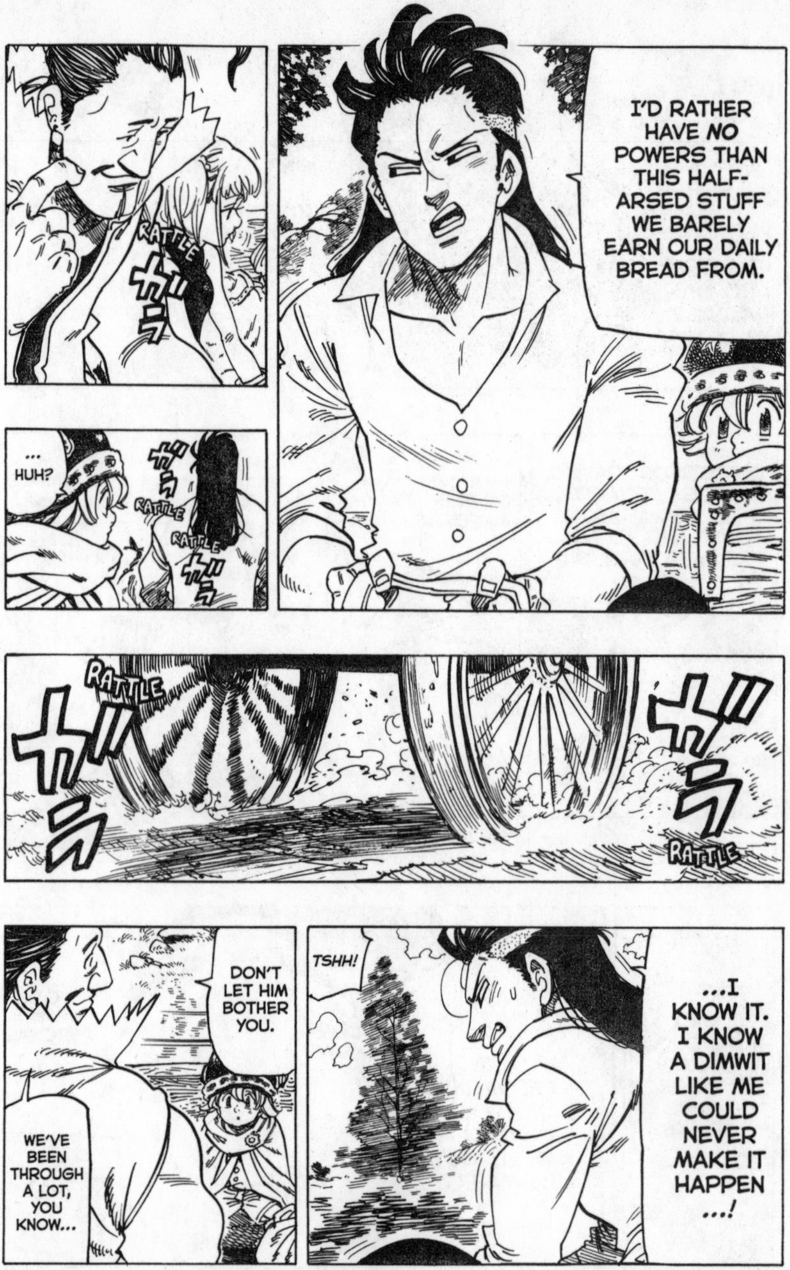
I'D RATHER HAVE *NO* POWERS THAN THIS HALF-ARSED STUFF WE BARELY EARN OUR DAILY BREAD FROM.
ガラ
RATTLE
ガラ
RATTLE
...HUH?
ガラ
RATTLE
ガラ
RATTLE
RATTLE
ガラ
...I KNOW IT. I KNOW A DIMWIT LIKE ME COULD NEVER MAKE IT HAPPEN ...!
TSHH!
DON'T LET HIM BOTHER YOU.
WE'VE BEEN THROUGH A LOT, YOU KNOW...

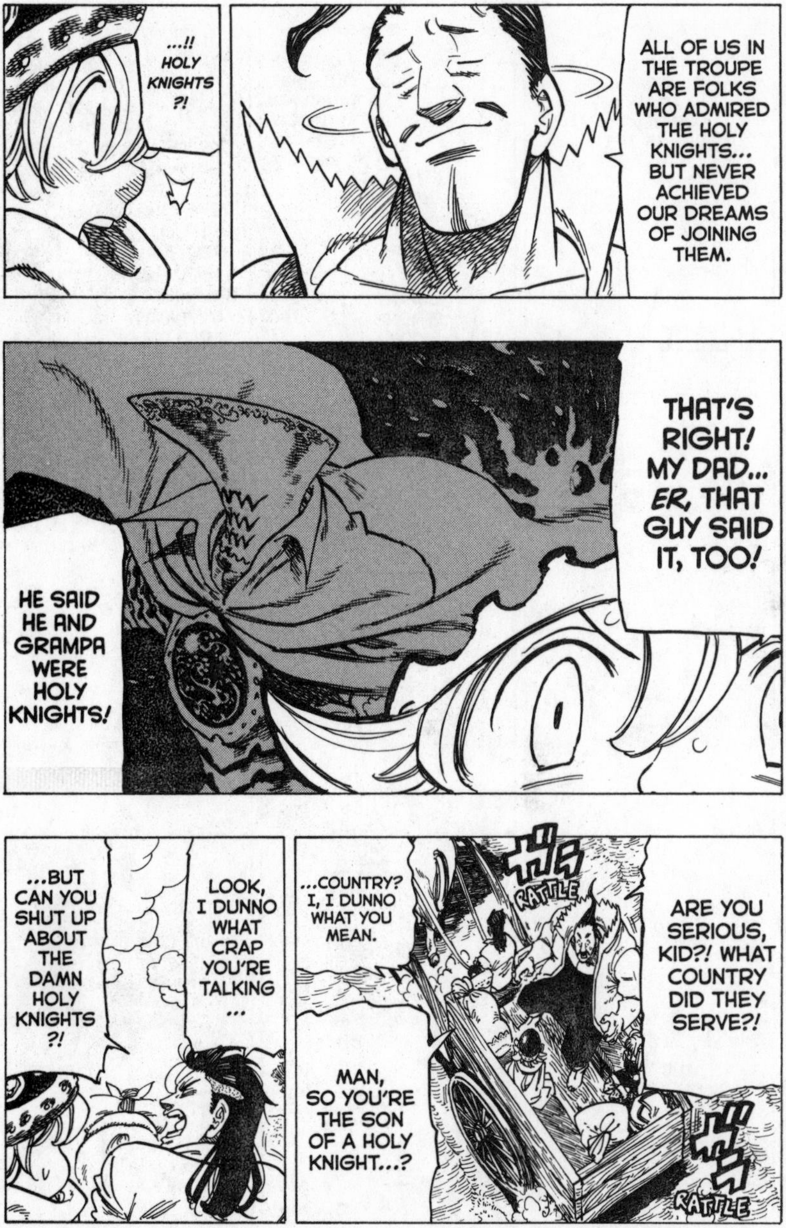
ALL OF US IN THE TROUPE ARE FOLKS WHO ADMIRED THE HOLY KNIGHTS... BUT NEVER ACHIEVED OUR DREAMS OF JOINING THEM.
...!! HOLY KNIGHTS ?!
THAT'S RIGHT! MY DAD... *ER,* THAT GUY SAID IT, TOO!
HE SAID HE AND GRAMPA WERE HOLY KNIGHTS!
RATTLE
ARE YOU SERIOUS, KID?! WHAT COUNTRY DID THEY SERVE?!
...COUNTRY? I, I DUNNO WHAT YOU MEAN.
MAN, SO YOU'RE THE SON OF A HOLY KNIGHT...?
RATTLE
LOOK, I DUNNO WHAT CRAP YOU'RE TALKING ...
...BUT CAN YOU SHUT UP ABOUT THE DAMN HOLY KNIGHTS ?!

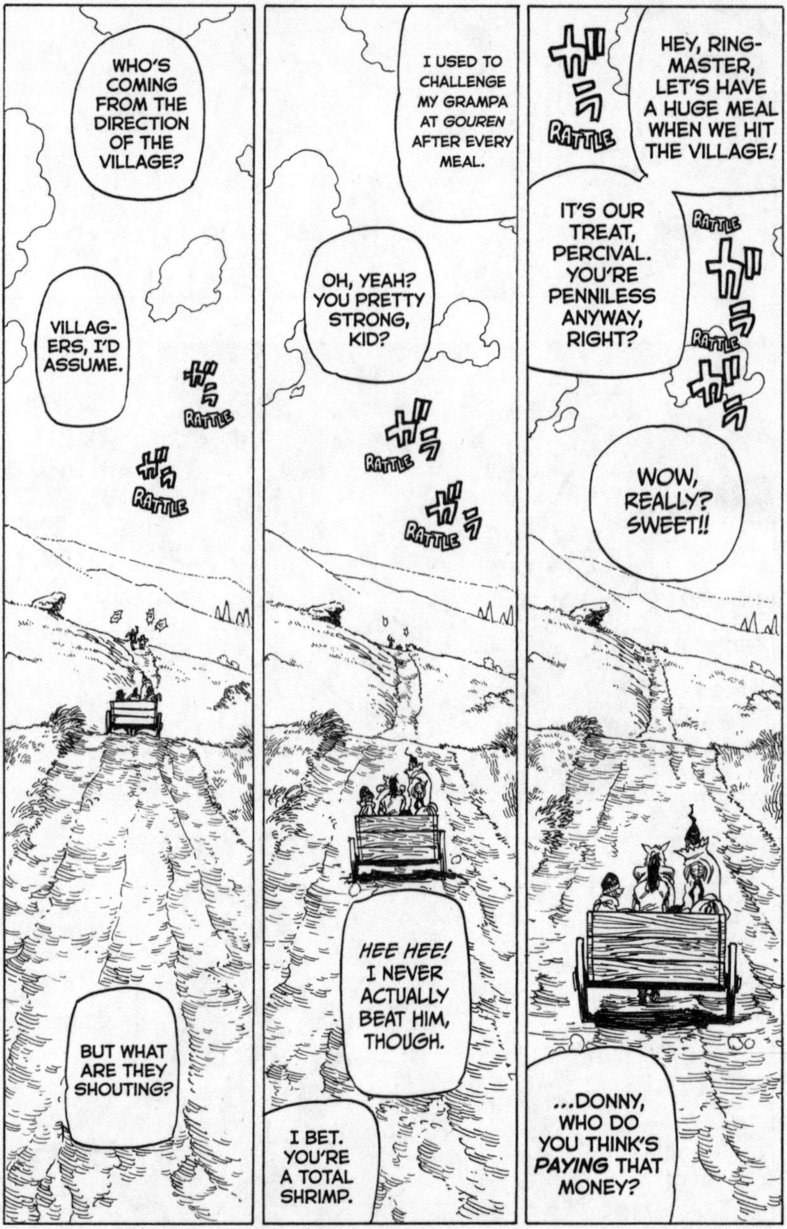
HEY, RING-MASTER, LET'S HAVE A HUGE MEAL WHEN WE HIT THE VILLAGE!
ガラ RATTLE
IT'S OUR TREAT, PERCIVAL. YOU'RE PENNILESS ANYWAY, RIGHT?
ガラ RATTLE
ガラ RATTLE
ガラ
WOW, REALLY? SWEET!!
...DONNY, WHO DO YOU THINK'S *PAYING* THAT MONEY?
I USED TO CHALLENGE MY GRAMPA AT *GOUREN* AFTER EVERY MEAL.
OH, YEAH? YOU PRETTY STRONG, KID?
ガラ RATTLE
ガラ RATTLE
HEE HEE! I NEVER ACTUALLY BEAT HIM, THOUGH.
I BET. YOU'RE A TOTAL SHRIMP.
WHO'S COMING FROM THE DIRECTION OF THE VILLAGE?
VILLAG-ERS, I'D ASSUME.
ガラ RATTLE
ガラ RATTLE
BUT WHAT ARE THEY SHOUTING?

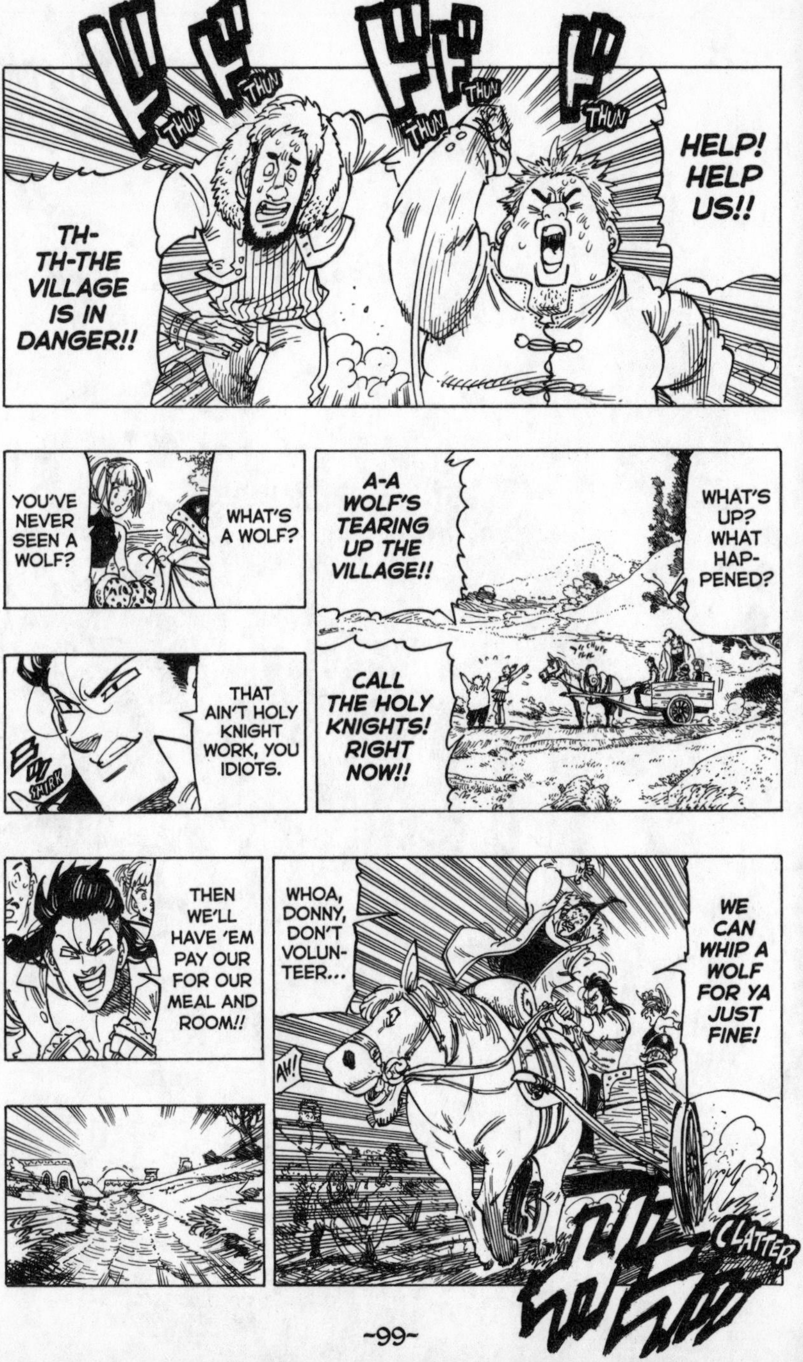
THUN THUN THUN THUN THUN
HELP! HELP US!!
TH- TH-THE VILLAGE IS IN DANGER!!
WHAT'S UP? WHAT HAP- PENED?
A-A WOLF'S TEARING UP THE VILLAGE!!
CALL THE HOLY KNIGHTS! RIGHT NOW!!
WHAT'S A WOLF?
YOU'VE NEVER SEEN A WOLF?
THAT AIN'T HOLY KNIGHT WORK, YOU IDIOTS.
SMIRK
WE CAN WHIP A WOLF FOR YA JUST FINE!
WHOA, DONNY, DON'T VOLUN- TEER...
AH!
CLATTER
THEN WE'LL HAVE 'EM PAY OUR FOR OUR MEAL AND ROOM!!

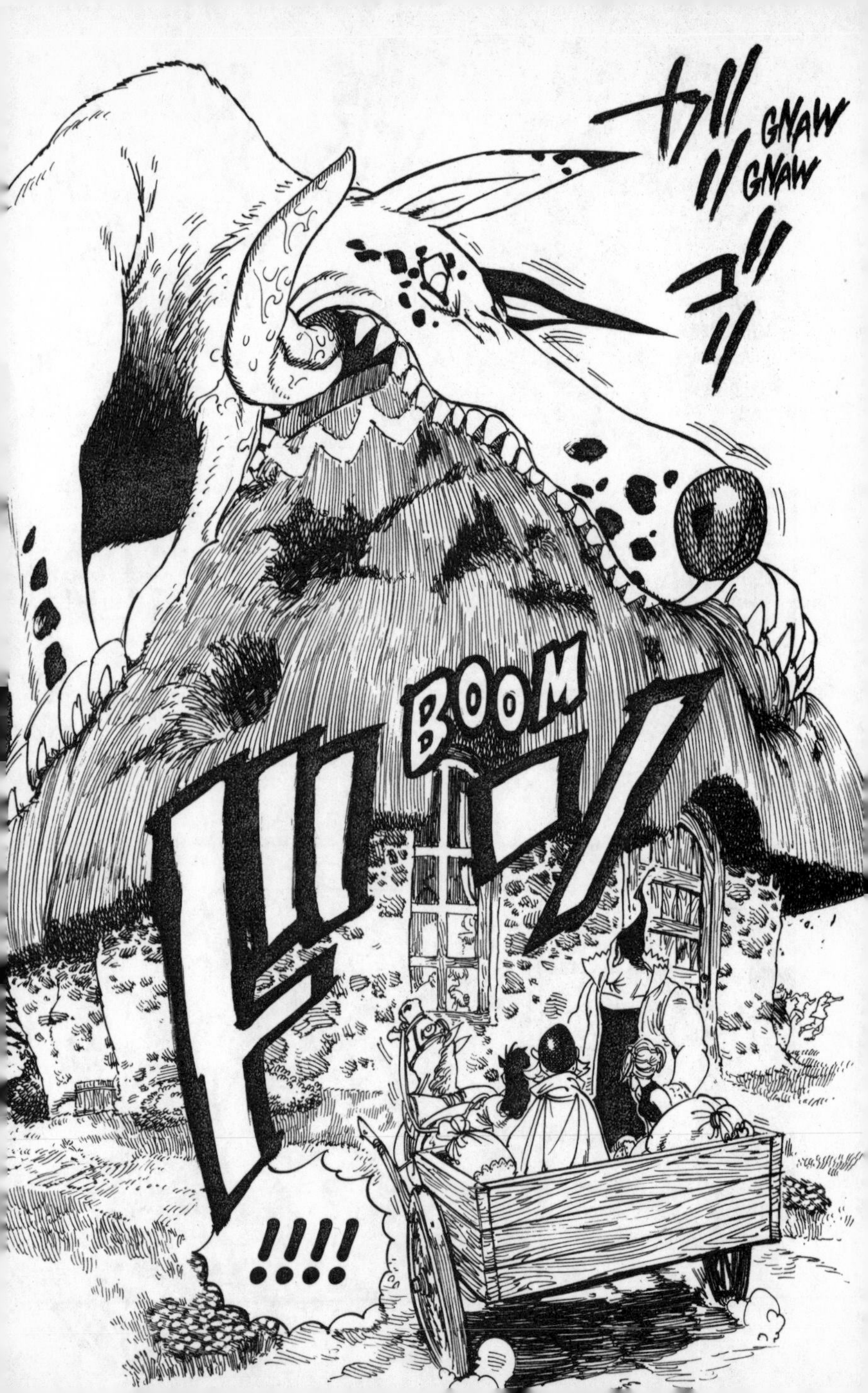
ガリ
GNAW
ゴリ
GNAW
ドーン
BOOM
!!!!

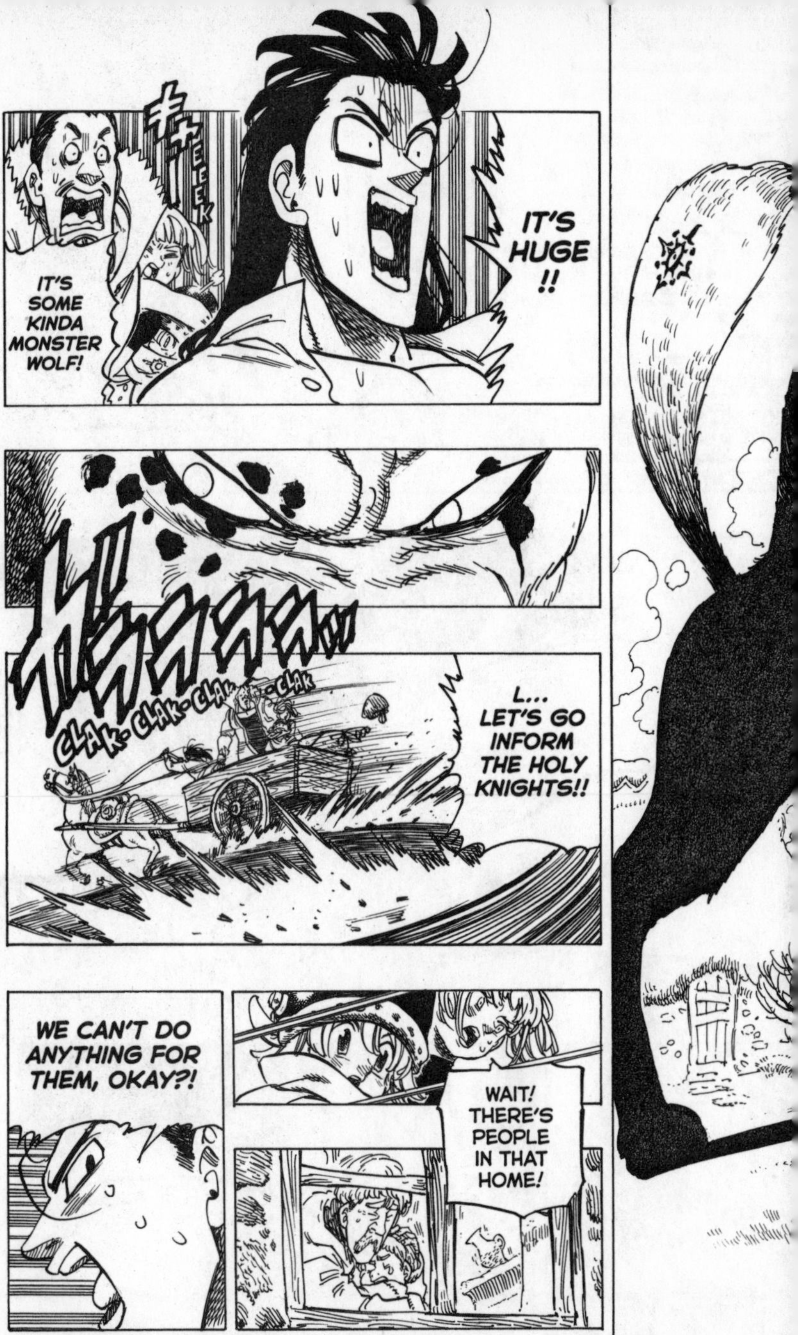
IT'S HUGE!!
EEEK
IT'S SOME KINDA MONSTER WOLF!
CLAK-CLAK-CLAK-CLAK
L... LET'S GO INFORM THE HOLY KNIGHTS!!
WAIT! THERE'S PEOPLE IN THAT HOME!
WE CAN'T DO ANYTHING FOR THEM, OKAY?!

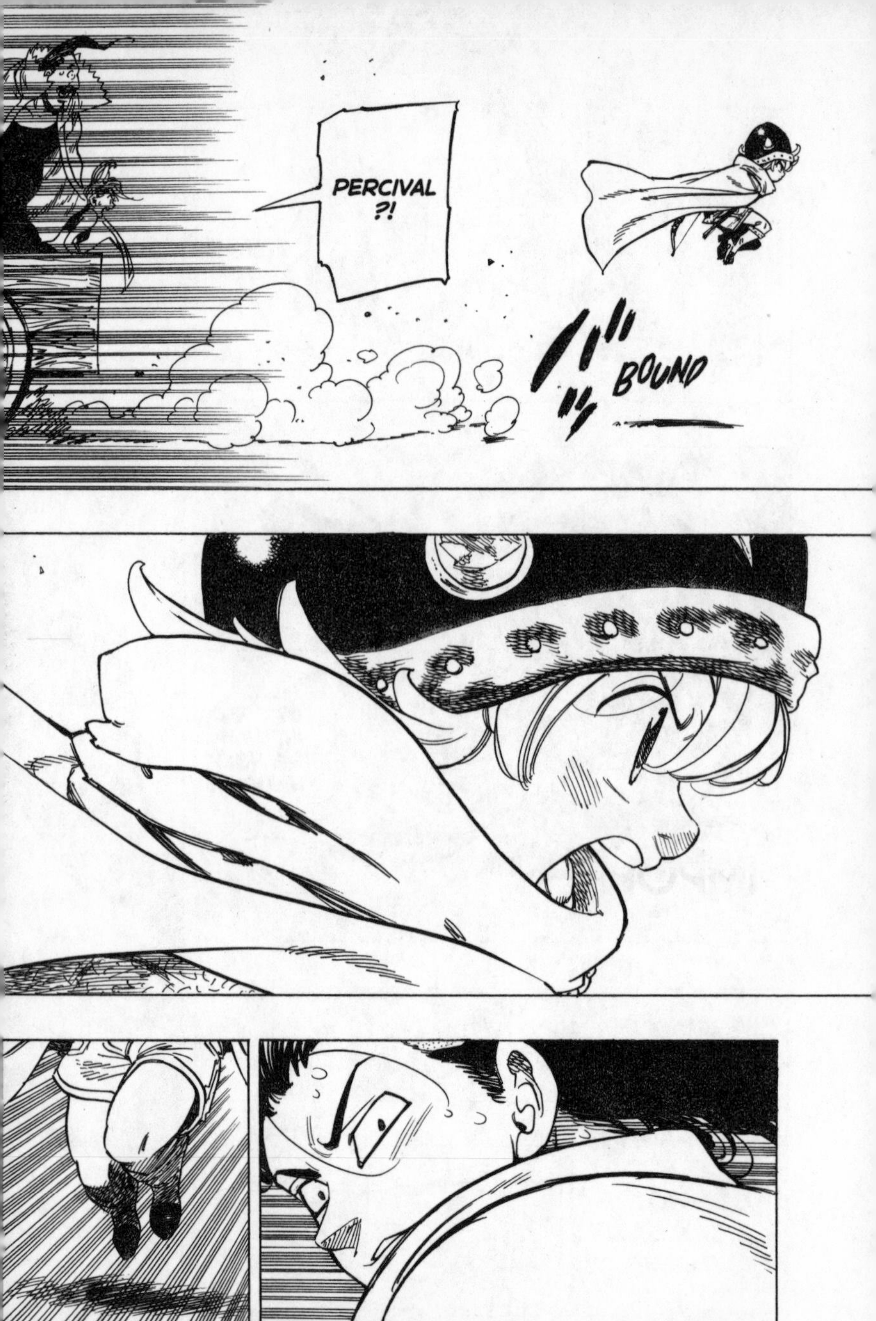
BOUND
PERCIVAL ?!

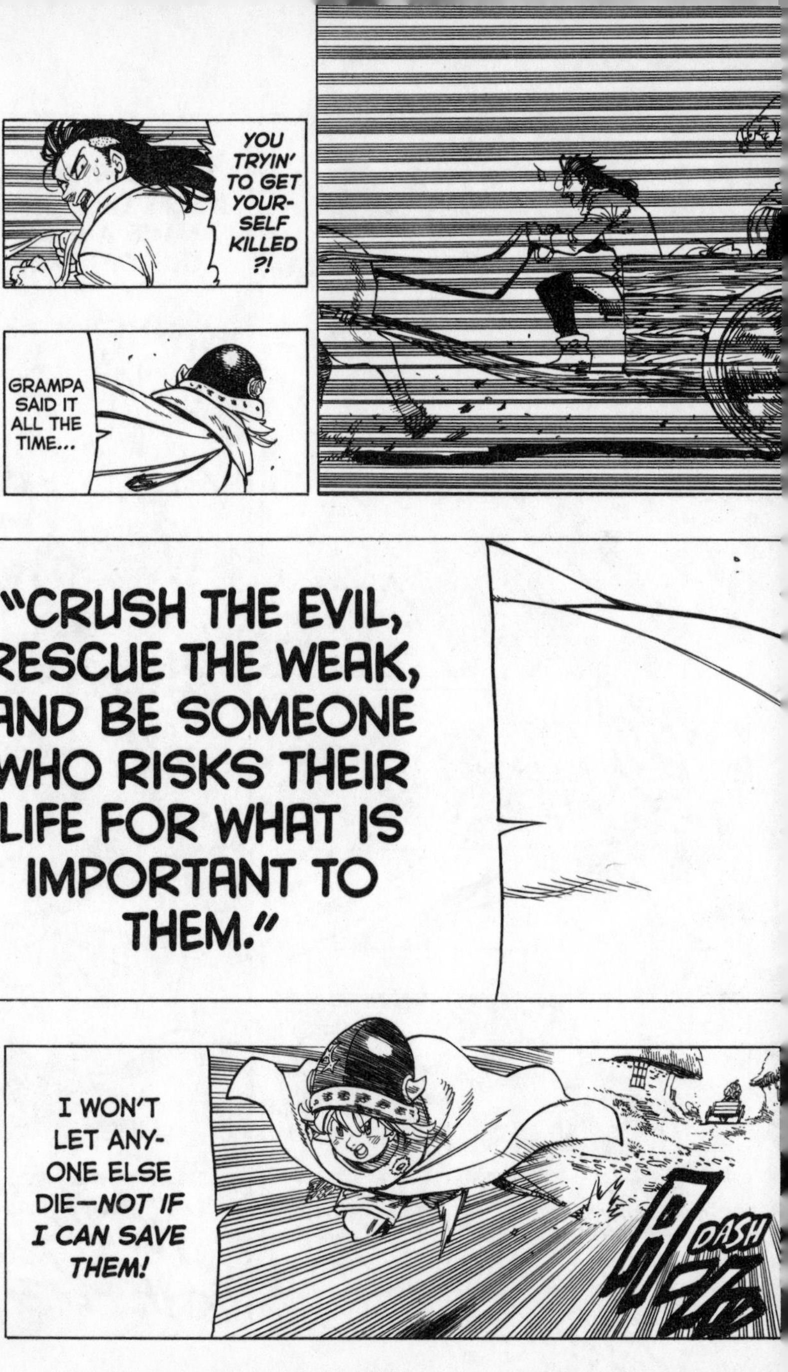
YOU TRYIN' TO GET YOURSELF KILLED ?!
GRAMPA SAID IT ALL THE TIME...
"CRUSH THE EVIL, RESCUE THE WEAK, AND BE SOMEONE WHO RISKS THEIR LIFE FOR WHAT IS IMPORTANT TO THEM."
I WON'T LET ANYONE ELSE DIE—*NOT IF I CAN SAVE THEM!*
DASH

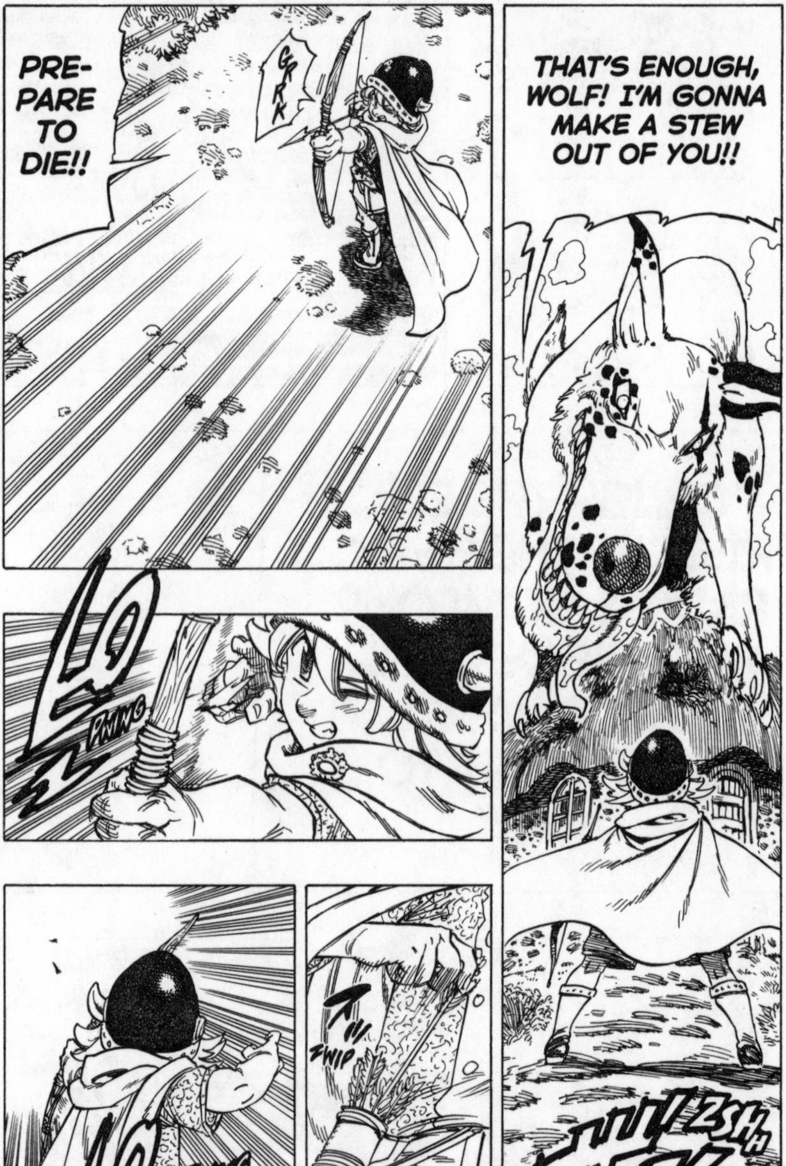
THAT'S ENOUGH, WOLF! I'M GONNA MAKE A STEW OUT OF YOU!!
ZSHH
PRE-PARE TO DIE!!
GRRK
PWING
ZWIP
PWING

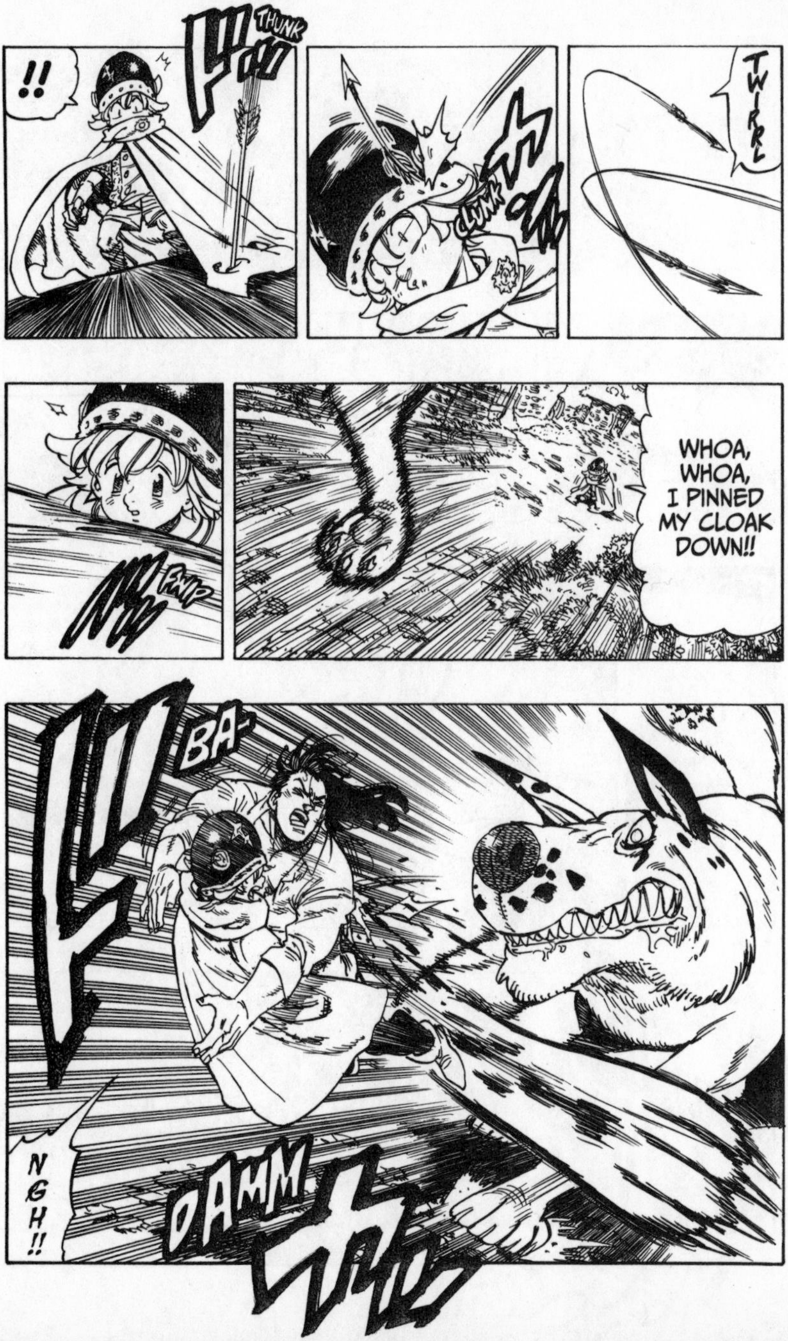
TWIRL
CLUNK
!!
THUNK
WHOA, WHOA, I PINNED MY CLOAK DOWN!!
FWIP
BA-
DAMM
NGH!!

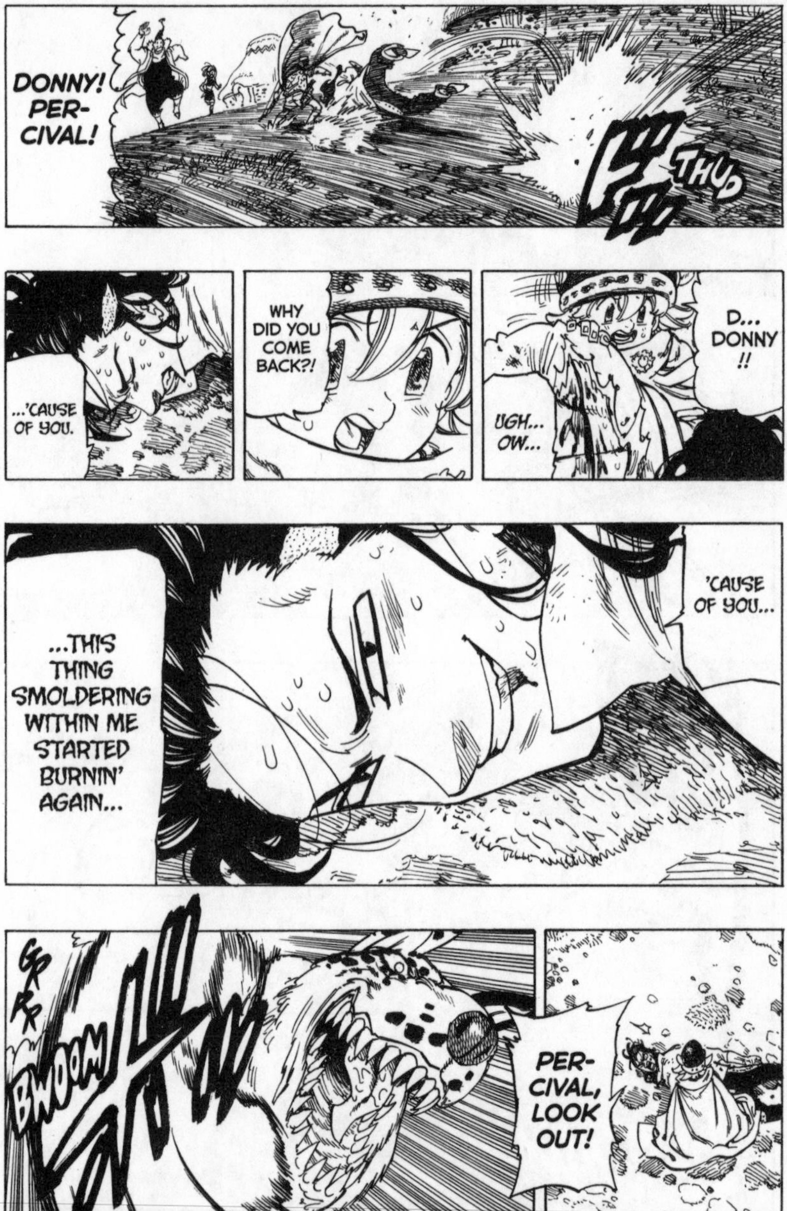
THUD
DONNY! PER-CIVAL!
D... DONNY !!
UGH... OW...
WHY DID YOU COME BACK?!
...'CAUSE OF YOU.
'CAUSE OF YOU...
...THIS THING SMOLDERING WITHIN ME STARTED BURNIN' AGAIN...
PER-CIVAL, LOOK OUT!
GRRR
BWOOM

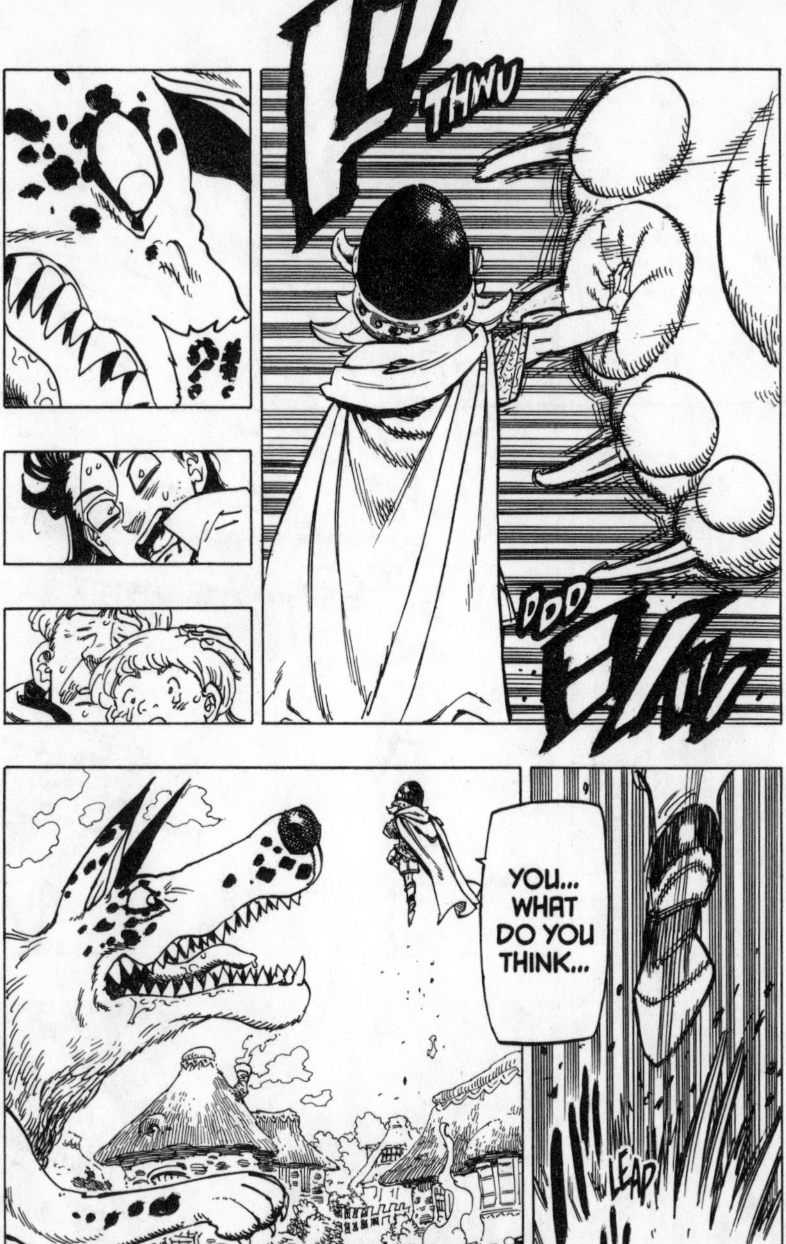
THWU
?!
LEAP
YOU... WHAT DO YOU THINK...

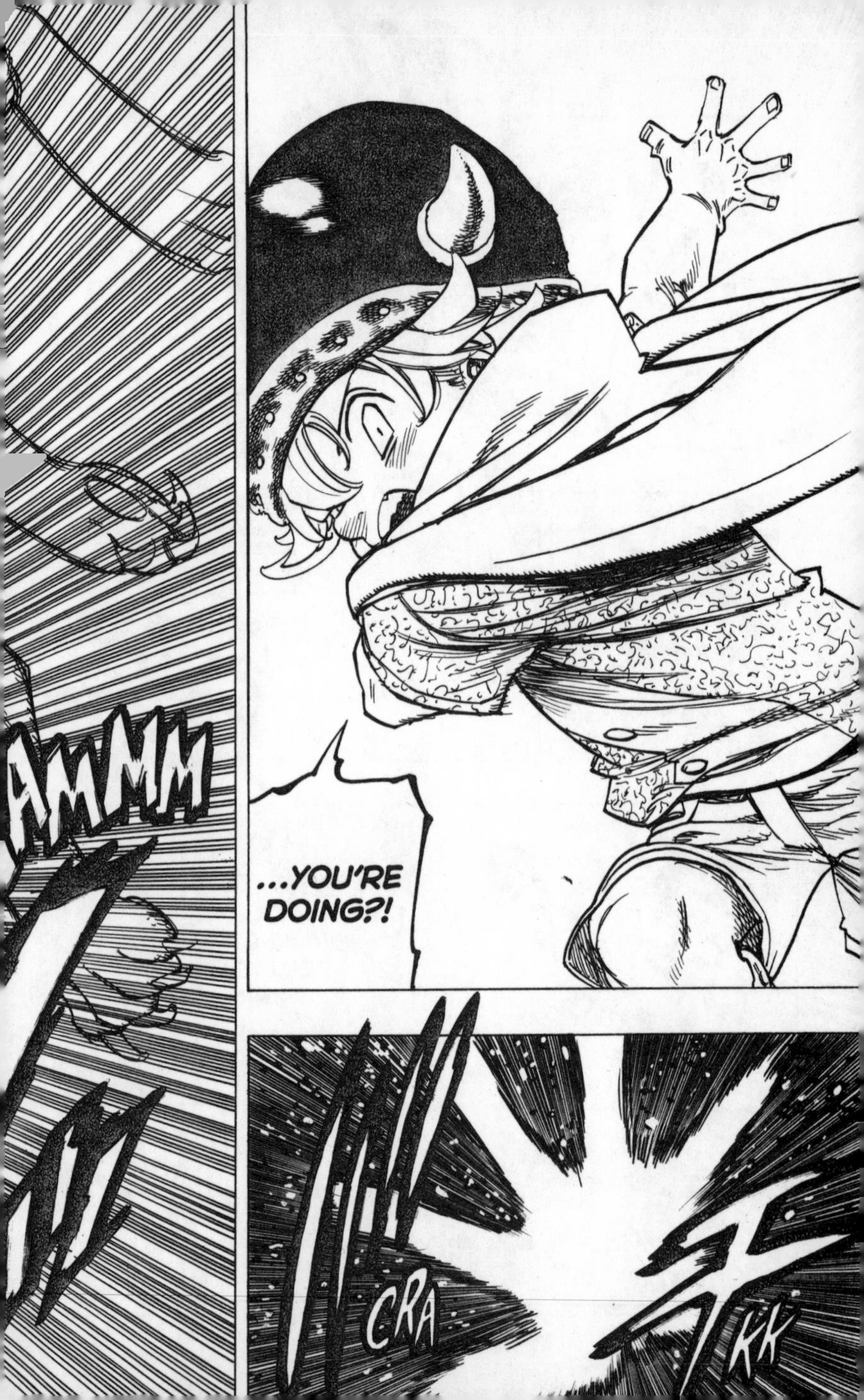
...YOU'RE DOING?!
CRA
KK
AMMM

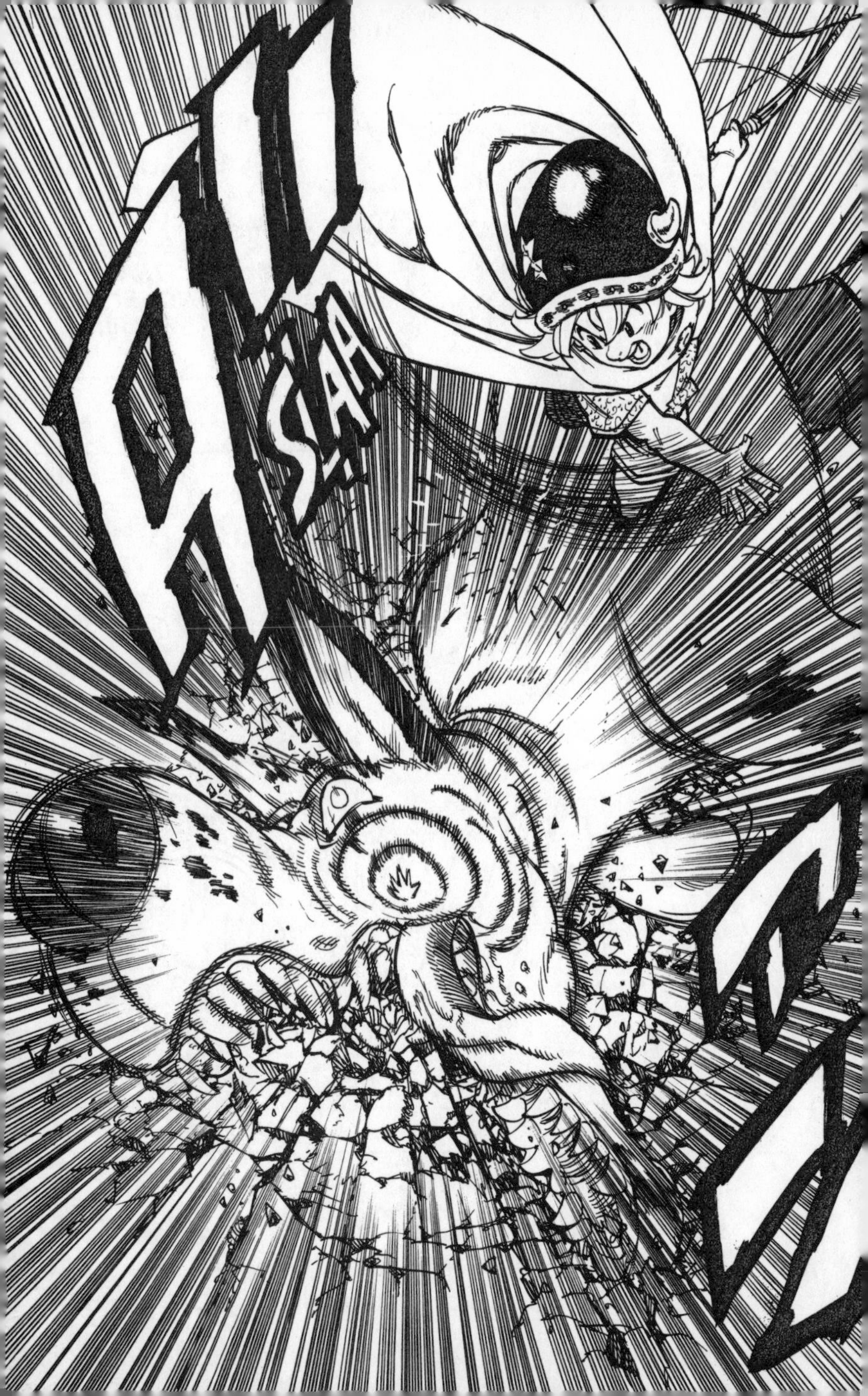

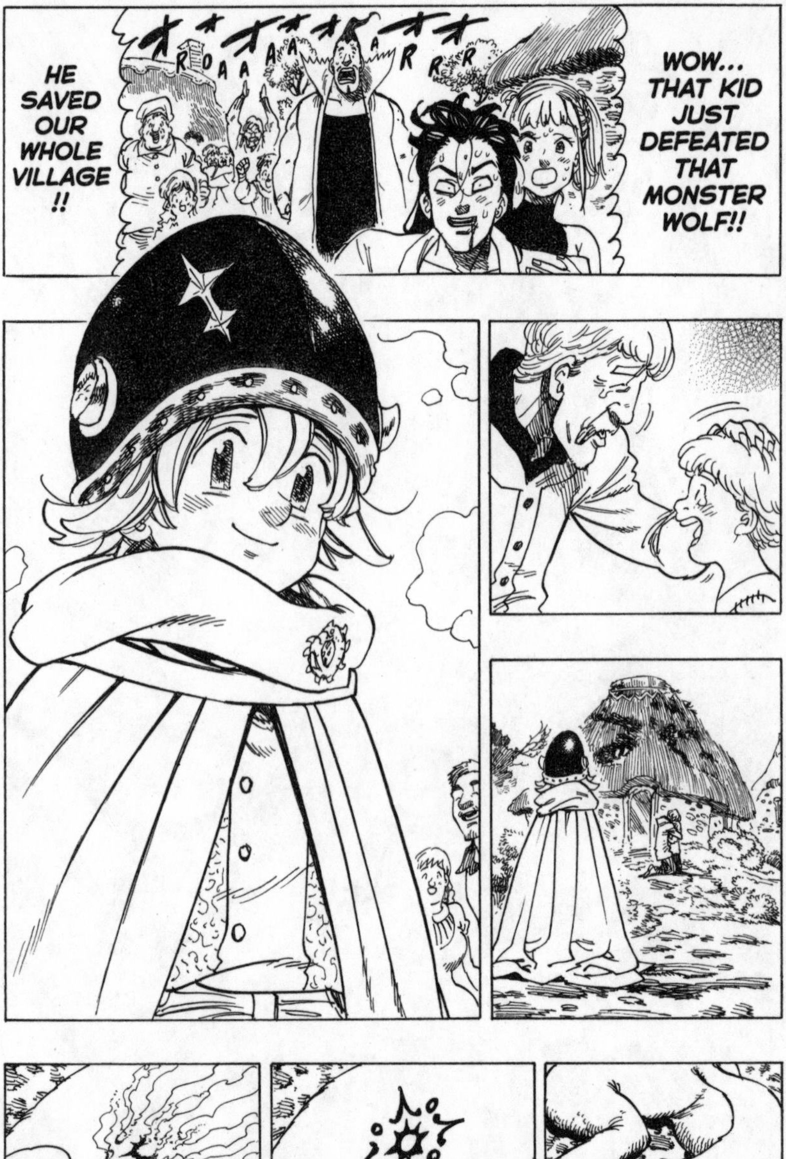
WOW... THAT KID JUST DEFEATED THAT MONSTER WOLF!!
ROAAAAARRR
HE SAVED OUR WHOLE VILLAGE!!
FRIZZ...

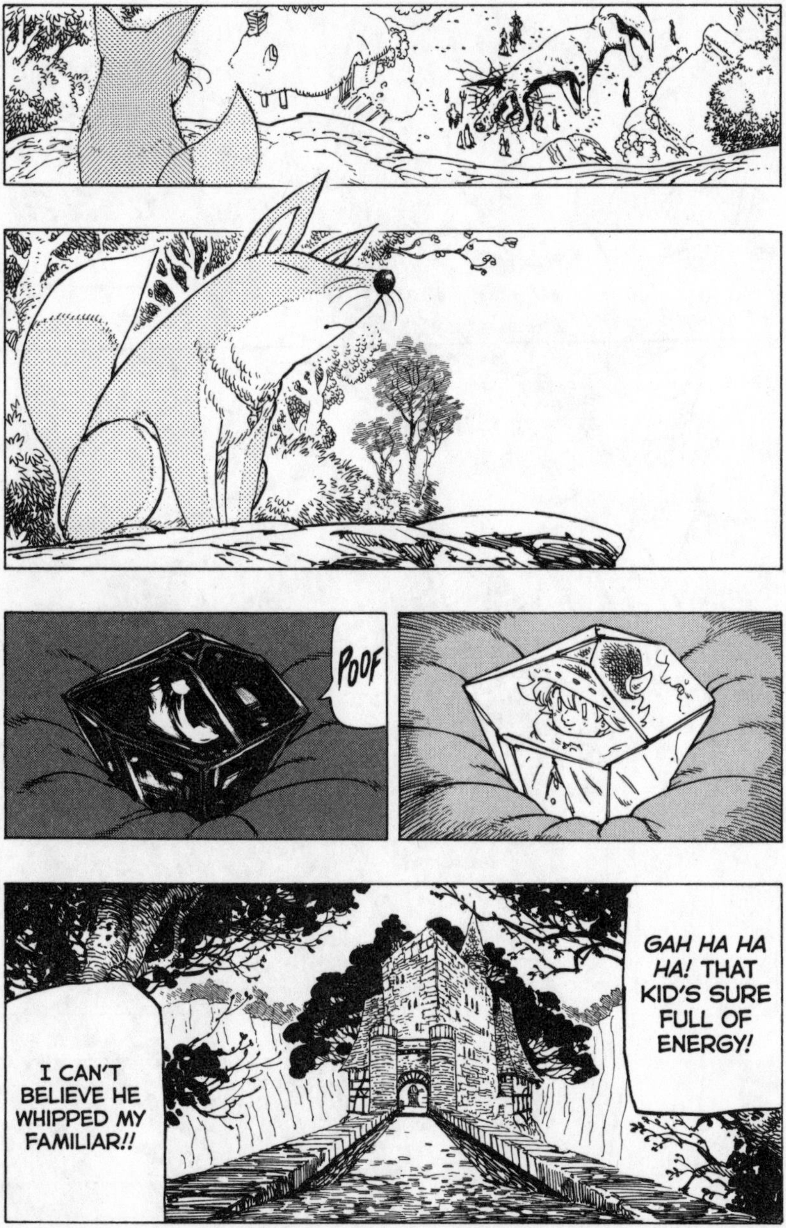
POOF
GAH HA HA HA! THAT KID'S SURE FULL OF ENERGY!
I CAN'T BELIEVE HE WHIPPED MY FAMILIAR!!

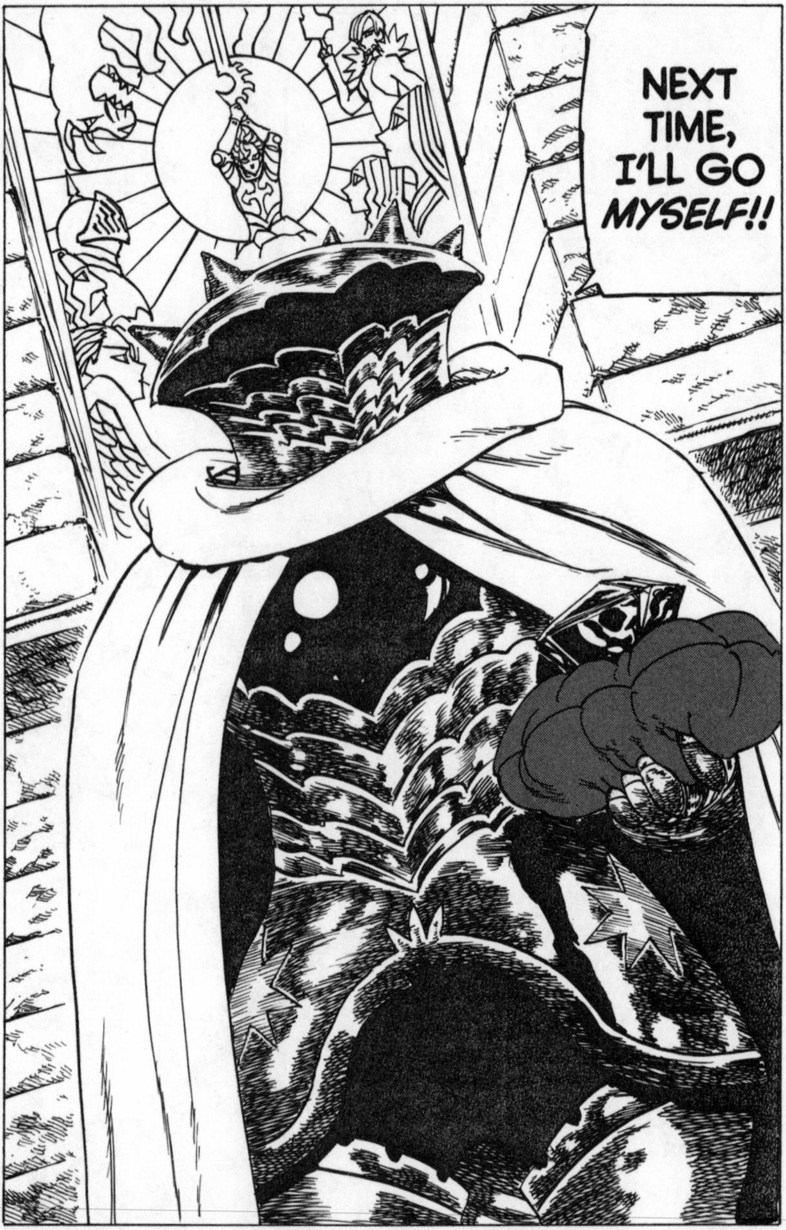
NEXT TIME, I'LL GO *MYSELF*!!

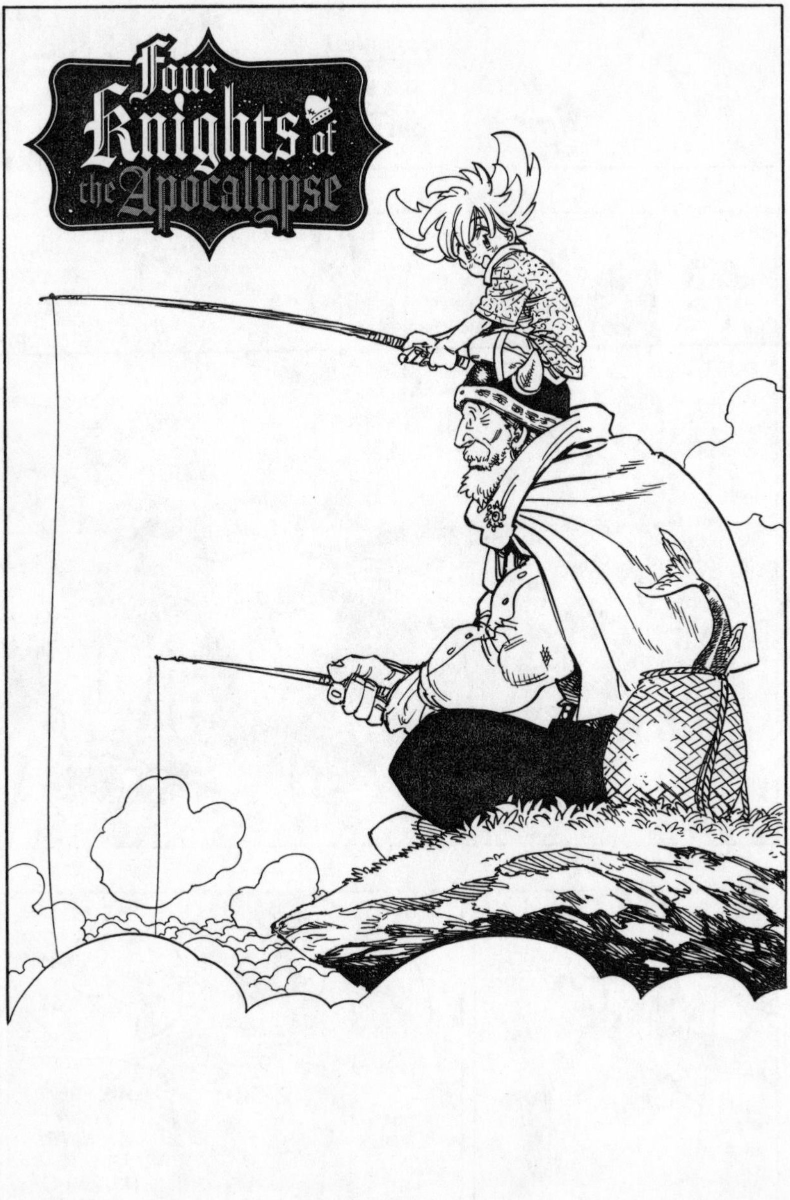
Four Knights of the Apocalypse

CHAPTER 3: ON FATHER'S TRAIL

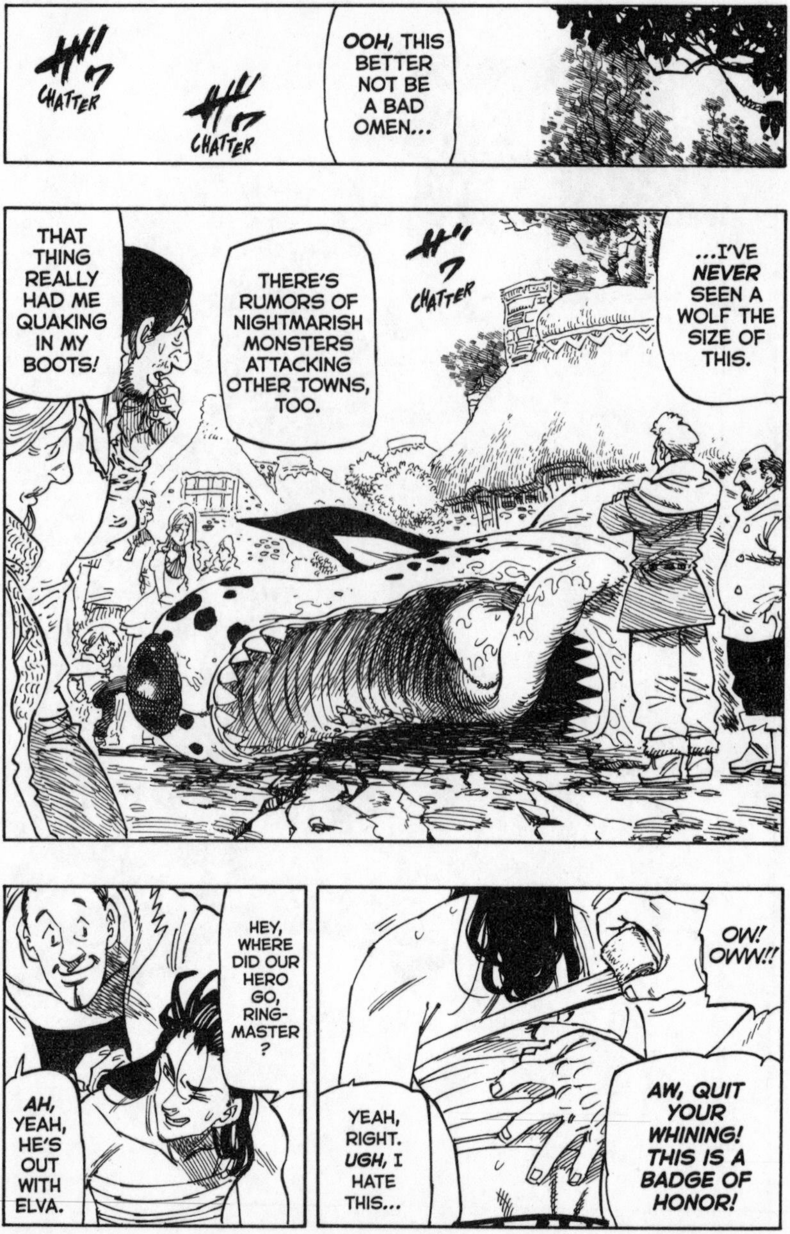
OOH, THIS BETTER NOT BE A BAD OMEN...
CHATTER
CHATTER
...I'VE NEVER SEEN A WOLF THE SIZE OF THIS.
CHATTER
THERE'S RUMORS OF NIGHTMARISH MONSTERS ATTACKING OTHER TOWNS, TOO.
THAT THING REALLY HAD ME QUAKING IN MY BOOTS!
OW! OWW!!
AW, QUIT YOUR WHINING! THIS IS A BADGE OF HONOR!
YEAH, RIGHT. UGH, I HATE THIS...
HEY, WHERE DID OUR HERO GO, RING-MASTER?
AH, YEAH, HE'S OUT WITH ELVA.

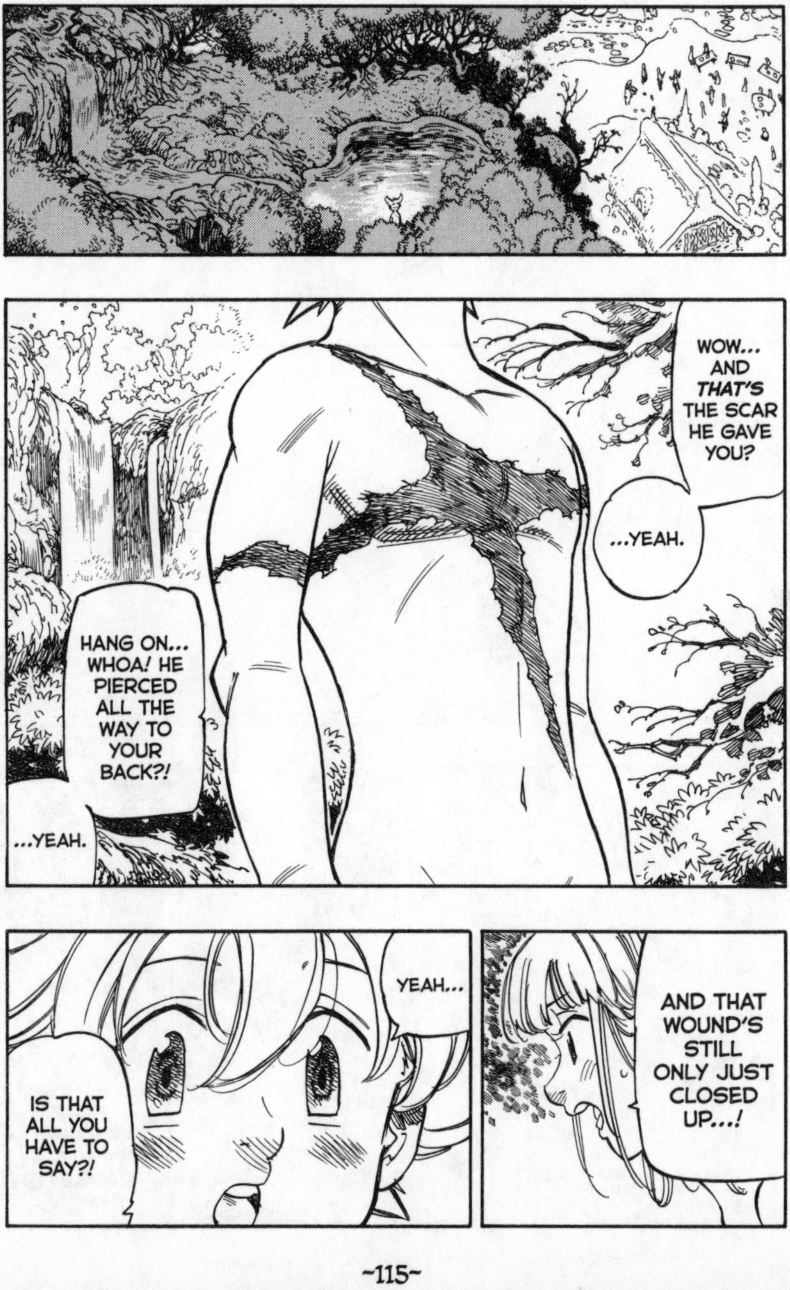
WOW... AND *THAT'S* THE SCAR HE GAVE YOU?
...YEAH.
HANG ON... WHOA! HE PIERCED ALL THE WAY TO YOUR BACK?!
...YEAH.
AND THAT WOUND'S STILL ONLY JUST CLOSED UP...!
YEAH...
IS THAT ALL YOU HAVE TO SAY?!

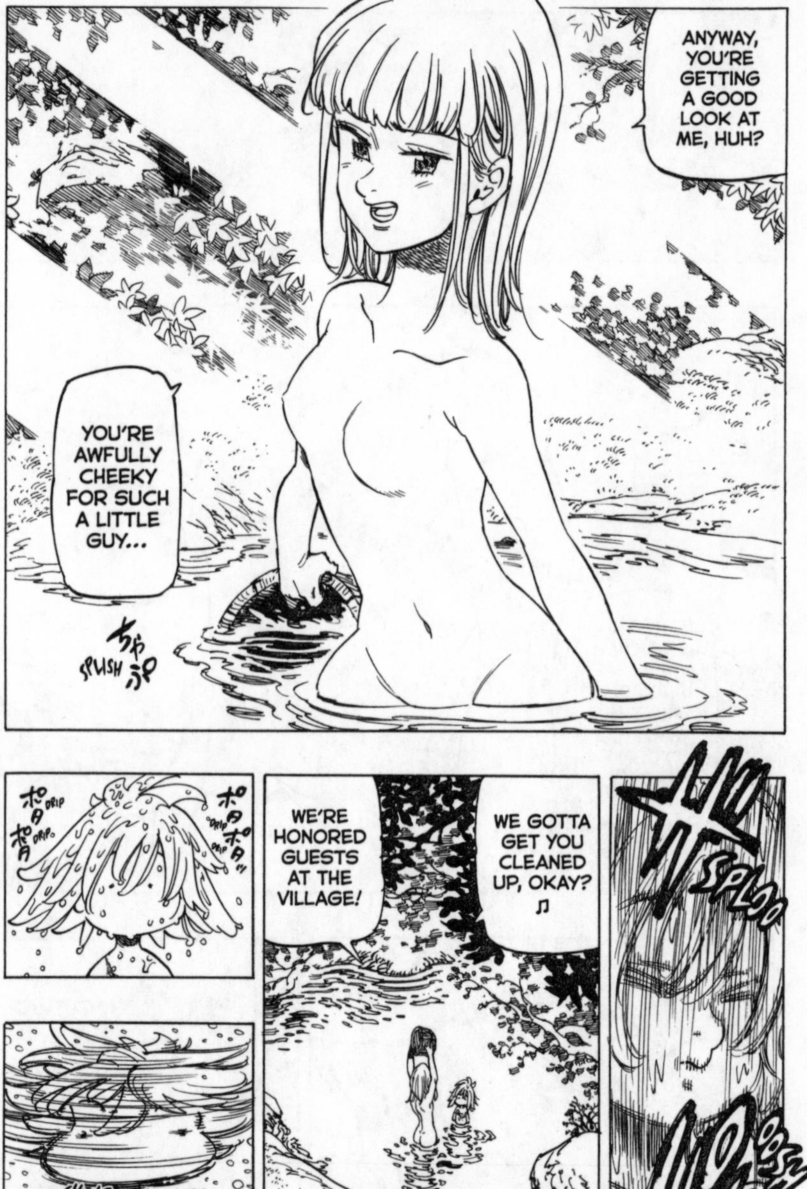

ANYWAY, YOU'RE GETTING A GOOD LOOK AT ME, HUH?
YOU'RE AWFULLY CHEEKY FOR SUCH A LITTLE GUY...
SPLISH
SPLOO
OOSH
WE GOTTA GET YOU CLEANED UP, OKAY? ♫
WE'RE HONORED GUESTS AT THE VILLAGE!
DRIP DRIP DRIP DRIP
SHWIP WIP WIP

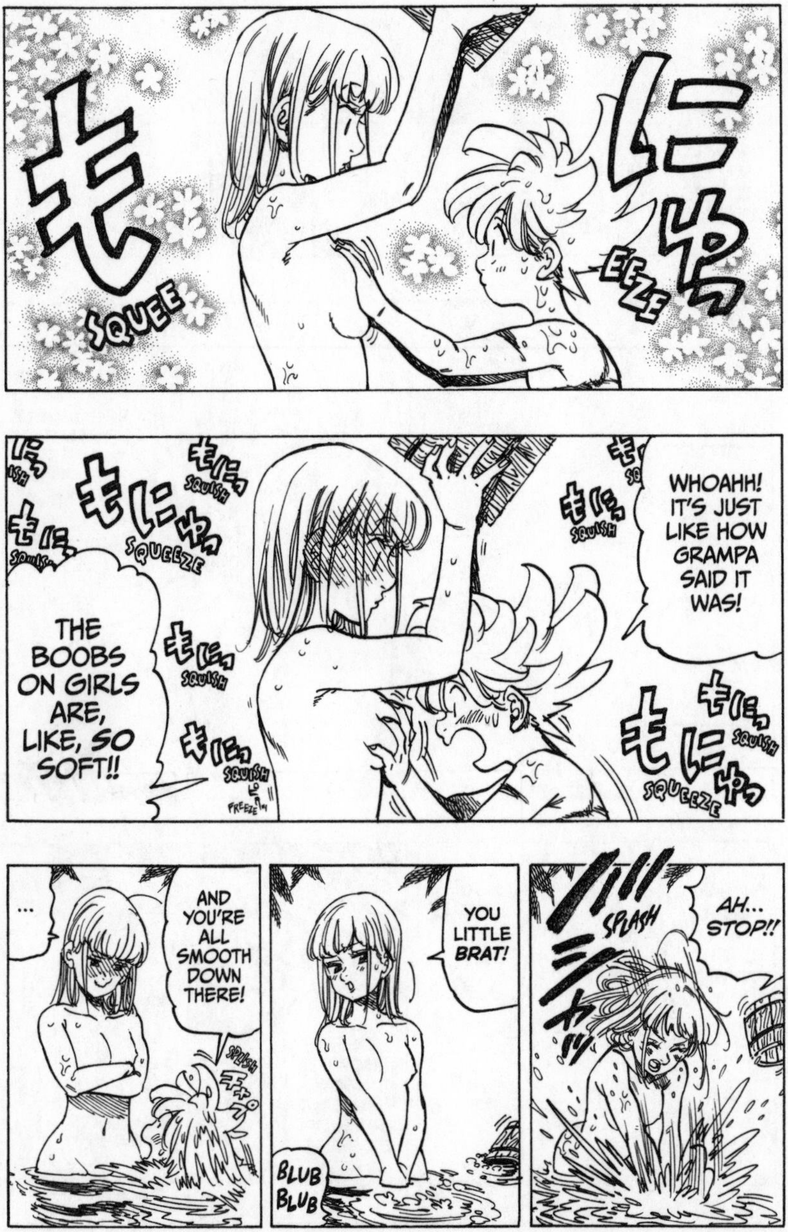
にゅ
EEZE
も
SQUEE
WHOAHH! IT'S JUST LIKE HOW GRAMPA SAID IT WAS!
SQUISH
SQUEEZE
SQUISH
SQUISH
SQUEEZE
SQUISH
THE BOOBS ON GIRLS ARE, LIKE, SO SOFT!!
SQUISH
SQUISH
FREEZE
AH... STOP!!
SPLASH
YOU LITTLE BRAT!
BLUB BLUB
AND YOU'RE ALL SMOOTH DOWN THERE!
...
SPLISH

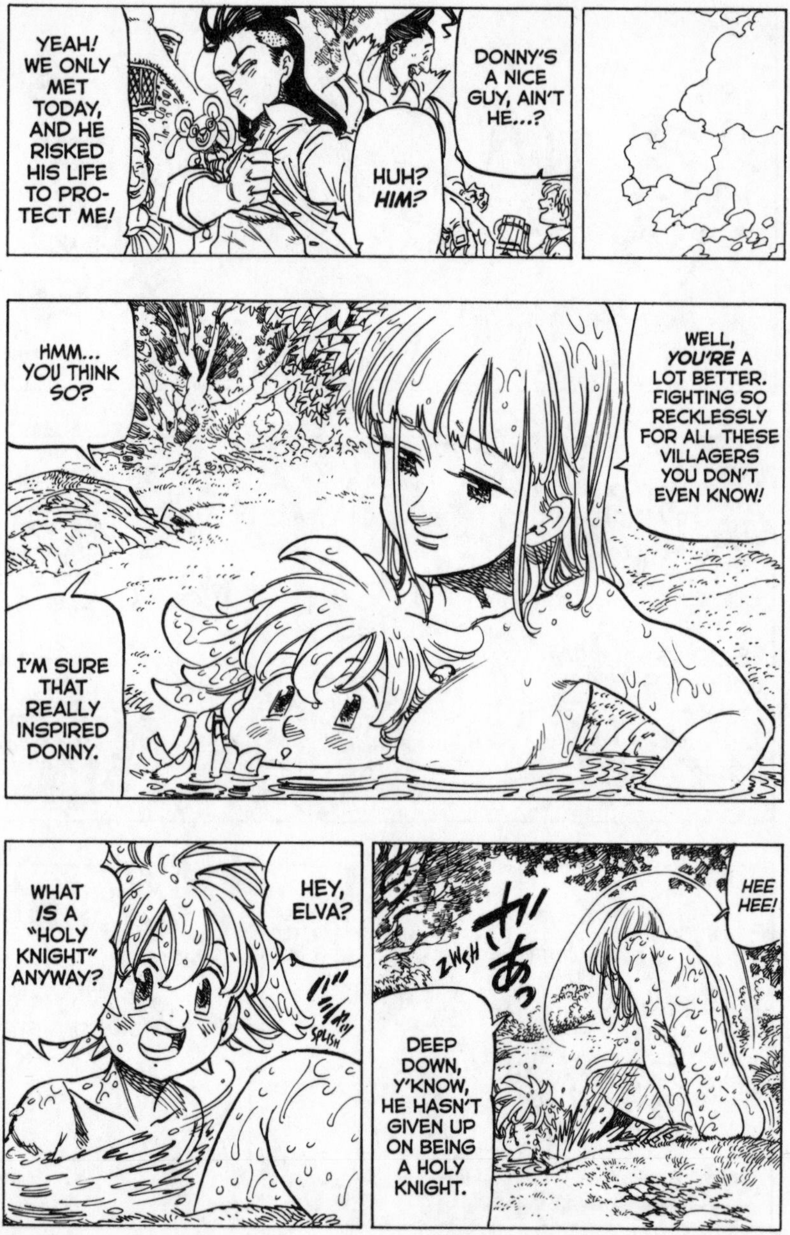
DONNY'S A NICE GUY, AIN'T HE...?
HUH? *HIM?*
YEAH! WE ONLY MET TODAY, AND HE RISKED HIS LIFE TO PRO-TECT ME!
WELL, *YOU'RE* A LOT BETTER. FIGHTING SO RECKLESSLY FOR ALL THESE VILLAGERS YOU DON'T EVEN KNOW!
HMM... YOU THINK SO?
I'M SURE THAT REALLY INSPIRED DONNY.
HEE HEE!
ざあっ
ZWSH
DEEP DOWN, Y'KNOW, HE HASN'T GIVEN UP ON BEING A HOLY KNIGHT.
HEY, ELVA?
WHAT *IS* A "HOLY KNIGHT" ANYWAY?
SPLISH

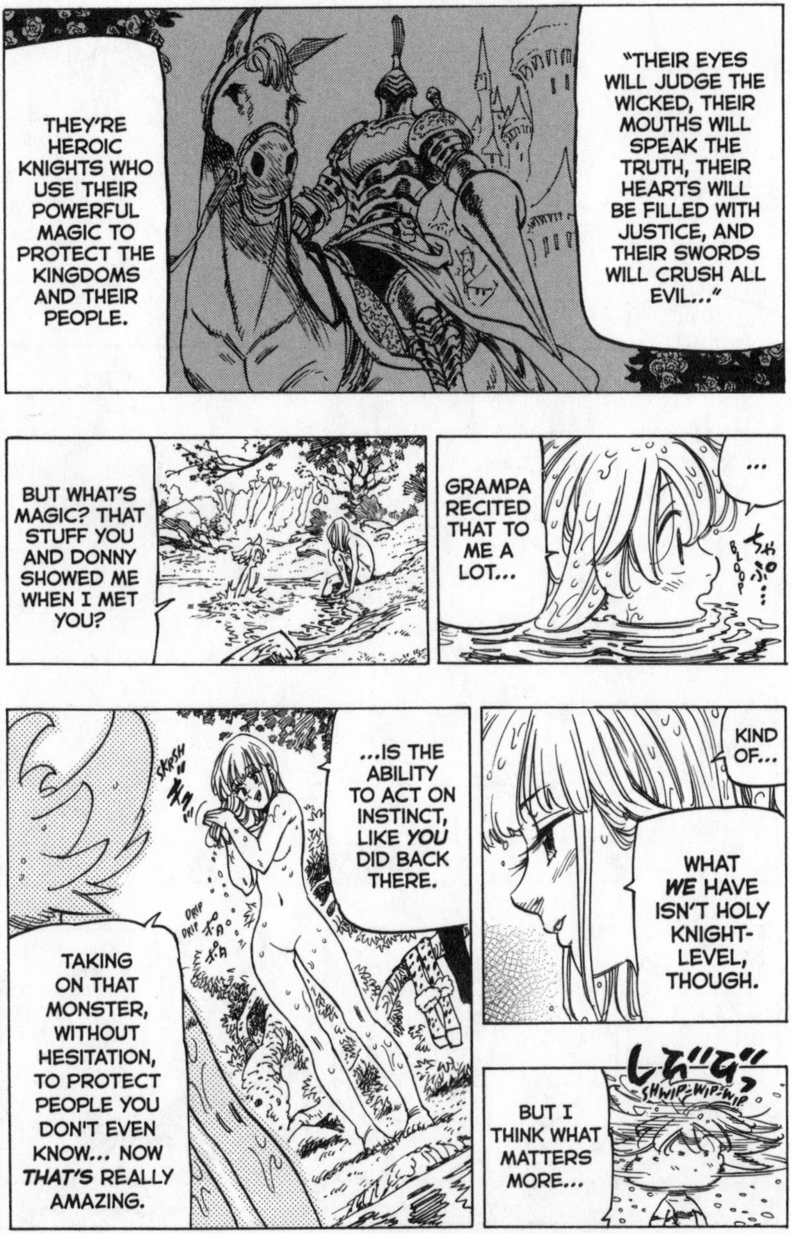
"THEIR EYES WILL JUDGE THE WICKED, THEIR MOUTHS WILL SPEAK THE TRUTH, THEIR HEARTS WILL BE FILLED WITH JUSTICE, AND THEIR SWORDS WILL CRUSH ALL EVIL..."
THEY'RE HEROIC KNIGHTS WHO USE THEIR POWERFUL MAGIC TO PROTECT THE KINGDOMS AND THEIR PEOPLE.
...
GRAMPA RECITED THAT TO ME A LOT...
BLOOP
BUT WHAT'S MAGIC? THAT STUFF YOU AND DONNY SHOWED ME WHEN I MET YOU?
KIND OF...
WHAT *WE* HAVE ISN'T HOLY KNIGHT-LEVEL, THOUGH.
SHWIP-WIP-WIP
BUT I THINK WHAT MATTERS MORE...
...IS THE ABILITY TO ACT ON INSTINCT, LIKE *YOU* DID BACK THERE.
SKRSH
DRIP DRIP
TAKING ON THAT MONSTER, WITHOUT HESITATION, TO PROTECT PEOPLE YOU DON'T EVEN KNOW... NOW *THAT'S* REALLY AMAZING.

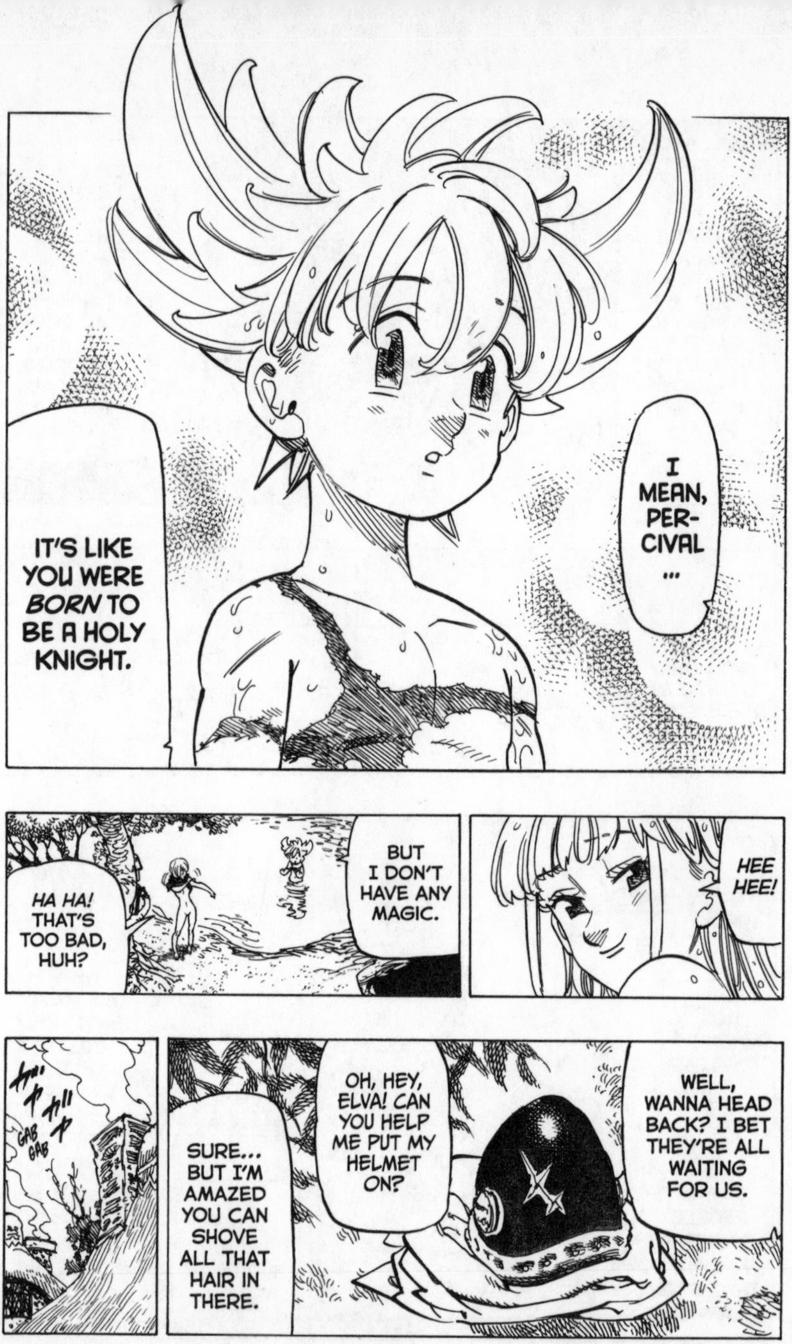
I MEAN, PERCIVAL...
IT'S LIKE YOU WERE *BORN* TO BE A HOLY KNIGHT.
HEE HEE!
BUT I DON'T HAVE ANY MAGIC.
HA HA! THAT'S TOO BAD, HUH?
WELL, WANNA HEAD BACK? I BET THEY'RE ALL WAITING FOR US.
OH, HEY, ELVA! CAN YOU HELP ME PUT MY HELMET ON?
SURE... BUT I'M AMAZED YOU CAN SHOVE ALL THAT HAIR IN THERE.
GAB GAB

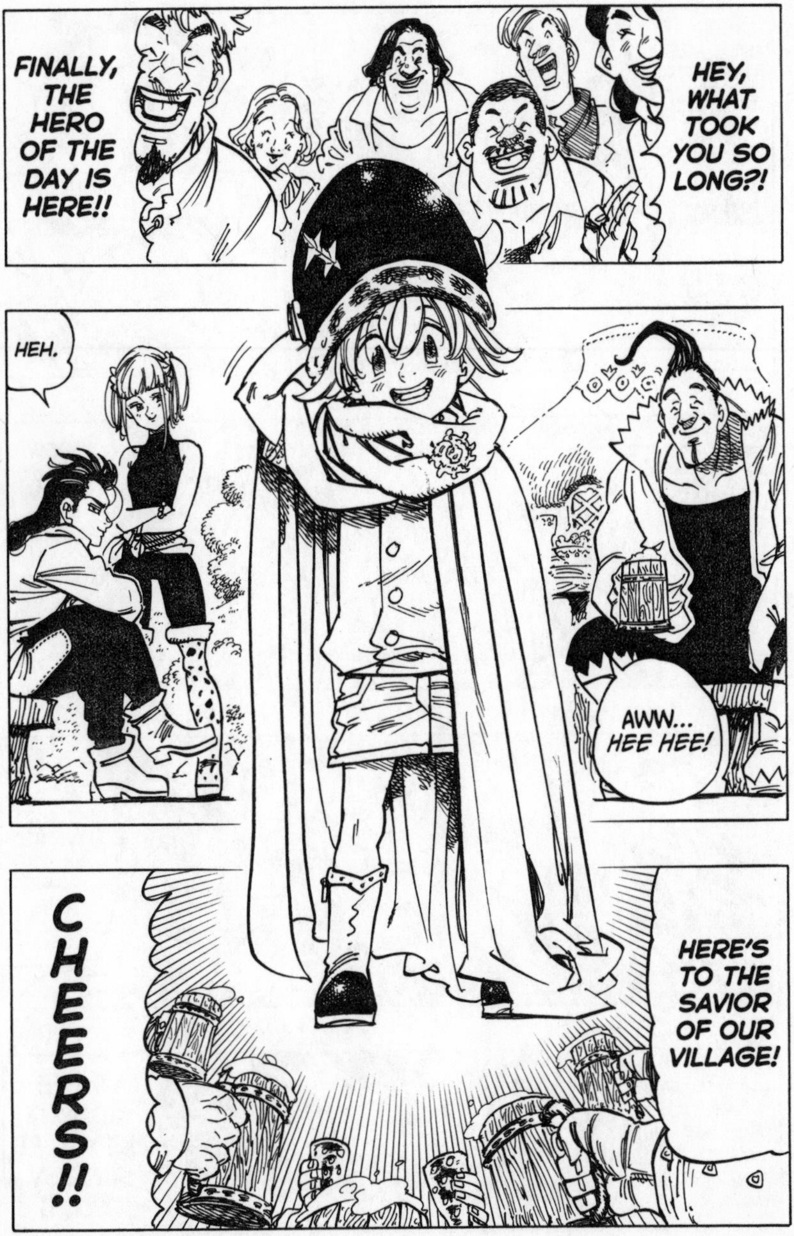
HEY, WHAT TOOK YOU SO LONG?!
FINALLY, THE HERO OF THE DAY IS HERE!!
AWW... HEE HEE!
HEH.
HERE'S TO THE SAVIOR OF OUR VILLAGE!
CHEERS!!

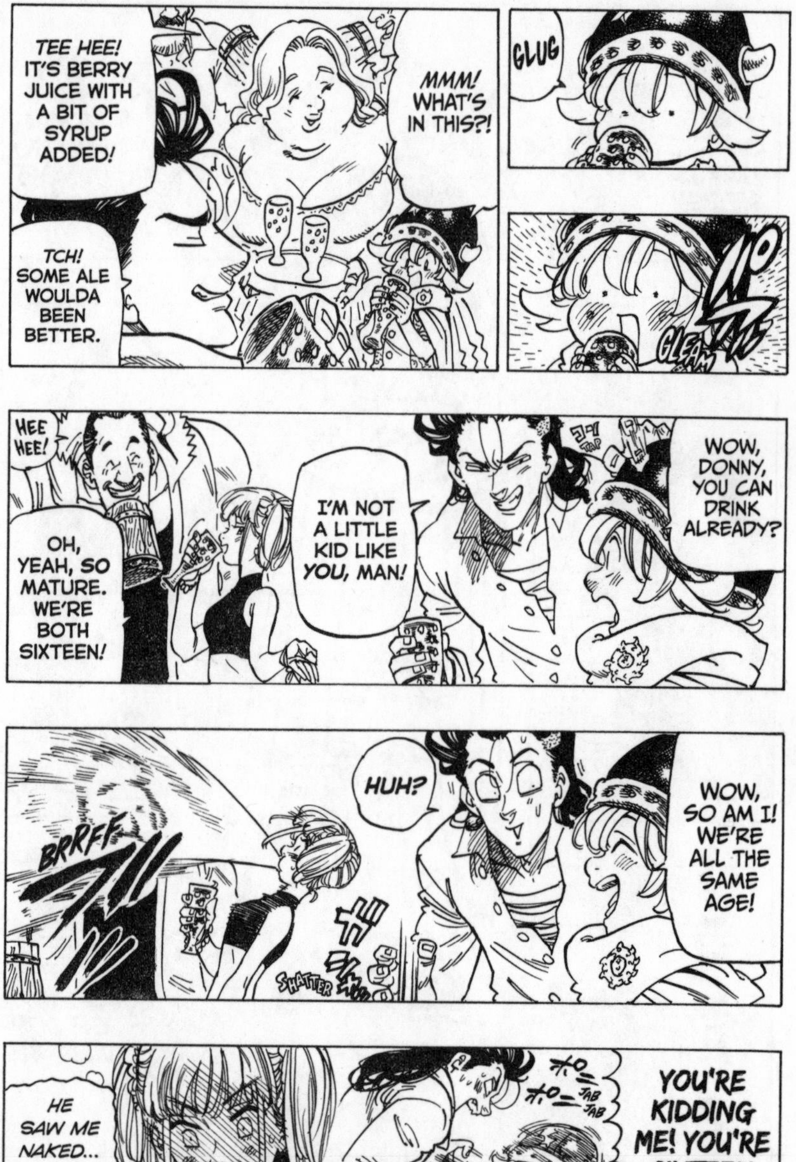
GLUG
GLEAM
MMM! WHAT'S IN THIS?!
TEE HEE! IT'S BERRY JUICE WITH A BIT OF SYRUP ADDED!
TCH! SOME ALE WOULDA BEEN BETTER.
WOW, DONNY, YOU CAN DRINK ALREADY?
JAP
I'M NOT A LITTLE KID LIKE YOU, MAN!
HEE HEE!
OH, YEAH, SO MATURE. WE'RE BOTH SIXTEEN!
WOW, SO AM I! WE'RE ALL THE SAME AGE!
HUH?
SHATTER
BRRFF
YOU'RE KIDDING ME! YOU'RE SIXTEEN TOO?!!
JAB JAB
HE SAW ME NAKED... AND FELT ME UP...

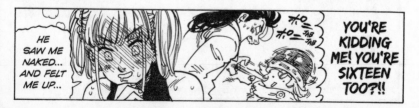

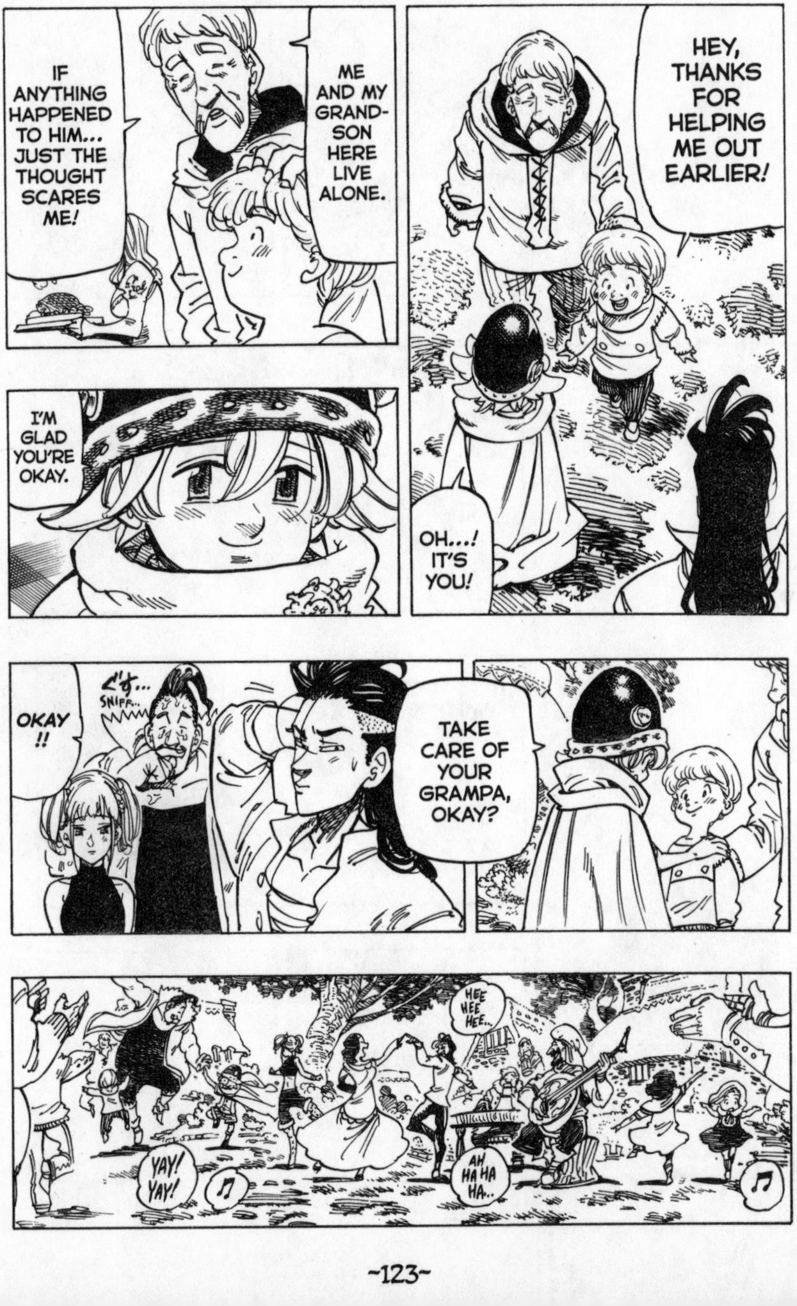
HEY, THANKS FOR HELPING ME OUT EARLIER!
OH...! IT'S YOU!
ME AND MY GRANDSON HERE LIVE ALONE.
IF ANYTHING HAPPENED TO HIM... JUST THE THOUGHT SCARES ME!
I'M GLAD YOU'RE OKAY.
TAKE CARE OF YOUR GRAMPA, OKAY?
ぐす...
SNIFF...
OKAY!!
HEE HEE HEE...
♪
AH HA HA HA...
YAY! YAY!
♪

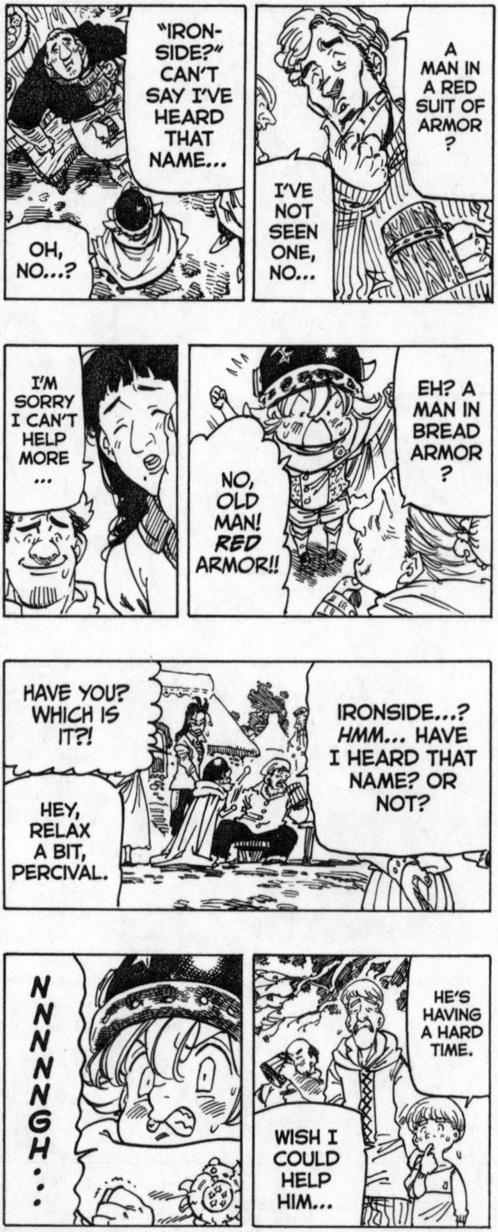
A MAN IN A RED SUIT OF ARMOR?
I'VE NOT SEEN ONE, NO...
"IRON-SIDE?" CAN'T SAY I'VE HEARD THAT NAME...
OH, NO...?
EH? A MAN IN BREAD ARMOR?
NO, OLD MAN! *RED* ARMOR!!
I'M SORRY I CAN'T HELP MORE...
IRONSIDE...? *HMM...* HAVE I HEARD THAT NAME? OR NOT?
HAVE YOU? WHICH IS IT?!
HEY, RELAX A BIT, PERCIVAL.
HE'S HAVING A HARD TIME.
WISH I COULD HELP HIM...
NNNNNGH...

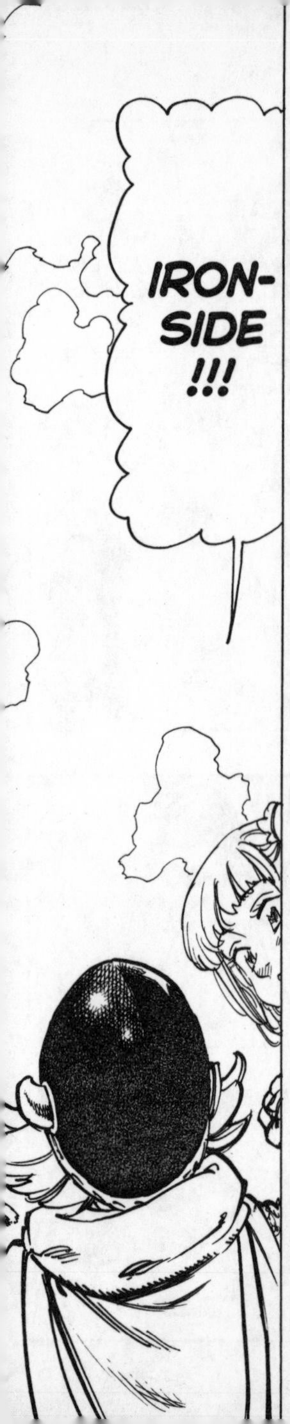
IRON-SIDE!!!

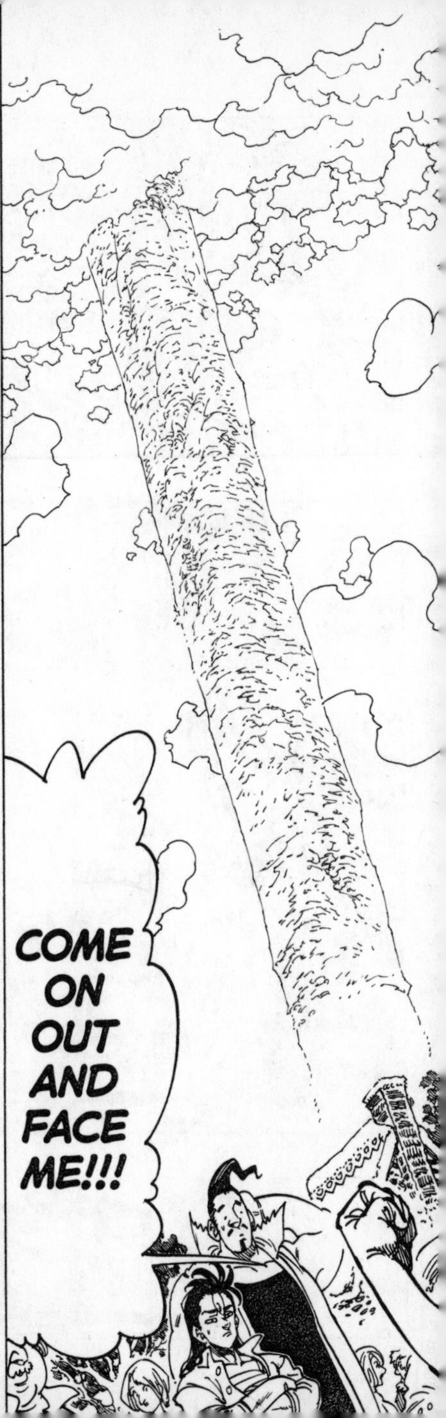
COME ON OUT AND FACE ME!!!
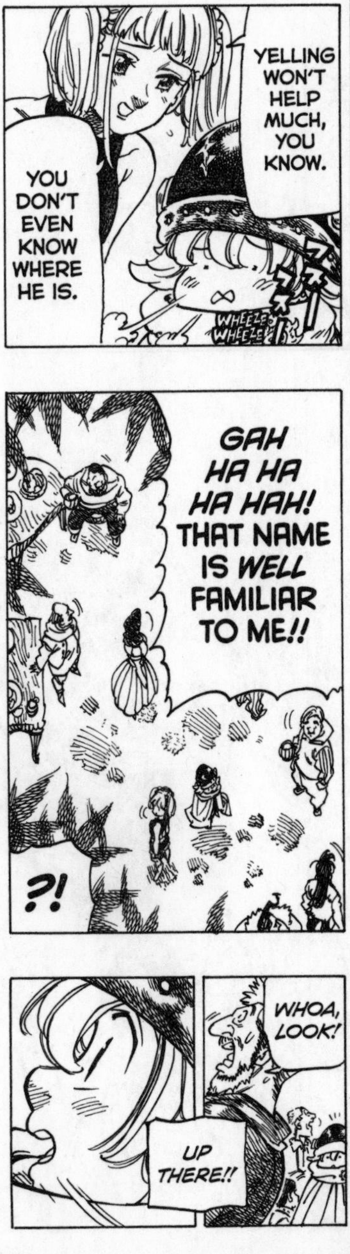
YELLING WON'T HELP MUCH, YOU KNOW.
YOU DON'T EVEN KNOW WHERE HE IS.
WHEEZE WHEEZE
GAH HA HA HA HAH! THAT NAME IS *WELL* FAMILIAR TO ME!!
?!
WHOA, LOOK!
UP THERE!!

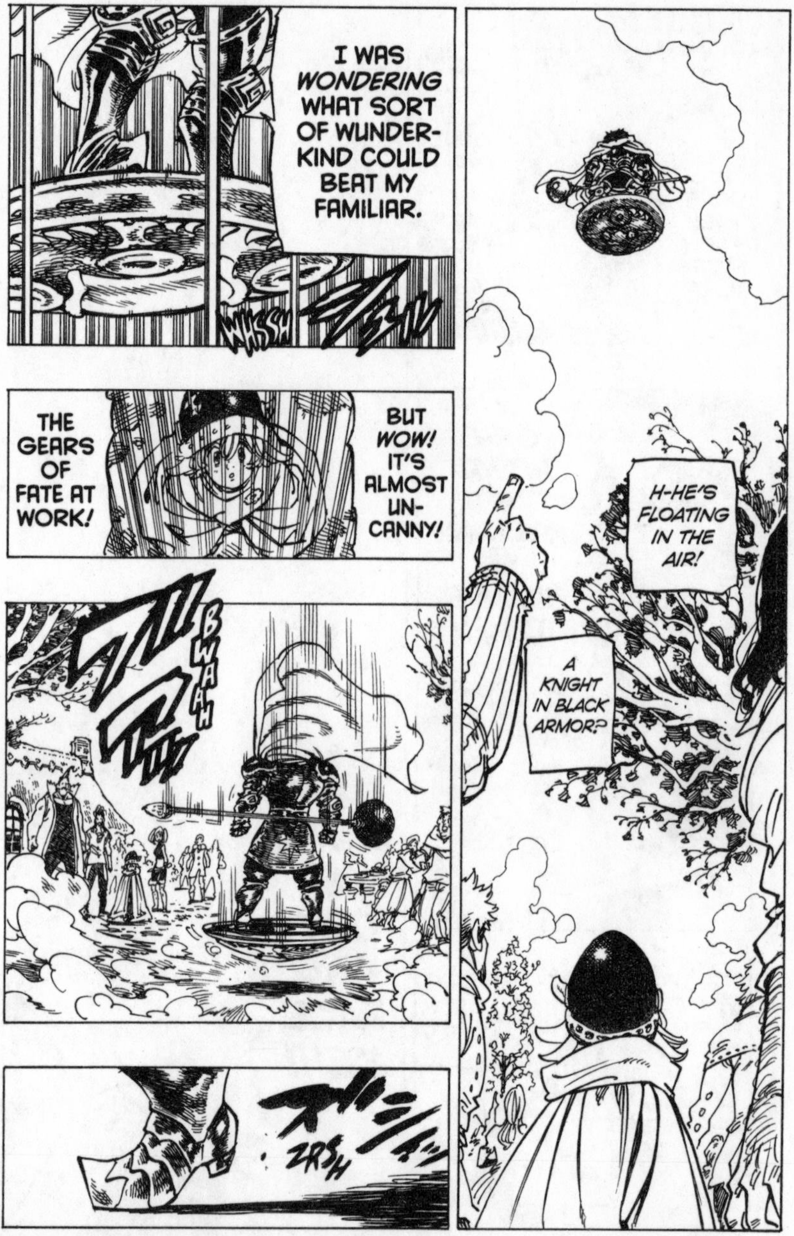

H-HE'S FLOATING IN THE AIR!
A KNIGHT IN BLACK ARMOR?
I WAS *WONDERING* WHAT SORT OF WUNDER-KIND COULD BEAT MY FAMILIAR.
WHSSH
BUT *WOW!* IT'S ALMOST UN-CANNY!
THE GEARS OF FATE AT WORK!
BWAAAH
ZRSH

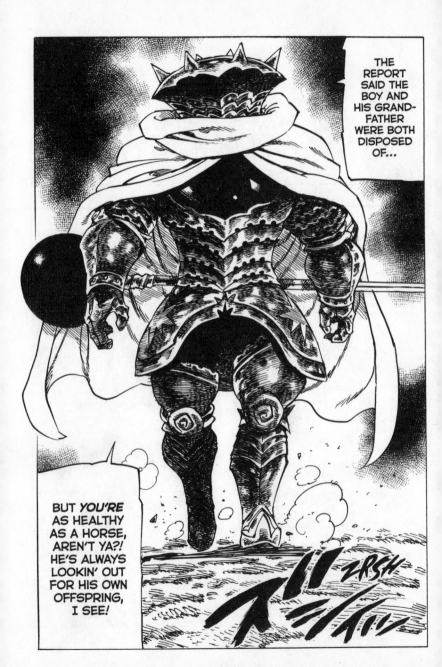

THE REPORT SAID THE BOY AND HIS GRANDFATHER WERE BOTH DISPOSED OF...

BUT *YOU'RE* AS HEALTHY AS A HORSE, AREN'T YA?! HE'S ALWAYS LOOKIN' OUT FOR HIS OWN OFFSPRING, I SEE!

ZRSH

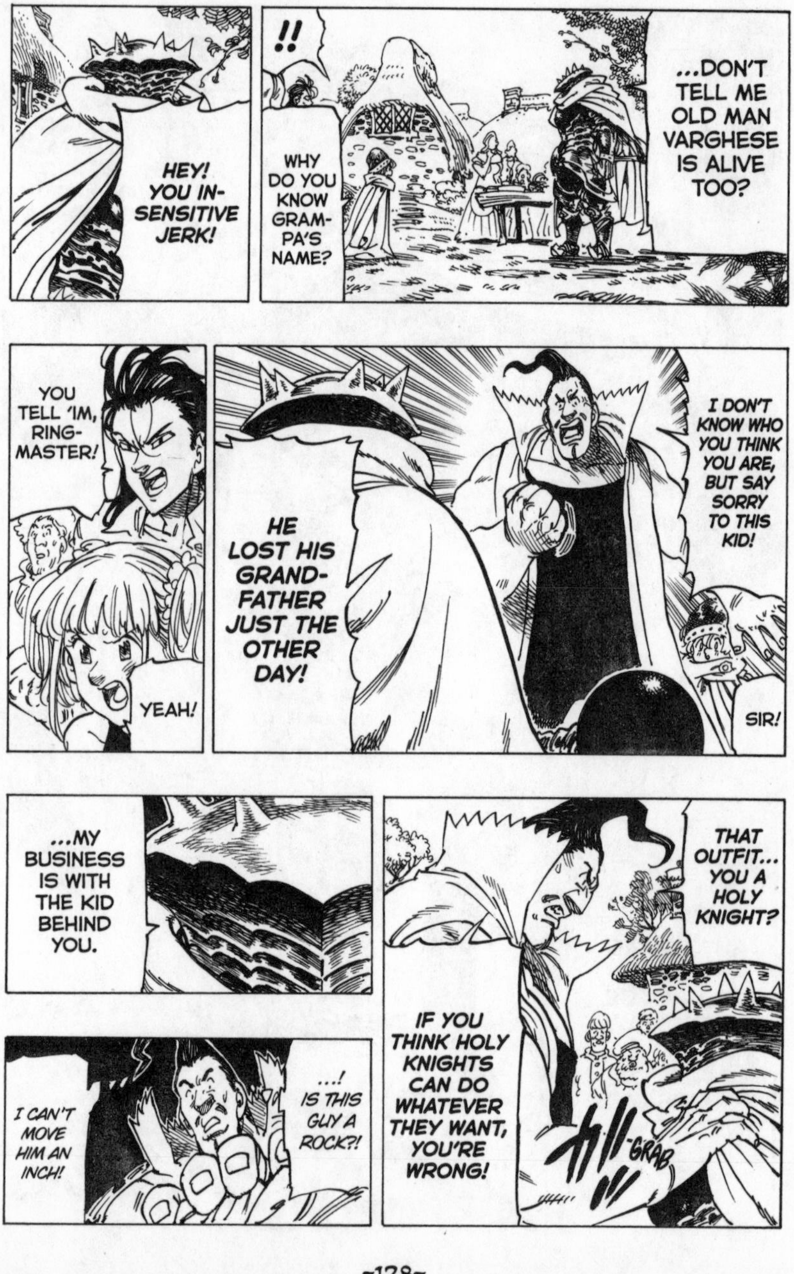
...DON'T TELL ME OLD MAN VARGHESE IS ALIVE TOO?
!!
WHY DO YOU KNOW GRAM-PA'S NAME?
HEY! YOU IN-SENSITIVE JERK!
I DON'T KNOW WHO YOU THINK YOU ARE, BUT SAY SORRY TO THIS KID!
HE LOST HIS GRAND-FATHER JUST THE OTHER DAY!
SIR!
YOU TELL 'IM, RING-MASTER!
YEAH!
THAT OUTFIT... YOU A HOLY KNIGHT?
IF YOU THINK HOLY KNIGHTS CAN DO WHATEVER THEY WANT, YOU'RE WRONG!
-GRAB
...MY BUSINESS IS WITH THE KID BEHIND YOU.
...! IS THIS GUY A ROCK?!
I CAN'T MOVE HIM AN INCH!

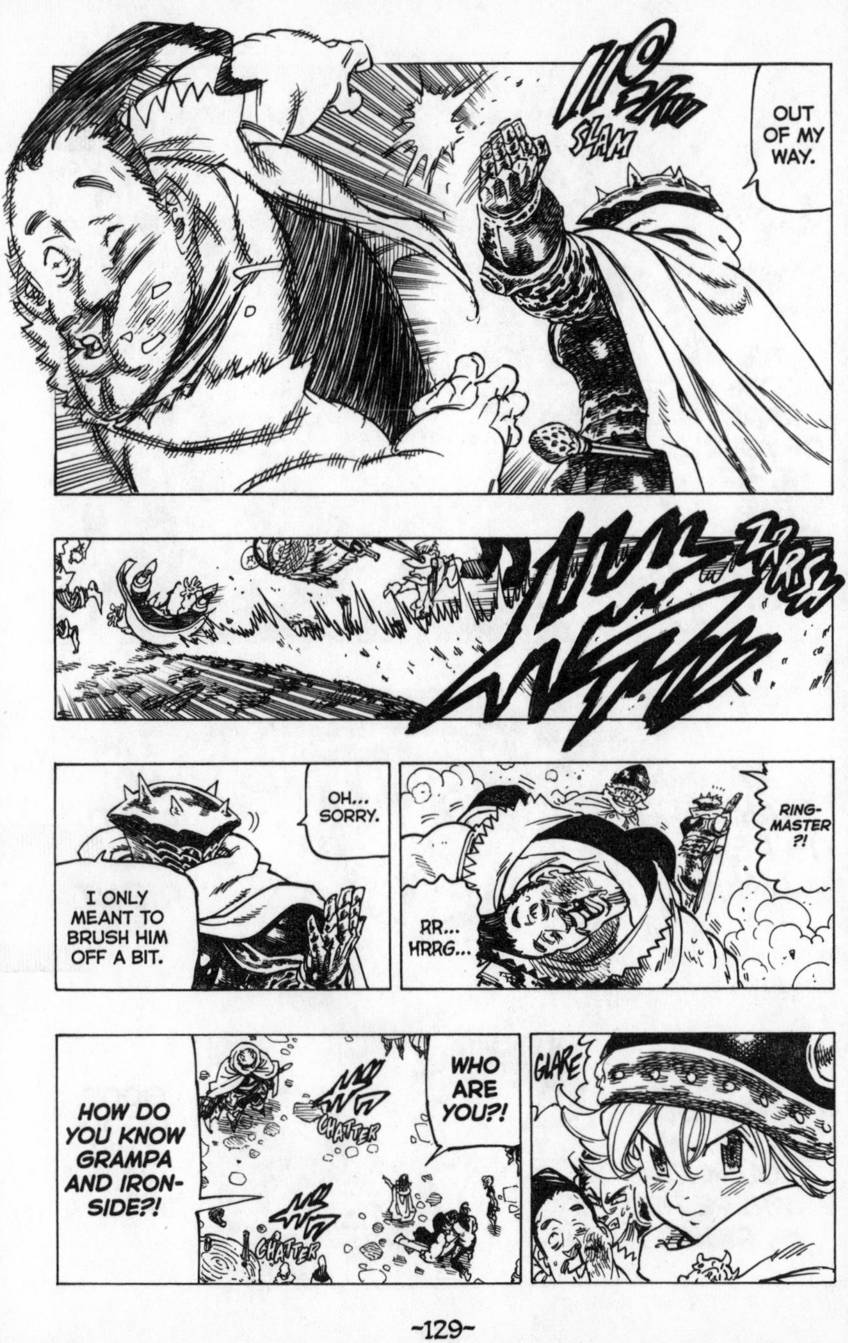
SLAM
OUT OF MY WAY.
ZRRSH
RING-MASTER?!
RR... HRRG...
OH... SORRY.
I ONLY MEANT TO BRUSH HIM OFF A BIT.
GLARE
WHO ARE YOU?!
CHATTER
HOW DO YOU KNOW GRAMPA AND IRON-SIDE?!
CHATTER

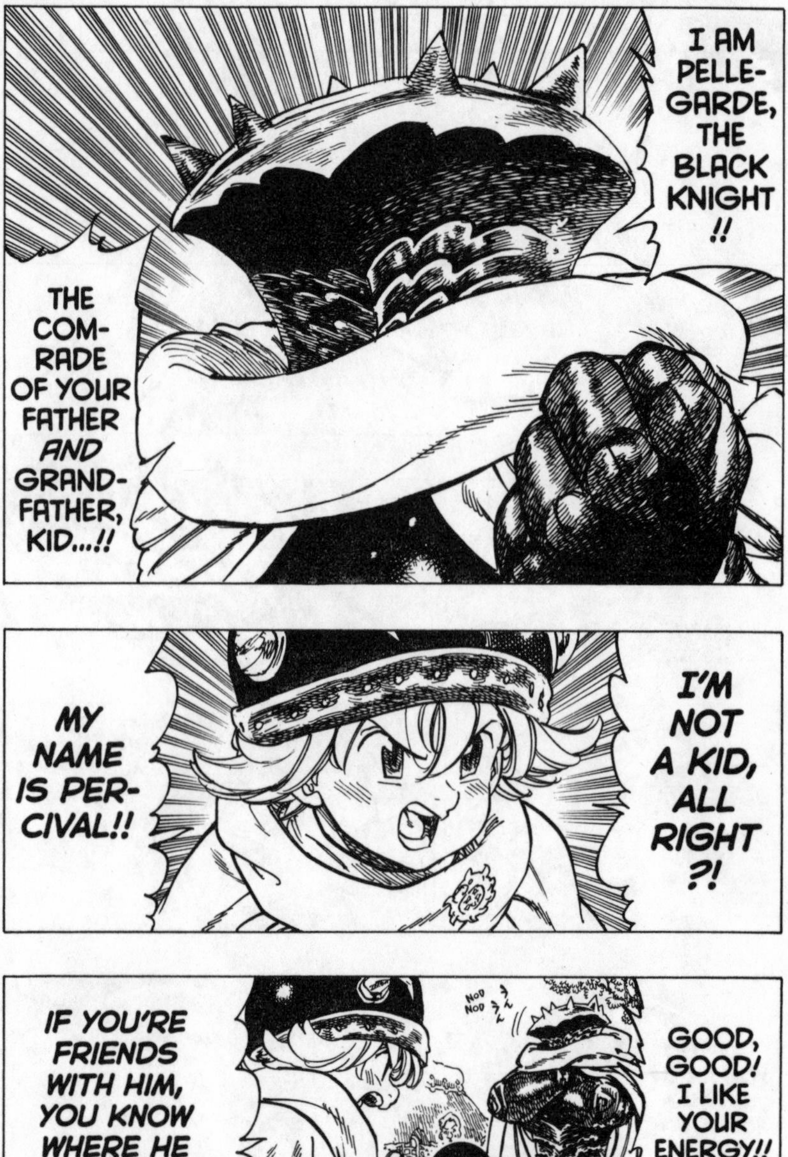
I AM PELLE-GARDE, THE BLACK KNIGHT!!
THE COMRADE OF YOUR FATHER *AND* GRANDFATHER, KID...!!
I'M NOT A KID, ALL RIGHT?!
MY NAME IS PERCIVAL!!
NOD NOD
GOOD, GOOD! I LIKE YOUR ENERGY!!
IF YOU'RE FRIENDS WITH HIM, YOU KNOW WHERE HE IS, RIGHT?!

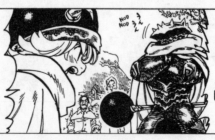

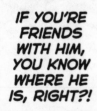

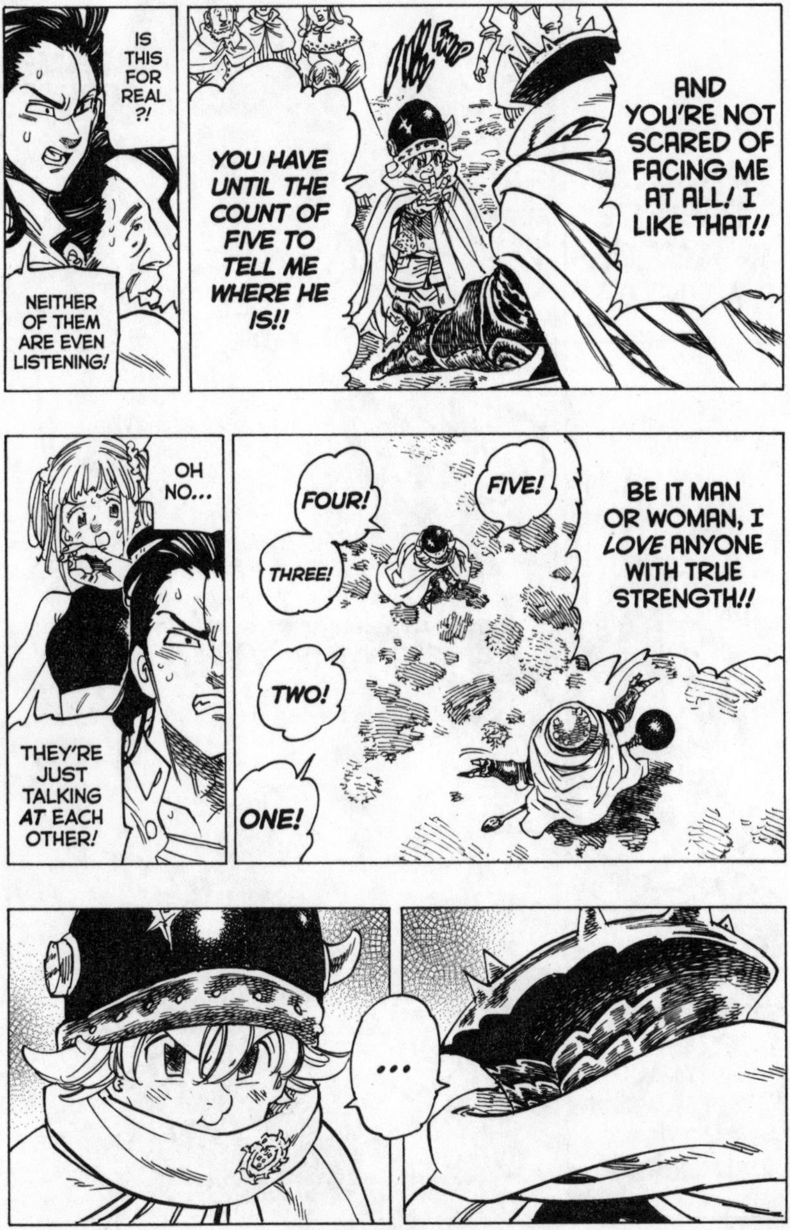
AND YOU'RE NOT SCARED OF FACING ME AT ALL! I LIKE THAT!!
YOU HAVE UNTIL THE COUNT OF FIVE TO TELL ME WHERE HE IS!!
IS THIS FOR REAL?!
NEITHER OF THEM ARE EVEN LISTENING!
BE IT MAN OR WOMAN, I LOVE ANYONE WITH TRUE STRENGTH!!
FIVE!
FOUR!
THREE!
TWO!
ONE!
OH NO...
THEY'RE JUST TALKING AT EACH OTHER!
...

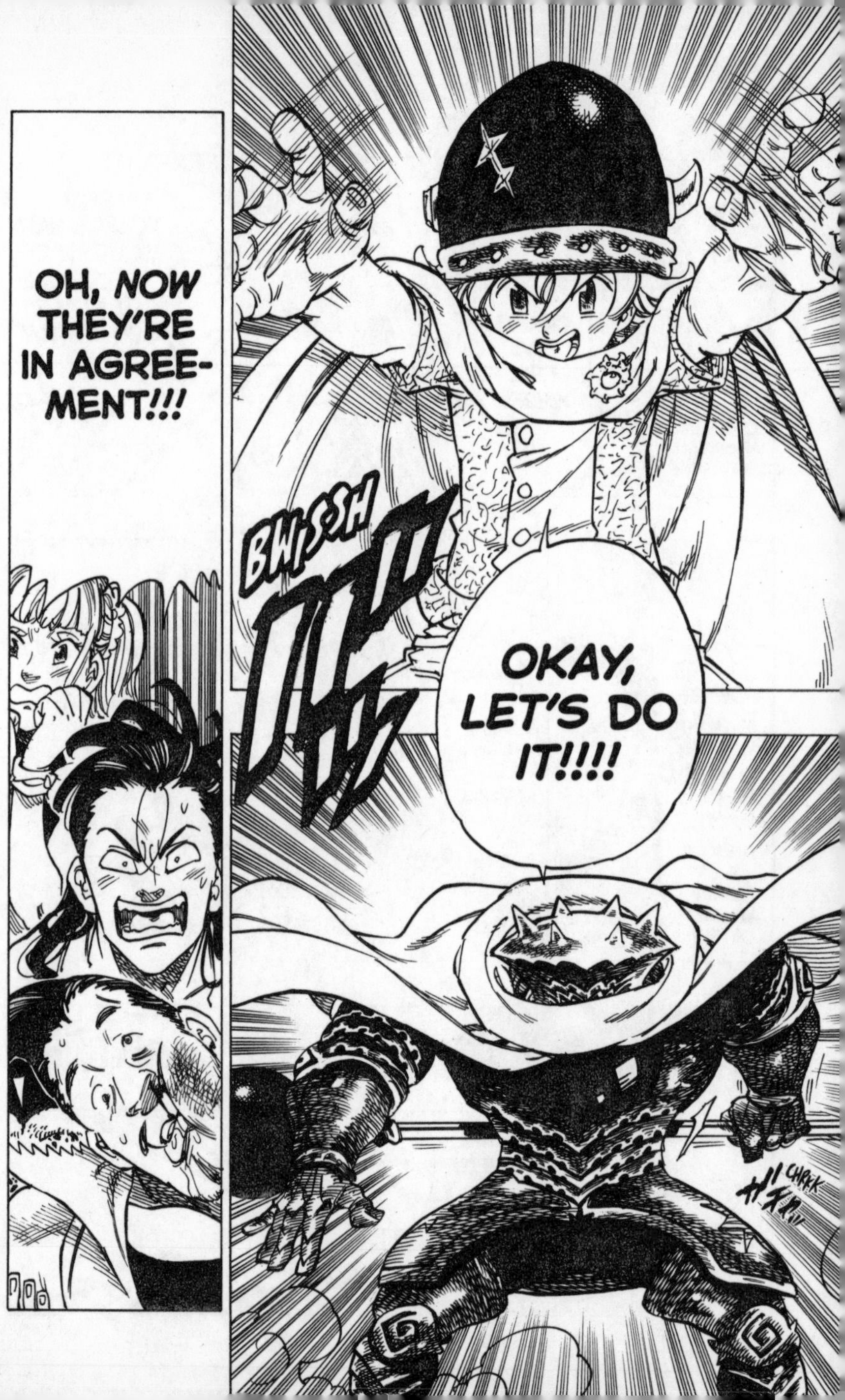
BWISSH
OKAY, LET'S DO IT!!!!
CHAKK
OH, *NOW* THEY'RE IN AGREEMENT!!!

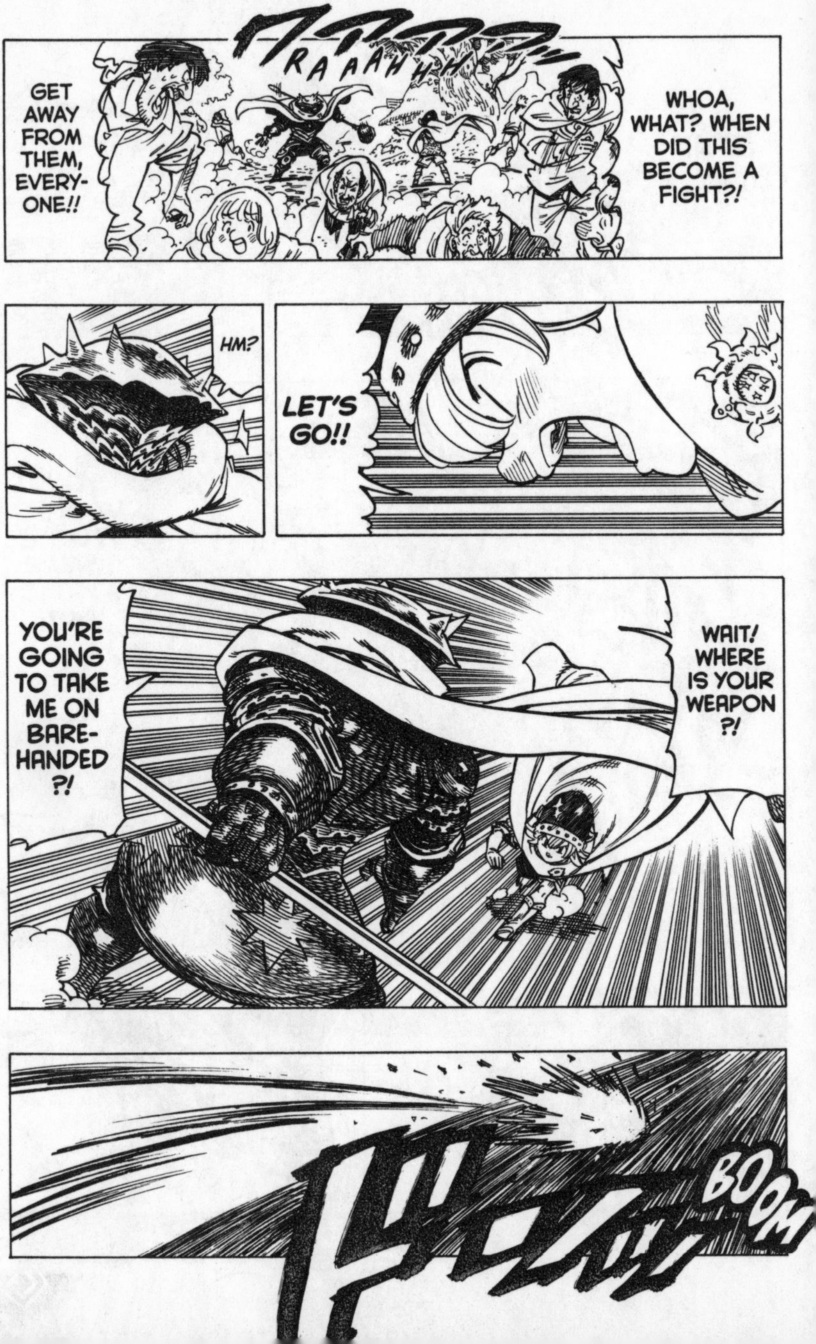
RAAAHHH
WHOA, WHAT? WHEN DID THIS BECOME A FIGHT?!
GET AWAY FROM THEM, EVERYONE!!
LET'S GO!!
HM?
WAIT! WHERE IS YOUR WEAPON?!
YOU'RE GOING TO TAKE ME ON BAREHANDED?!
BOOM

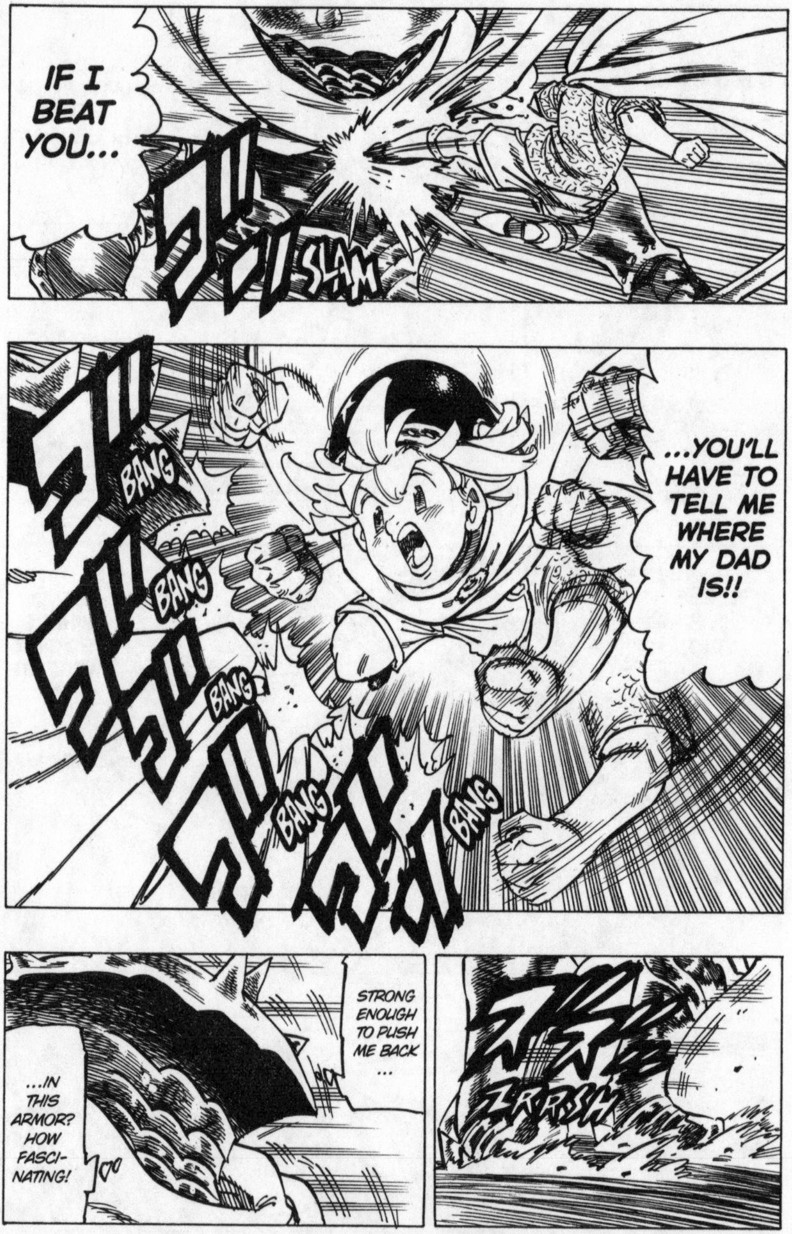
IF I BEAT YOU...
SLAM
...YOU'LL HAVE TO TELL ME WHERE MY DAD IS!!
BANG
BANG
BANG
BANG
BANG
ZRRRSCH
STRONG ENOUGH TO PUSH ME BACK ...
...IN THIS ARMOR? HOW FASCI- NATING!

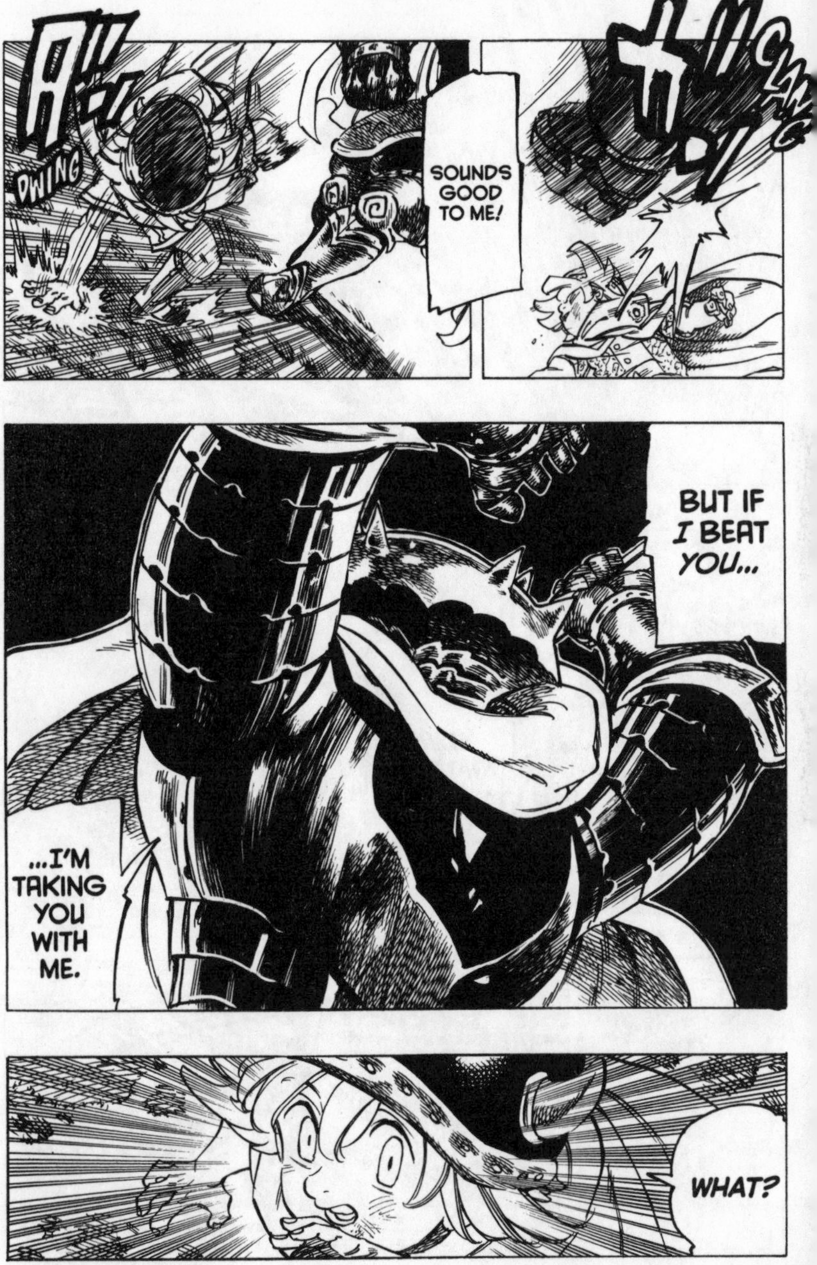
CLANG
DWING
SOUNDS GOOD TO ME!
BUT IF I BEAT YOU...
...I'M TAKING YOU WITH ME.
WHAT?

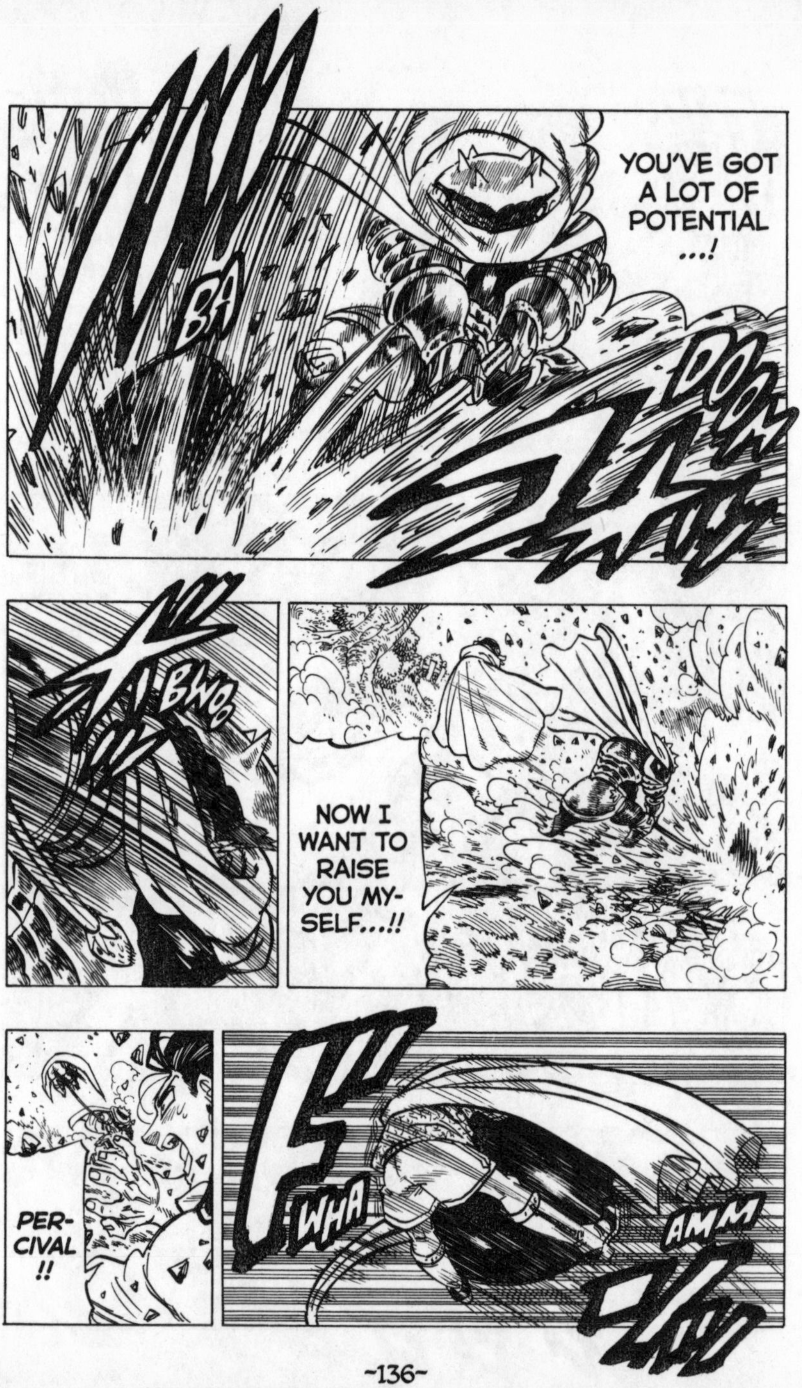
YOU'VE GOT A LOT OF POTENTIAL ...!
BA
DOOM
NOW I WANT TO RAISE YOU MY-SELF...!!
BWOO
WHA
AMM
PER-CIVAL !!

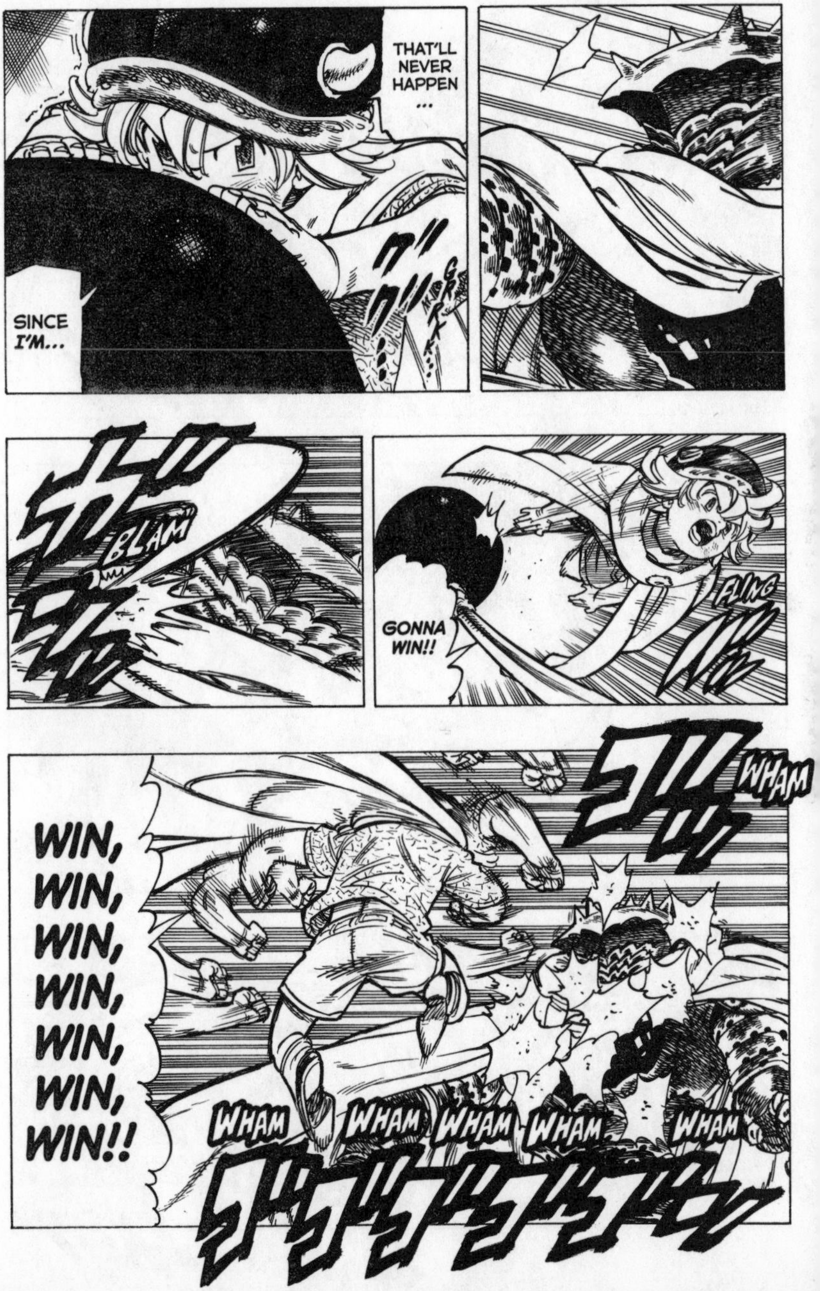
THAT'LL NEVER HAPPEN ...
GRRK...
SINCE I'M...
FLING
GONNA WIN!!
BLAM
WHAM
WIN, WIN, WIN, WIN, WIN, WIN, WIN!!
WHAM
WHAM
WHAM
WHAM
WHAM

!!

GRRRRIP

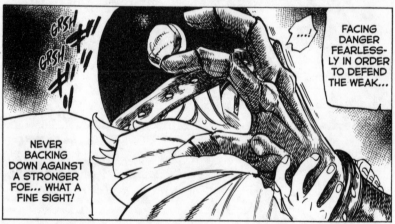

GRSH !!
GRSH !!

....!

FACING DANGER FEARLESSLY IN ORDER TO DEFEND THE WEAK...

NEVER BACKING DOWN AGAINST A STRONGER FOE... WHAT A FINE SIGHT!

WHAM

BUT YOU CAN'T DO MUCH BAREHANDED.

P... PERCIVAL !!

AHH! HE GOT HIM!!

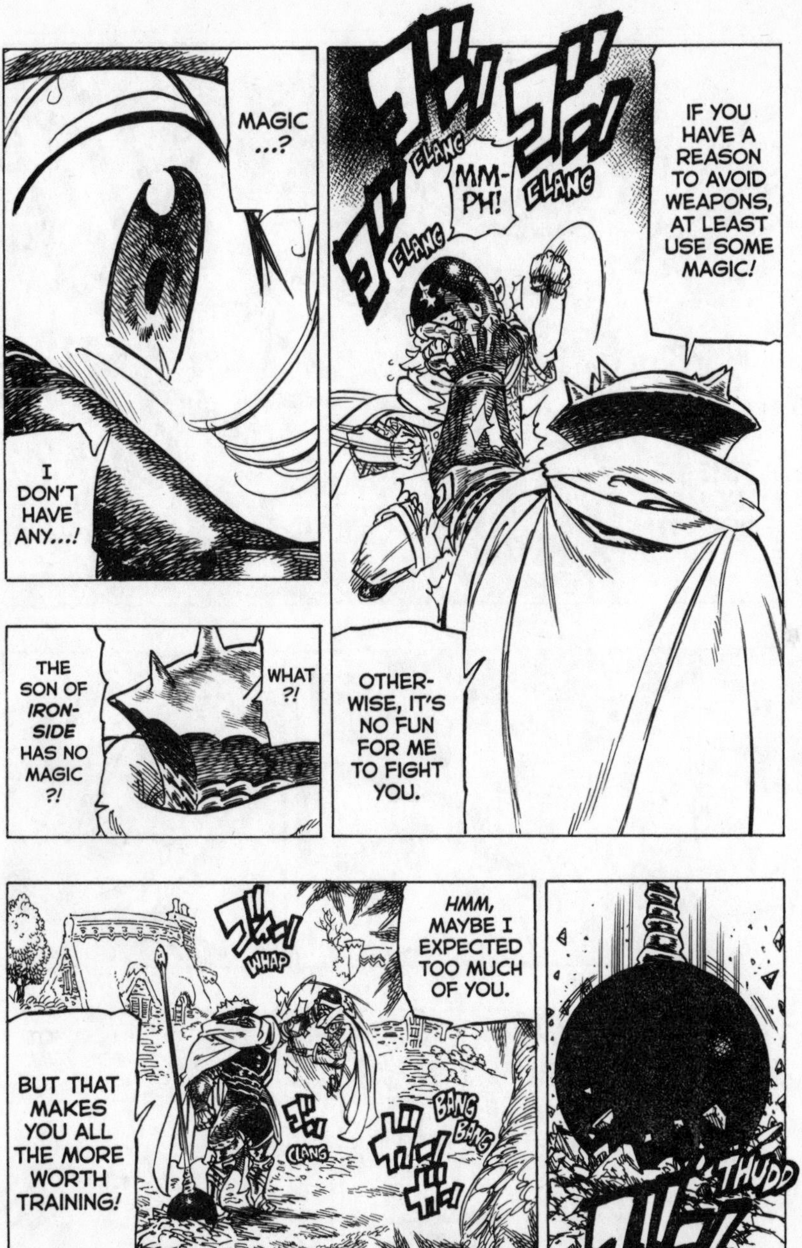
IF YOU HAVE A REASON TO AVOID WEAPONS, AT LEAST USE SOME MAGIC!
CLANG
CLANG
MM-PH!
CLANG
OTHERWISE, IT'S NO FUN FOR ME TO FIGHT YOU.
MAGIC ...?
I DON'T HAVE ANY...!
WHAT ?!
THE SON OF *IRONSIDE* HAS NO MAGIC ?!
THUDD
HMM, MAYBE I EXPECTED TOO MUCH OF YOU.
WHAP
BANG BANG
CLANG
BUT THAT MAKES YOU ALL THE MORE WORTH TRAINING!

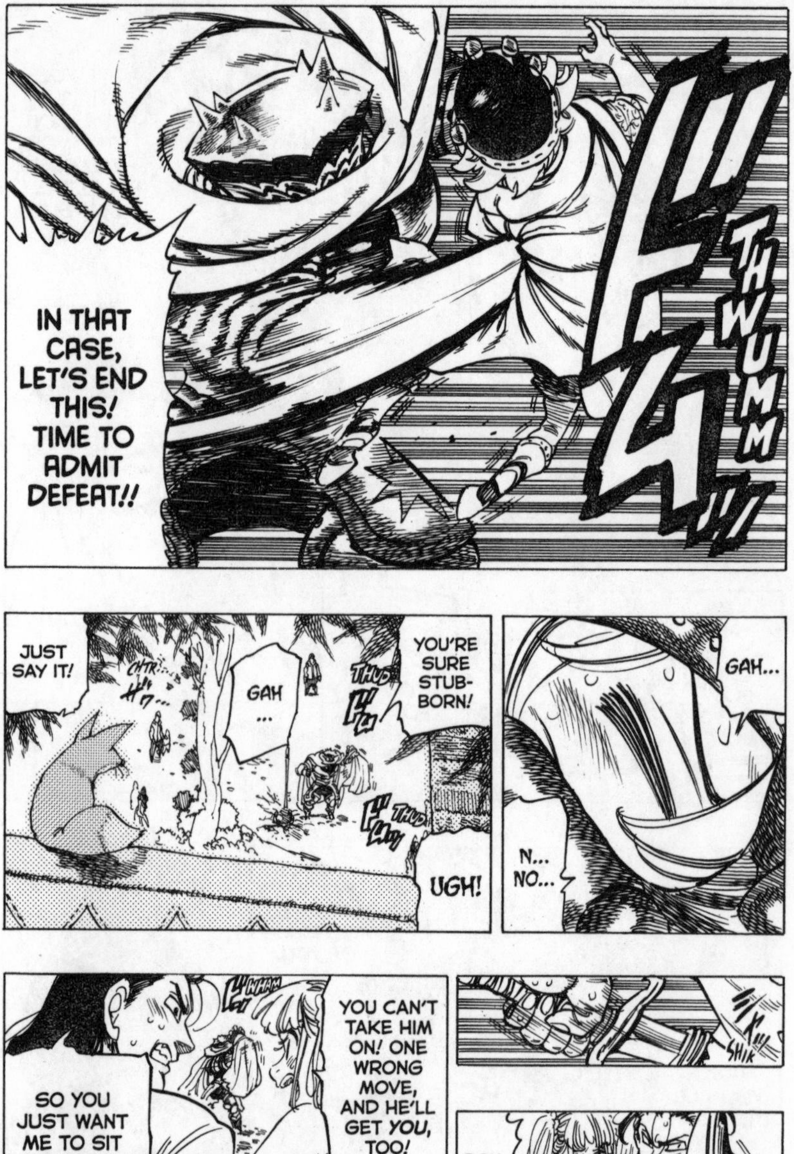
THWUMM
IN THAT CASE, LET'S END THIS! TIME TO ADMIT DEFEAT!!
GAH...
N... NO...
YOU'RE SURE STUBBORN!
THUD
GAH ...
JUST SAY IT!
CHTR
THUD
UGH!
SHIK
DONNY!
WHAM
YOU CAN'T TAKE HIM ON! ONE WRONG MOVE, AND HE'LL GET *YOU*, TOO!
SO YOU JUST WANT ME TO SIT AND WATCH THIS...?!

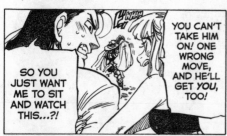

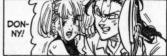

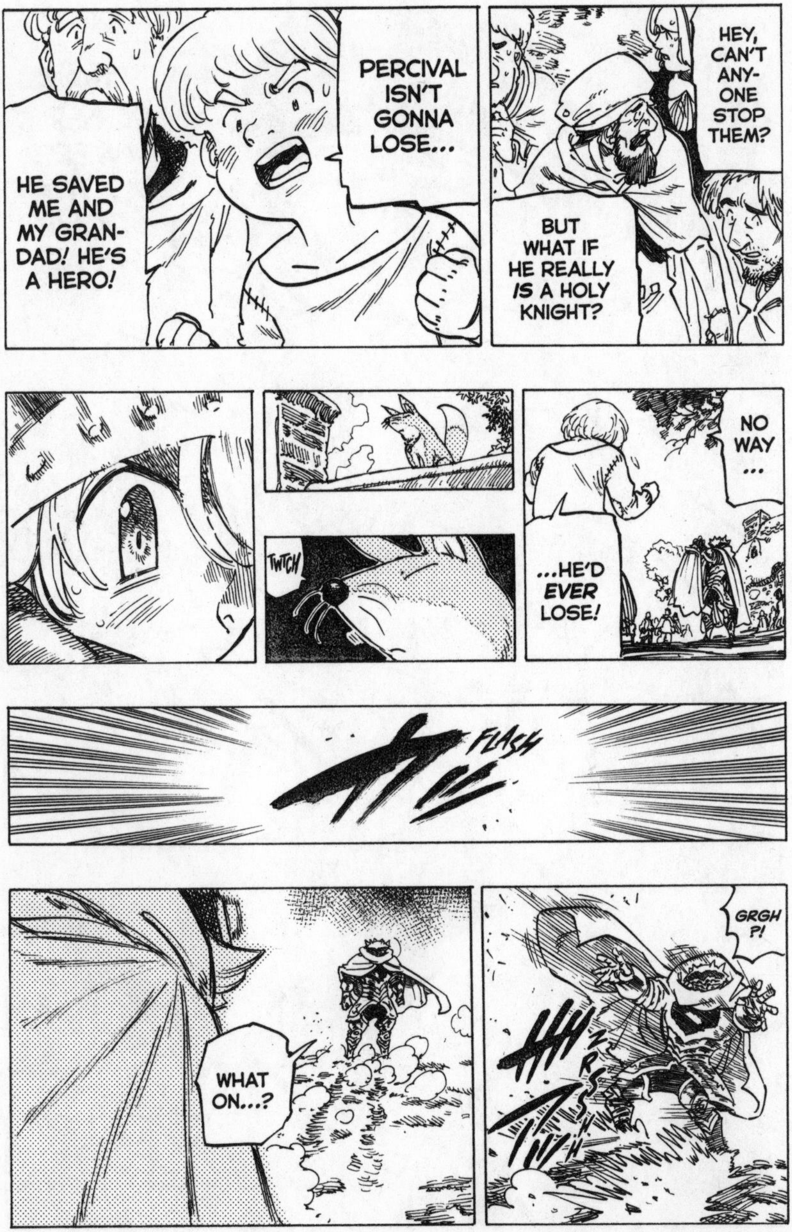
HEY, CAN'T ANY-ONE STOP THEM?
BUT WHAT IF HE REALLY *IS* A HOLY KNIGHT?
PERCIVAL ISN'T GONNA LOSE...
HE SAVED ME AND MY GRAN-DAD! HE'S A HERO!
NO WAY...
...HE'D *EVER* LOSE!
TWITCH
FLASH
GRGH ?!
ZRSHH
WHAT ON...?

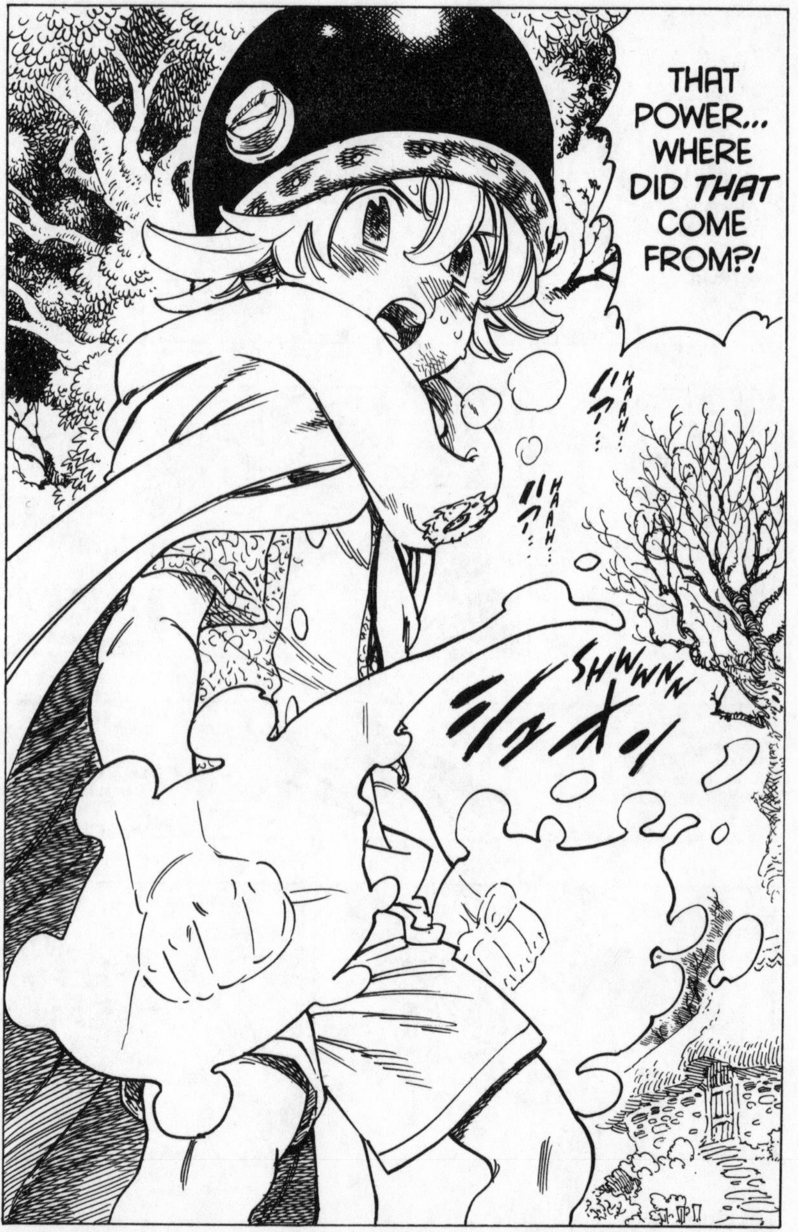
THAT POWER... WHERE DID *THAT* COME FROM?!
HAAH...
HAAH...
SHWWNN

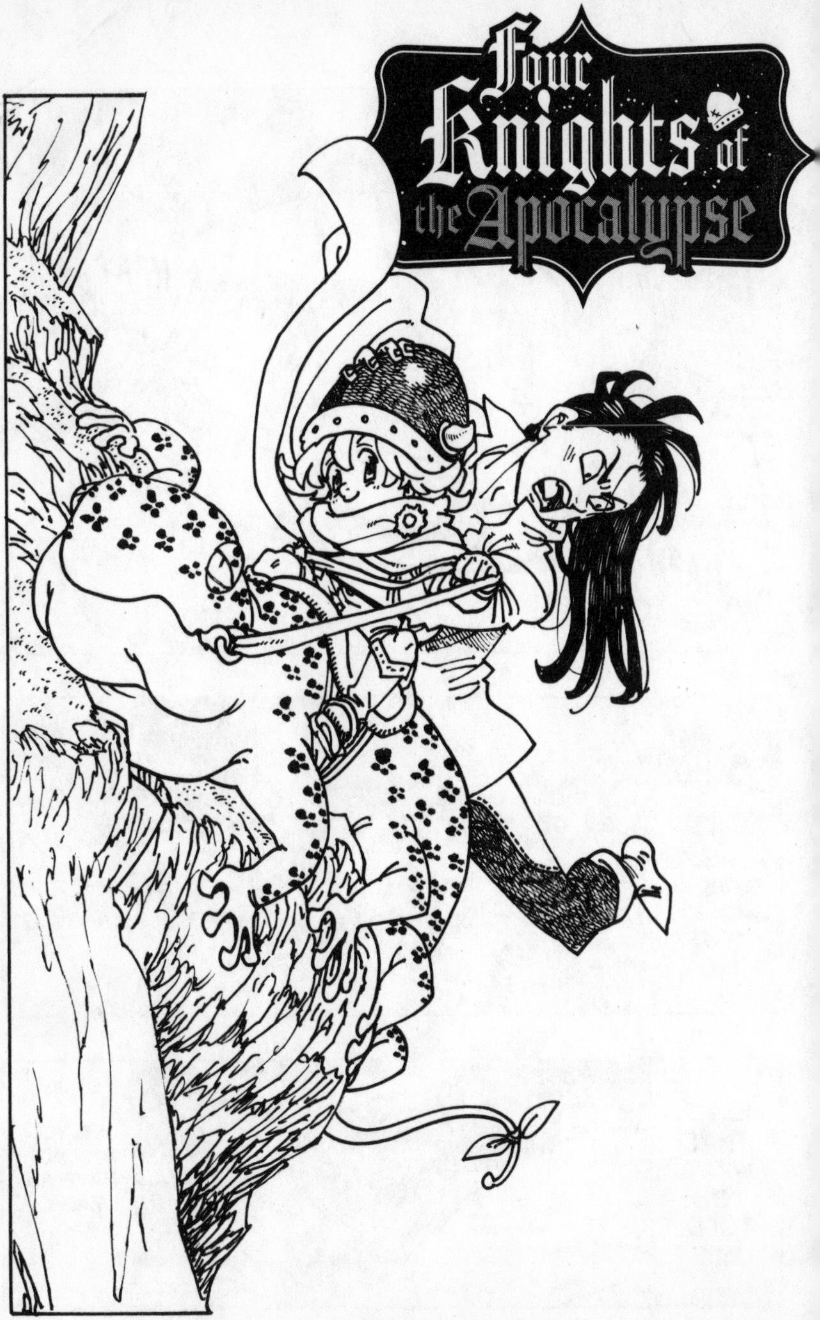
Four Knights of the Apocalypse

CHAPTER 4: THE UNKNOWN FORCE

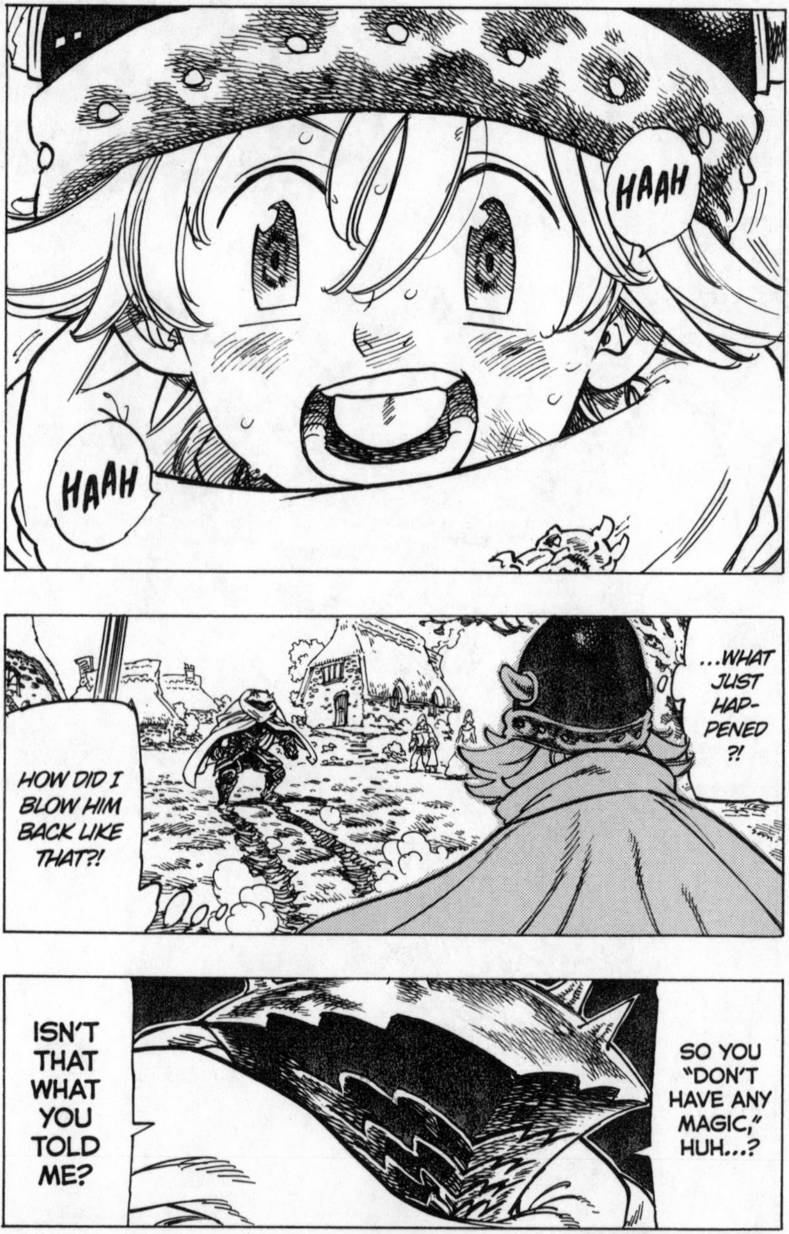
HAAH
HAAH
...WHAT JUST HAP-PENED ?!
HOW DID I BLOW HIM BACK LIKE THAT?!
SO YOU "DON'T HAVE ANY MAGIC," HUH...?
ISN'T THAT WHAT YOU TOLD ME?

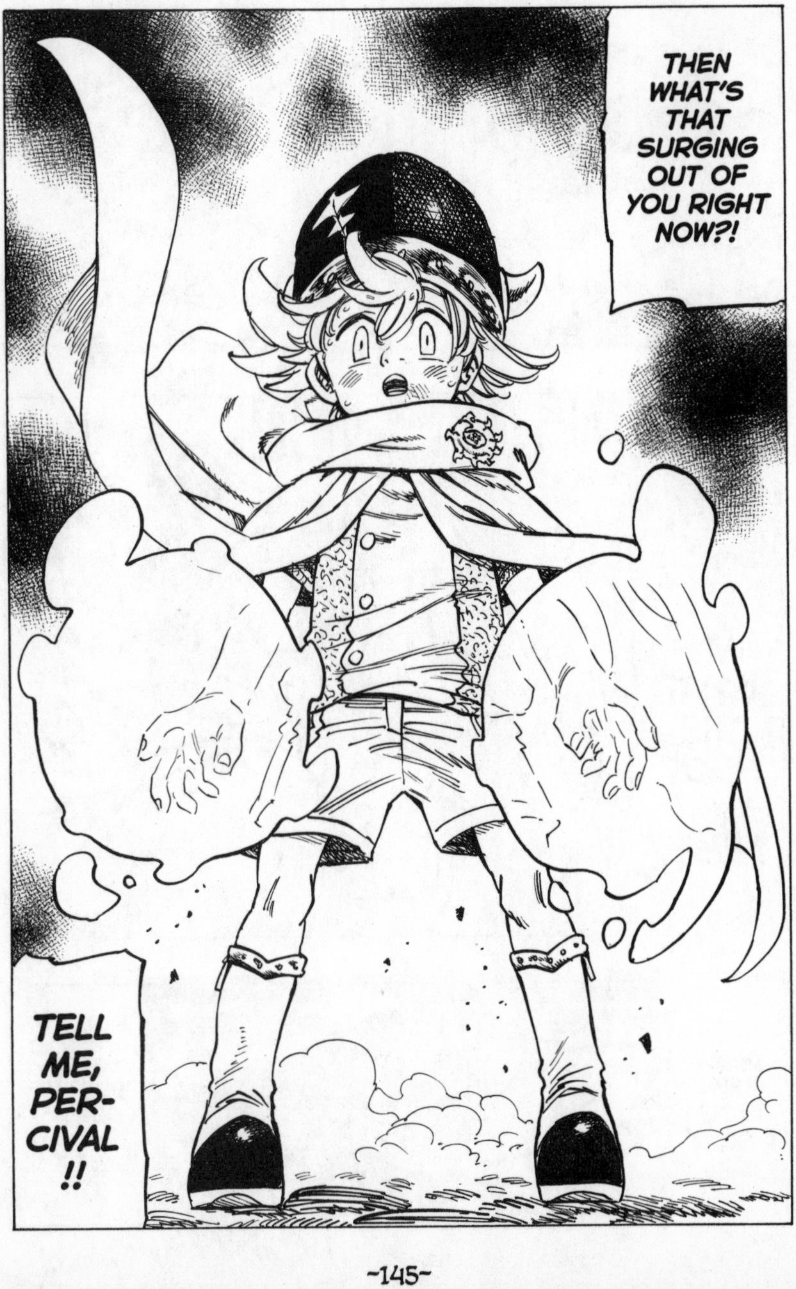
THEN WHAT'S THAT SURGING OUT OF YOU RIGHT NOW?!
TELL ME, PER-CIVAL !!

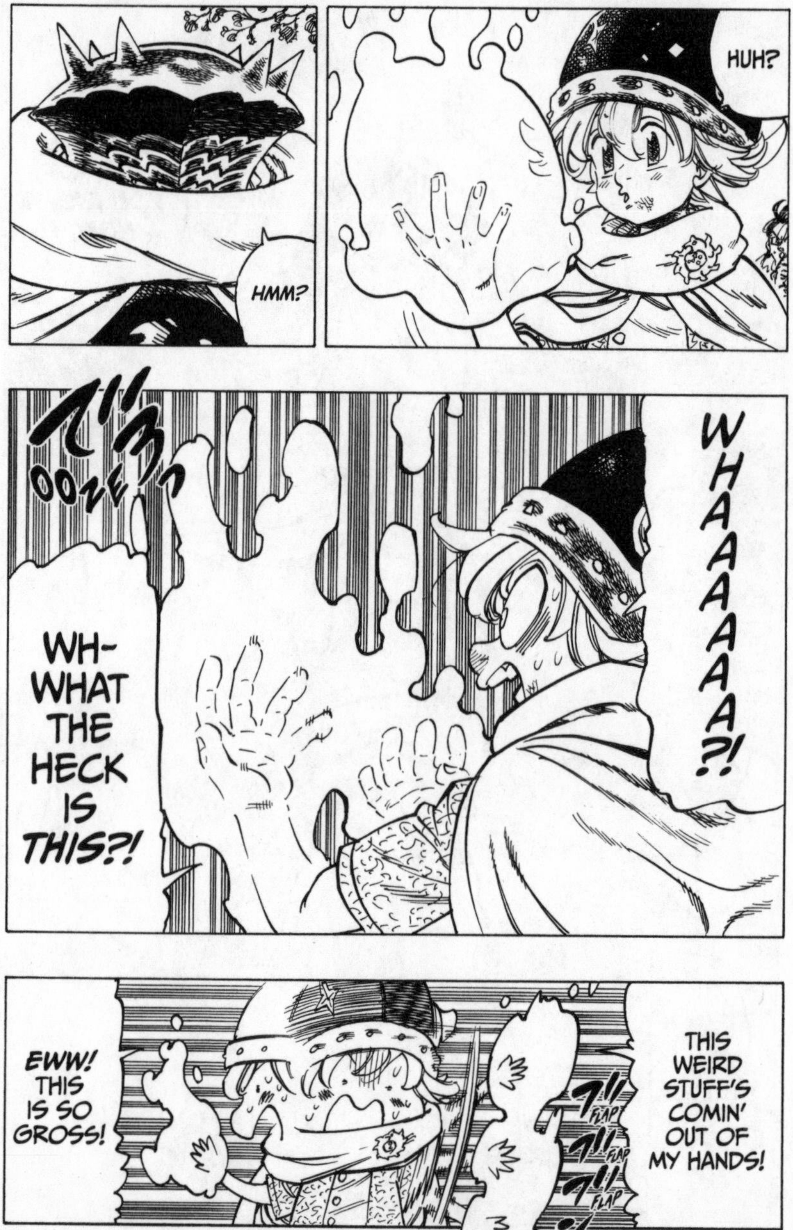
HUH?
HMM?
WHAAAAAAA?!
OOZE
WH-WHAT THE HECK IS THIS?!
THIS WEIRD STUFF'S COMIN' OUT OF MY HANDS!
FLAP
FLAP
FLAP
FLAP
EWW! THIS IS SO GROSS!

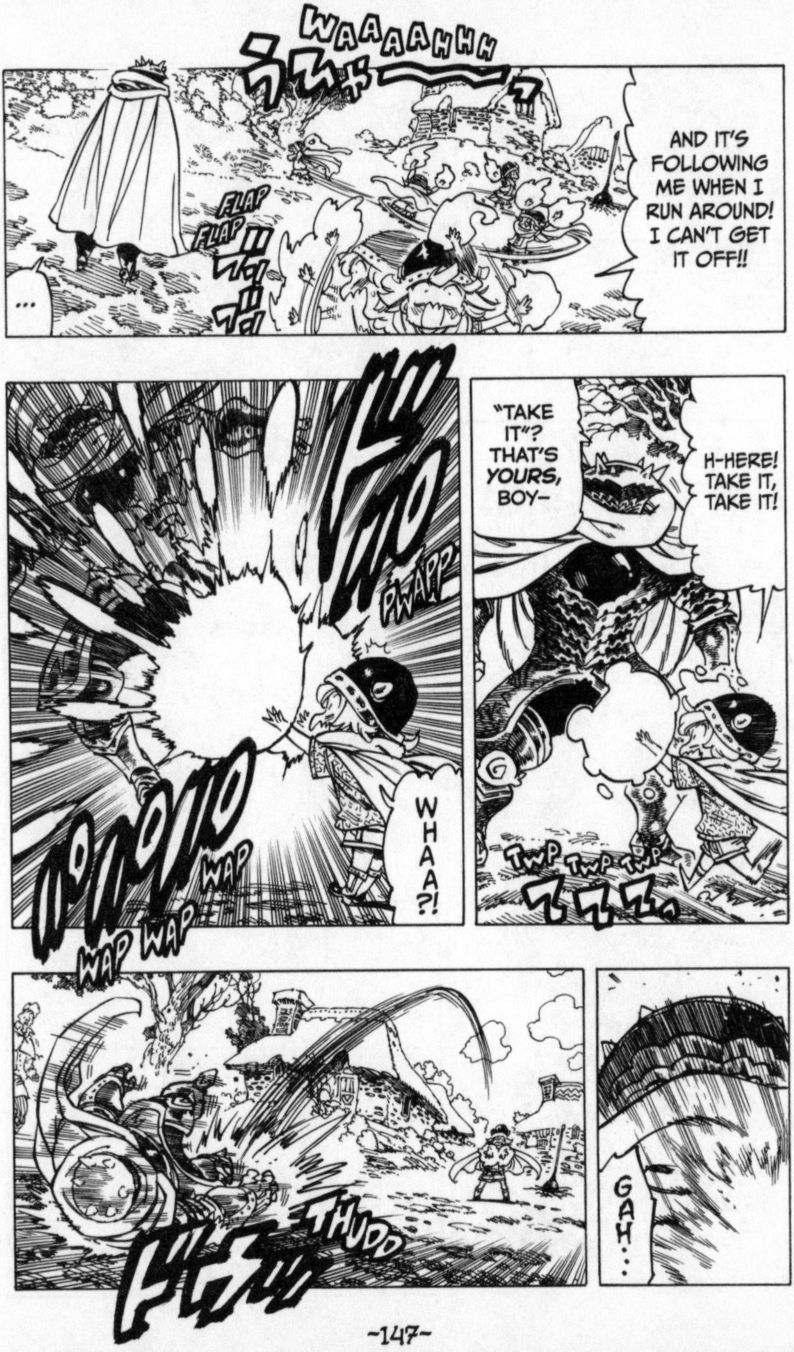
WAAAAAHHH
AND IT'S FOLLOWING ME WHEN I RUN AROUND! I CAN'T GET IT OFF!!
FLAP FLAP
...
H-HERE! TAKE IT, TAKE IT!
"TAKE IT"? THAT'S YOURS, BOY–
TWP TWP TWP
PWAPP
WHAAA?!
WAP WAP WAP
GAH...
THUDD

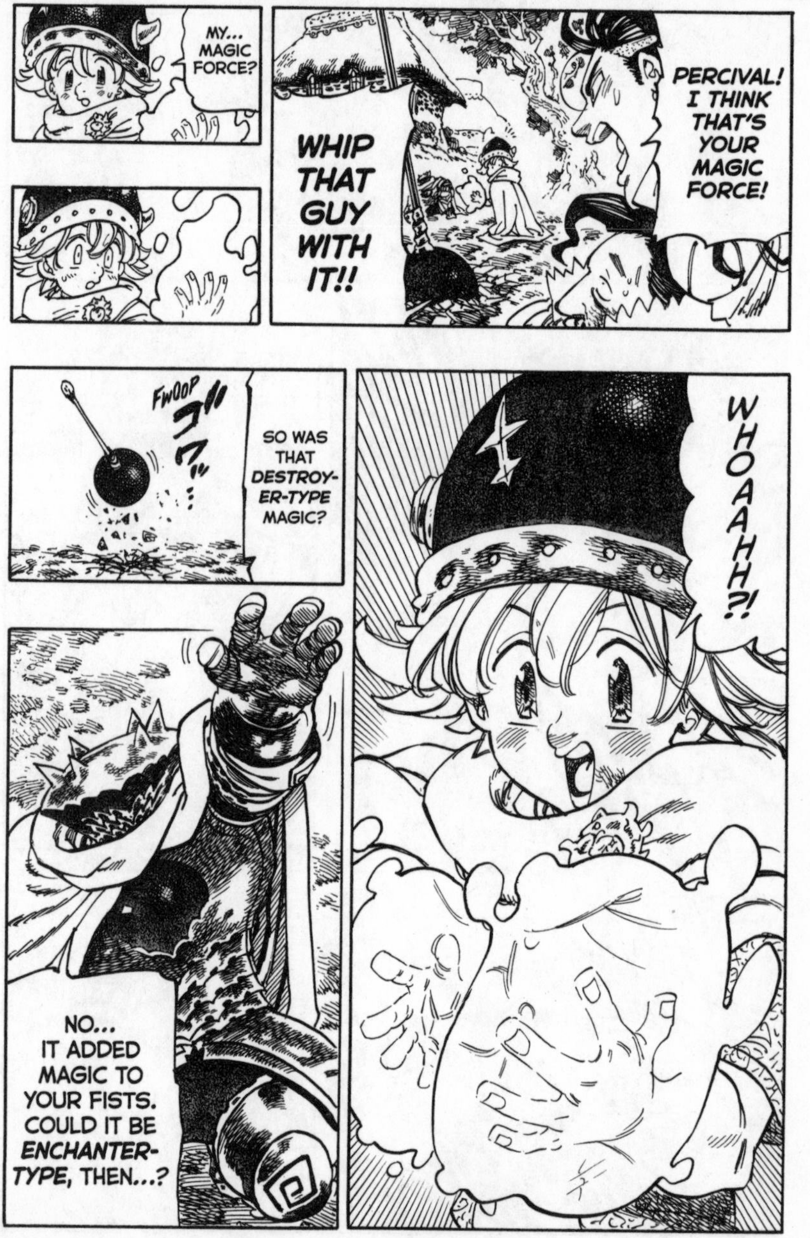
PERCIVAL! I THINK THAT'S YOUR MAGIC FORCE!
WHIP THAT GUY WITH IT!!
MY... MAGIC FORCE?
WHOAAHH?!
FWOOP
SO WAS THAT DESTROYER-TYPE MAGIC?
NO... IT ADDED MAGIC TO YOUR FISTS. COULD IT BE ENCHANTER-TYPE, THEN...?

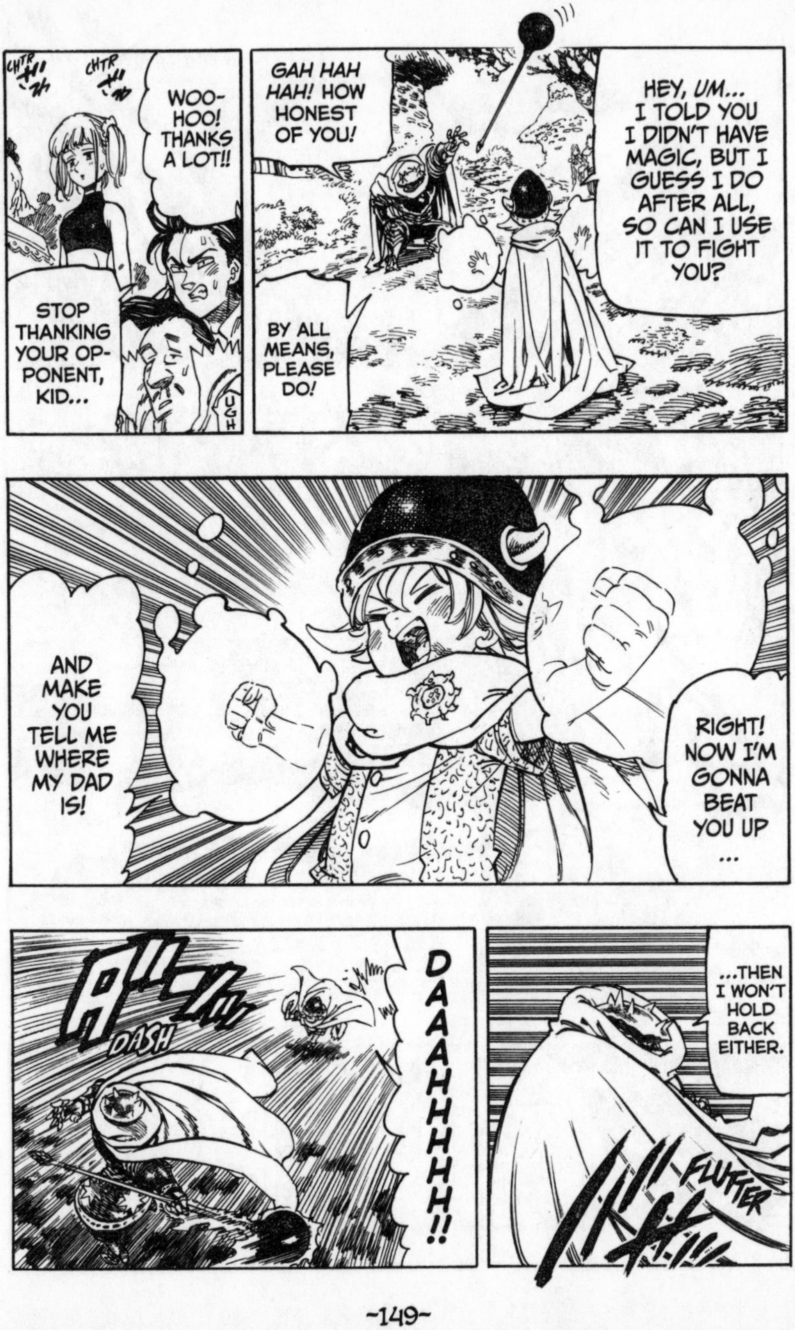
HEY, UM... I TOLD YOU I DIDN'T HAVE MAGIC, BUT I GUESS I DO AFTER ALL, SO CAN I USE IT TO FIGHT YOU?
GAH HAH HAH! HOW HONEST OF YOU!
BY ALL MEANS, PLEASE DO!
CHTR
CHTR
WOO-HOO! THANKS A LOT!!
STOP THANKING YOUR OP-PONENT, KID...
UGH
RIGHT! NOW I'M GONNA BEAT YOU UP ...
AND MAKE YOU TELL ME WHERE MY DAD IS!
...THEN I WON'T HOLD BACK EITHER.
FLUTTER
DAAAAHHHHHH!!
DASH

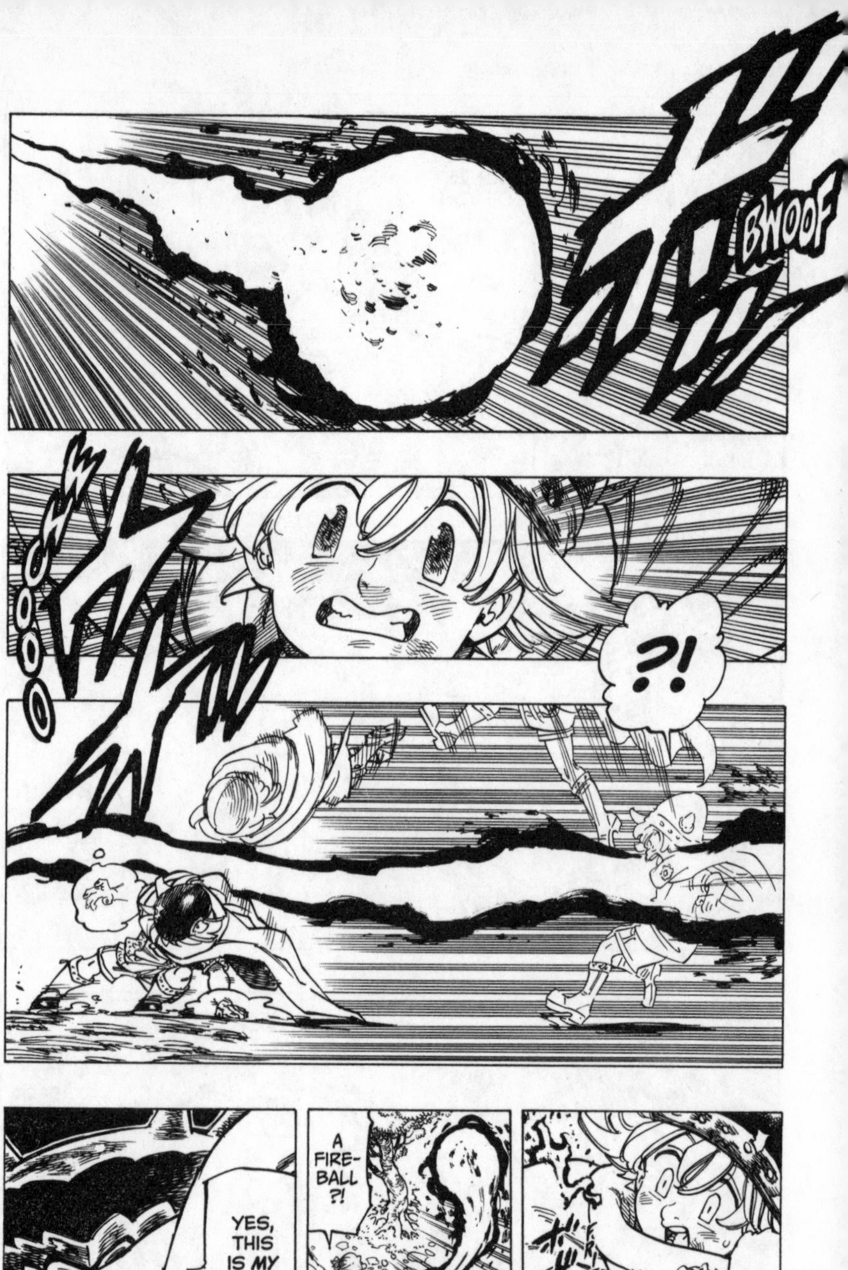
BWOOF
?!
WHOOOO
FRIZZ
OW!
A FIRE-BALL ?!
YES, THIS IS MY MAGIC–

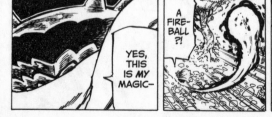

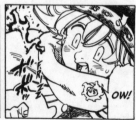

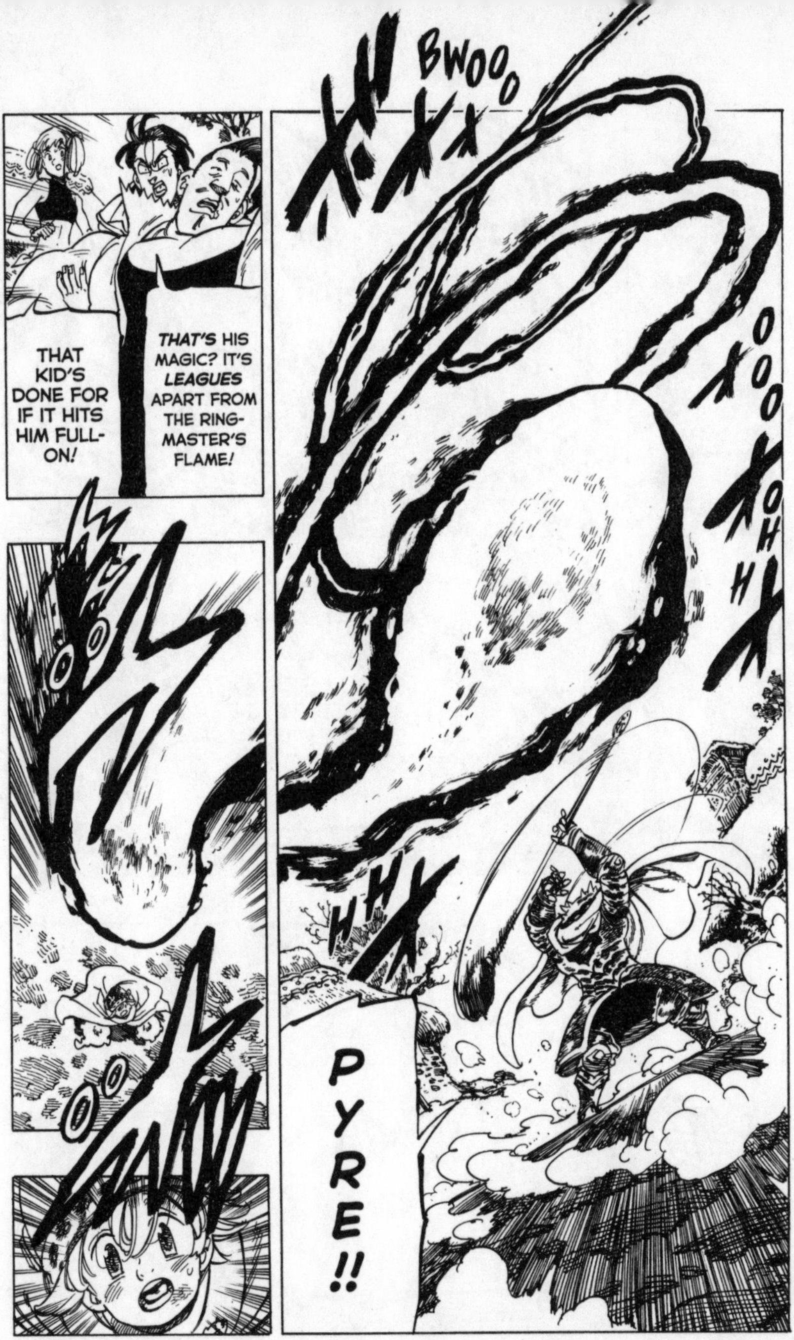
BWOOOOOOOHHHHH
PYRE!!
THAT'S HIS MAGIC? IT'S *LEAGUES* APART FROM THE RING-MASTER'S FLAME!
THAT KID'S DONE FOR IF IT HITS HIM FULL-ON!

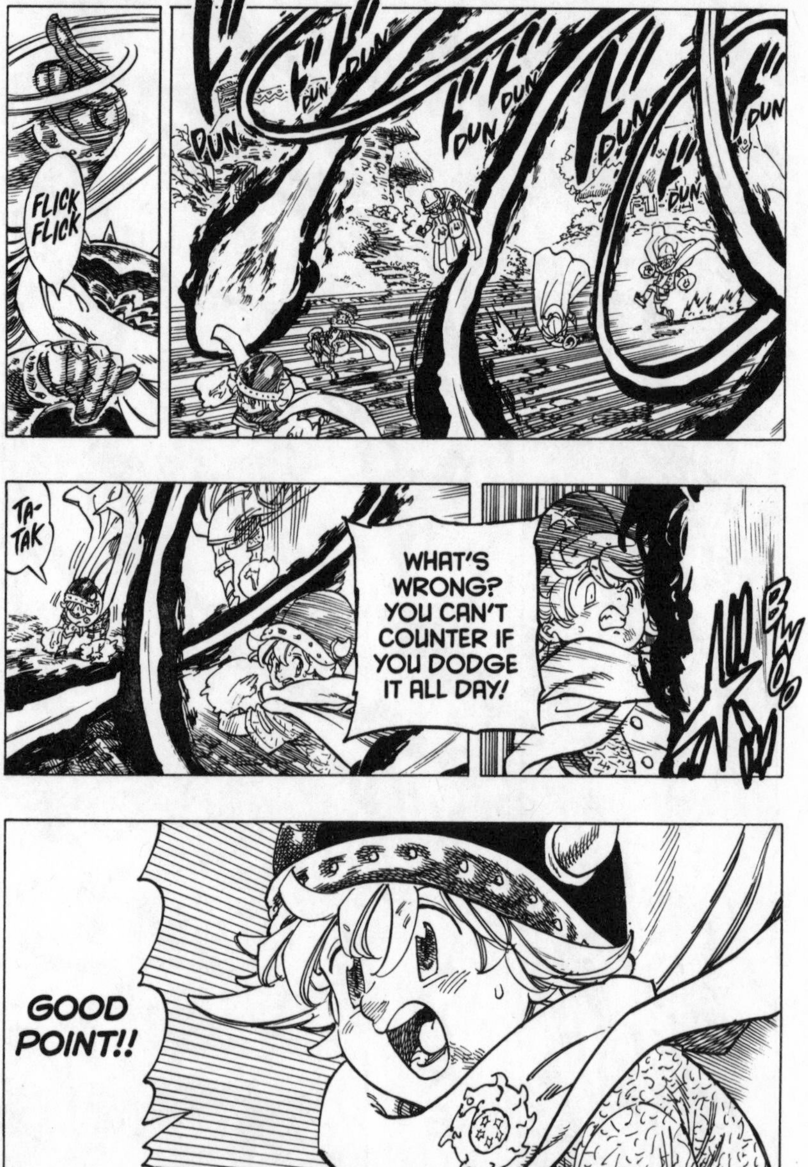
DUN
DUN
DUN
DUN
DUN
DUN
DUN
DUN
FLICK FLICK
BWOOM
WHAT'S WRONG? YOU CAN'T COUNTER IF YOU DODGE IT ALL DAY!
TA-TAK
GOOD POINT!!

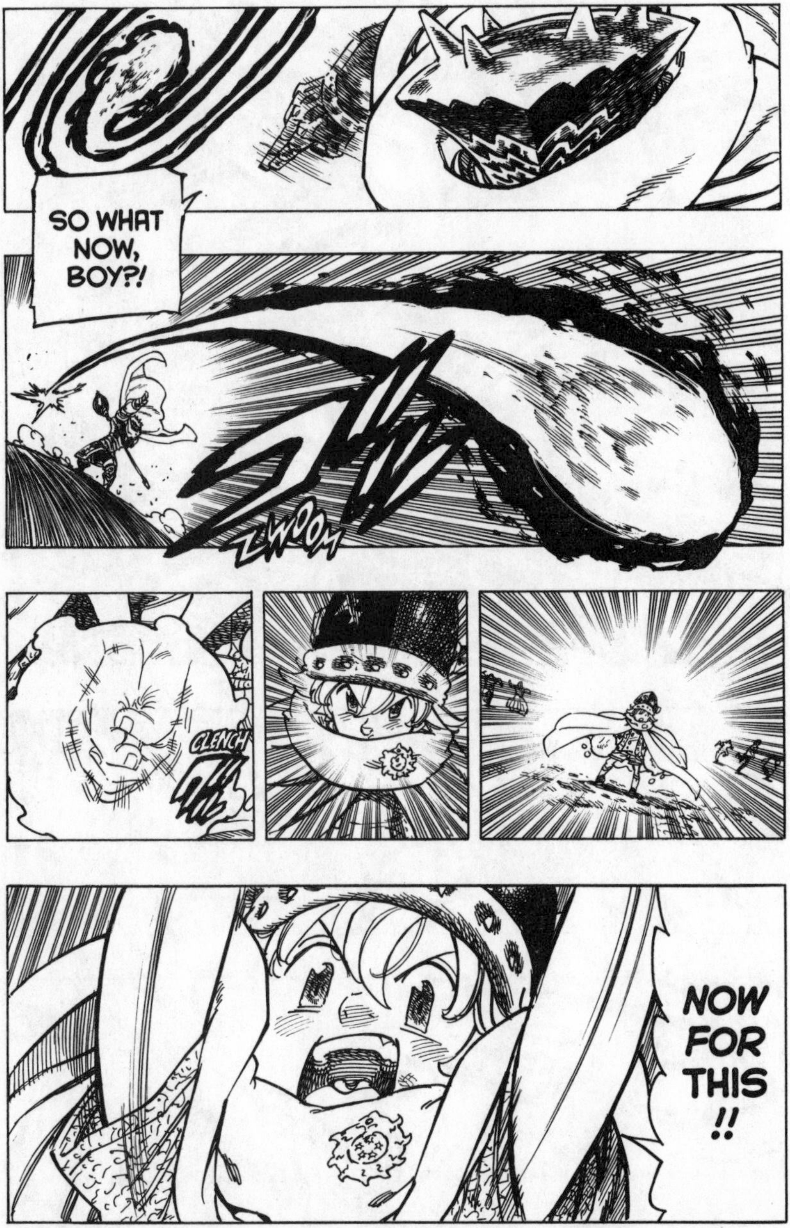
SO WHAT NOW, BOY?!
ZWOOM
CLENCH
NOW FOR THIS!!

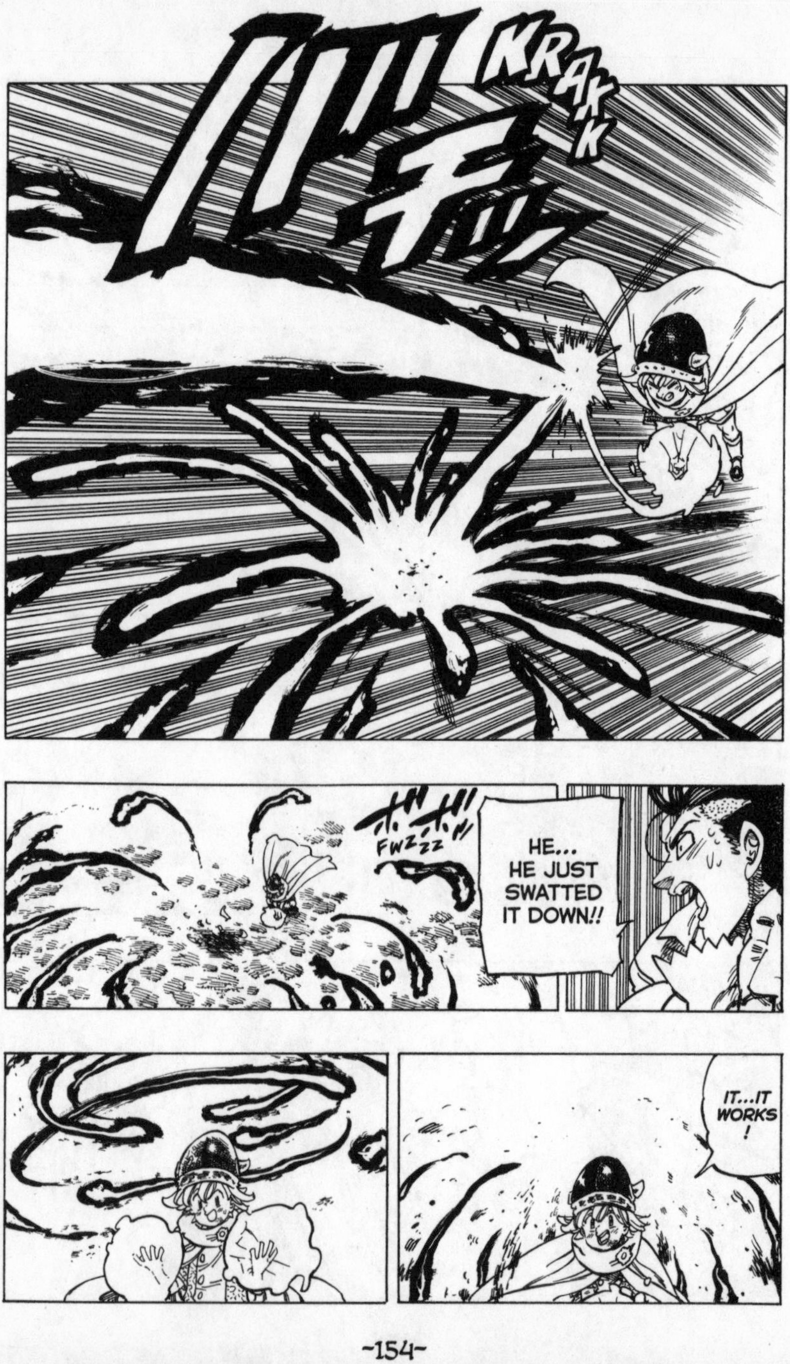
KRAKK
FWZZZ
HE... HE JUST SWATTED IT DOWN!!
IT...IT WORKS!

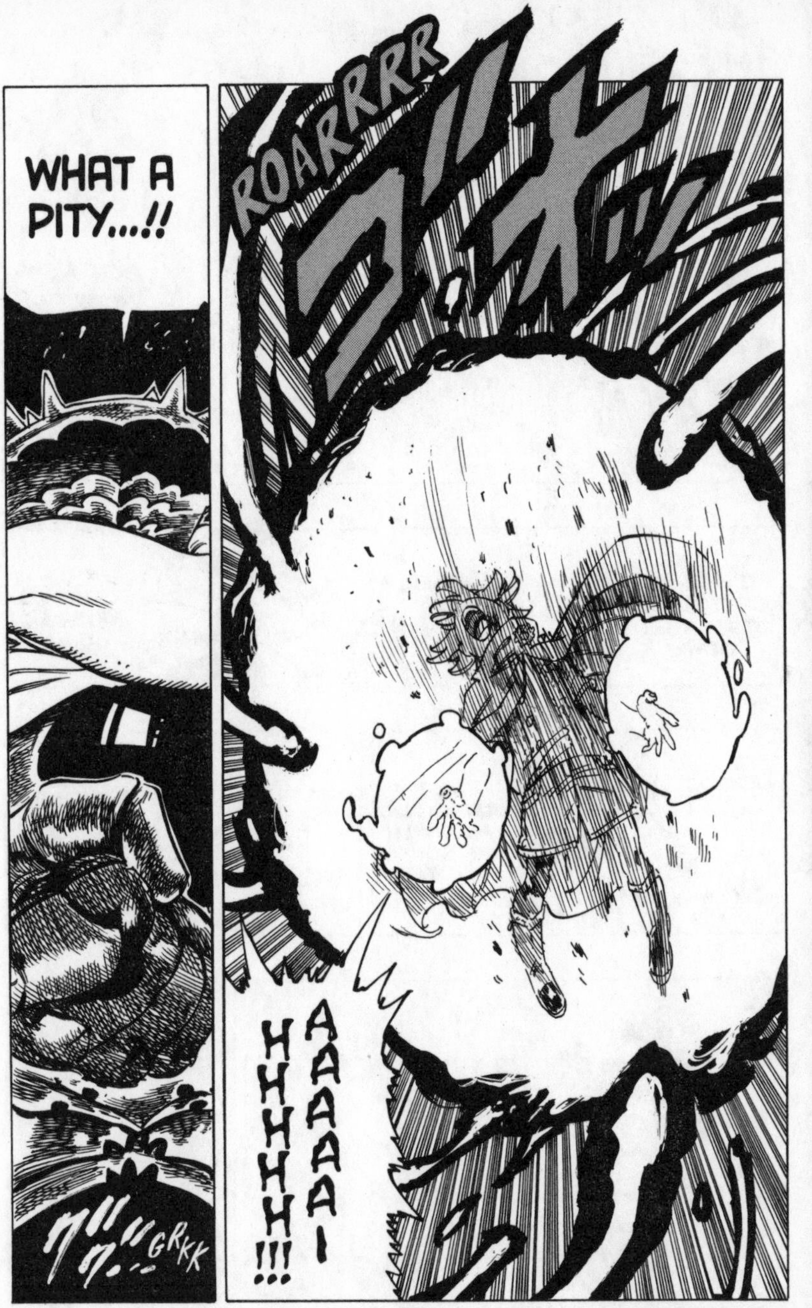
ROARRRR
AAAAAAI
HHHHHH!!!
WHAT A PITY...!!
GRKK

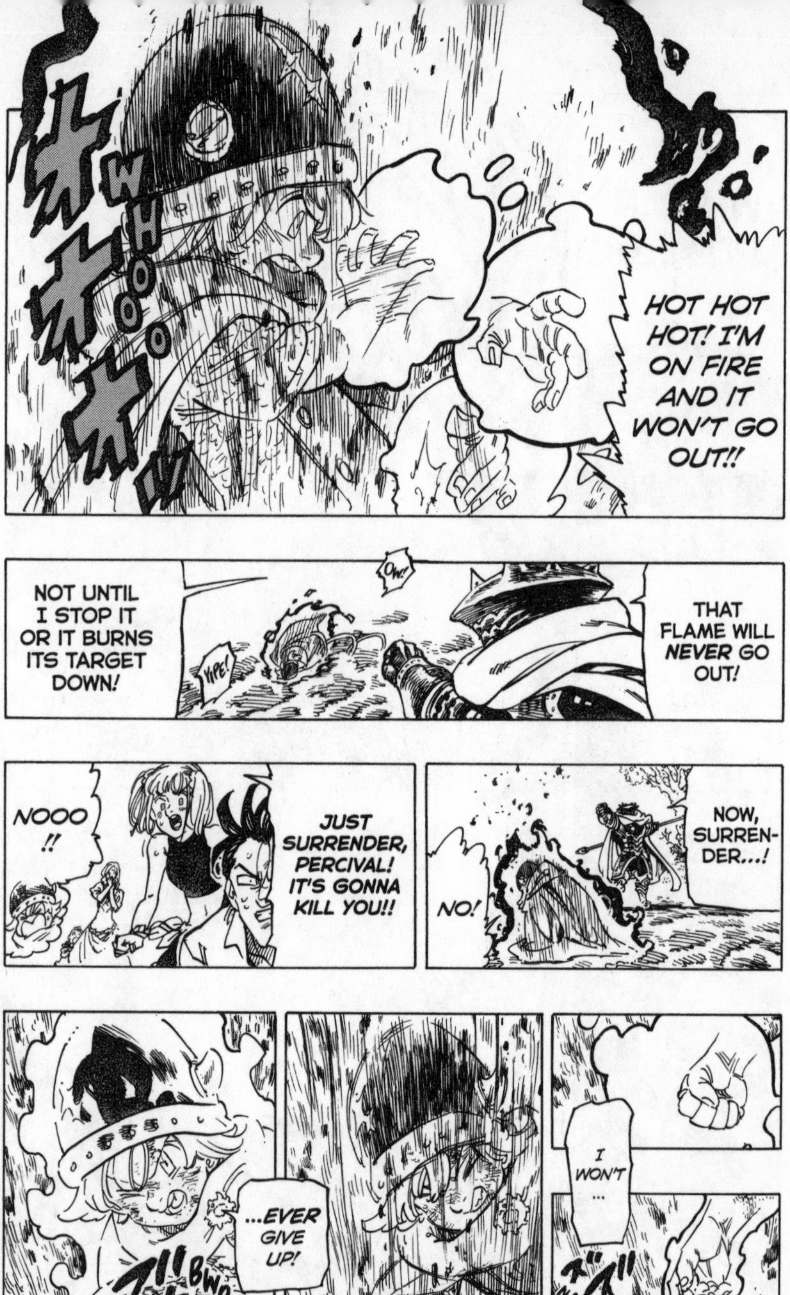
HOT HOT HOT! I'M ON FIRE AND IT WON'T GO OUT!!
WHOOOO
THAT FLAME WILL NEVER GO OUT!
OW!
YIPE!
NOT UNTIL I STOP IT OR IT BURNS ITS TARGET DOWN!
NOW, SURREN-DER...!
NO!
JUST SURRENDER, PERCIVAL! IT'S GONNA KILL YOU!!
NOOO !!
I WON'T ...
NRRZ
...EVER GIVE UP!
BWOOO

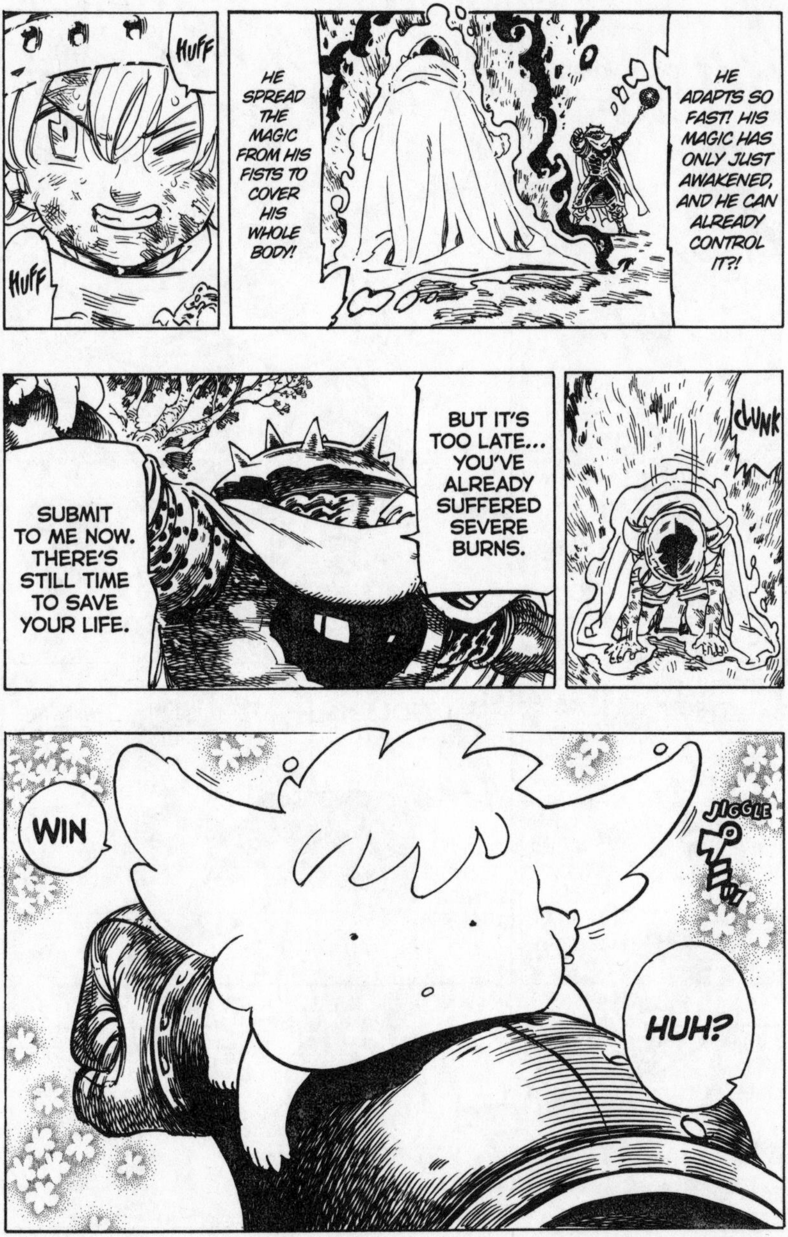
HE ADAPTS SO FAST! HIS MAGIC HAS ONLY JUST AWAKENED, AND HE CAN ALREADY CONTROL IT?!
HE SPREAD THE MAGIC FROM HIS FISTS TO COVER HIS WHOLE BODY!
HUFF
HUFF
CLUNK
BUT IT'S TOO LATE... YOU'VE ALREADY SUFFERED SEVERE BURNS.
SUBMIT TO ME NOW. THERE'S STILL TIME TO SAVE YOUR LIFE.
JIGGLE
WIN
HUH?

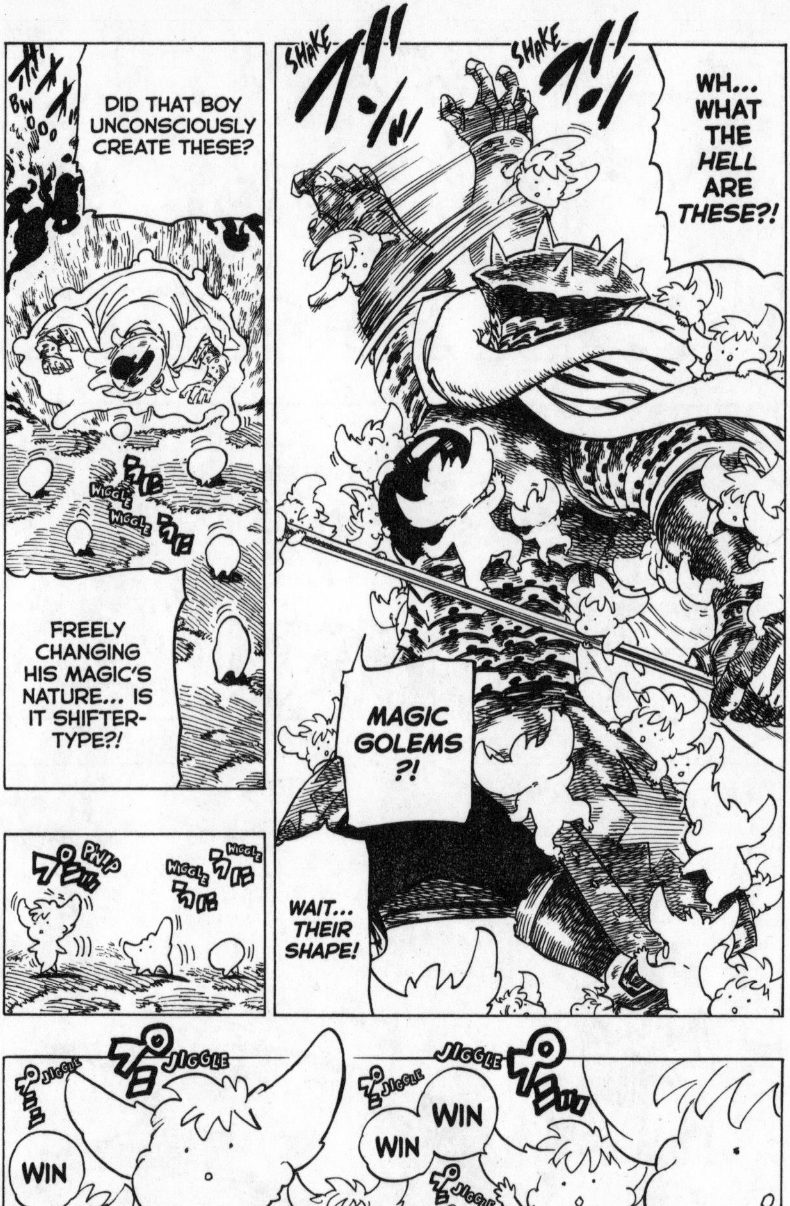
WH... WHAT THE HELL ARE THESE?!
SHAKE
SHAKE
MAGIC GOLEMS ?!
WAIT... THEIR SHAPE!
BWOOO
DID THAT BOY UNCONSCIOUSLY CREATE THESE?
WIGGLE
WIGGLE
FREELY CHANGING HIS MAGIC'S NATURE... IS IT SHIFTER-TYPE?!
WIGGLE
WIGGLE
PWIP
JIGGLE
JIGGLE
WIN
WIN
JIGGLE
JIGGLE
JIGGLE
WIN

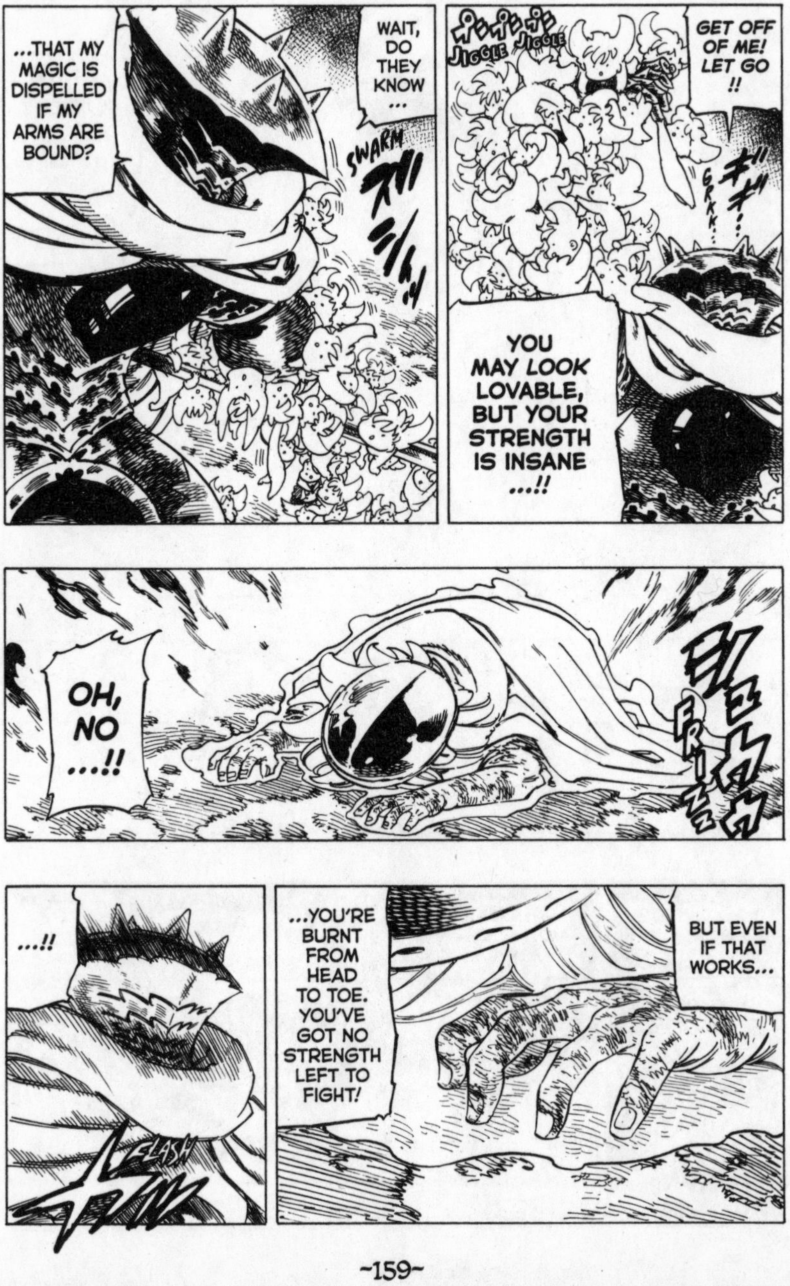
GET OFF OF ME! LET GO !!
JIGGLE JIGGLE
GRAKK...
YOU MAY *LOOK* LOVABLE, BUT YOUR STRENGTH IS INSANE ...!!
WAIT, DO THEY KNOW ...
...THAT MY MAGIC IS DISPELLED IF MY ARMS ARE BOUND?
SWARM
FRIZZ
OH, NO ...!!
BUT EVEN IF THAT WORKS...
...YOU'RE BURNT FROM HEAD TO TOE. YOU'VE GOT NO STRENGTH LEFT TO FIGHT!
...!!
FLASH

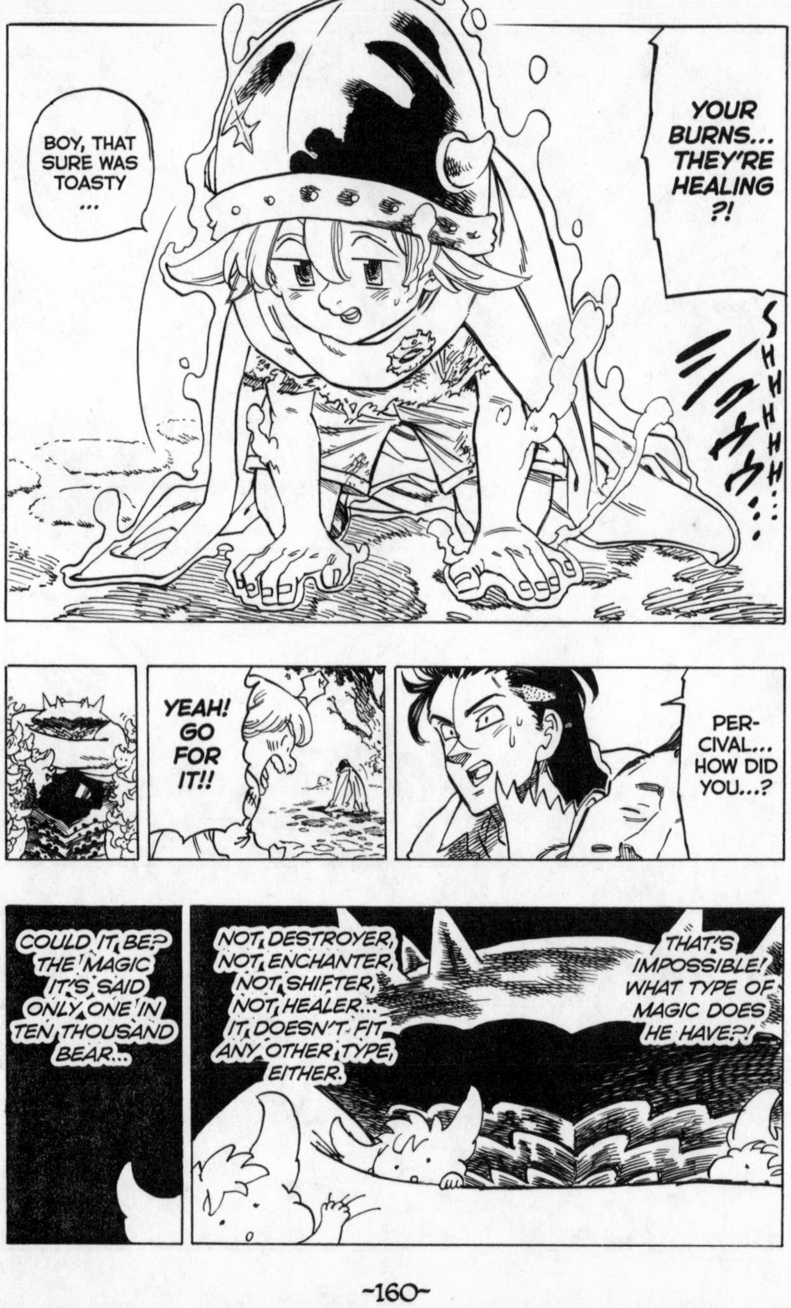
YOUR BURNS... THEY'RE HEALING ?!
SHHHHH...
BOY, THAT SURE WAS TOASTY ...
PER-CIVAL... HOW DID YOU...?
YEAH! GO FOR IT!!
THAT'S IMPOSSIBLE! WHAT TYPE OF MAGIC DOES HE HAVE?!
NOT DESTROYER, NOT ENCHANTER, NOT SHIFTER, NOT HEALER... IT DOESN'T FIT ANY OTHER TYPE, EITHER.
COULD IT BE? THE MAGIC IT'S SAID ONLY ONE IN TEN THOUSAND BEAR...

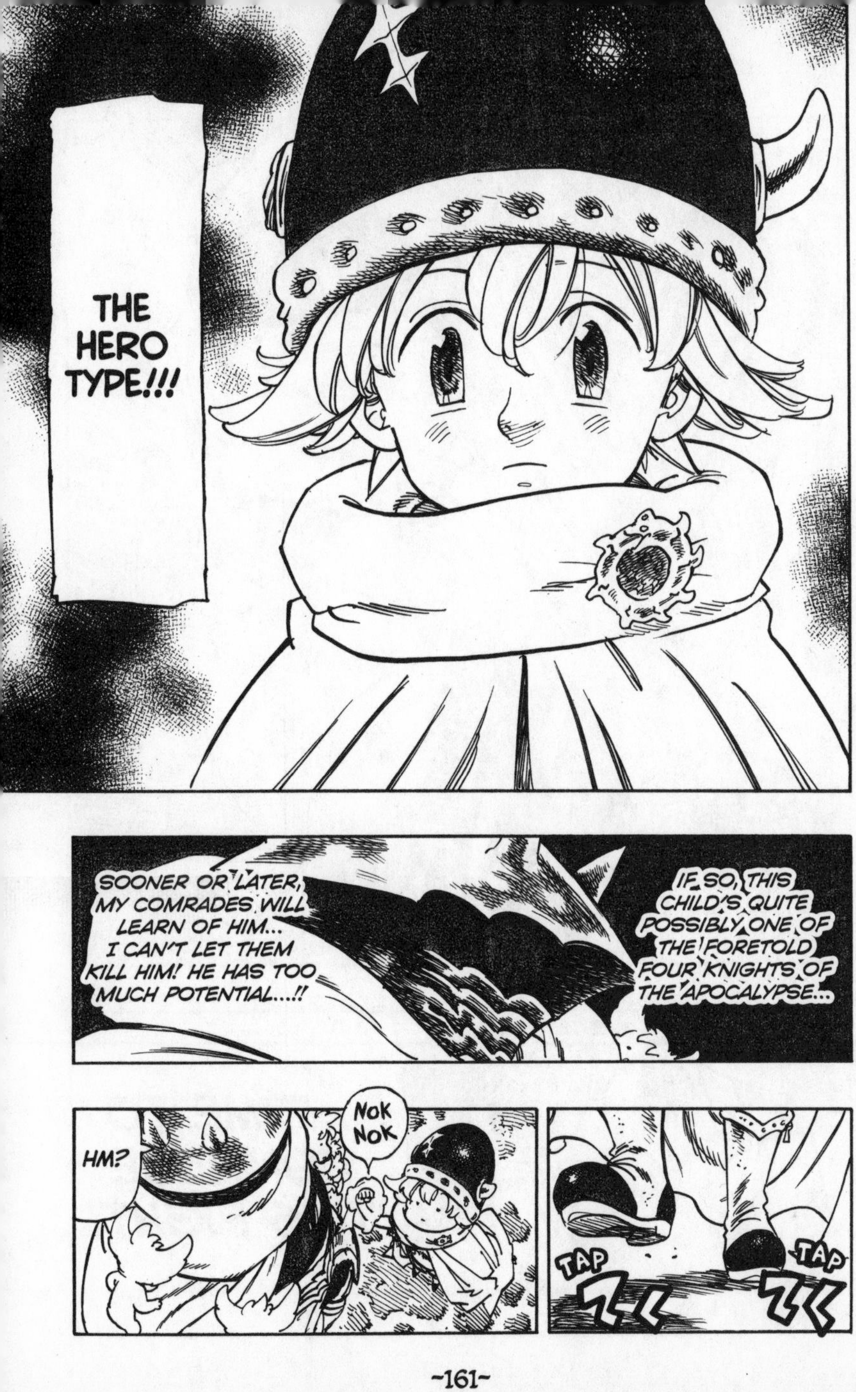
THE HERO TYPE!!!
IF SO, THIS CHILD'S QUITE POSSIBLY ONE OF THE FORETOLD FOUR KNIGHTS OF THE APOCALYPSE...
SOONER OR LATER, MY COMRADES WILL LEARN OF HIM... I CAN'T LET THEM KILL HIM! HE HAS TOO MUCH POTENTIAL...!!
TAP
TAP
NOK NOK
HM?

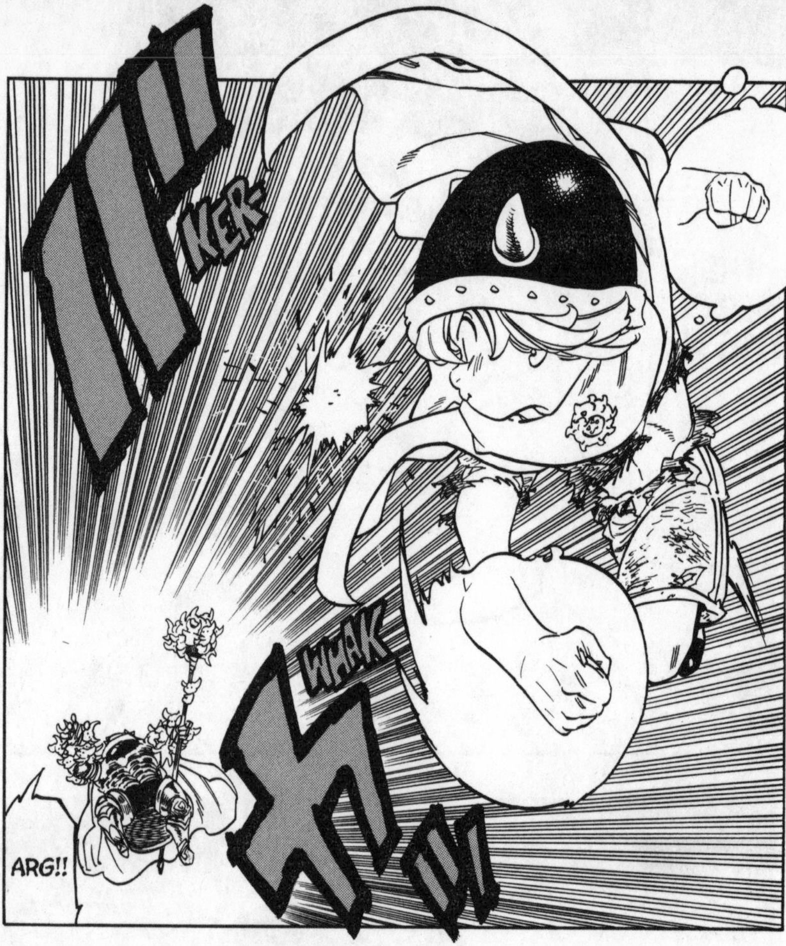
KER-
WHAK
ARG!!
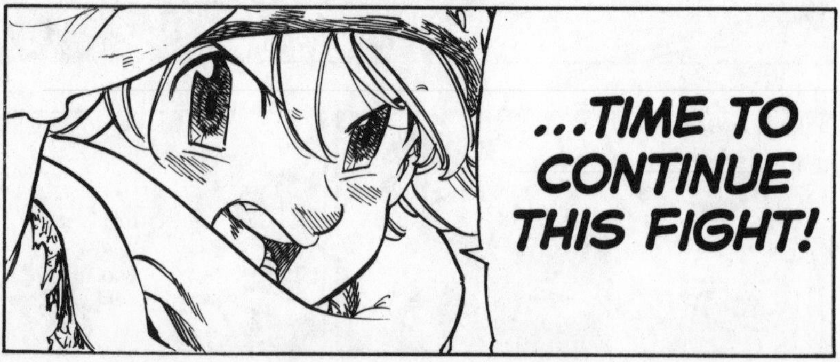
...TIME TO CONTINUE THIS FIGHT!

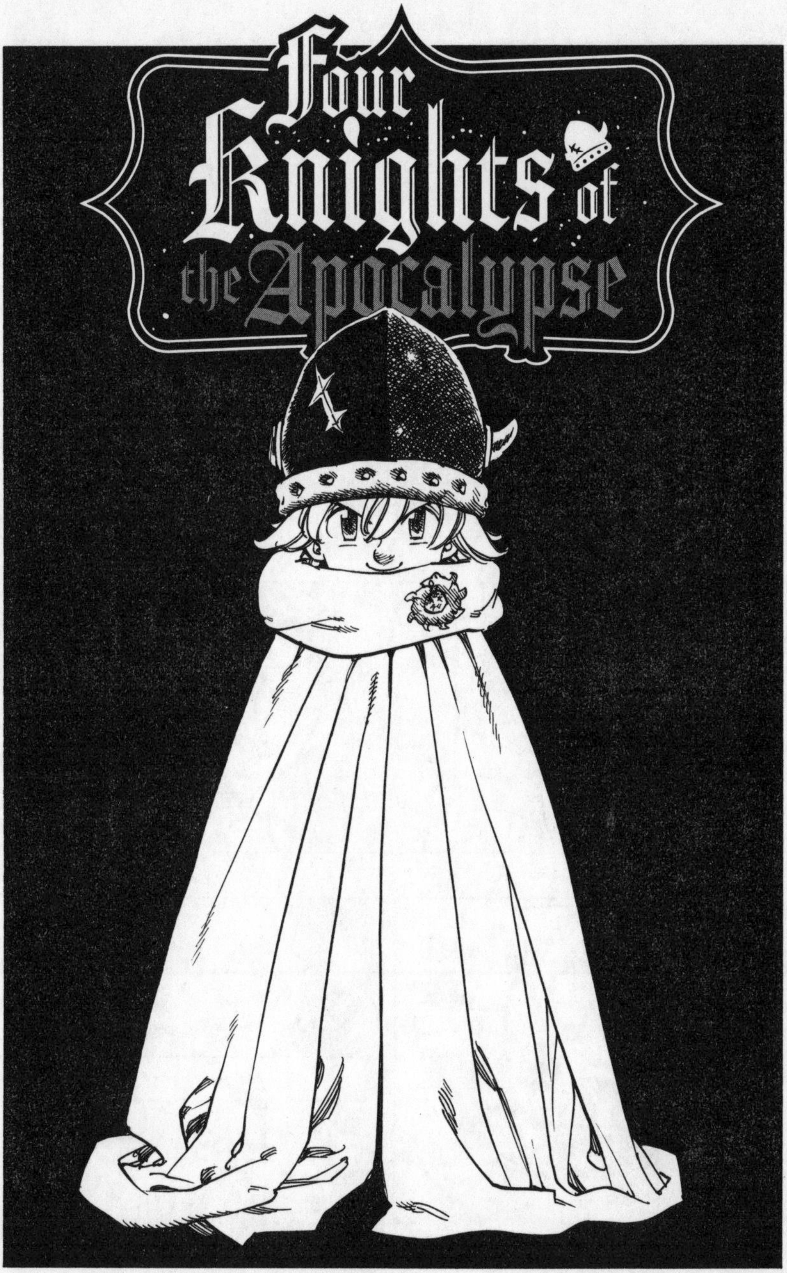
Four
Knights of
the Apocalypse

CHAPTER 5: THE FOUR KNIGHTS OF THE APOCALYPSE

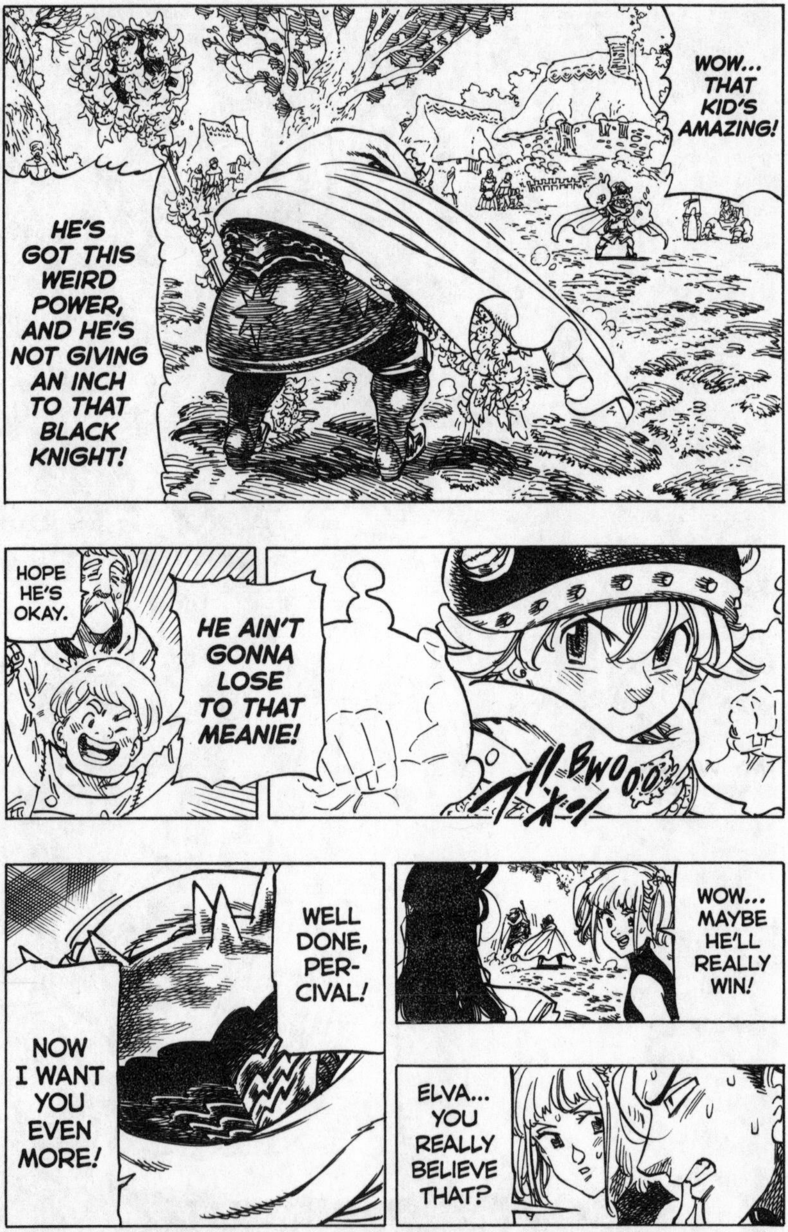
WOW... THAT KID'S AMAZING!
HE'S GOT THIS WEIRD POWER, AND HE'S NOT GIVING AN INCH TO THAT BLACK KNIGHT!
BWOOO
HOPE HE'S OKAY.
HE AIN'T GONNA LOSE TO THAT MEANIE!
WOW... MAYBE HE'LL REALLY WIN!
ELVA... YOU REALLY BELIEVE THAT?
WELL DONE, PER-CIVAL!
NOW I WANT YOU EVEN MORE!

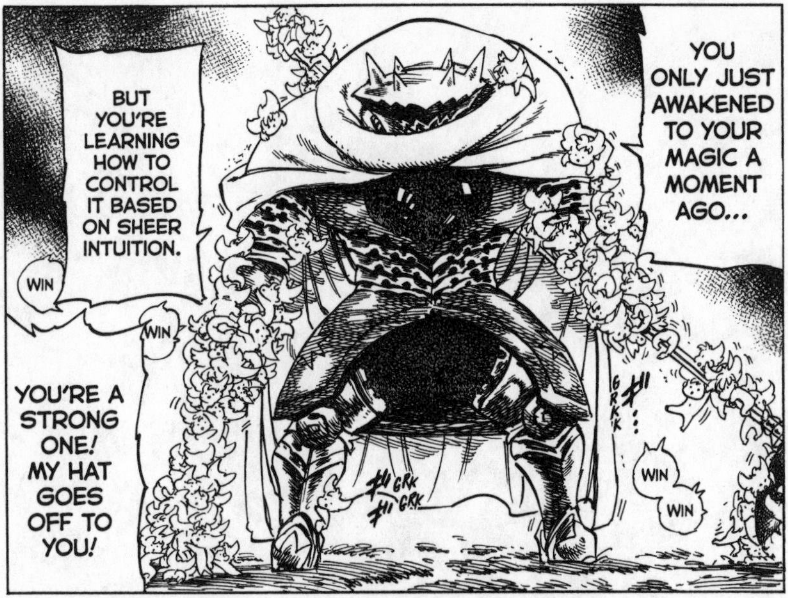
YOU ONLY JUST AWAKENED TO YOUR MAGIC A MOMENT AGO...
BUT YOU'RE LEARNING HOW TO CONTROL IT BASED ON SHEER INTUITION.
WIN
WIN
GRKK
WIN
WIN
GRK
GRK
YOU'RE A STRONG ONE! MY HAT GOES OFF TO YOU!

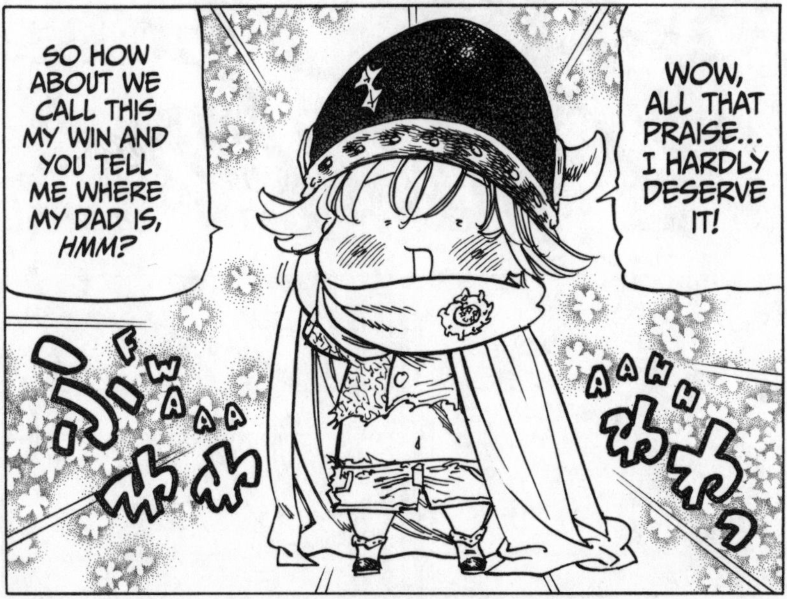
WOW, ALL THAT PRAISE... I HARDLY DESERVE IT!
SO HOW ABOUT WE CALL THIS MY WIN AND YOU TELL ME WHERE MY DAD IS, *HMM?*
AAHH
FWAAAA

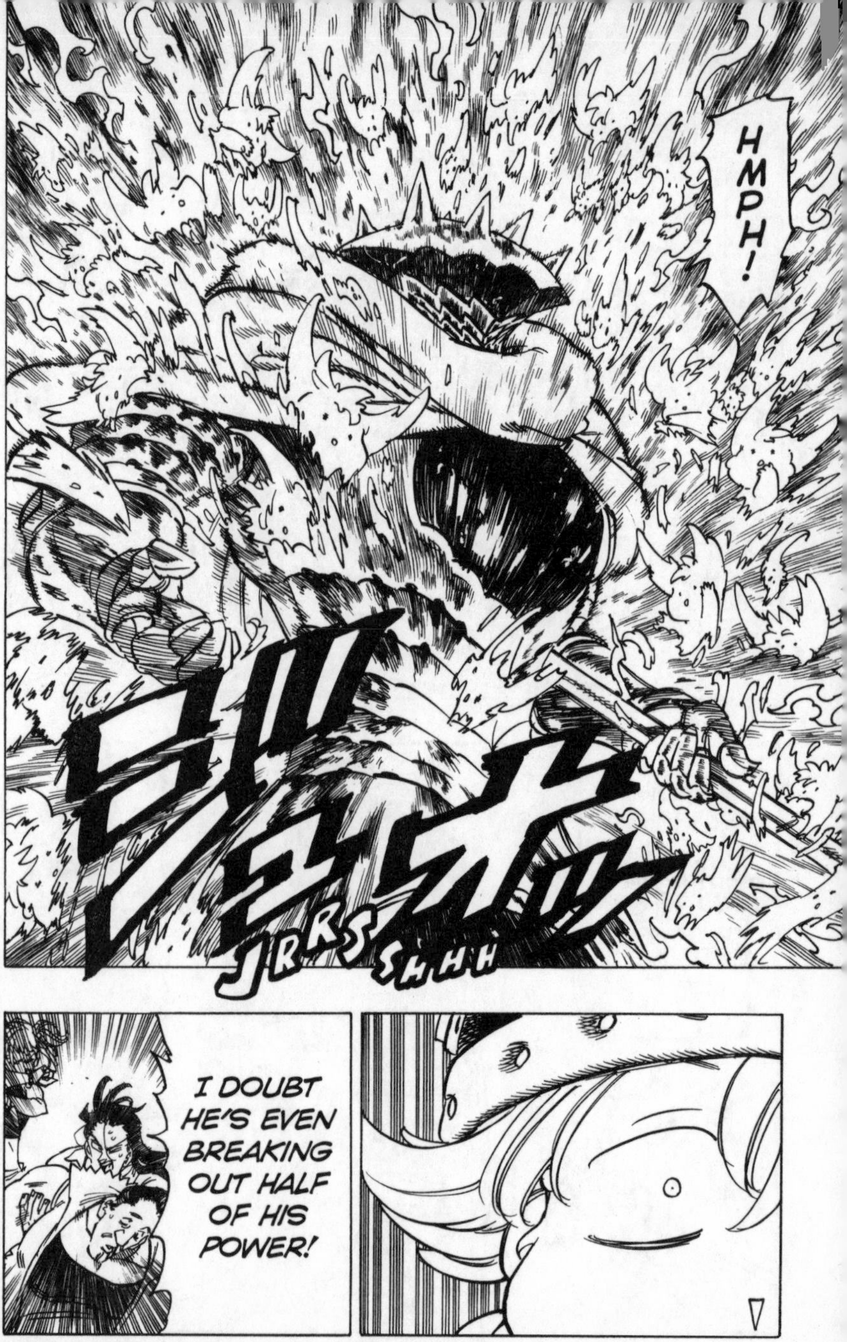
HMPH!
JRRSSHHH
I DOUBT HE'S EVEN BREAKING OUT HALF OF HIS POWER!

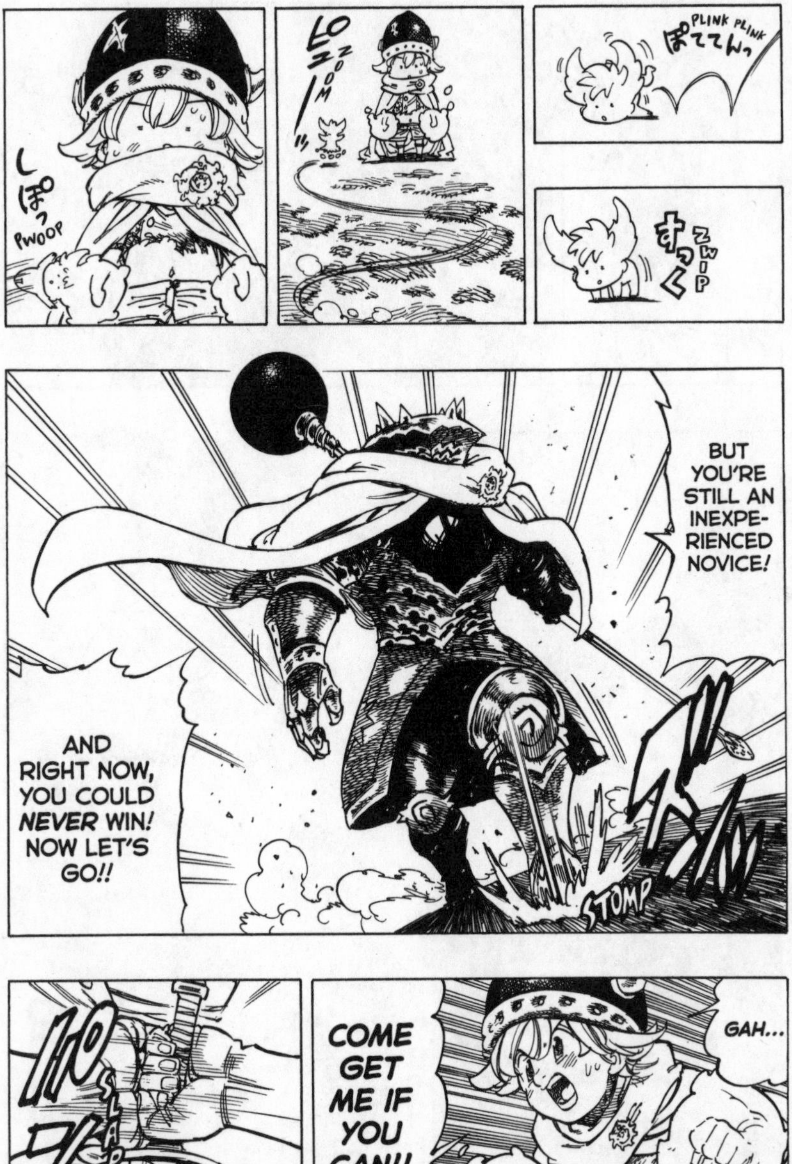
PLINK PLINK
ぽててんっ
すっく
ZWIP
ZOOM
しぽっ
PWOOP
BUT YOU'RE STILL AN INEXPERIENCED NOVICE!
AND RIGHT NOW, YOU COULD *NEVER* WIN! NOW LET'S GO!!
STOMP
GAH...
COME GET ME IF YOU CAN!!
SLAP

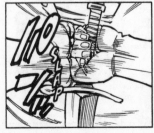

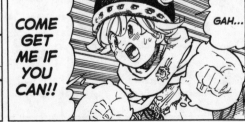

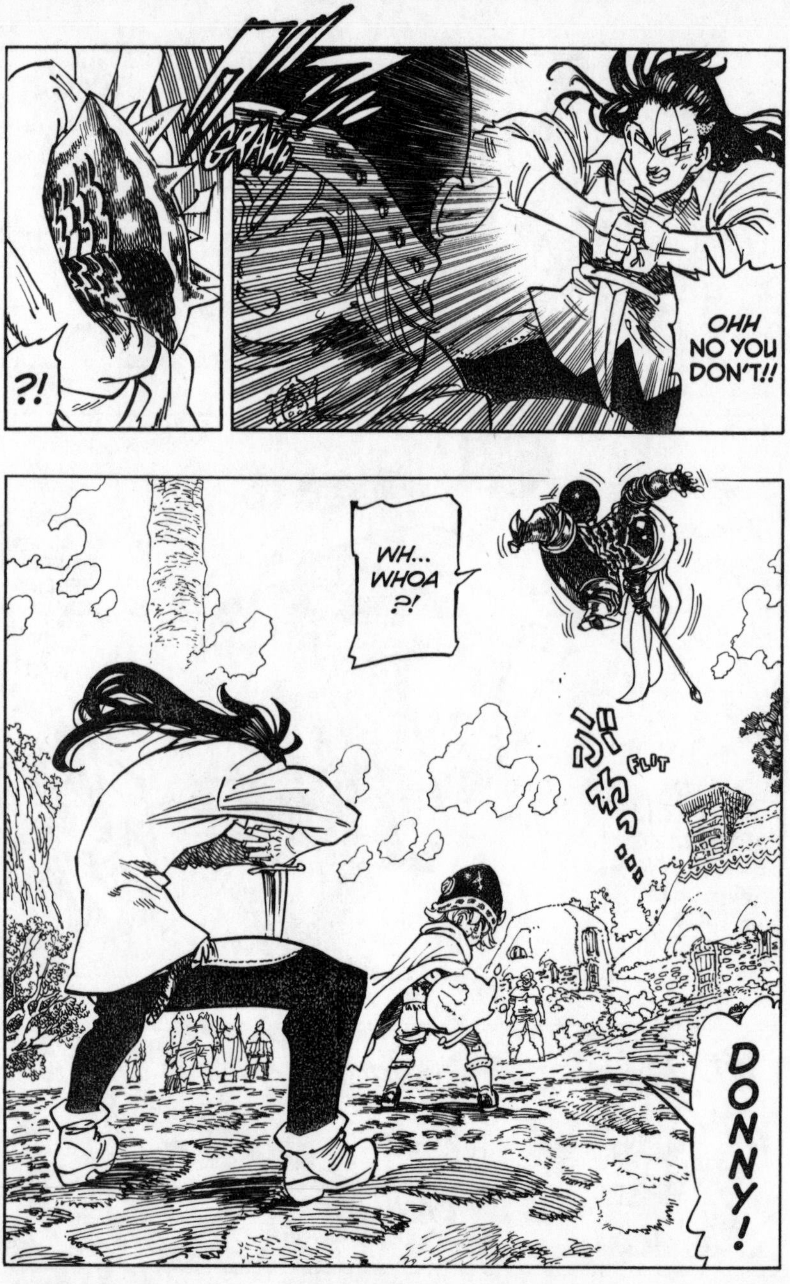
OHH NO YOU DON'T!!
GRAHH
?!
WH... WHOA ?!
FLIT
DONNY!

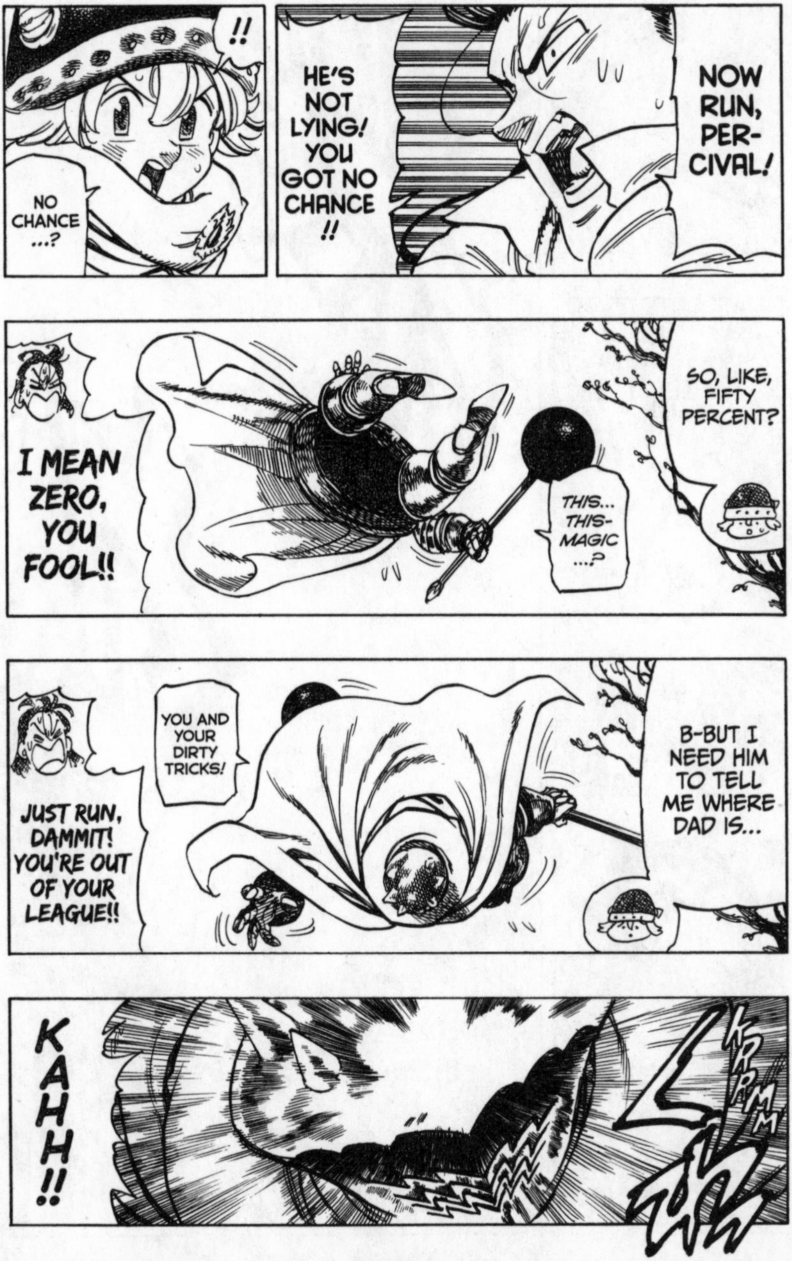
NOW RUN, PER-CIVAL!
HE'S NOT LYING! YOU GOT NO CHANCE!!
!!
NO CHANCE ...?
SO, LIKE, FIFTY PERCENT?
THIS... THIS-MAGIC ...?
I MEAN ZERO, YOU FOOL!!
B-BUT I NEED HIM TO TELL ME WHERE DAD IS...
YOU AND YOUR DIRTY TRICKS!
JUST RUN, DAMMIT! YOU'RE OUT OF YOUR LEAGUE!!
KRRMM
KAHH!!

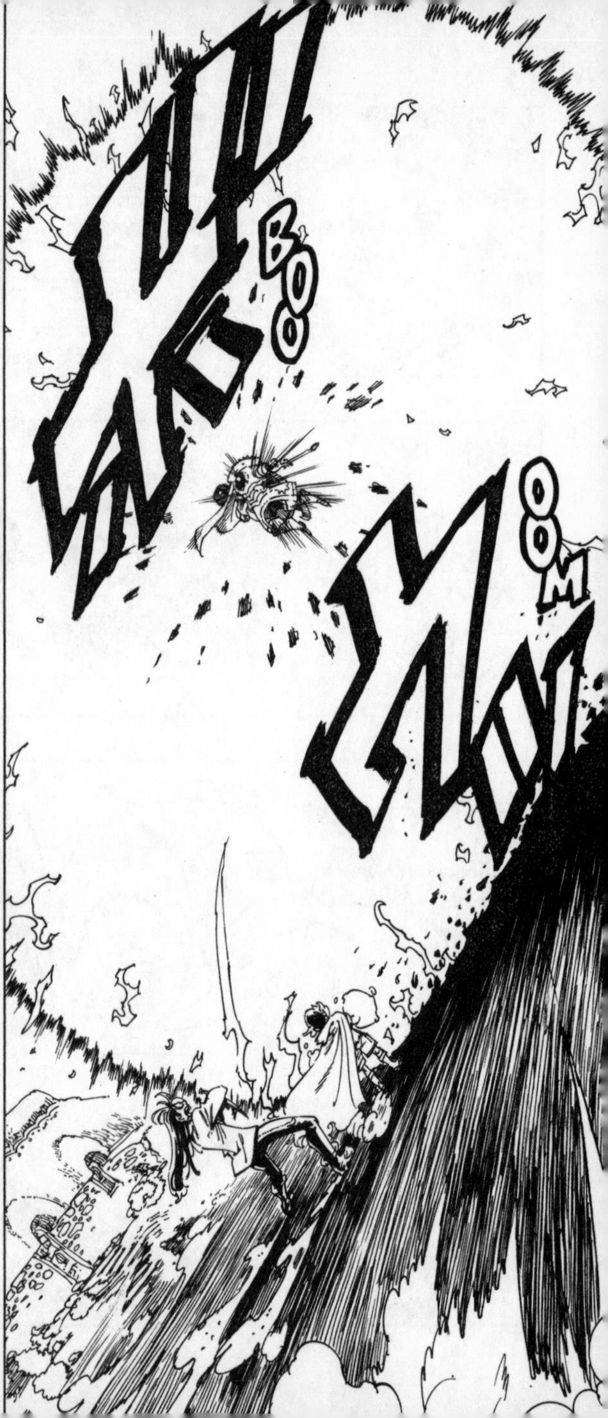
BOOO
OOM
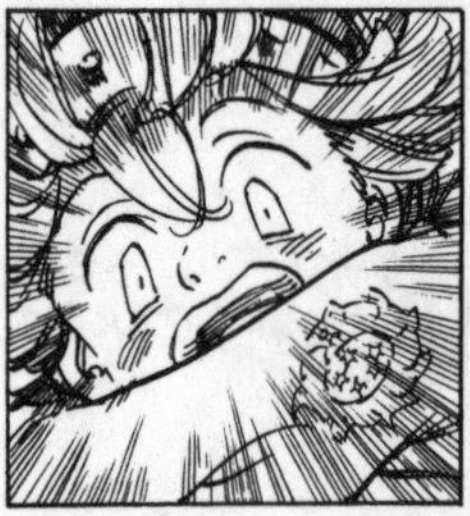
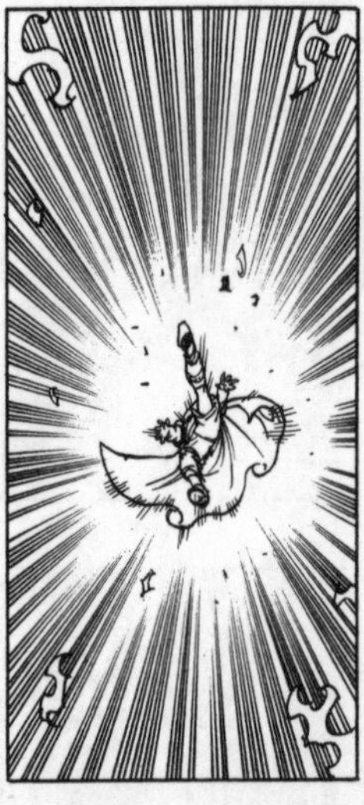
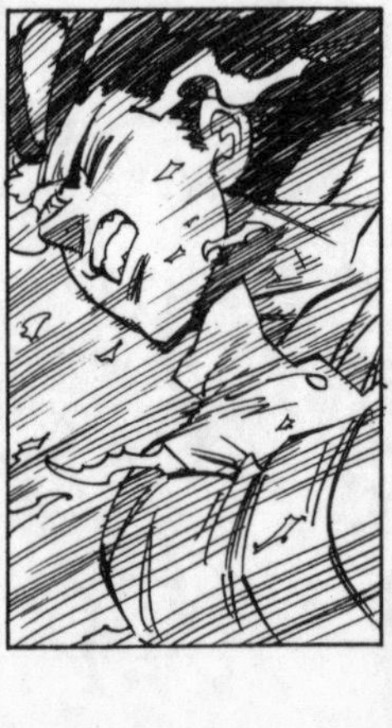

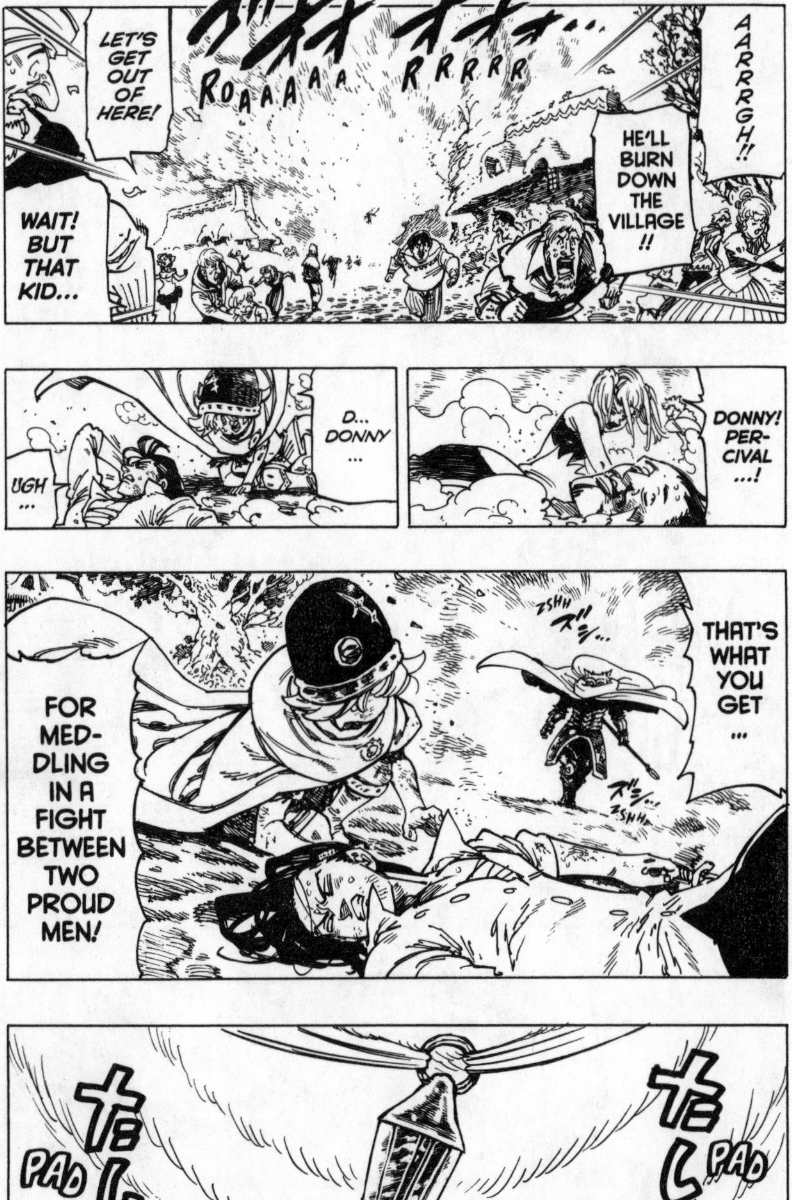
AARRRGH!!
HE'LL BURN DOWN THE VILLAGE!!
ROAAAAA RRRRR
LET'S GET OUT OF HERE!
WAIT! BUT THAT KID...
DONNY! PERCIVAL...!
D... DONNY...
UGH...
ZSHH
THAT'S WHAT YOU GET...
FOR MEDDLING IN A FIGHT BETWEEN TWO PROUD MEN!
ZSHH
PAD
PAD

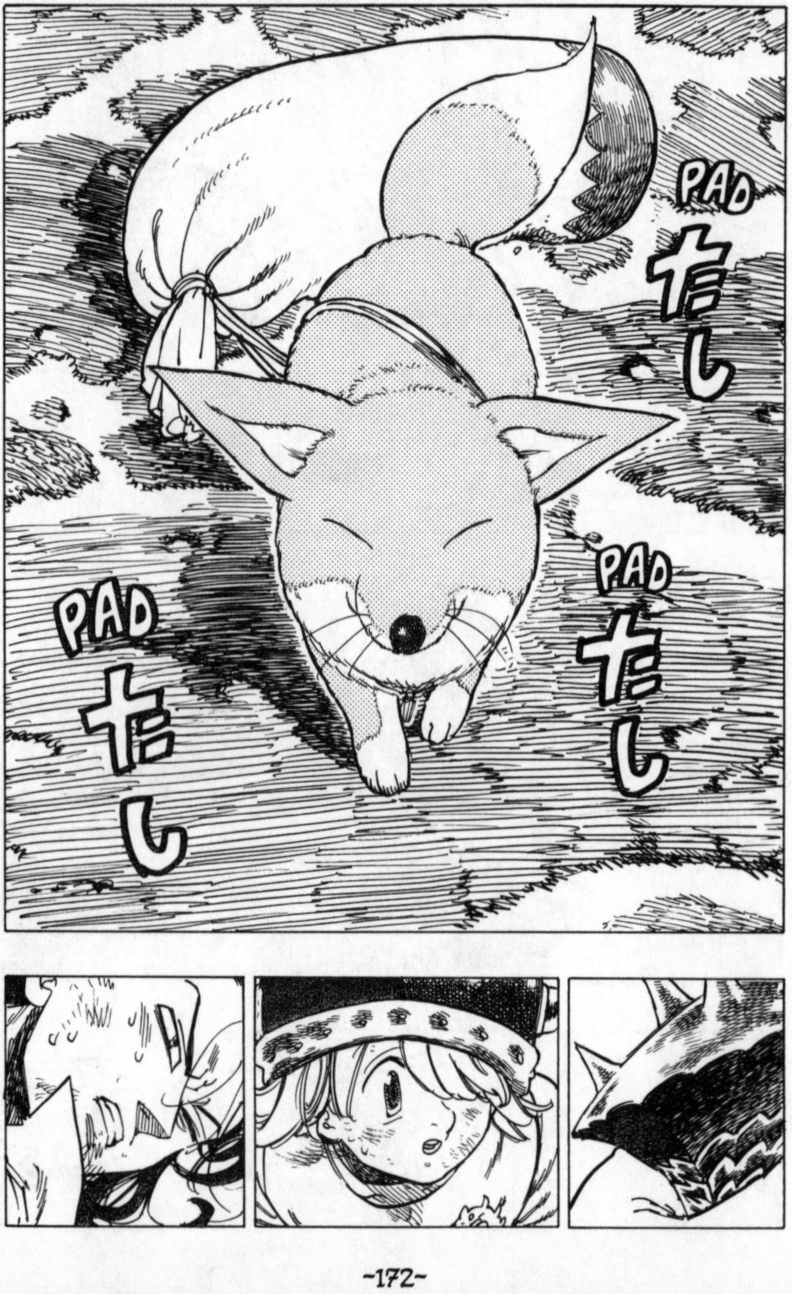
PAD
たし
PAD
たし
PAD
たし

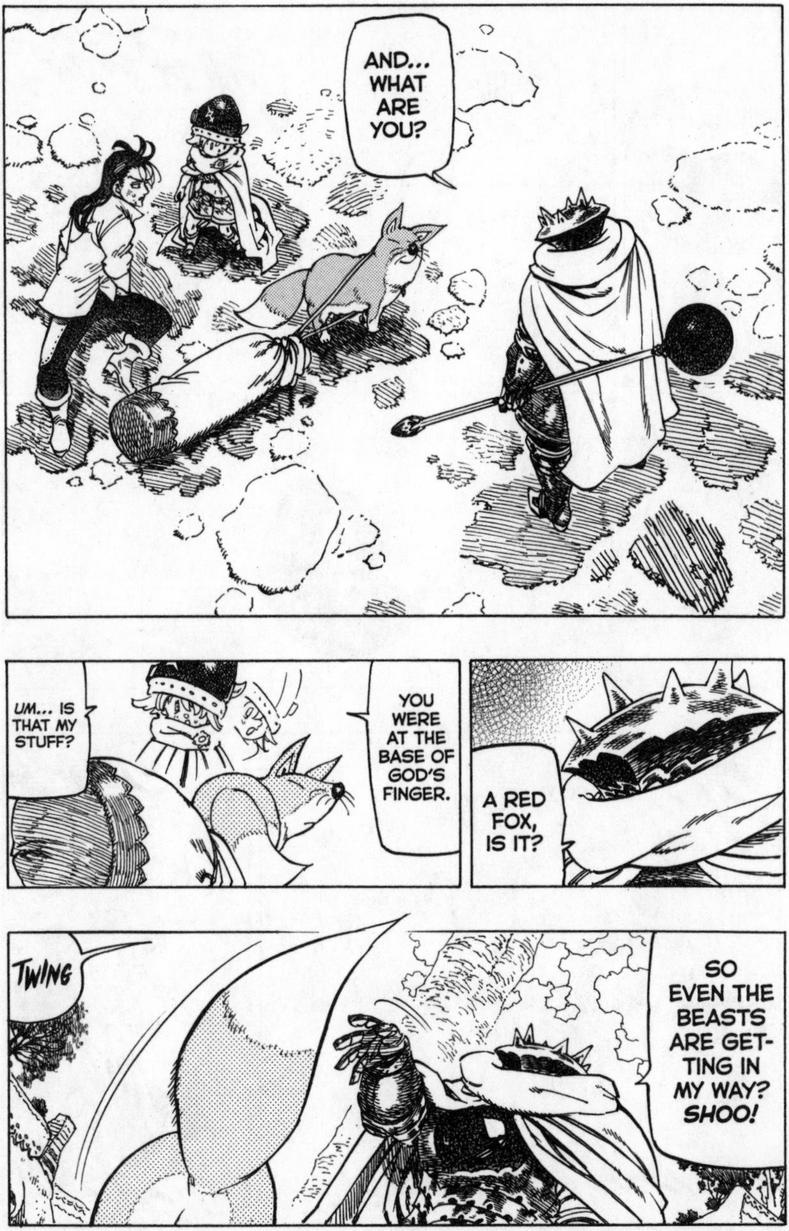
AND... WHAT ARE YOU?
A RED FOX, IS IT?
YOU WERE AT THE BASE OF GOD'S FINGER.
UM... IS THAT MY STUFF?
SO EVEN THE BEASTS ARE GET-TING IN MY WAY? SHOO!
TWING

PLIP

FWIP FWIP FWIP FWIP

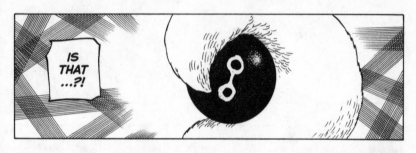
IS THAT ...?!

WHSH

FLAAAAAAAA ASH

W... WAIT!

FLING

FLAM

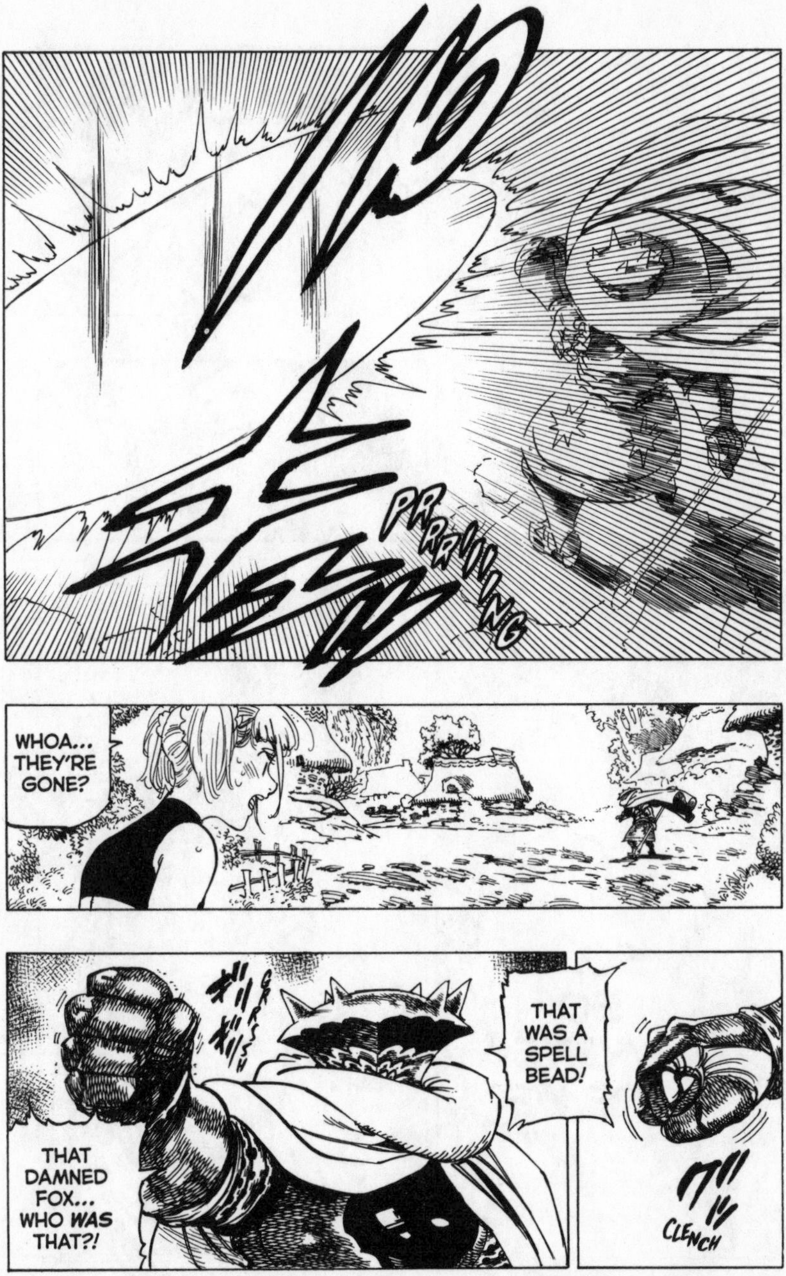
PRRIIIING
WHOA... THEY'RE GONE?
CLENCH
THAT WAS A SPELL BEAD!
GRRSSH
THAT DAMNED FOX... WHO *WAS* THAT?!

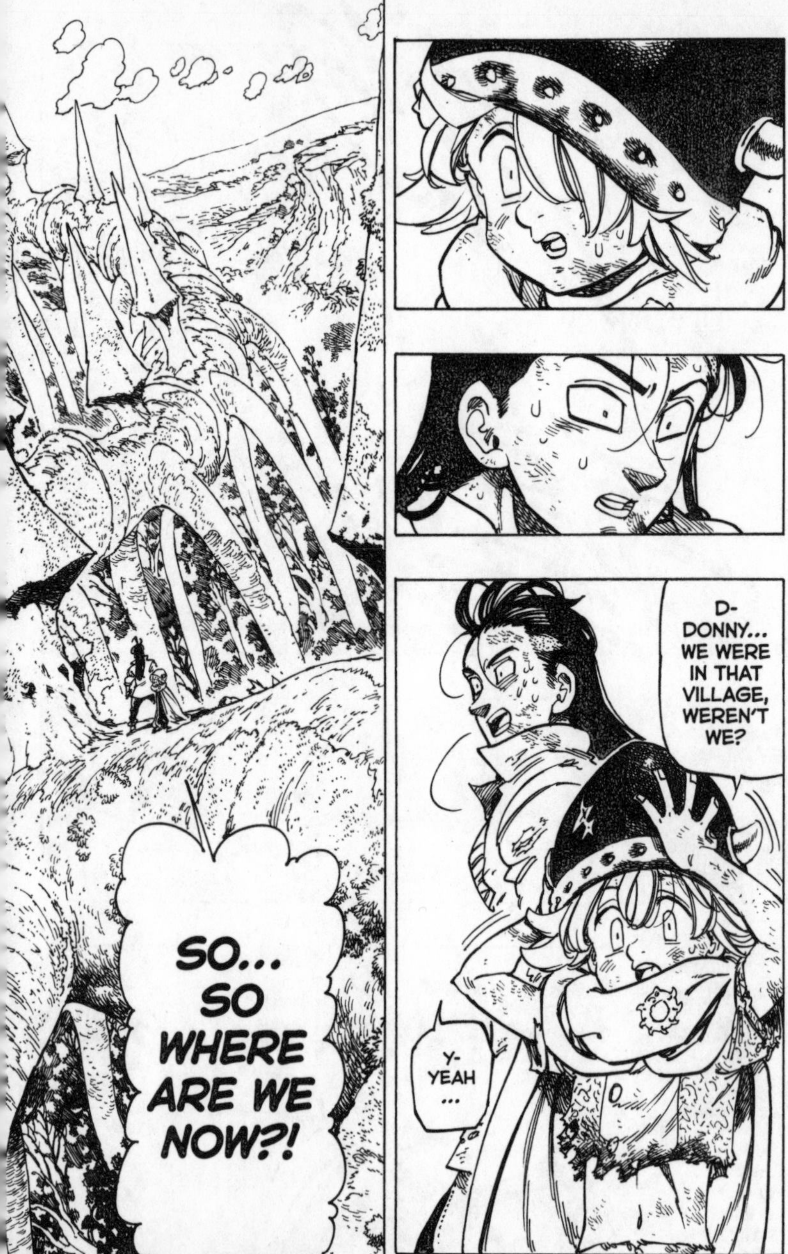
D-DONNY... WE WERE IN THAT VILLAGE, WEREN'T WE?
Y-YEAH ...
SO... SO WHERE ARE WE NOW?!

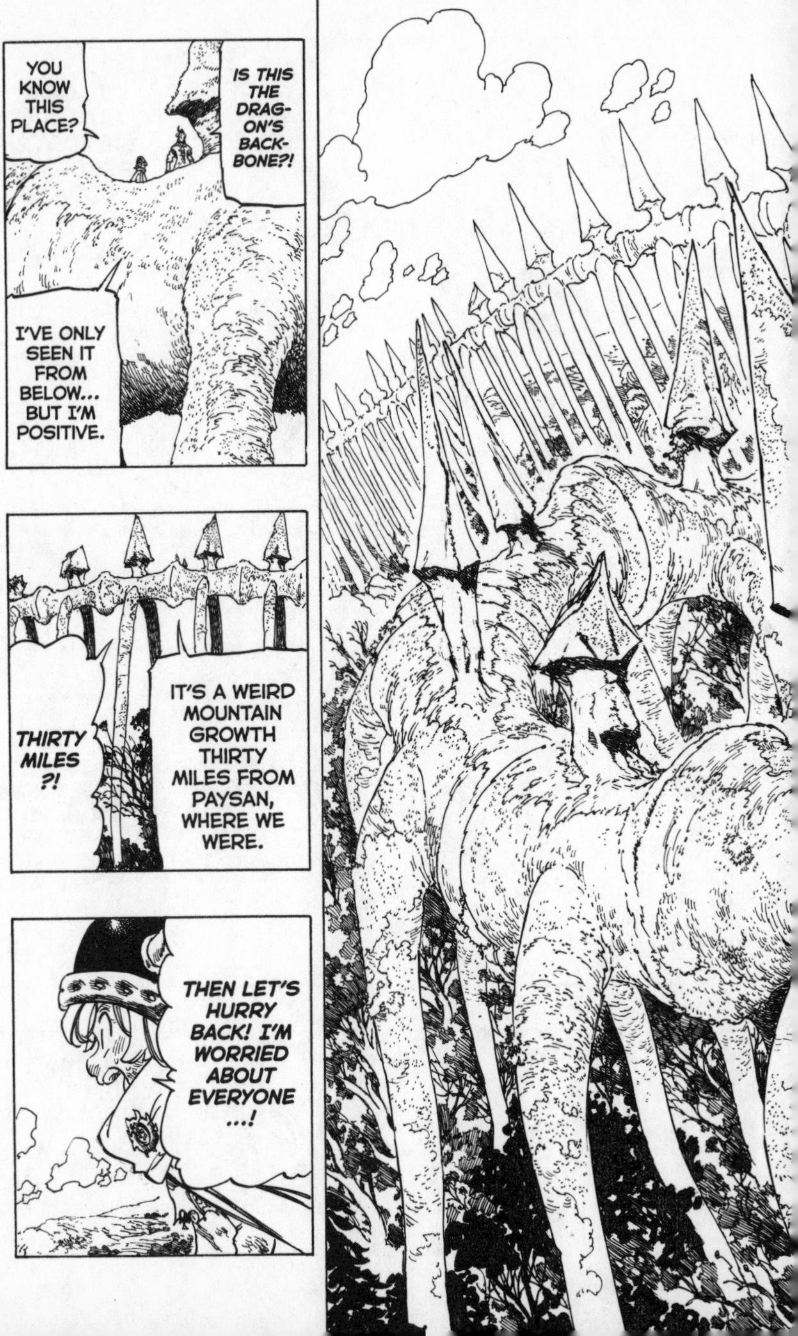
IS THIS THE DRAGON'S BACKBONE?!
YOU KNOW THIS PLACE?
I'VE ONLY SEEN IT FROM BELOW... BUT I'M POSITIVE.
IT'S A WEIRD MOUNTAIN GROWTH THIRTY MILES FROM PAYSAN, WHERE WE WERE.
THIRTY MILES ?!
THEN LET'S HURRY BACK! I'M WORRIED ABOUT EVERYONE ...!

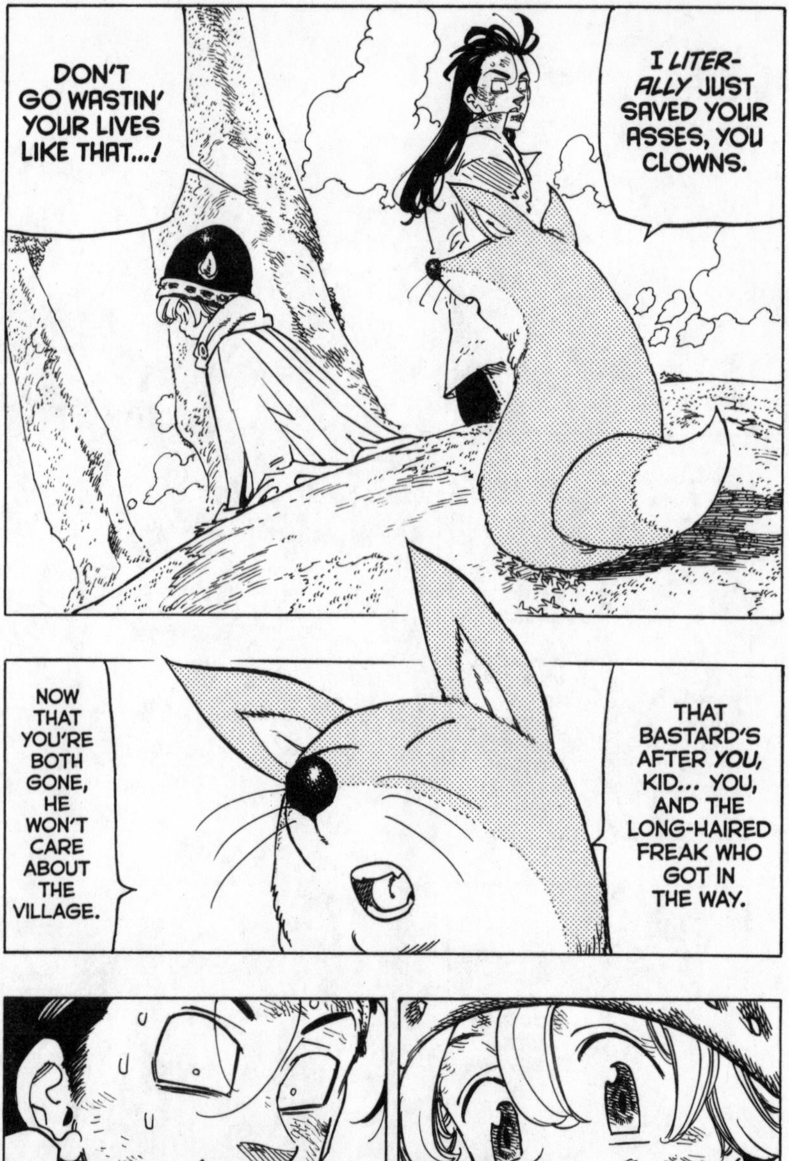
I LITERALLY JUST SAVED YOUR ASSES, YOU CLOWNS.
DON'T GO WASTIN' YOUR LIVES LIKE THAT...!
THAT BASTARD'S AFTER YOU, KID... YOU, AND THE LONG-HAIRED FREAK WHO GOT IN THE WAY.
NOW THAT YOU'RE BOTH GONE, HE WON'T CARE ABOUT THE VILLAGE.
IT ...

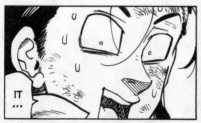

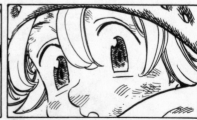

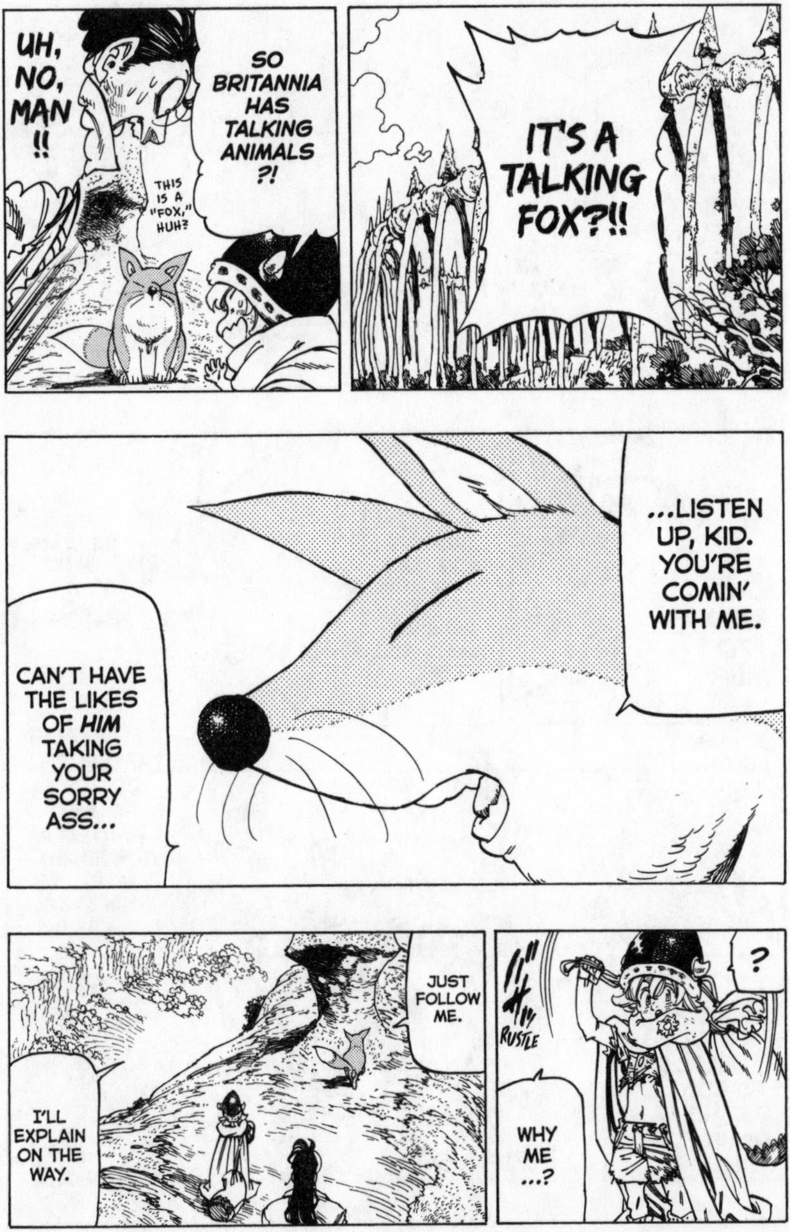
IT'S A TALKING FOX?!!
SO BRITANNIA HAS TALKING ANIMALS ?!
UH, NO, MAN !!
THIS IS A "FOX," HUH?
...LISTEN UP, KID. YOU'RE COMIN' WITH ME.
CAN'T HAVE THE LIKES OF *HIM* TAKING YOUR SORRY ASS...
?
RUSTLE
WHY ME ...?
JUST FOLLOW ME.
I'LL EXPLAIN ON THE WAY.

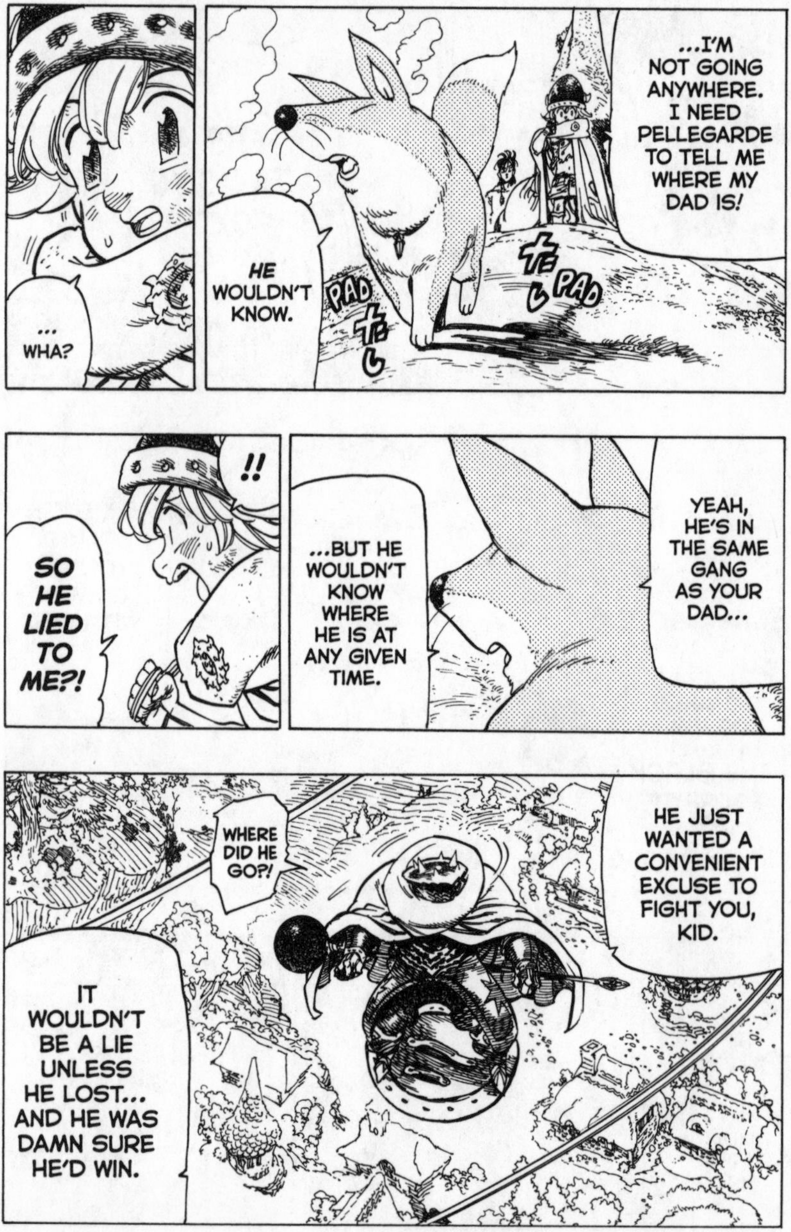
...I'M NOT GOING ANYWHERE. I NEED PELLEGARDE TO TELL ME WHERE MY DAD IS!
PAD
PAD
HE WOULDN'T KNOW.
... WHA?
YEAH, HE'S IN THE SAME GANG AS YOUR DAD...
...BUT HE WOULDN'T KNOW WHERE HE IS AT ANY GIVEN TIME.
!!
SO HE LIED TO ME?!
HE JUST WANTED A CONVENIENT EXCUSE TO FIGHT YOU, KID.
WHERE DID HE GO?!
IT WOULDN'T BE A LIE UNLESS HE LOST... AND HE WAS DAMN SURE HE'D WIN.

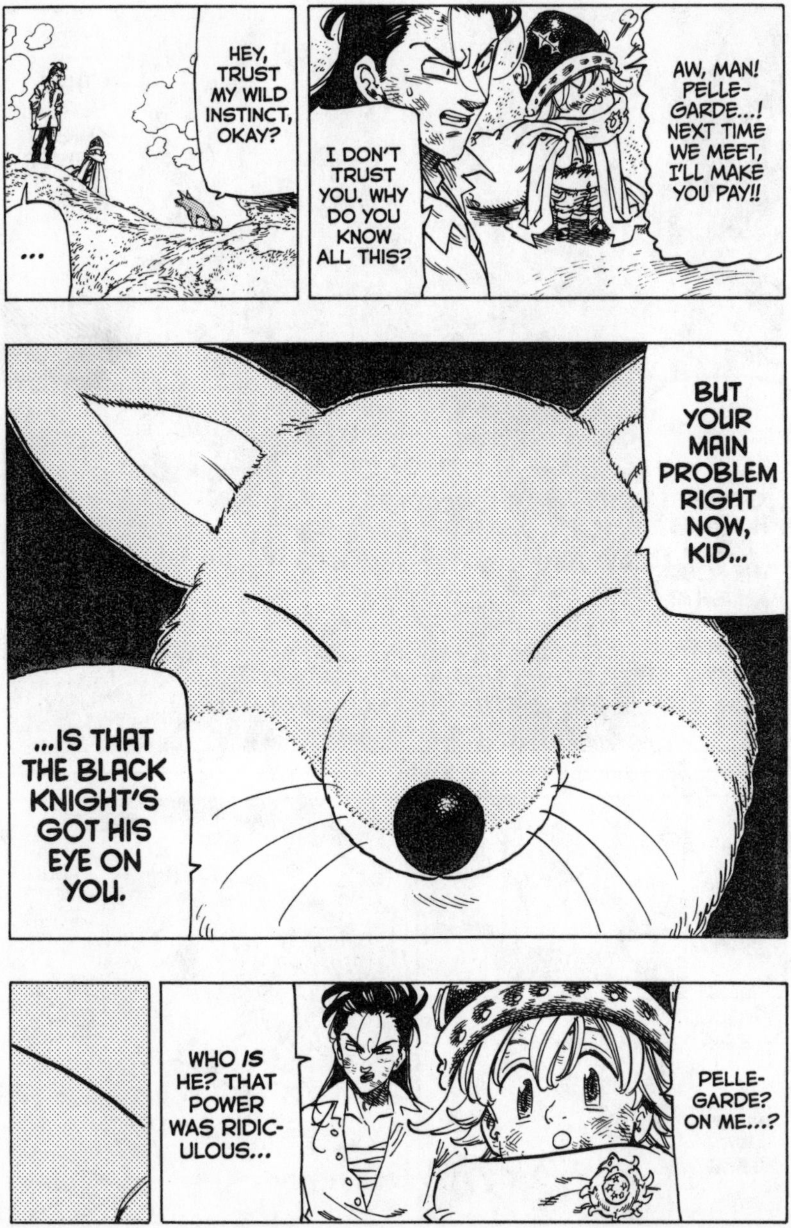
AW, MAN! PELLE-GARDE...! NEXT TIME WE MEET, I'LL MAKE YOU PAY!!
I DON'T TRUST YOU. WHY DO YOU KNOW ALL THIS?
HEY, TRUST MY WILD INSTINCT, OKAY?
...
BUT YOUR MAIN PROBLEM RIGHT NOW, KID...
...IS THAT THE BLACK KNIGHT'S GOT HIS EYE ON YOU.
PELLE-GARDE? ON ME...?
WHO *IS* HE? THAT POWER WAS RIDIC-ULOUS...

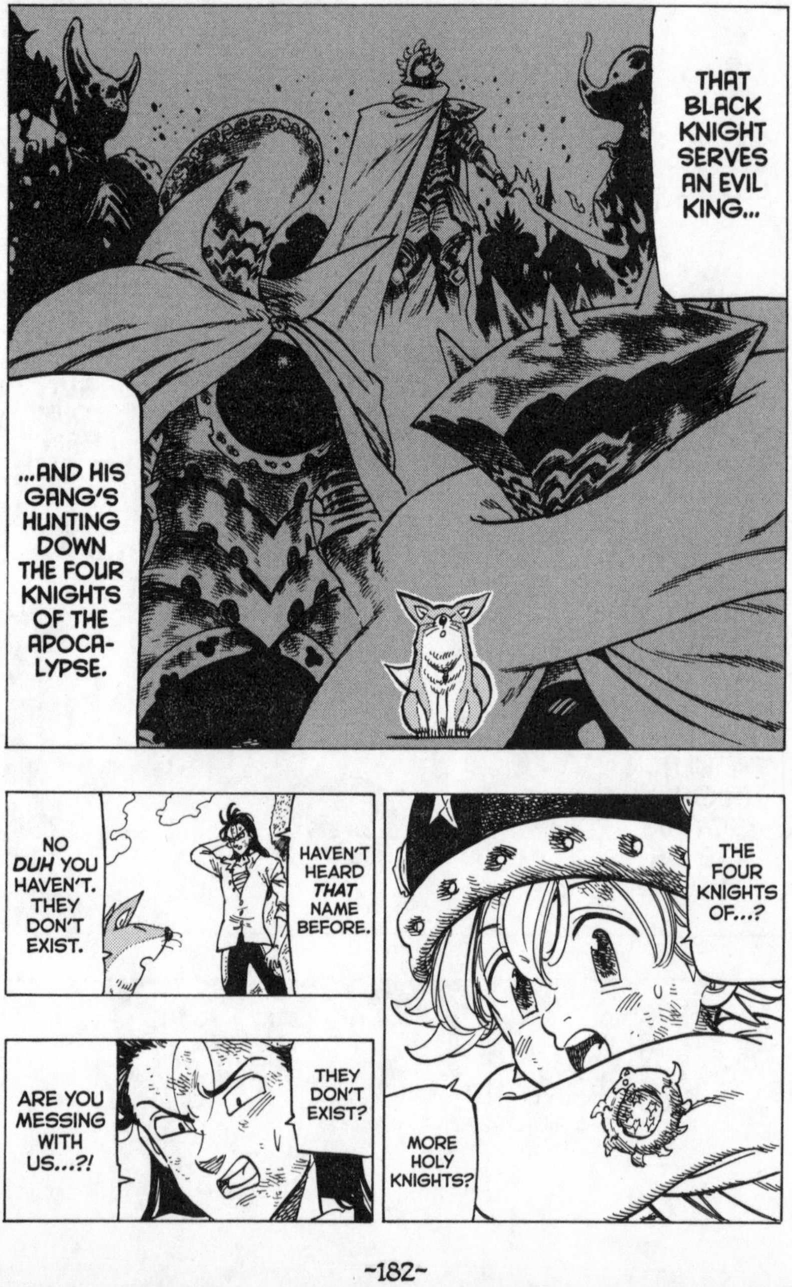
THAT BLACK KNIGHT SERVES AN EVIL KING...
...AND HIS GANG'S HUNTING DOWN THE FOUR KNIGHTS OF THE APOCA-LYPSE.
THE FOUR KNIGHTS OF...?
MORE HOLY KNIGHTS?
HAVEN'T HEARD *THAT* NAME BEFORE.
NO *DUH* YOU HAVEN'T. THEY DON'T EXIST.
THEY DON'T EXIST?
ARE YOU MESSING WITH US...?!

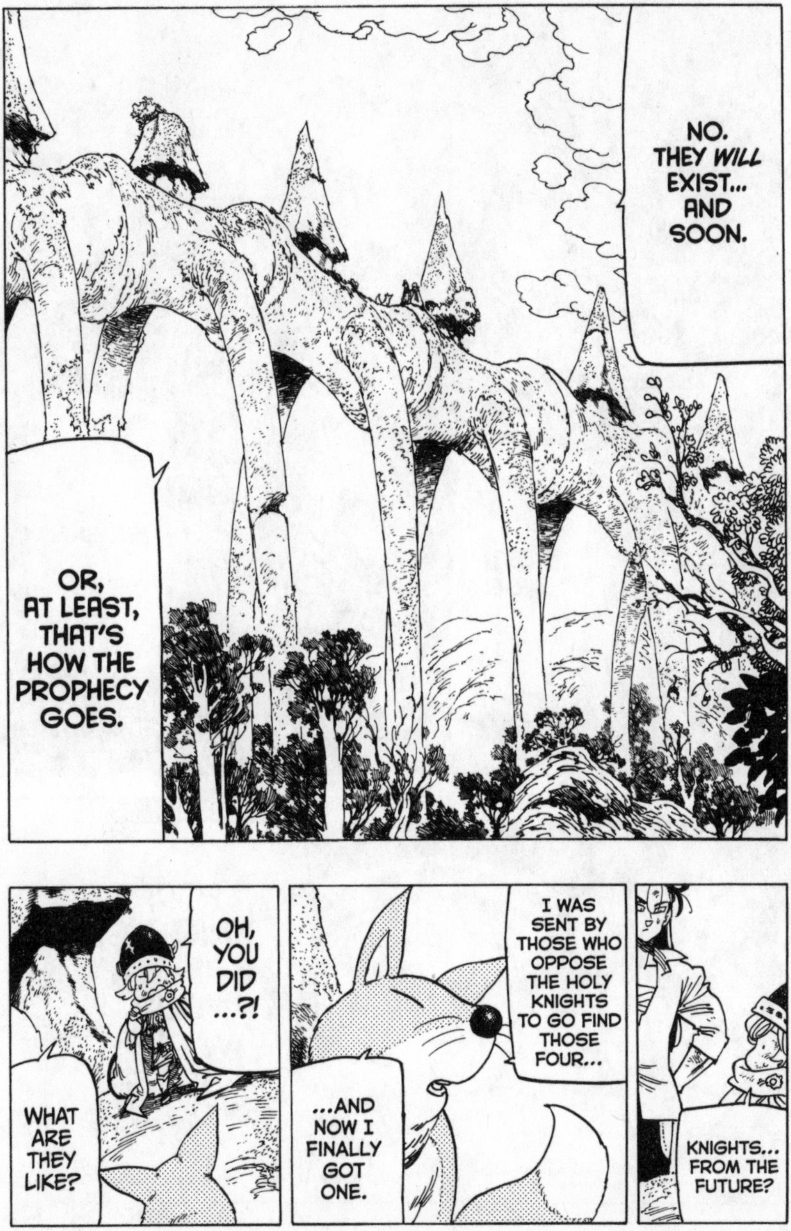
NO. THEY *WILL* EXIST... AND SOON.
OR, AT LEAST, THAT'S HOW THE PROPHECY GOES.
KNIGHTS... FROM THE FUTURE?
I WAS SENT BY THOSE WHO OPPOSE THE HOLY KNIGHTS TO GO FIND THOSE FOUR...
...AND NOW I FINALLY GOT ONE.
OH, YOU DID ...?!
WHAT ARE THEY LIKE?

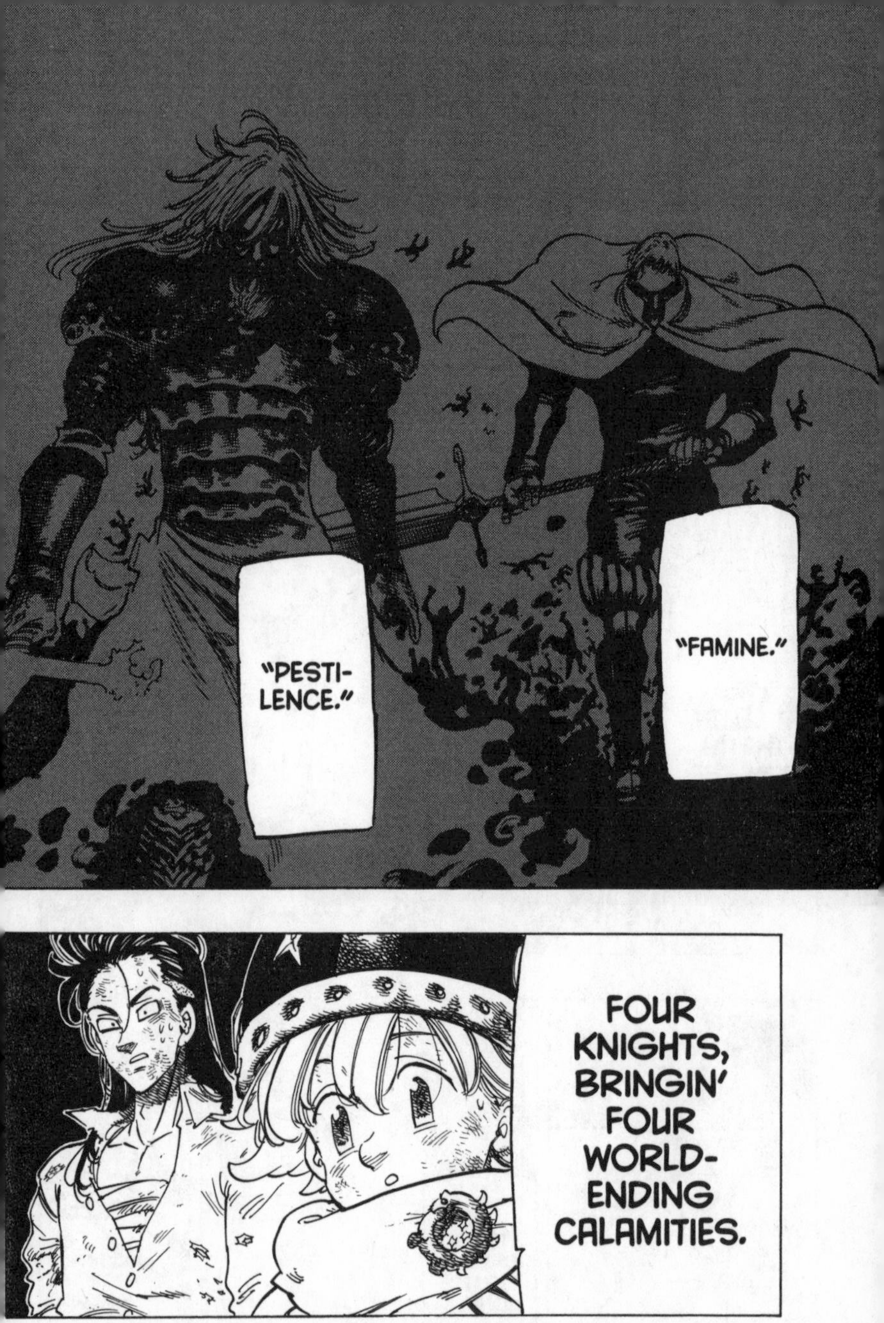
"FAMINE."
"PESTI-
LENCE."
FOUR KNIGHTS, BRINGIN' FOUR WORLD-ENDING CALAMITIES.

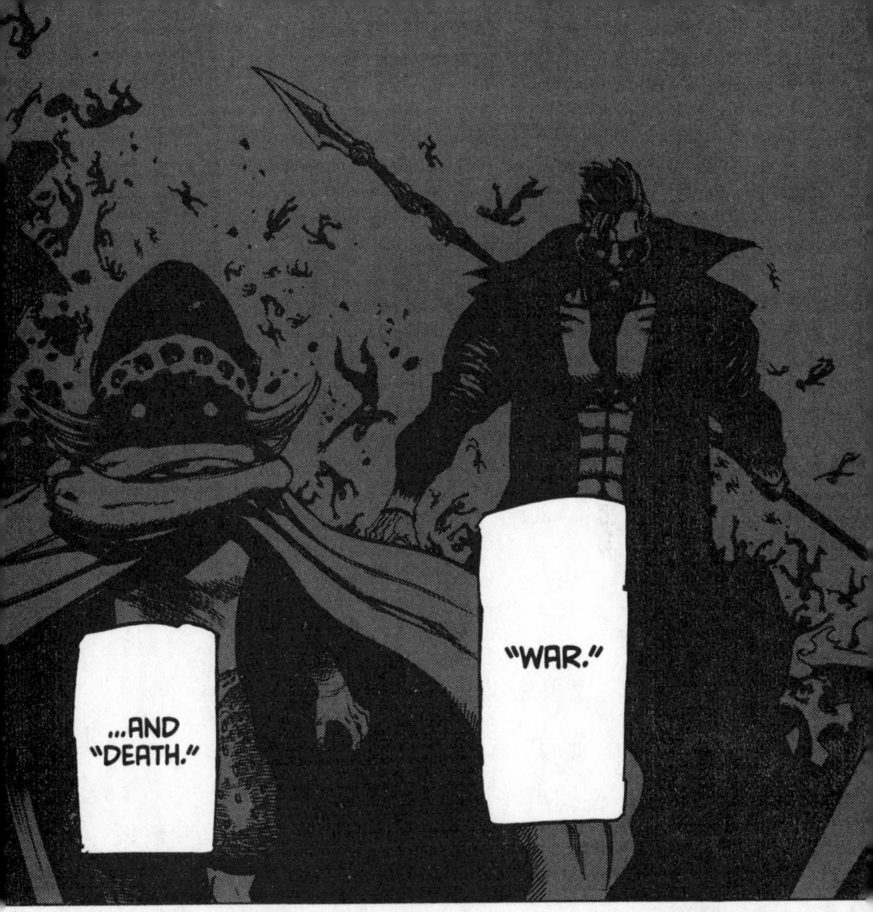
"WAR."
...AND "DEATH."

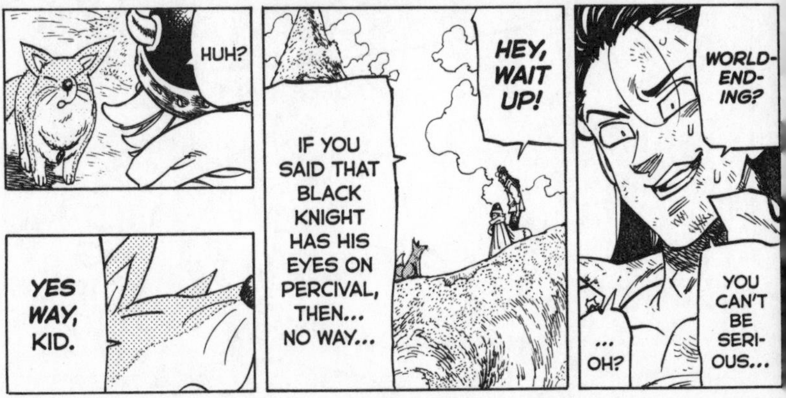
WORLD-ENDING?
YOU CAN'T BE SERI-OUS...
...OH?
HEY, WAIT UP!
IF YOU SAID THAT BLACK KNIGHT HAS HIS EYES ON PERCIVAL, THEN... NO WAY...
HUH?
YES WAY, KID.

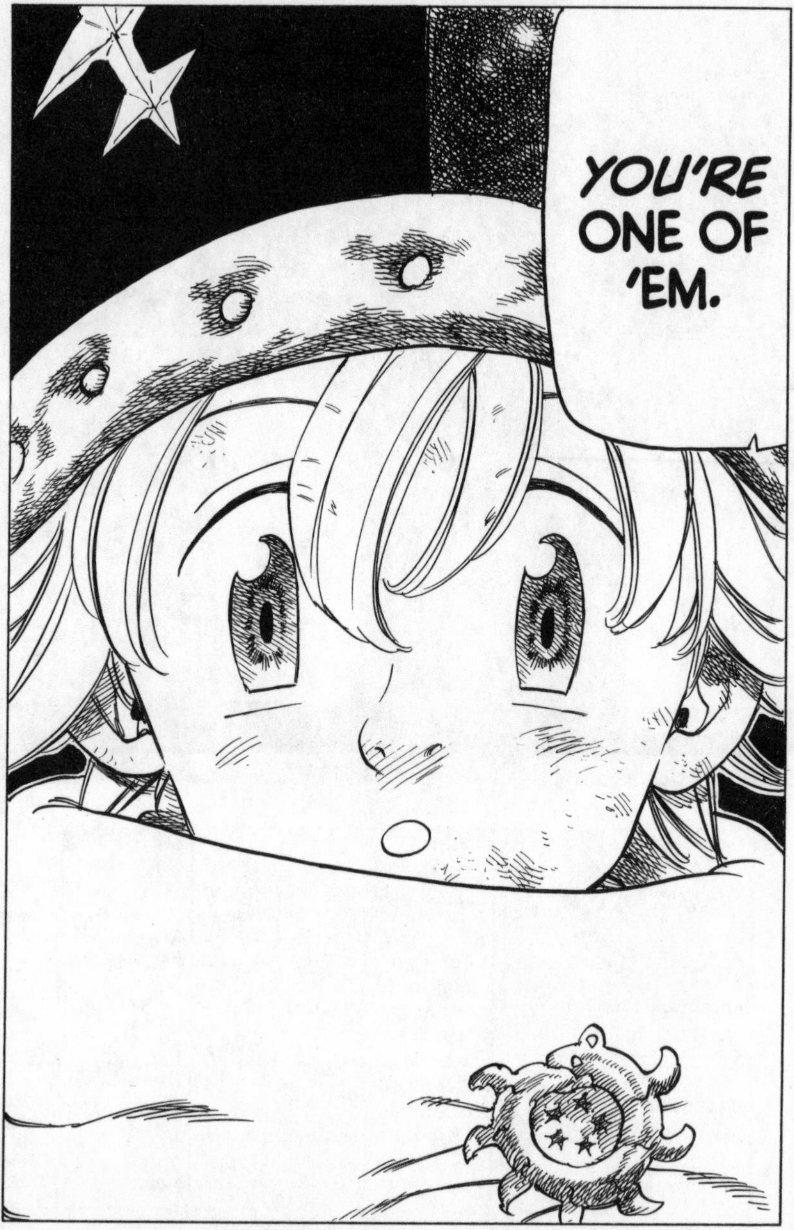
YOU'RE ONE OF 'EM.

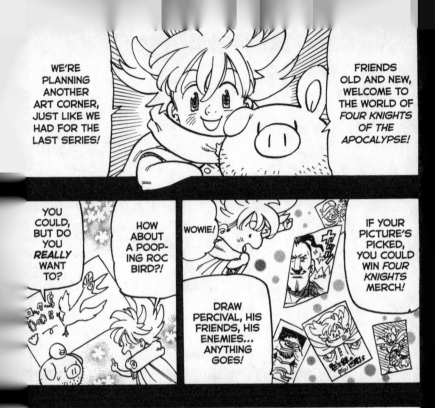

FRIENDS OLD AND NEW, WELCOME TO THE WORLD OF FOUR KNIGHTS OF THE APOCALYPSE!
WE'RE PLANNING ANOTHER ART CORNER, JUST LIKE WE HAD FOR THE LAST SERIES!
IF YOUR PICTURE'S PICKED, YOU COULD WIN FOUR KNIGHTS MERCH!
WOWIE!
DRAW PERCIVAL, HIS FRIENDS, HIS ENEMIES... ANYTHING GOES!
HOW ABOUT A POOPING ROC BIRD?!
YOU COULD, BUT DO YOU REALLY WANT TO?

SUBMIT YOUR DRAWING!

- ART MUST BE ON A POSTCARD OR POSTCARD-SIZED PAPER.
- WRITE YOUR NAME AND ADDRESS ON THE BACK OF YOUR PICTURE! YOU CAN INCLUDE COMMENTS IF YOU WANT. ALL ART WILL BE PRINTED IN BLACK AND WHITE, EVEN IF YOU SUBMIT IT IN COLOR.
- COPYING NAKABA SUZUKI'S ART STYLE IS FINE, OF COURSE, BUT COPYING PICTURES DRAWN BY OTHER FANS IS DEFINITELY NOT OKAY.

IF YOUR PIECE IS PRINTED, YOU'LL GET SPECIAL MERCH!
THE BEST PIECE IN EACH VOLUME WILL RECEIVE THE "SPECIAL AWARD" AND AN AUTOGRAPH!

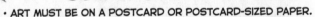

SEND SUBMISSIONS TO:
KODANSHA WEEKLY SHONEN MAGAZINE ATTN: FOUR KNIGHTS OF THE APOCALYPSE ART TROOP
2-12-21 OTOWA, BUNKYO WARD, TOKYO PREFECTURE 112-8001

NOTE: SUBMISSIONS WILL BE GIVEN TO THE ARTIST. PLEASE UNDERSTAND THAT THIS INCLUDES ANY ADDRESS, NAME, OR OTHER PERSONAL INFORMATION WRITTEN ON SAID SUBMISSIONS.

HIGH!! HIGH!! PERCIVAL!

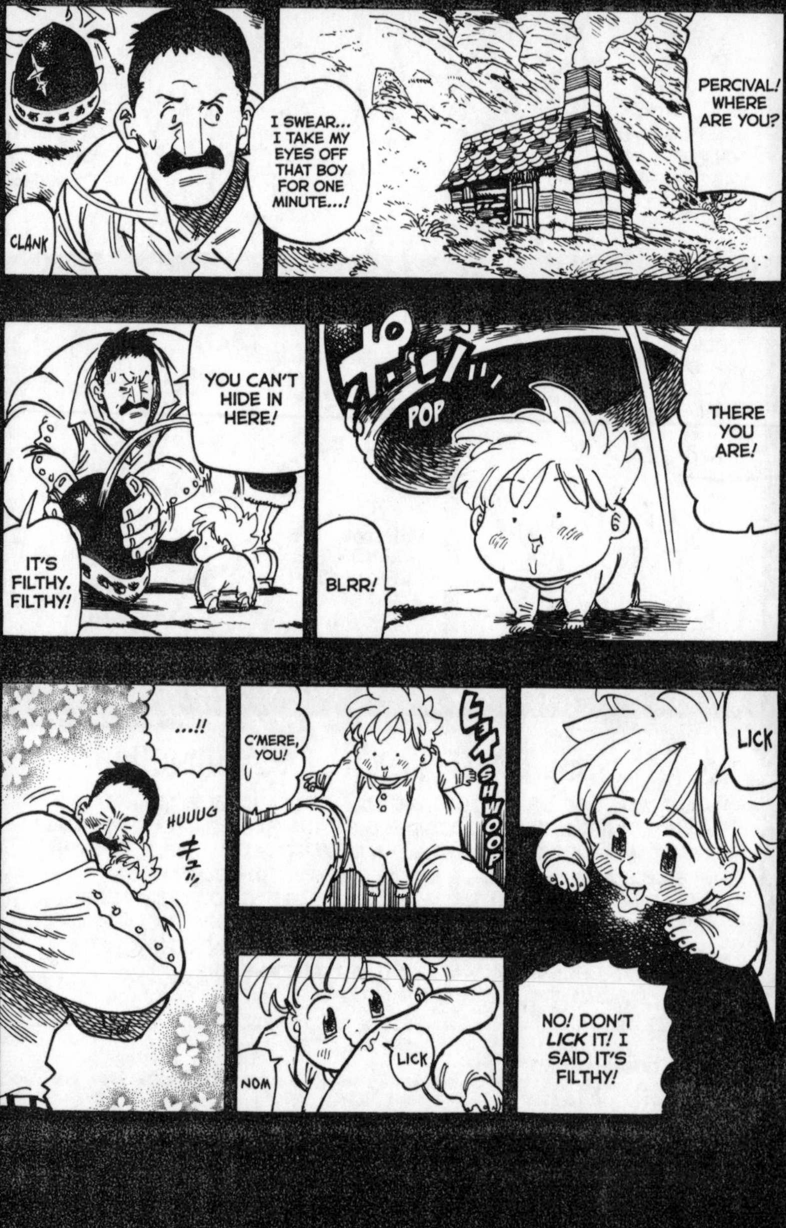
PERCIVAL! WHERE ARE YOU?
I SWEAR... I TAKE MY EYES OFF THAT BOY FOR ONE MINUTE...!
CLANK
THERE YOU ARE!
POP
BLRR!
YOU CAN'T HIDE IN HERE!
IT'S FILTHY. FILTHY!
LICK
NO! DON'T *LICK* IT! I SAID IT'S FILTHY!
SHWOOP
C'MERE, YOU!
LICK
NOM
...!!
HUUUG

HIGH!! HIGH!! PERCIVAL!

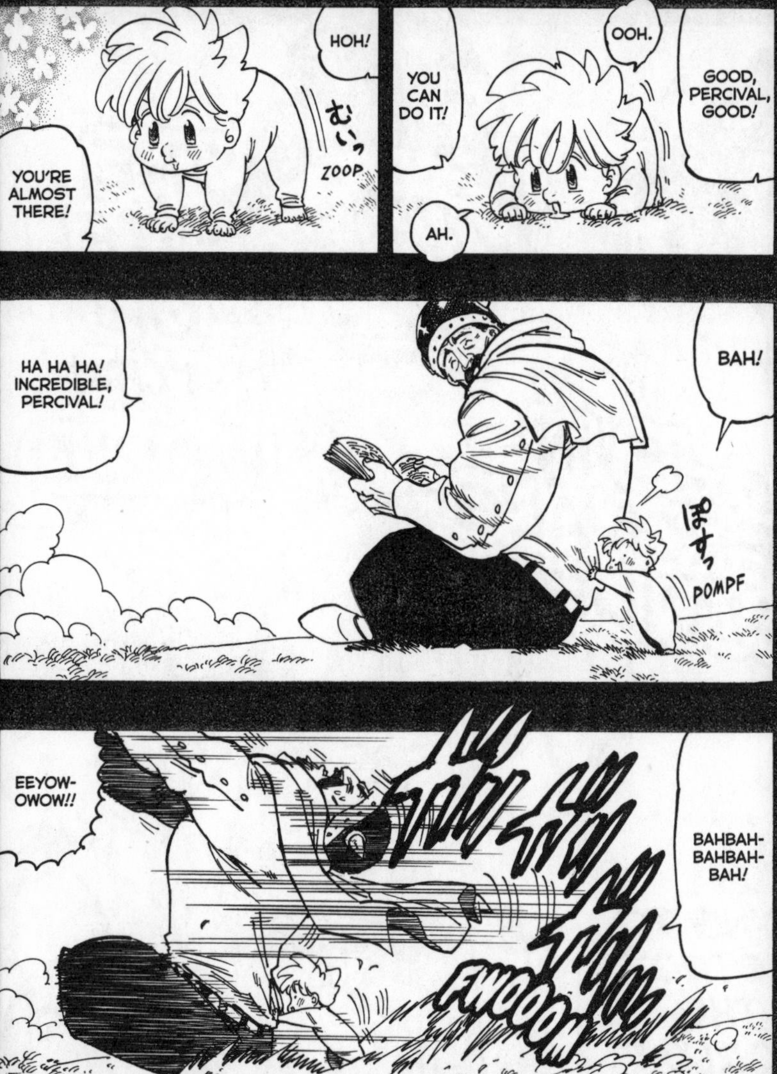

GOOD, PERCIVAL, GOOD!
OOH.
YOU CAN DO IT!
AH.
HOH!
むいっ
ZOOP
YOU'RE ALMOST THERE!
BAH!
ぽすっ
POMPF
HA HA HA! INCREDIBLE, PERCIVAL!
BAHBAH-BAHBAH-BAH!
FWOOOM
EEYOW-OWOW!!

END

no one ever expected!!

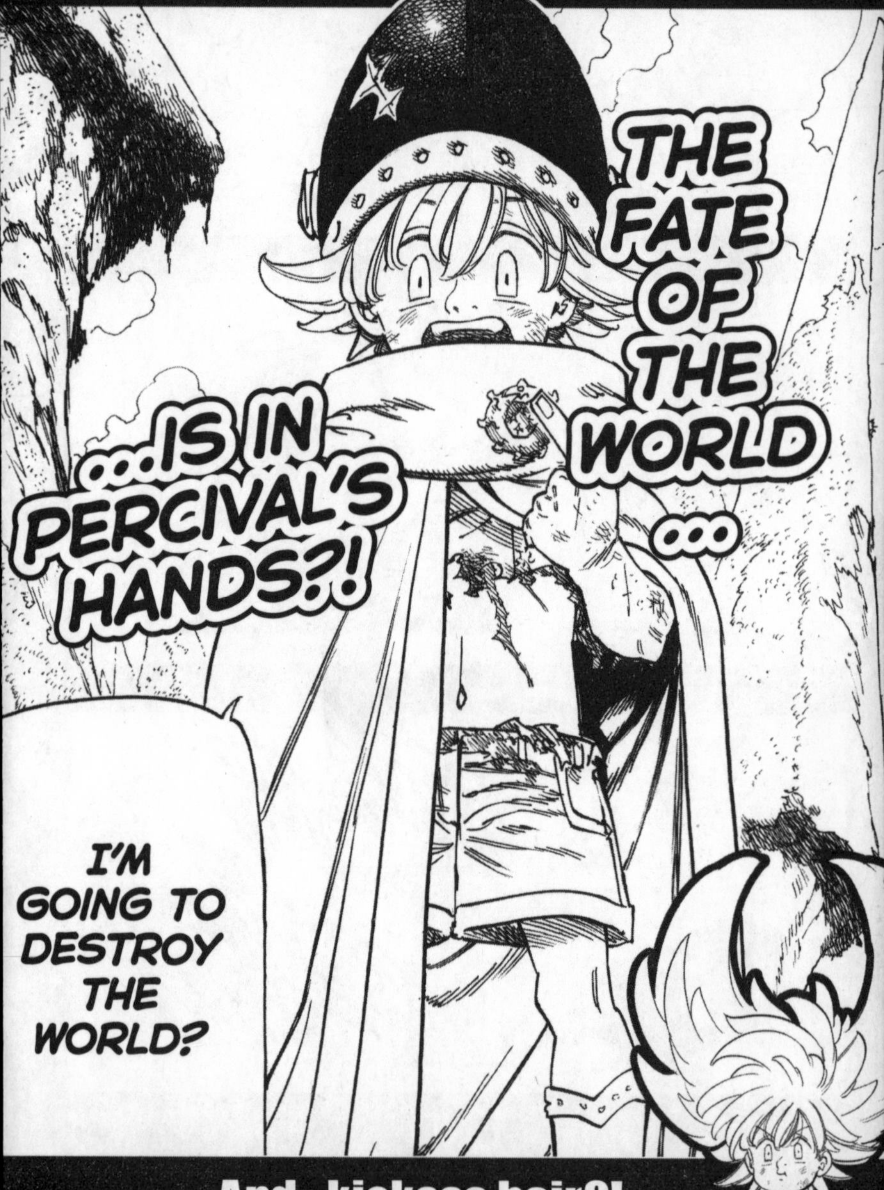
THE FATE OF THE WORLD ...
...IS IN PERCIVAL'S HANDS?!
I'M GOING TO DESTROY THE WORLD?

And...kickass hair?!

A Kodansha Trade Paperback Original

The Seven Deadly Sins: Four Knights of the Apocalypse 1 copyright © 2021 Nakaba Suzuki
English translation copyright © 2022 Nakaba Suzuki

Published in the United States by
Kodansha USA Publishing, LLC, New York.

Publication rights for this English edition arranged through
Kodansha Ltd., Tokyo.

First published in Japan in 2021 by Kodansha Ltd., Tokyo
as *Mokushiroku no Yonkishi 1*.

ISBN 978-1-64651-452-6

Printed in the United States of America.

1st Printing

Translation: Kevin Gifford
Additional translation: Kevin Steinbach
Lettering: Darren Smith
Additional lettering and layout: AndWorld Design
Editing: Aimee Zink
YKS Services LLC/SKY Japan, Inc.
Kodansha USA Publishing edition cover design by Matt Akuginow

Publisher: Kiichiro Sugawara

Director of Publishing Services: Ben Applegate
Associate Director of Publishing Operations: Stephen Pakula
Publishing Services Managing Editors: Alanna Ruse, Madison Salters
Production Managers: Emi Lotto, Angela Zurlo

KODANSHA.US

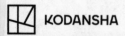

KODANSHA